Japanese Diaspora and Migration Reconsidered

In contrast to most studies of migration, which assume that migrants arrive from less developed countries to the industrialised world, where they suffer from discrimination, poor living conditions and downward social mobility, this book examines a different sort of diaspora – descendants of Japanese migrants or "Nikkei" – in Bolivia, who, after a history of organised migration, have achieved middle-class status in a developing country, while enjoying much symbolic capital among the majority population. Based on extensive original research, the book considers the everyday lives of Nikkei and their identity, discusses how despite their relative success they remain not fully integrated into Bolivia's imperfect pluricultural society and explores how they think about, and relate to, Japan.

Yvonne Siemann completed her doctorate at the University of Lucerne, Switzerland.

Japan Anthropology Workshop Series

For a full list of available titles please visit: www.routledge.com/Japan -Anthropology-Workshop-Series/book-series/SE0627

Series editor:
Joy Hendry, Oxford Brookes University

Editorial Board:
Pamela Asquith, University of Alberta
Eyal Ben Ari, Kinneret Academic College, Sea of Galilee
Christoph Brumann, Max Planck Institute for Social Anthropology, Munich
Henry Johnson, Otago University
Hirochika Nakamaki, the Suita City Museum

Religion in Japanese Daily Life
David C. Lewis

Escaping Japan
Reflections on Estrangement and Exile in the Twenty-First Century
Edited by Blai Guarné and Paul Hansen

Women Managers in Neoliberal Japan
Gender, Precarious Labour and Everyday Lives
Swee-Lin Ho

Global Coffee and Cultural Change in Modern Japan
Helena Grinshpun

Inside a Japanese Sharehouse
Caitlin Meagher

Mental Health and Social Withdrawal in Contemporary Japan
Nicolas Tajan

Japanese Diaspora and Migration Reconsidered
Yvonne Siemann

Revitalization and Internal Colonialism in Rural Japan
Timo Thelen

Japanese Diaspora and Migration Reconsidered

Yvonne Siemann

LONDON AND NEW YORK

First published 2022
by Routledge
4 Park Square, Milton Park, Abingdon, Oxon OX14 4RN

and by Routledge
605 Third Avenue, New York, NY 10158

Routledge is an imprint of the Taylor & Francis Group, an informa business

© 2022 Yvonne Siemann

The right of Yvonne Siemann to be identified as author of this work has been asserted in accordance with sections 77 and 78 of the Copyright, Designs and Patents Act 1988.

All rights reserved. No part of this book may be reprinted or reproduced or utilised in any form or by any electronic, mechanical, or other means, now known or hereafter invented, including photocopying and recording, or in any information storage or retrieval system, without permission in writing from the publishers.

Trademark notice: Product or corporate names may be trademarks or registered trademarks, and are used only for identification and explanation without intent to infringe.

British Library Cataloguing-in-Publication Data
A catalogue record for this book is available from the British Library

Library of Congress Cataloging-in-Publication Data
A catalog record has been requested for this book

ISBN: 978-1-032-13243-3 (hbk)
ISBN: 978-1-032-13247-1 (pbk)
ISBN: 978-1-003-22829-5 (ebk)

DOI: 10.4324/9781003228295

Typeset in Times New Roman
by Deanta Global Publishing Services, Chennai, India

A Julia Yoshino (1937–2019)

A Rosario Rios (1955–2012)

Meiner Mutter (1949–2019)

The book is a revised version of a PhD thesis at the University of Lucerne, Switzerland, with the title "The Nikkei in Santa Cruz: An Ethnographic Analysis of Japanese Descendants' Ethnic Identities in Bolivia", submitted in 2019.

Contents

List of figures	viii
Preface	ix
Acknowledgements	xi
A note on pseudonyms, transcriptions, translations, photos and currencies	xiii

1	Introduction	1
2	History of Japanese migration to Bolivia	19
3	How ethnic identities justify symbolic capital	50
4	The daily creation of ethnic boundaries	86
5	Dynamics of inclusion and exclusion in the *comunidad japonesa*	110
6	Nikkei ethnic associations' rise and decline	138
7	Nikkei networks in Latin America and beyond	168
8	Searching for an economic basis	185
9	How the Nikkei relate to the Bolivian state	210
10	Conclusion	238

Glossary	245
References	247
Index	273

Figures

2.1	Santa Cruz' central plaza.	20
2.2	Map of Japan.	22
2.3	Current numbers of Japanese descendants in the Americas.	30
2.4	Map of Bolivia.	35
2.5	Club Social ceremonial hall at the central plaza in 2007.	39
2.6	Residential areas Santa Cruz between Second and Third Ring Road.	40
2.7	Map of Santa Cruz de la Sierra.	47
3.1	Migrants' suitcase at the museum of Japanese migration, La Paz.	60
3.2	Fresh fruits and vegetables from Colonia Okinawa.	64
3.3	Mural at a ropeway station in La Paz, celebrating 40 years of Japanese cooperation in Bolivia.	67
3.4	Automobile advertisement in the streets of Santa Cruz.	80
3.5	Kimono Fashion Show.	83
4.1	Callisthenics [*rajio taisō*] before Japanese class in Santa Cruz.	100
5.1	Place of residence of the members of Centro Social.	114
5.2	Keirōkai (Respect for the Aged Festival) in Centro Social Japonés.	121
5.3	Ryūkyūkoku Matsuridaiko at Feria de Comunidades Extranjeras.	135
6.1	Centro Social Japonés with Policonsultorio Nikkei.	140
6.2	Okinawa Kenjinkai building.	141
6.3	ANBJ building.	142
6.4	Origami shown at Sociedad Japonesa de La Paz.	148
6.5	The shishimai or lion dance at Hōnensai.	150
6.6	Cleaning the sports ground after undōkai in La Paz.	152
7.1	Volleyball players from different countries at Confra 2014.	170
7.2	Kachaashi at Wakamono Taikai in Düsseldorf.	181
8.1	Entrance to a Japanese restaurant.	198
8.2	Chicken house in San Juan.	200
8.3	CAICO's noodle factory.	204
9.1	Shelter with graffiti at the entrance to San Juan.	211

Preface

Japanese Diaspora and Migration Reconsidered : Nikkei Identities in a Bolivian City

Yvonne Siemann, a young scholar from Switzerland, has contributed a precious ethnographic work on Nikkei (Japanese abroad) identities in Latin America. Her fieldwork was based in Santa Cruz, the second largest city in Bolivia, but Santa Cruz in lowland Bolivia is little known by the Japanese or even by the North Americans and Europeans. In the outskirts of Santa Cruz, there exist two Japanese settlements named Colonia San Juan and Colonia Okinawa. Both *colonias* were established after the Second World War as agricultural communities by the Japanese immigrants. They have survived for more than half a century, while maintaining a strong Japanese identity nourished by the first generation (Issei). But the author turned her eyes to the second and third generations (Nisei and Sansei) who moved to Santa Cruz where most of them enjoy a relatively prosperous life as middle-class citizens.

The author conducted her fieldwork for 16 months in 2013/2014 for a PhD thesis, collecting data mainly through around 100 interviews. She communicated with her interview partners mostly in Spanish, so barely communicated with Issei, nor does she cite any academic publications written in Japanese. However, the main target of research was the identities of Nisei and Sansei in the city and the author was fortunately well informed by the English and Spanish/Portuguese publications of important works conducted by Japanese scholars.

Her doctoral thesis is now transformed into a volume of Japan Anthropology Workshop (JAWS) Series, which is composed of 10 chapters, including Introduction and Conclusion. What is unique is that the author begins her description as if it were an essay and often uses narratives of informants as the headline of a section. For example, "Chino (Chinese)" in Chapter 2, "Barefoot but happy" in Chapter 3, "Don't stain your family's name" in Chapter 4 and "The Nikkei has to eat more manioc" in Chapter 9. This shows that she takes interviewees' concrete expressions into account and avoids discussions becoming too abstract. Therefore, it is readable and easy to follow. One almost feels that this ethnography is a chain of interesting narratives which pauses periodically at chapter conclusions.

The main theme of this volume is Nikkei ethnic identities in an urban setting. Generally speaking, "Japanese-ness" and "Japanese values" are contrasted with

x *Preface*

"Bolivianisation", whereas the former ones are considered as a source of success by the Japanese themselves. There are, however, other peculiar characteristics to be reconsidered in Santa Cruz, she argues. One is that the Japanese identities are not common or equal, for the majority of Nikkei are of Okinawan descent, due to the proximity of Colonia Okinawa. Second, Nikkei communities have survived not only by their hard-working efforts rooted in "Japanese values" but also with the financial and symbolic support of Japan, particularly through the governmental organization named JICA. Third, younger generations of Nikkei are striving to extend their network through Pan-American associations such as APN. On the other hand, Nikkei seldom seek political power within the Bolivian state, which becomes the fourth point. Other points such as *dekasegi* (work migration) to Japan shall be found as you go on reading.

Before closing this preface, I would like to emphasise the author's comparative perspectives with regard to Nikkei identities. Since 2009, Bolivia has taken its official name as "Pluricultural State of Bolivia". And the Nikkei can be part of it as an ethnic group, though it has never been sought by the Nikkei. Intermittent references to Mennonites offer a unique comparison to contextualise Nikkei identities within Bolivia, not to mention indigenous people. As to the neighbouring countries, Bolivian issues are frequently compared with Peruvian cases, but also Brazilian and Paraguayan ones are dealt with whenever necessary. The reader can be well assured to be provided with rich resources to reconsider the Japanese diaspora in Latin American countries and their migration to urban areas, making use of a focus on the Nikkei in Santa Cruz, Bolivia.

Hirochika Nakamaki
October 2020

Acknowledgements

It is impossible to write a book alone. While I know that the list will be incomplete, I want to thank the following persons who supported me during the research process:

My parents for their support of my studies.

The Graduate School of the University of Lucerne, the SSLAS and CUSO for financial support.

My supervisors Bettina Beer and Wolfram Manzenreiter for their guidance.

Don Gardner, Araceli Mendiluce, Érica Hatugai, Carlos Torrico, Pablo Barriga, Peter Larsen, Ayumi Takenaka, Peter Bernardi, Julius Riese, Chen Yi, Clara Koller, Willem Church, Anke Moesinger, Ibrahim Ankaoglu, Laurent Goetschel and Mark Goodale for comments and Elise Voerkel, Simon Foppa, Urs Marbet, Freddy Ulloa Peñaloza, Martina Bonenberger, Melanie Nertz, Rebekka Khaliefi, Laetitia della Bianca, Chiaki Kinjo and Doris Bacalzo for commenting on one or more chapters.

Noriko Ogita and Freddy Ulloa Peñaloza for helping me with language issues.

Carolina Schneider and her family, Camila Jara and her family, Narumi and Naomi Nishizawa, Fumio and Yoko Mita, Erika Higa and her family, as well as Francisca de Oliveira Calegari, Eida Magalhães, Nacira Flores and her family, Rosario Rios and her family, Sachika Nakachi, Nanako Yogi, Ritsuko Fujimoto and Nelly Masemi Mbembi for hosting me in Bolivia, Brazil, Paraguay and Japan.

Max Steiner, Nacira Flores and Arturo Zamorano for their help in the administrative process.

Corina Ashimine, Coty Kishimoto, Eiki Nishizawa, Susana Nishizawa, Eiko Igei, Etsuko Inoue, Hiroaki Yamashiro, Jorge Kuba, Rosemery Rodríguez, Lidia Miyasato, Santiago Nishizawa, Teruyuki Taira, Tokiko Takeno, Javier Guibu, Rina Ikeda, Toru Higa, Analía Torres, Virginia Benavides, Freddy Ulloa Peñaloza, Lane Ryo Hirabayashi, Érica Hatugai, Hajime Tsuboi, Dahil Melgar, Huascar Morales, Ronan Alves Pereira, Nobutoshi Sato, Takashi Aniya, Ken'ichi Kuwabara, Kinjo Shimabukuro, Taku Suzuki, Kozy Amemiya, Katsumi Bani, Chizu Fukui, Satoshi Higa, Chiaki Kinjo, Masaru Tonoshiro, Rebeca Gonzalez, Shigeru Aniya, Masashi Kinoshita, Shigeru Kojima, Toshio Yanagida, Toru Higa, Fumino Shima, Ikuro Nishizawa, Zaida Kaihara, Jhonnatan Torres Casanoba, Jenny Maydana, Emi Kasamatsu, Alessandra Pellegrini, João Sardinha, José Luis

xii *Acknowledgements*

Mendoza Condori, Rosana Albuquerque and the late Takeshi Kamiya, for their help in finding documents and for their assistance in the research process.

Ryūkyūkoku Matsuridaiko Boribia Shibu for the good company and the beautiful moments we passed together.

Finally, it would not have been possible to write this book without my interview partners, be they Nikkei or not. I am very thankful that you shared your experiences with me.

A note on pseudonyms, transcriptions, translations, photos and currencies

It was often not possible to decontextualise information or to change details about interview partners or situations. On the one hand, Japanese descendants are not numerous in Bolivia, on the other hand, some details may be necessary to understand the argument. I am aware that many interview partners will be identifiable for insiders. Nevertheless, I have changed all interview partners' names except for three individuals who are public personalities or who comment on their publications cited in the book.

I transcribe Japanese terms according to *rōmaji* conventions. Japanese names are transcribed following the order first name – last name, without using macrons, as they would be written in Bolivia.

All interview translations are mine. In the few cases in which I have translated sentences from literature, it is noted.

All photos are mine.

During the time of fieldwork, one U.S. dollar was equivalent to approximately 6.9 bolivianos and to around 110 yen.

"Different people have asked me about the most important thing in life. They ask me: "What do you think?" Well, it's difficult to say [...]. But for me, it's the encounter [...]. Sometimes we aren't really aware, it's just an encounter with one person or another. And out of that, many things emerge and develop. Including business transactions, friendships, or even courtship, marriage. [...] An encounter can even change an individual or a life to the worse or to the better. [...] But what's important is that everything, the bad in life, the good in life, starts with an encounter."

An Issei entrepreneur in Santa Cruz

1 Introduction

The sound of enthusiastic cheering and applause fills the air in the Coliseo Don Bosco sports hall in Santa Cruz de la Sierra, a city of 1.5 million inhabitants in the Bolivian lowlands. Bolivia's male futsal[1] team is playing against Argentina for the tournament title. The match becomes increasingly exciting: both teams are equally strong, and they play in overtime. Although the stands are half-empty, the atmosphere is great: fans of all ages jump up and down, cheering to encourage their team. Given the location of the tournament, the majority supports Bolivia, waving flags, shouting "*Viva Bolivia*" and beating large, red barrel drums. When the ball ends in the corner next to the Argentinean goal, the Bolivian supporters scream out of disappointment. The Argentinean team sees a chance, runs towards the Bolivian goal – but the attack fails. Suddenly, everything happens very fast: a Bolivian player sidesteps an Argentinean, conquers the ball, skates forward, passes to his teammate who shoots and – Bolivia wins the gold medal!

Even though this football match might seem typical for a Latin American setting, in the eyes of most Bolivians and Argentineans, the participants would not pass as "normal" representatives of either country. The players were all of Japanese origin, just like most of their supporters. The game was part of the Confra tournament for Nikkei [Japanese descendants] in Latin America. The 21st edition in January and February 2014 took place in Bolivia for the first time. Around 700 Nikkei competed against each other in futsal, baseball, volleyball, table tennis, golf, athletics and judo in Santa Cruz and nearby Colonia Okinawa. Apart from the Bolivian participants, most others had come from Argentina, Paraguay, Brazil, Peru and Mexico for this four-day event.

During Confra, national symbols of different Latin American countries were omnipresent – already in the inauguration ceremony at Santa Cruz' largest stadium Estadio Tahuichi Aguilera, a singer performed Bolivia's national anthem and the participants defiled behind national flags in sports suits of the same colours. During the tournament, some Bolivian Nikkei commented on a participant's "typically Argentinean behaviour" or recognised the Paraguayan Nikkei by their "typically Paraguayan" habit of drinking cold *tereré* infusion and carrying around large thermos tanks. Moreover, organisers also invited a non-Nikkei *caporales* dance group, using the inauguration ceremony to present "traditional Bolivian culture" to the foreign guests.

DOI: 10.4324/9781003228295-1

2 Introduction

Japanese national symbols were highly visible as well. The country's anthem and flag constituted a self-evident component of the inauguration ceremony, and the Japanese ambassador in Bolivia held a speech to welcome the Nikkei from abroad. By taking part in the tournament, all participants openly identified with a Japanese origin. They supposed that their common ancestry meant shared experiences, similar habits and values as well as an affinity with Japanese descendants from other Latin American countries. Posters in the streets of Santa Cruz announced "*700 deportistas japoneses por primera vez en Bolivia*" [700 Japanese athletes for the first time in Bolivia], with the reference "*Evento de la comunidad japonesa*" [Event of the Japanese community]. On a closer look, all these representations were interwoven with displays of regional identities, such as the Okinawa sumo contest, the presentation of the Okinawan dance Ryūkyūkoku Matsuridaiko or the Bolivian participants' green-white jackets with the name "Santa Cruz" and the corresponding arms.

Although different teams competed against each other, totally excited or deeply disappointed after winning or losing a match, the organising committee explained that the event aimed above all at the fraternisation between Nikkei from different countries. It was composed by a group of friends of Japanese origin from Santa Cruz and the nearby colonies. Accordingly, the name of the tournament derives from the word *confraternización* [fraternisation]. Confra is a site to propagate and actively create a supranational Nikkei identity.

By emphasising the commitment to their respective country of residence, organisers intended to show a specific representation of Japanese descendants to non-Nikkei *cruceñas* and *cruceños*,[2] invited as spectators to witness the "Japanese migration success story." Confra organisers convincingly presented Japanese descendants as successful, cosmopolitan and respected citizens of foreign origin able to carry out a large and costly international event. Indeed, the mere fact that they were able to afford a plane ticket to Bolivia showed that Confra participants practically all belonged to the middle class, despite the implicit or explicit mention of their ancestors' humble origin as migrant farmers.

This was probably also the first time that the term "Nikkei" was used in Bolivia on a broad basis. "Nikkei" as a self-designation has emerged in the course of Pan-American Nikkei conventions like COPANI, emphasising Latin America or the respective countries of residence as a core referent. At one meeting, the following working definition of Nikkei emerged: "Someone who has one or more ancestors from Japan, and/or anyone who self-identifies as a Nikkei," although not everybody accepted the latter part of the definition (Hirabayashi and Kikumura-Yano 2002: 155). In her introduction to the *Encyclopedia of Japanese Descendants in the Americas*, Nikkei anthropologist Akemi Kikumura-Yano (2002b: 3) defines Nikkei more precisely as

> all Japanese emigrants and their descendants who, while acknowledging their Japanese ancestry, have created unique communities within various national contexts throughout the Americas. The term also includes persons

Introduction   3

of mixed racial descent who identify themselves as Nikkei, as well as those who have returned to Japan but retain identities separate from the native Japanese.

This means that Nikkei identity is a construction that implies "a dynamic process of selection, reinterpretation, and synthesis of cultural elements" (ibid.).

The term "Nikkei"/"Nikkeijin" combines the element "*nichi*," referring to the sun but also to Japan, with "*kei*," meaning "descent." Finally, "*jin*" stands for "people." For the sake of variety, I will use the term "(Bolivian) Nikkei" interchangeably with the expression "(Japanese) descendants (in Bolivia)". I am aware that while "Nikkei" may be the dominant term in literature, it is not necessarily used by all Japanese descendants at all times, and much less by non-Nikkei. Japanese Bolivians may speak about themselves as "*descendientes (de japoneses)*" [(Japanese) descendants] or as "*japoneses*"/"*nihonjin*" (Japanese). In interviews, some later-generation[3] Nikkei explicitly presented themselves as "*cambas japoneses*" [Japanese lowland Bolivians] or "*bolivianos de sangre japonesa*" [Bolivians of Japanese blood]. Most non-Nikkei Bolivians, however, simply call them "*japoneses*" or even "*chinos*" [Chinese]. In and outside the group, several ways of identification coexist and influence each other.

As the Confra example illustrates, Nikkei ethnic identities in the city of Santa Cruz de la Sierra, Bolivia are complex, layered, situational and sometimes contradictory. But this study's main argument is that all these expressions of identity are intrinsically linked to the Nikkei's middle-class status. While migration scholarship has often presented migrants as poor and marginalised, my study explores the relations and interactions between Nikkei ethnic identity, symbolic capital and diasporic links to Japan. The example of Nikkei in Bolivia gives insights into Latin American and Japanese societies as well as the possibilities and limits of ethnic minorities.

Ethnic identities in the nation-state

Focusing on the descendants of migrants who arrived after the Second World War (post-war Nikkei for short), I will show in this study how they negotiate their ethnic identity, especially in the urban environment while interacting with non-Nikkei, whereas their being part of the middle class plays a decisive role for identity constructions. I describe how different identifications emerge, which practices are attached to them and under which conditions they are negotiated. At the same time, the Nikkei example shows many contradictions between multiple sources of identity, such as the fact that Asian descendants are denied full membership status in Bolivian society. Furthermore, I will lay specific emphasis on strategies to use ethnic identity as symbolic capital (Bourdieu 1989) and on the influence of diasporic relations, for example through financial aid from the Japanese government. When I study Nikkei identities in Bolivia, I also examine the "fuzzy boundaries": descendants of partly non-Japanese origin, recent Japanese migrants, Nikkei from neighbouring countries and non-Nikkei acquaintances.

4   *Introduction*

Thereby, this book concentrates on some aspects that have so far not received much attention in migration research and in Bolivian studies. First, most migration scholars have been studying movements to North America and Western Europe, neglecting migration within or between Africa, Asia and Latin America under sometimes very different circumstances (see, for example, Lan 2003). Second, research on Bolivia has concentrated on indigenous and socioeconomically disadvantaged groups but seldom on the middle and upper classes (Barriga Dávalos 2016; Shakow 2014). Third, Bolivianists have rarely discussed minorities of recent immigrant origin (apart from Nikkei studies, see studies on the Mennonites such as Hedberg 2007). One reason is the small number of foreign migrants compared to neighbouring countries such as Chile, Brazil and Argentina. Still, the cultural and socioeconomic influence of European, Latin American, Asian and other immigrants was essential also for Bolivia. I argue that minorities like the Nikkei, although generally outside the focus of attention, provide valuable insights into the society they live in, showing us how ethnic and national identities interact with class.

Compared to Brazil and Peru, research on the around 13,000 Nikkei in Bolivia, about 2,400 of them in the Santa Cruz area, is scarce. The existing studies have been carried out almost exclusively in the *colonias*[4] (Akamine Núñez 2004; Kunimoto 2013b; Parejas Moreno 1981; Wakatsuki and Kunimoto 1985; Suzuki 2010; Kunimoto 1990). In addition, descendants themselves have published several books with a historical focus (see, for example, Koronia Okinawa Nyūshoku 50 Shūnen Kinenshi Hensan Iinkai 2005; Santa Kurusu Chūō Nihonjinkai Sōritsu 50 Shūnen Kinenshi 2006; Sociedad Japonesa de La Paz 2012). Nevertheless, my ethnographic study focuses on the daily interactions among Nikkei and between Nikkei and non-Nikkei. It suggests that the urban environment is an interesting place to explore the negotiation of ethnic boundaries due to a variety of possible identifications and social relations. At the same time, I am aware that it is not possible to rigidly separate descendants' lives in Santa Cruz and the *colonias*.

To understand the multiple ethnic identifications of Nikkei in Santa Cruz, one has to take into account that identity, in general, is both a construction and a dynamic, performative act, marked by ambivalence, complexity and breaks. Collective, as well as individual identities are based on a seemingly contradictory relation between sameness, consistency and coherence, but they hold an individual facet related to authenticity and peculiarity. This process does not occur in a vacuum: discrepancies may emerge between different expectations, for example, in the course of social mobility or migration. In other words, contradictions are inherent to identity (Müller 2011).

As Eriksen (2013: 282) notes, ethnic identity means "the enduring and systematic communication of cultural differences between groups considering themselves to be distinct. It appears whenever cultural differences are made relevant in social interaction." An ethnic group like the Nikkei can be understood as an imagined community in the sense of Anderson (2006): it is not the group as such but the idea which persists. Ethnic identity as the social or subjective affiliation of an individual to an ethnically defined group is not given, but socially constructed

Introduction 5

and marked by ambivalences and flexibility, constituting a complex set of different resources, processes and constructions. It is performed in and influenced by specific cultural, social, political, economic and historical contexts. However, in popular discourse, the Nikkei often draw on seemingly innate characteristics and a mythic-historical heritage, namely the group's association with a common territory of origin or common "blood." Members of ethnic groups are related by symbolic kinship, assume a common ancestry and history as well as shared values, norms and culture, supposing the group to be clearly definable (Wimmer 2013: 177ff.). They legitimise ethnic boundaries through stereotypes, generalised characterisations based on some subjectively chosen characteristics as ideological legitimations.

Relationships are central to ethnic identity; a group[5] like the Nikkei cannot exist without a minimum of contact with others (Barth 1994). Internal and external definitions influence each other; hence, it can be useful to distinguish groups, corresponding to the internal definition, from categories, referring to external ideas of the collectivity (Eriksen 2010: 106ff.; Jenkins 1994: 52ff.). Although the Nikkei might construct an ethnic boundary towards non-Nikkei, cultural influences and mutual contacts obviously exist. Collective ethnic identities are often strengthened and not weakened during such interactions. As Gans (1979) underlines, groups may become practically identical in their cultural practices while they consciously choose specific ethnic symbols such as food, dances and set expressions in their ancestors' language to present an essentialised version of their place of origin. Thereby, ethnic identity has adopted new meanings in contexts of migration, globalisation and capitalism (Appadurai 1996: 139ff.; Eriksen 2010: 39f.; Jenkins 1997: 29ff.). It is essential to differentiate between culture and ethnic identity – as my study shows, ethnic identity can become highly ambivalent when ethnic and cultural boundaries are incongruent. Nevertheless, the cultural content and the boundary influence each other – the content legitimises the boundary (Jenkins 1997: 123).

It is important for this study to consider that humans may also behave strategically when drawing ethnic boundaries, since it may mean gaining access to tangible resources and non-material benefits. Moreover, new formulations of identity can be a key for ethnic mobilisation, often with reference to a discourse on human, social and other rights (Glidden 2011). Finally, in their book on ethnic branding, Comaroff and Comaroff (2009) cite examples of collectivities that merchandise their seemingly unique ethnic identities on a national or even global level, thereby substantially influencing group definitions through essentialisation and abstraction. However, reducing ethnic identity to a simple manipulation tool would be an oversimplification: while my study shows that it is often useful to identify as Nikkei, it demonstrates that ethnic identity has an affective dimension as well. The sense of ethnic membership usually emerges during early childhood and is difficult to change.

I will focus on ethnic differences, but Wimmer (2013: 8) points out that the difference between ethnic identity and race is not always clear-cut. Race means categorising human beings based on actual or assumed characteristics, be they

6 Introduction

visible or not, supposedly inherited and shared by members of one group (Beer 2002: 47). Although assuming the existence of different human races is highly problematic, the term is still used in popular discourse.

Nevertheless, the significance of ethnic identity should not be overestimated. Several interview partners felt that class or gender can be far more relevant in daily life. I also describe various cases of individuals who position themselves or are positioned at the margins or in an ambivalent position. Finally, when choosing a specific concept, this also influences the nature of data – if one looks for ethnic identity, one will find it everywhere, Eriksen (2010: 177f.) holds: "[W]hen all is said and done, ethnicity is a social and cultural product which anthropologists contribute to creating."

Obviously, Nikkei in Bolivia do not live in a legal and political vacuum. Since nation-states and ethnic groups seldom overlap, national territories commonly host one or more ethnic minorities (Tambiah 1994).[6] One can speak of a layered sense of membership: through one's attachment to an ethnic group, one may also make claims of being part of a nation-state. To achieve a common national identity, nation-states try to create an official version of culture, remembering past events for current needs or even inventing rituals to connect past, present and future (Hobsbawm 2008). In the 19th century, many European nation-states implemented a cultural standardisation policy for their heterogeneous populations which had formerly been differentiated first of all by formal hierarchies (Anderson 2006); Japan followed the example during the Meiji era. Today, popular discourse supposes that Japanese national and ethnic identities overlap (Lie 2001; Murphy-Shigematsu 1993).

But some states like Bolivia do not fit the model of ethnic homogeneity at all, propagating a different kind of nationalism. Although at times they restricted the entry of specific groups, most states in the Americas saw immigration as part of their nation-building process – even Bolivia with low immigration rates. At the beginning of the 20th century, Franz Tamayo (1986) propagated *mestizaje* of whites and indigenous people as an ideal for Bolivia – notions that later influenced the revolution of 1952 (Soruco 2006; Stefanoni 2010). Nationalism, in this case, is rather connected to discourses of civil society and equal rights; even though discrimination on ethnic grounds has been a recurring feature of Bolivian society. Nevertheless, neither in Bolivia nor in other Latin American countries did these ideas refer to the incorporation of recent migrants from Japan or elsewhere in Asia. As a result, Latin Americans of Asian origin, generally citizens[7] of their country of residence, are mostly regarded as foreigners. After Evo Morales' election as Bolivian president in 2005, his administration implemented ambitious and contradictory measures to create a "plurinational" state – but unlike indigenous groups, Nikkei as an ethnic minority did not obtain specific rights in the new constitution.

The nation-state can adopt a range of different strategies regarding rights, access to resources and modes of participation of different ethnic groups. It may request minorities to fully assimilate into the majority population; individuals and groups may be rewarded for assimilation or punished for non-assimilation.

Introduction 7

Moreover, a state can try to highlight differences, creating ethnic categories. By assuming a bounded view of culture, it may mean that some people are deprived of rights because they belong to a specific group, as in South Africa during apartheid. But it can also mean that an individual is able to participate in society while maintaining a distinct cultural and religious identity (Castles and Miller 2009: 247ff.). I will discuss the Nikkei's relation to plurinationalism in Chapter 9.

As a reaction to such disadvantages, individuals or collectivities can try to assimilate into the majority society by abandoning non-desired cultural elements and customs. Apart from isolation, they may also overcommunicate common features with the dominant group, intending to exploit the categorisation system to their own advantage. They can, finally, turn stigmatised elements into positive symbols or opt for a mixed strategy (Eriksen 2010: 123f.; Jenkins 1997: 70f.; Wimmer 2013: 58ff.).

Classical theories of migrants' incorporation into the receiving society follow a binary model of "here" and "there": over time, migrants and their offspring continually assimilate into the majority population (see, e.g., Eisenstadt 1954; Gordon 1964). Although these assumptions have not proven completely wrong in empirical studies, contemporary scholars argue that changes do not necessarily occur in a linear way and that the relations between migrants, their descendants and the sending and receiving countries' societies are much more complex (Åkesson 2011). In the case of Nikkei in Bolivia, interacting factors on a micro-, meso- and macro-level as well as remigration and ongoing relationships with Nikkei in third countries continuously influence identity constructions.

The importance of diasporic connections

Diasporic links to Japan as "relation to a referent-origin" (Dufoix 2008: 3) remain important also to later-generation Nikkei. The term "diaspora" has been applied especially in contexts of prolonged community formation in different countries. According to Faist (2010: 12f.), it was originally used for religious or ethnic minorities, forced to live outside their country of origin, while it also implied isolation from the receiving society and the wish to return to a real or imagined homeland.[8] Diasporas should be understood as "dynamic relationships between space, time and identity" (Manzenreiter 2017b: 108); they refer to a shared collective memory, imaginations of the past and a place of origin as well as to ongoing relations with co-ethnics in third countries. Through such relations, they incorporate, reinterpret and redefine different cultural practices in a continuous process while nevertheless maintaining multiple interactions with the receiving society – therefore, diasporas should not be understood as a bounded group, but rather as a set of practices.[9]

It is very important to consider that many Nikkei in Bolivia have drawn to Japan also as a source of financial support. Identifying as a Japanese descendant is economically useful in a Latin American context. These identifications are not only negotiated on the micro-level, but are also influenced by the meso-level or even macro-level context of state administrations, global finance and international

8   *Introduction*

relations. Although understated in Nikkei narratives, I point out that the descendants' current prosperity was possible only because of the financial, material and knowledge-based help by the Japanese state, mainly via the Japanese International Cooperation Agency (JICA). Japanese passports also offered the Nikkei tangible opportunities during the Japanese economic boom, the so-called bubble economy, in the late 1980s and early 1990s: earning money in Japan as *dekasegi*[10] migrants contributed to the Nikkei's middle-class status in Bolivia. However, because Japan itself is not the same country as it was 50 or 100 years ago, I want to emphasise that the meaning of being Nikkei has changed over time. Although diasporic relations to their country of origin may not always be empowering or satisfactory for the individual, they have been generally positive for the Nikkei.

Diasporic links to co-ethnic in other countries do not exist per se, but are reproduced through specific practices. Hence, when I compare Nikkei in Bolivia to Japanese descendants in other countries, I do not assume that they automatically behave in an identical way or feel close to each other (Ang 2004). Still, several parallels can be observed not least due to prolonged contact, a comparable social environment and a similar immigration history. Hence, some try to create a supranational Nikkei identity at events such as the previously mentioned Confra sports tournament.

Nevertheless, research on the border-crossing practices of migrants' offspring is scarce. Although later generations may be less intensely engaged than their parents or grandparents, Levitt and Jaworsky (2007: 134) point out that at different moments in life, values or connections may become important also for them. Even though popular opinion might not agree, most scholars think that engaging in the country of origin and the country of destination is not contradictory (Åkesson 2011).

At the same time, controlling citizens or their offspring abroad is essential for states trying to obtain resources. Sending states' engagement includes a broad range of activities, incentives and policies for citizens abroad. Japan hoped that emigration would alleviate domestic unemployment and it urged migrants to assist in the organisation of further migration projects. Until today, some states explicitly encourage citizens to remit, to connect to each other or to invest in the country of origin. Supporting overseas citizens also means demonstrating power on a political, economic or cultural level. States organise or sponsor exchange programmes as described in Chapters 7 and 8, hoping that participants will then advocate the interests of these countries. Also, regional governments like Okinawa Prefecture engage in such diasporic activities in order to increase their political influence, sometimes entering into competition with the national administration. However, little research exists on the importance of specific subnational actors so far (Sahoo 2006: 95ff.).

A success story?

Diasporic networks can also mean power in one's country of residence. Therefore, the Confra tournament was also meant to demonstrate the Nikkei's economic

Introduction 9

well-being and good reputation as a tiny minority. Unlike many studies on discriminated migrants, literature has usually presented Japanese migration to Latin America as a success story. The Nikkei are well-respected while they have seldom suffered from stigmatisation and discrimination. Instead, Kikumura-Yano (2002b: 3) notes that "'Nikkei-ness' is also a dynamic cultural resource, especially in Latin America, where 'being Nikkei' is not a matter of 'race' per se but rather 'a pragmatic ethnic network of potential opportunities.'"

The pursuit of recognition from others, be they migrants or not, appears to be a universal human feature. Nevertheless, few authors have dealt with the definition of "prestige" as other people's respect and admiration towards an individual or group based on one's behaviour or position in society. With Thorstein Veblen, Max Weber, Marcel Mauss and Georg Simmel as predecessors, Pierre Bourdieu introduces the term "symbolic capital" for such cultural, economic, social or physical resources of a group or individual. He defines it as "the form that the various species of capital assume when they are perceived and recognized as legitimate" (Bourdieu 1989: 17), requiring a more or less conscious consensus. Actors try to defend or even improve their position in society, creating boundaries of distinction to others who enjoy less symbolic capital. As Bourdieu (1989: 23) writes: "Symbolic capital is a credit; it is the power granted to those who have obtained sufficient recognition to be in a position to impose recognition." Symbolic capital may lead to symbolic power, the ability to influence which social practices count as right and valuable: "The power to impose and to inculcate a vision of divisions, that is, the power to make visible and explicit social divisions that are implicit, is political power par excellence" (ibid.). According to Bourdieu (1979b), such distinctions depend on economic capital such as income and property; but they also relate to social capital, actual or potential social networks as well as to cultural capital such as education, skills and manners. Hence, following his theory of the conversion of capitals, symbolic capital can be translated into other forms of capital or vice-versa; it may, for example, be objectified in the form of an aristocratic title.[11] While economic capital may result in symbolic capital, the latter also legitimises the former: symbolic capital is useful to find work, social support and other resources. Being associated with modernity may also lead to symbolic capital (Mooney 2011).

Whereas classical texts on ethnic identity like Barth (1994) neglected questions of inequality between groups, socio-cultural notions and aspects of power influence each other, creating complex webs of inequalities. The case of Japanese migration to Bolivia demonstrates that migrant minorities are not per se regarded as a threat to a nation's economy, public security and welfare system or its cultural identity – although popular discourse in Europe may currently point to another direction. Also, academic literature usually describes ethnic minorities as socially and economically disadvantaged, a situation caused by both legislation and generalised negative stereotypes, since the majority generally controls political and economic institutions, sets cultural standards and rewards or punishes a specific habitus. Concrete disadvantages with direct consequences for a minority's social mobility can be precarious schooling, living

10 *Introduction*

and working conditions or reduced access to welfare. Especially the status as non-citizen means a legal handicap. All this is not the case for the Nikkei, but experiences of being verbally excluded because of phenotype, ethnic identity or cultural practices can mean inequality with the majority population as well, even though they may not lead to concrete disadvantages.[12] As Khosravi (2010: 93f.) observes:

> Immigrants and even their children are regarded as guests. One is regarded as a guest as long as one is regarded as an immigrant. An immigrant cannot be a host for the simple reason that she or he is a guest whose presence is expected to be only temporary. A guest is always a stranger; there is an asymmetric power relationship between host and guest. This relationship is violent. It requires a definite gratitude. Guests are expected to display their gratitude for being tolerated. Naturalization ceremonies, which may include kissing the flag, manifest the expectation of gratitude.

Against this background, I argue that the equation "migrant/ethnic minority = disadvantaged" is an oversimplification and reflects the general lack of research on more influential minorities, like highly qualified foreigners or lifestyle migrants (Benson and Osbaldiston 2016; Koser and Salt 1997). While no group is omnipotent in a given society, an ethnic minority may control a significant share of material and immaterial resources and may even impose its definitions onto another collectivity. However, few studies have described how such minorities attain and negotiate this position and how they interact with other groups (see, e.g., Klein 2012; Ley 2010; Ong 2005; Salverda 2015; Schmidt-Lauber 1998; Takenaka 2003b; Tsuda 1999).

Nikkei in Bolivia and elsewhere often identify as part of the middle class. While Salverda (2015) writes about Franco-Mauritians as an "ethnic elite"[13] which dominates large parts of the economy, the Nikkei's political, social, cultural or economic influence is comparatively much less important. Although they are not able to impose their vision of the world, they enjoy much symbolic capital among the majority population – following Scott (2003: 157), they constitute an advantaged group, but not an elite.

As Heiman et al. (2012: 9) write, "class" describes the experiences and practices of everyday life: culture produces and reproduces social privilege. While embracing economic-maximising strategies to maintain a comfortable standard of living in a capitalist context, "[m]iddle-class people are those in between, those neither corrupted by deprivation, nor debauched by excess," Liechty (2003: 69) writes in his study on Kathmandu's middle class. In the Nikkei case, too, rhetorics of morality naturalise this state-of-being; since, as Liechty (2003: 15) states, "cultural practices of the middle class disguise its class privileges (its economic and political powers) behind seemingly non-economic rhetorics of honor, achievement, and so on." All over the world, the middle class is marked by ambiguity, vulnerability as well as ambivalent relations with modernity. However, it depends on cultural, ethnic and national determinants and has to be defined through local practices. Also to the inside, the middle class is heterogeneous in orientation and follows differing interests and competing lifestyles (Pina-Cabral 2000).

While Bourdieu writes that ethnic identity can lead to symbolic capital, he does not develop this idea further. However, the Nikkei's ethnic boundary-making practices frequently overlap with social boundaries: behavioural patterns like manners, aspirations, modes of consumption, lifestyles and moral values help to create and recreate class (Bourdieu 1979a; Cohen 1992; Lamont 1992). Moreover, in Bolivia and Latin America in general, differences not only in culture but also in phenotype are often equated with markers of someone's socioeconomic background. According to Salverda (2015: 14), a common ethnic origin or even distinct physical features are useful when trying to create cohesion in a socially distinct group like the Franco-Mauritian elite: "Any overlap with ethnic characteristics contributes favourably to organizing itself particularistically, as ethnic groups tend to have a strong conviction that they share exclusive cultural characteristics, and a history different from other groups."

In this context, Nikkei identity seems to be a positive asset rather than something to be ashamed of. In contrast to the concept of "middlemen minorities," well-off but unbeloved foreign merchants who lack contacts with local residents (Bonacich 1973), the Nikkei's prosperity has almost never caused resentments from non-Nikkei Latin Americans. However, few researchers on Japanese Latin Americans have explicitly discussed this topic, except for Tsuda (1999: 210) who calls Japanese Brazilians a "positive minority" because of their prosperity above average, but does not further develop the concept except for the following short definition:

> Positive minorities are groups that are numerically small and that are not the dominant political power holders in a society, but that enjoy a generally higher socioeconomic status than the majority of the populace and whose distinctive cultural qualities and social position are respected if not admired.

Finally, the term "model minority" has been used for citizens of East Asian origin especially in the U.S. While the social, political and historical context is different here, they nevertheless share some characteristics with Nikkei in Latin America. The U.S. Americans of East Asian origin enjoy symbolic capital since they are considered outstandingly successful in academia and economy. Consistent with a neoliberal worldview, they seem to rely on their own forces to attain prosperity. However, the term has been heavily criticised since it means that such a group does not question existing power relations and does not denounce discrimination – their symbolic capital stems from the fulfilment of social obligations, but they are not able to define which social practices count as right. The term also implies that Asian Americans are regarded as foreigners despite being U.S. citizens (Li and Wang 2008; Wang 2008).

It is essential to note here that no advantaged group[14] is omnipotent and that symbolic capital has its limits, too. A group is powerful only in relation to other actors: the field of action determines specific forms of power. Hence, it is

12 *Introduction*

continuously challenged to maintain its position in society, resulting in complex and ambivalent relations to the majority population. Although Bourdieu (1989: 22) shortly acknowledges that "there are always, in any society, conflicts between symbolic powers that aim at imposing the vision of legitimate divisions, that is, at constructing groups," many authors have not focused enough on this unstable balance. Especially in the case of easily identifiable groups of foreign origin, conflicts may arise when a monopoly is at stake: the majority population might suddenly turn hostile and, as Tambiah (1994: 439) notes, "[f]oreign specialized minorities are thus vulnerable to the policies of forcible ejection and/or dispossession by governments promoting the interests of 'indigenous' minorities." Groups like the Nikkei usually avoid too much public attention and open conflict, fearing becoming an easy target during times of change. As Salverda (2015: 16) summarises, such a group's position in society is highly ambivalent: "That Franco-Mauritians' white-skin colour can be a threat to their position, however, does not exempt it from a symbolic distinction that can equally work in their favour – a nuance often missed."

Reflections on fieldwork and ethnographic methodology

The present research project is based on approximately 16 months of fieldwork in the city of Santa Cruz de la Sierra, Bolivia, mainly in 2013/2014, with short-term stays between 2009 and 2019. I have, furthermore, collected information in Colonia Okinawa, San Juan and La Paz as well as in Asunción, Paraguay, and Curitiba, Brasília and São Paulo, Brazil. I have also travelled to Kōbe, Tōkyō, Yokohama and Okinawa Prefecture, Japan.

I realised around 100 interviews, most of them between one and one-and-a-half hours; several actors I interviewed more than once. Moreover, informal conversations were an important source of information: short remarks on somebody's behaviour may lead to new aspects to be covered, and accidental encounters with acquaintances sometimes turned into discussions on the Nikkei's role in Santa Cruz' society.

Most interview partners were later-generation descendants of post-war migrants. Furthermore, I also interviewed some post-war Issei, pre-war descendants as well as some Brazilian, Peruvian and Paraguayan Nikkei, recent Japanese immigrants and non-Nikkei Bolivians who are married to Nikkei, work for Nikkei institutions, have frequent contact with Nikkei or have done research on Santa Cruz region. Their age span was 20–80 years, but most were Nisei and Sansei in their 30s, 40s and 50s. I realised the interviews in Spanish and exceptionally in Portuguese. This language choice might have limited the range of possible interviewees since carrying out an interview in Japanese would have been difficult for me, but my focus was on the current experiences of Nisei and Sansei who are all fluent Spanish speakers.

I found many interview partners through a snowball system that automatically directed me to some well-known association members. Depending on their leaders, some associations were enthusiastic to invite me to their activities, whereas others seemed indifferent and hardly reacted to interview requests. However, relying solely on this strategy often leads to individuals regarded as "typical." Especially through the recommendation of non-Nikkei, I also spoke with individuals who did not identify as Nikkei despite being of Japanese origin. Finally, I contacted some interview partners specifically because of their role in associations or because I had previously heard about them.

In order to cross-check information and to complement interviews, I did participant observation in daily life and during events. No "Japantown" exists in Santa Cruz, but the best place to meet Nikkei or other Asian descendants is Calle Antonio Vaca Diez, also known as Calle Adán Gutiérrez, a small but busy street close to Los Pozos market with several Asian shops, offices and the headquarters of Okinawa Kenjinkai association. One can also meet many Nikkei in Centro Social Japonés, the other important Nikkei association, principally on Saturdays after Japanese school.

Fieldwork is not a linear process, but unanticipated delays and difficulties may bring valuable insights into the research topic. Fieldwork also depends on strokes of luck, but, as Yano (2003: 292) notes: "[S]erendipity does not just happen, but is partly bestowed, partly earned, and partly exploited." Fortunately, accessing the field was not as difficult as stereotypes on the "closed Japanese" suggest. It became evident that the Nikkei are in a comfortable social position and that the research topic is relatively uncontroversial. Interview partners did not ask for affiliations, business cards or formal letters, although an informal introduction by a mutual acquaintance proved to be helpful in two cases.[15] We often met spontaneously at the interview partner's office during working hours, in restaurants, cafes and at their homes. I soon gained some insight into people's biographies and knew whom I could ask to obtain specific information. I also learned about the position of interview partners in Nikkei networks, enabling me to contextualise their accounts. As Hardacre (2003: 84) emphasises, fieldwork is not an on-off experience, but contacts can be useful for further studies and pragmatic reasons, thereby concluding that "it has usually been my experience that genuine friendships arise spontaneously in the course of fieldwork."

Suzuki (2010: 15) as a male researcher observed that accessing female research participants in Colonia Okinawa was not easy, but I as a woman also encountered more difficulties in accessing female circles than male ones. Even though several women were eager to give their opinion, males tended to be more used to dealing with outsiders and discussing research-related topics.

Upon speaking about my research outside the Nikkei community, I usually encounter blank astonishment since the topic is new to most interlocutors outside Latin America and Japan. The Nikkei are generally not considered "really Bolivian," unlike Quechua, Aymara, Guaraní or other indigenous groups – consequently, the literature in Spanish, English and other languages on such groups is abundant compared to non-indigenous urban Bolivians. Nevertheless, for most Bolivian Nikkei, it was simply natural to become a research topic. For many of the interview partners, it was clearly not the first time to be interviewed, and they were often aware that especially Japanese researchers have been interested in their fate. Several of them had also read one or more books on Japanese migration.

14 *Introduction*

A side effect of this familiarity with Nikkei studies was that interview partners often assumed that I was a historian and recommended Issei as eyewitnesses to me – many visitors are interested in the *colonias'* history above all. Some also urged me to focus on the *colonias* since they considered them "more authentic." Unlike what Suzuki (2010: 15) experienced in the rural environment of Colonia Okinawa, "student" was a category urban Nikkei accepted since most of them were university graduates. Whereas post-war Nikkei generally took my interest for granted, especially pre-war interview partners were grateful for my attention, thereby expressing their disappointment with Japan and post-war descendants who, according to them, did not care about their fate.

Power relations are central to social relations and to fieldwork. Anthropologists have often consciously chosen to study poor and marginalised groups, trying to give them a voice. A researcher is, in most cases, considered to possess financial means, information, education and access to institutions, being more mobile and enjoying more symbolic capital, whether or not this is true. In my research, I often felt the opposite – it was rather a case of "studying up" (Nader 1972). Many Nikkei own spacious houses or apartments, sometimes in gated communities, and may travel abroad for holidays to other American countries, Japan or Europe. I did not have material goods, information or connections to offer in exchange for an interview – nor was that expected. After an interview or event, they often offered to drive me home, a frequent practice among middle-class *cruceñas* and *cruceños*; otherwise, I relied on buses and shared taxis, regarded as a means of transport for lower classes and students in Santa Cruz.

Hauser-Schäublin (2008: 38) writes that being a participant observer means having an inconspicuous role, in other words, not being a leader or organiser. As a short-term visitor, one does not enjoy all rights but does not need to fulfil all obligations; hence, possibilities to participate might be limited (Bestor 2003). Rules for acceptance or non-acceptance exist for each situation, leading to a whole bunch of possible engagements that cannot be exactly repeated on a later occasion. I regularly assisted in Day Service activities for the elderly and participated in Okinawan-style Ryūkyūkoku Matsuridaiko dance. While especially Okinawan descendants identified me as a dance group member and appreciated my representing Okinawan culture in Bolivia, some people had difficulties in understanding the concept of participant observation – one elderly lady complained about me sitting around idly in Multimercado Okinawa. Because I used to spend time at Centro Social Japonés on Saturdays after Japanese school, others assumed that I was waiting for a child. Furthermore, I bought food in Nikkei shops, had meals in Japanese restaurants, became a regular visitor of the associations' celebrations and enrolled for a Japanese course. After some time, I noticed that many descendants talked to me in Spanish mixed with Japanese words or implicitly assumed that I knew people or events they were talking about; I interpreted this as a sign that people had become accustomed to my presence.

Nikkei interview partners often tried to find similarities between Japan and Central Europe, for instance, regarding low crime rates or the lack of corruption, supposing that there was a common understanding between us because of similar

Introduction 15

expectations and experiences. They often supposed me to be organised and on time or to have an attitude towards work they did not expect from non-Nikkei Bolivians. They also appreciated when I demonstrated my knowledge about Japan and got excited whenever I drank green tea without sugar – "you drink tea like a Japanese!" – or when I told them about my preference for dishes such as *soba, udon, anko* or even *mochi* – I have experienced that few people outside East Asia like these rice cakes due to their particular rubber-like consistency …! Often, the highly welcomed result was that they invited me to a Japanese meal. Furthermore, because I am fluent in Chinese, I could impress some Nikkei by reading Japanese *kanji* characters, since many are merely familiar with *hiragana* and *katakana*.[16]

It is sometimes suggested that being an insider gives more advantage during the process of gathering information, whereas one may also suggest that outsiders will more easily notice what seems normal to group members. Consequently, it is necessary to seek closeness without losing the distance. I do not know if I, as a non-Japanese and non-Nikkei, had an advantage. At least in two cases, it turned out to be easier to obtain an appointment when I declared myself not Bolivian. In one of these cases, my comments on a calendar in the interview partner's shop were essential because it showed the famous wood bridge in Lucerne, the Kapellbrücke, next to my university. Fortunately, non-Nikkei Bolivian interview partners, too, turned out to be open to my questions.

At the same time, without an attempt to justify all their actions, I cannot deny that I felt sympathetic towards my interview partners. Similar to what Salverda (2015: 18) writes, while I have been trying to be critical, I recognise that also the Nikkei in Bolivia are subject to specific external circumstances and that they are not necessarily interested in challenging them since it might eventually mean losing their existence.

Outline

Chapter 2 presents the background of Japanese migration to Bolivia. I focus first on the socioeconomic circumstances in Japan and Okinawa from the late 19th century onwards. This includes an analysis of Japan's attitude towards ethnic minorities, its emigration policies as well as the receiving countries' motivations to accept foreigners. I furthermore provide an outline of Japanese migration to the Americas in general and present an overview of Bolivian history since the late 19th century, with a particular focus on the Bolivian lowlands and regional identity discourses and, of course, Japanese migration to Bolivia.

In Chapter 3, I highlight how post-war Nikkei have achieved middle-class status in Bolivia. They present a narrative on supposedly superior "Japanese values" while implicitly or explicitly distancing themselves from non-Nikkei. On a closer look, Japan's support for descendants abroad has been essential as has been work migration to Japan. I also describe how Bolivian Nikkei have benefitted from favourable media images on a macro-level. However, the situation remains double-faced: descendants are frequently identified as foreigners or even as *chinos*

16 *Introduction*

[Chinese]; therefore, they actively try to present themselves as "well-integrated" model migrants who have contributed to Bolivia's well-being.

Chapter 4 discusses how post-war Nikkei define the *comunidad japonesa* (Japanese community) while negotiating ethnic boundaries in daily life. While many descendants declare to feel an affinity to this "large family," Nikkei association leaders often try to present a homogeneous community to the outside. Endogamy has contributed to creating a distinctive ethnic identity. At the same time, Nikkei both identify with and distance themselves from the *cruceño* middle class and hope to resist the perceived loss of values by sending their children to Japanese school. Some also try to propagate "Japanese values" at work. All this occurs with an implicit or explicit reference to Japan, but many Nikkei's relation to that country is becoming increasingly ambivalent.

Nevertheless, not everybody with Japanese ancestors identifies as Nikkei or is readily accepted by other Nikkei as part of the *comunidad japonesa*. Therefore, Chapter 5 shows a variety of ambiguities and contradictions. Nikkei in Bolivia and elsewhere often differentiate themselves according to generation, language skills, regional origin and their ancestors' time of arrival. Individual attitudes towards the *comunidad* are becoming increasingly heterogeneous. Finally, I examine descendants of partly non-Japanese origin, recent Japanese migrants, Nikkei from neighbouring countries and non-Nikkei acquaintances, their identities and their role in the *comunidad*.

Associations have played an essential role in the definition of Nikkei identities. In Chapter 6, I resume their efforts to construct an ethnic identity through cultural activities. Whereas religious associations remain seldom in the Japanese diaspora, ethnic associations wish to ensure a favourable representation to the outside while trying to maintain the relation with Japan. However, they lose members because of internal tensions and differing expectations. In times of increasing financial difficulties, their future is uncertain.

These developments stand in contrast to the growing importance of Pan-American Nikkei events as discussed in Chapter 7. For some time, Japanese and especially Okinawan descendants all over the Americas have been meeting for sports tournaments, conventions or youth meetings. The popularity of such events also illustrates the Nikkei's self-confidence as middle-class citizens, resulting in a changing relationship with Japan and in new definitions of Nikkei identity on a supranational level.

Bolivian Nikkei identify more and more as Bolivians, but they are nevertheless challenged to maintain their economic basis at a time when Japanese state support is decreasing. Chapter 8 describes how the Nikkei have been struggling to translate their socioeconomic success from the *colonias* to urban areas. Bolivian Nikkei entrepreneurs outside agriculture remain rare and few descendants have taken advantage of their ethnic origin to establish business relations with Japan. Despite Japan's popularity in Bolivia, Nikkei do not merchandise their ethnic identity. Moreover, it is questionable if the younger generations are well prepared for the Bolivian job market. Even in the *colonias*, socioeconomic stability is not guaranteed: whereas the two Nikkei agricultural cooperatives are widely

Introduction 17

recognised as role models, a closer look reveals that they are challenged in an increasingly competitive environment.

Chapter 9 focuses on the Nikkei's distanced relationship with the Bolivian state. Many descendants consider corruption an inherent ill of Bolivian society, pointing to their supposed moral superiority as Japanese descendants and considering themselves victims of the state rather than as its citizens. While Japanese diplomacy has occasionally supported the Nikkei in land conflicts, they did not need to invest in networks for a long time, and, as a result, their power in the Bolivian political arena remains limited. As the case of a Nikkei mayor demonstrates, the polarised political climate makes it difficult for outsiders to assert themselves even at the local level. Nevertheless, Nisei and Sansei increasingly argue for more participation in Bolivian civil society, but with few tangible results so far.

Notes

1 A kind of five-a-side football which is played indoors and which is popular especially in Latin America.
2 The term refers to the inhabitants of Santa Cruz, both the city and the department. It is considered to be a neutral designation, unlike the word *camba* that implies an emotional attachment.
3 Taking Japan as a reference, Japanese descendants all over the world divide themselves into Issei [first generation], namely the migrants themselves, as well as Nisei [second generation], Sansei [third generation], Yonsei [fourth generation], etc. These designations are not used in a strict way: they often refer broadly to a specific age group independently of the individuals' generational affiliation.
4 I will use the term "*colonia*" since it is common among descendants and in literature to refer to this kind of agricultural settlement central to Latin American Nikkei imaginary. However, it is questionable if the term "*colonias*" is still justified since they are now regular municipalities according to Bolivian legislation, inhabited by a majority of non-Nikkei.
5 However, Eriksen (2010: 1) rightly observes that the term "group" is contradictory: "Does the non-immigrant population of Britain constitute a people, does it comprise several peoples [...], or does it rather form part of a Germanic, or an English-speaking, or an Atlantic, or a European people?"
6 Ethnic minorities are generally classified either as being of indigenous origin (Eriksen 2015: 360ff.), often related to premodern modes of production, or as minorities of forced or voluntary migration. The latter usually live in urban areas and are integrated into the capitalist system. In the following sections, I will focus on the latter type.
7 Legal citizenship or nationality, according to Vink and Bauböck (2013: 622), "is a status that creates a legal bond between individuals and a state and endows these individuals with certain rights and obligations". I will not distinguish the two terms, although Jones-Correa (2001) puts forward that nationality does not mean enjoying all legal citizenship rights, for example, if absentee voting is not permitted. Bolivia and practically all states in the Americas automatically accept children born on their territory as citizens and do not object multiple citizenship. For individuals, multiple citizenship is often beneficial since it implies rights in more than one country. Some states, however, may also consider multiple allegiances to be dangerous: Japan, that merely applies jus sanguinis, officially allow its citizens to hold only one nationality.

18   *Introduction*

8   "Diaspora" has been a more politicised term than "transnationalism": states have been using the term to pursue nationalist agendas and political projects. However, the meaning of "diaspora" has changed and expanded in recent years; both are now often used interchangeably.

9   For further discussion on this concept see, e.g., Butler (2001), Dufoix (2008) and White (2003).

10   *Dekasegi* stands for temporary work migration (Kikumura-Yano 2002b: 3). However, it now mostly refers to the migration of Latin American Nikkei to Japan where they generally work in jobs that do not require high qualifications. This term is widely used among Bolivian Nikkei to refer to descendants' work migration to Japan.

11   However, his definition of symbolic capital is not without contradictions. Bourdieu remains vague on how to theorise the lack of symbolic capital. Unfortunately, complex relations of inequality remain unaddressed as well, e.g., cases like the wealthy but unpopular middlemen minorities described below, although Bourdieu (1989: 21) admits that "[S]ymbolic order is not formed in the manner of a market price, out of the mere mechanical addition of individual orders."

12   One has to bear in mind that perceptions of what constitutes discrimination are highly subjective.

13   Khan (2012: 362) defines elites broadly as "those who have vastly disproportionate control over or access to a resource". Similarly, Salverda and Abbink (2013: 1) describe elites as "a relatively small group within the societal hierarchy that claims and/or is accorded power, symbolic capital or command over others on the basis of a number of publicly recognised criteria, and aims to preserve an entrenched status thus acquired". Although systems cannot exercise power by themselves, they are important to explain how certain actors can exercise authority, Salverda (2015: 11) argues. When I refer to the "elite families" of Santa Cruz, I refer to a group of very prosperous interrelated European descendants who have been controlling most political and economic resources (Prado 2007: 157ff.)

14   Note that such groups are heterogeneous: while one may control large parts of the economy, another may exercise political power. Some actors have a disproportionate influence on cultural production, others dominate the military, the media, state administration, religious life or knowledge production (Dogan 2003).

15   Compared to Bestor et al. (2003: 14) who write that such formal introductions are of utmost importance in Japan.

16   The Japanese writing system combines several thousand *kanji* logographs and the syllabaries *hiragana* and *katakana*, each of them with 46 basic characters. Although Japanese language could theoretically be written in *hiragana* or *katakana* only, *kanji* help to clarify the meaning of homophones, especially in more abstract texts. In their majority, *kanji* maintain the meaning and physical shape of Chinese characters.

2 History of Japanese migration to Bolivia

The atmosphere is generally peaceful at Santa Cruz' main square Plaza 24 de Septiembre where families eat ice cream and feed doves. Elderly men play chess under *tajibo* trees flowering in yellow and rose, whereas other people buy coffee or fruit juice from waiters in white uniforms. The municipal guards seem bored, unless they oblige everybody to stand up when a band plays the national anthem on Monday morning. However, the green and white colours of the department's banner are much more visible around the main square and in the city than the red, yellow and green Bolivian flag. Santa Cruz has become the centre of the lowlands' autonomy movement: conflicts with the national government became prominent especially around 2008, and the plaza was an important site for noisy political demonstrations (Figure 2.1).

Like other Latin American cities, Santa Cruz is marked by a growing polarisation between different social strata. Potholes and garbage are part of the cityscape, as are chaotic markets and disabled persons singing pious songs in public transport. Many highlanders have settled in the more precarious residential areas in the city's south and east. Neighbourhoods such as Plan 3000 are characterised by a lack of basic services, poor socioeconomic indicators and uncontrolled growth. Meanwhile, some *cruceñas* and *cruceños* compare their hometown to Miami, referring to the omnipresent late-model SUVs, high-rise buildings, shopping malls and multinational agricultural companies, as well as to the countless beauty contests and glamorous parties. The city is also regarded as one of the country's most insecure places; urban life is associated with armed assault and drug trafficking. Palmasola, a prison managed by its inmates, has gained international notoriety. Consequently, the middle and upper class increasingly view the outside as potentially threatening. In 2006, those with financial means could choose between more than 160 gated communities (*condominios*), apartment houses and resorts that may offer access to facilities such as parks, swimming pools, tennis courts, golf courses, meeting halls, shops, etc. (Schoop 2008).

The city of Santa Cruz de la Sierra has become the largest city in the Bolivian lowlands and the capital of Santa Cruz Department. Even though Bolivia is generally associated with mountains, mines, salt lakes and lamas, the lowlands constitute around two-thirds of the country's surface area. Santa Cruz is located around 400 m above sea level on the shores of the Piraí River, more than 100 km east

DOI: 10.4324/9781003228295-2

Figure 2.1 Santa Cruz' central plaza.

of the Andean foothills. Because of its ring roads, it is nicknamed "*ciudad de la anillos*" [city of the rings]. Climate is hot and humid with heavy rainfalls mostly between November and February. For *cruceñas* and *cruceños*, this means benefitting from fruits like mangos, passion fruits and the local speciality *achachairú*, but also suffering from inundated streets and the omnipresence of mosquitos, potential vectors of diseases such as dengue and chikungunya. From May to September, cold air masses from the Antarctic can cause chilly temperatures, bringing public life almost to a halt. Especially, August is famous for strong winds, filling the city with dust, dry leaves and flying plastic bags.

The first Japanese reached the city of Santa Cruz at the beginning of the 20th century in the course of the so-called rubber boom, but most migrants arrived in the nearby *colonias* in the 1950s and 1960s. Santa Cruz was then still a quiet and relatively insignificant town and senior *cruceñas* and *cruceños* still remember how any heavy rainfall transformed the central streets into mud – one frequently finds these pictures of "old Santa Cruz" on calendars and posters. The city centre with the typically Hispano-American rectangular street grid and the single-storied houses still reflects the architecture of nearby villages, mostly lacking representative administrative and cultural buildings. Nevertheless, for the last 60 years, the city has grown enormously following the influx of migrants from the entire country: from around 43,000 inhabitants in the 1950s to approximately 1.5 million today. Santa Cruz as the department's capital has become Bolivia's economic centre with many subsidiaries of multinational companies, mainly related to agribusiness. The economic upturn is not only visible in the city itself, but also in the

History of Japanese migration to Bolivia   21

two Japanese colonies Colonia Okinawa and San Juan, a two- and three-hours' drive from the city, respectively. After the 1952 revolution and the following land reform, Bolivia, Japan and the United States signed two treaties to establish the two agricultural settlements, Colonia Okinawa and San Juan that have become two prosperous towns. The context of the development of a once almost forgotten territory to the economic motor of the entire country is central also to the history of Japanese migration to Bolivia.

A sociohistorical portrait of Japan

With roughly 127 million inhabitants by 2015, Japan covers a territory of 378,000 km². Hokkaidō, Honshu, Kyūshū and Shikoku are the largest of the 6,852 islands. Among the smaller islands is the Ryūkyū archipelago – located southwest of Kyūshū, it comprises over 100 islands, stretching over more than 600 km. The prefecture of Okinawa, roughly coinciding with this archipelago, has today around 1.5 million inhabitants (Sōmushō 2017). Japan's climate is mostly humid and subtropical, but since mountains dominate the central parts, few coastal plains are suitable for agriculture. Situated at the circumpacific ring of fire, active volcanoes are numerous and natural hazards such as earthquakes and tsunamis have repeatedly affected the country (Figure 2.2).

In the early 17th century, after the period of warring states, Japan was unified under the Tokugawa dynasty. Being able to combine political hegemony with economic power, the hereditary military rulers (*shōgun*) governed for the next 250 years with the emperor as the symbolic head of state. In the late 16th century, Portuguese traders had been the first Europeans to arrive in Kyūshū and soon, Jesuit missionaries set foot on Japanese soil.[1] The *shōgun* were increasingly afraid of losing power and opted for an isolationist policy *(sakoku)*: starting in 1630, no foreigners were allowed to enter Japan, although exceptions were made for some trade outposts. However, ideas from abroad did enter the country via books and trade goods. In 1429, the Ryūkyūs had become a unified kingdom focusing on trading relations with China and South East Asia, with Naha as its political and religious centre. The kingdom had to pay tribute to China and later to the Satsuma clan from Kagoshima (Molasky 2001; Zöllner 2006).

Europeans and North Americans increasingly challenged Japan's isolation. In 1853/54, Commodore Matthew Perry with his "black ships" forced Japan to sign a treaty with the United States on unequal terms. Agreements with other countries were made in the following years. Consequently, several economic branches entered into crisis, but reforms failed and some local rulers started challenging the Tokugawa's authority. The shogunate's end was marked by peasant insurgencies, price increases and famine (Jansen 2000; McClain 2002).

In 1868, Emperor Mutsuhito, better known as the Emperor Meiji, ascended the throne. Japan changed radically from a feudal country to an industrialised, capitalist and centralised nation with a constitution and an elected parliament. The government introduced a common national currency and the Western calendar, built railroads and a telegraph service and implemented a mass education system

22 *History of Japanese migration to Bolivia*

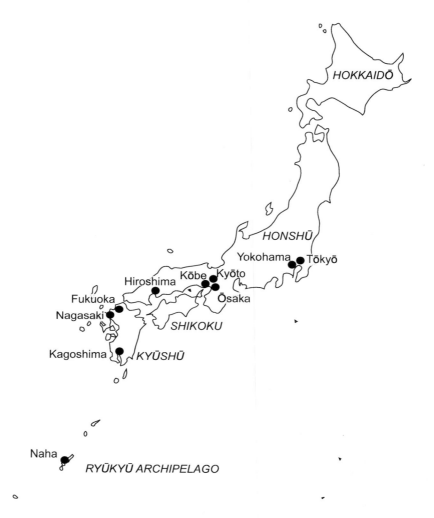

Figure 2.2 Map of Japan.

to catch up with the "West." Furthermore, Japan annexed the Ryūkyūs in 1879 (Gordon 2014; McClain 2002).

In the Meiji period and the subsequent Taishō era (1912–1926), economic inequalities resulted in several uprisings. Okinawa was treated as a colony to exploit and the collapse of sugar prices in the 1920s resulted in famine. Furthermore, in 1923, the Kantō earthquake devastated the Tōkyō area, causing more than 140,000 casualties (McClain 2002; Zöllner 2006). At the same time, Japan widened its influence in Eastern Asia in the first Sino–Japanese war (1894–1895) and in the Russian–Japanese war (1904–1905), colonising Hokkaidō, Taiwan and

History of Japanese migration to Bolivia   23

Korea and controlling Manchuria. In search of a better future, many Okinawans and mainland Japanese moved to the cities, others to the Japanese colonies in Asia or the Americas.

The Japanese government, dominated by ultranationalist and imperialist forces, aimed at establishing a new regional order with Japan at its head, provoking the outbreak of the Second World War in East Asia. The Allies bombed several cities in mainland Japan but the only major land combat on Japanese soil was the bloody Okinawa battle in 1944/45. Since Okinawans were regarded as potentially disloyal to Japan and the Emperor, they also came to fear the Japanese troops. Shuri Palace, the iconic symbol of the once independent kingdom, was destroyed and looted as well (Allen 2009; Hein and Selden 2003). It has been estimated that one-third to a quarter of the main island's population was killed (Kerr 1964: 472; Molasky 2001: 15). The war ended on 15 August 1945 with the Japanese Emperor declaring unconditional capitulation. Since the U.S. government was interested in the strategic location of the archipelago, it put Okinawa under the administration of the U.S. Civil Administration of the Ryūkyū Islands (USCAR). Before the occupation's end in 1972, USCAR built a number of military bases, occupying large areas of arable land.

In the Second World War, most Japanese cities had been devastated. Inflation and delinquency rates were high and essentials of life scarce. The situation was further aggravated when many settlers returned from the former Asian colonies: in 1945, Japan had 72 million inhabitants, but six years later, its population had grown to 85 million. (Yanagida 1998b: 67). Whereas migration to the Americas had ceased at the outbreak of the Second World War, many Japanese decided to migrate overseas again. The Japanese government required them to stay abroad permanently as recorded in their passports (Endōh 2009: 37). Only Brazil, Paraguay, Bolivia, Argentina and the Dominican Republic were willing to sign treaties to enable Japanese settlements, whereas Japan promised investments, loans and other benefits. The Ministry of Foreign Affairs as the responsible entity funded quasi-governmental migration offices in all prefectures as well as overseas. In 1974, these institutions eventually became part of the Japanese International Cooperation Agency (JICA) (Manzenreiter 2014). Many Okinawans decided to migrate abroad as well, supported by USCAR that feared revolts and the strengthening of communism on the islands (Amemiya 2002).

Japan's economy soon recovered, resulting in a so-called economic miracle: from 1950 to 1973, Japan's GDP grew more than 10% annually and in 1968, it had become the second highest in the world (Esmein 2009; Gordon 2014). This was mainly a consequence of massive investments in new technologies, well-trained employees and a favourable yen–dollar exchange. Loyalty to one's company and co-workers was highly valued and hard work rewarded with upward mobility. In socioeconomic terms, Japan remains a relatively homogeneous country with a substantial middle class (Lie 2001: 28ff.; Sugimoto 1997: 33f.). As a consequence of these economic developments, mass emigration came to an end in the 1960s. At the same time, many mostly young Latin American Nikkei came to Japan as so-called *dekasegi* workers in the 1980s and 1990s (see below).

24 *History of Japanese migration to Bolivia*

After the end of the Japanese asset price bubble of the late 1980s and early 1990s, present-day Japan faces challenges such as economic recession, low birth rates and an ageing society, conflicts with China and South Korea for war-related issues and territorial disputes as well as questions of gender equity and immigration. Japan's public debt accounts for more than twice its annual GDP (Jones and Fukawa 2015). Especially after the Tōhoku earthquake in March 2011, followed by a tsunami and a nuclear disaster, energy has become a controversial topic. Okinawa Prefecture continues to be Japan's least developed prefecture in socio-economic terms, lagging behind in per-capita income, employment rates, health indicators, level of education, etc. (Sōmushō 2015, 2016a, 2016b). Okinawa's *kichi mondai* (military base problem) continues to be an important topic in public debate (Inoue 2017). Apart from the military bases and tourism, Okinawa Prefecture relies economically on subsidies from Tōkyō – this may be one reason why independence movements do not play a major role (Allen 2009; Hein and Selden 2003; Nakasone 2002).

Defining Japanese-ness in Japan and abroad

Already in the 18th and 19th centuries, Japanese intellectuals developed ideologies of race and identity. Before 1945, this cultural nationalism was expressed in the idea of a united and harmonious racial community, related to an uninterrupted succession of divine emperors for more than 2,000 years (Murphy-Shigematsu 1993). The Imperial Rescript on Education from 1890 was one means to indoctrinate this nationalist ideology to students. Ideas about the uniqueness or even superiority of the Japanese gave rise to the so-called *nihonjinron* or discourses on Japanese-ness, a "commercialized expression of Japanese nationalism" (Dale 1986: 14). Academic, economic and political elites have been disseminating such concepts up to the present day, but they also appear in informal publications, for example in manuals for Japanese businesspersons wishing to deal with foreigners. They always suppose that the Japanese are fundamentally different from all others, notably from "Westerners." Ethnic affiliation is generally justified by supposedly immutable Japanese blood, geographical features and historical circumstances such as the prolonged isolation from other countries (Yoshino 1992, 2001). Such notions have also been reproduced in the non-Japanese research literature and popular discourse inside and outside Japan. I cannot count how often I have heard and read that the Japanese are difficult or impossible to understand.

Since the 1970s, the *nihonjinron* have experienced a rise in popularity. They strongly correlate the so-called economic miracle with the country's supposed egalitarian character and group-orientedness, claiming that the Japanese are ethnically and racially homogeneous. Compared to other highly industrialised countries, Japan's foreign population amounts to merely 1.5%, most of them citizens of neighbouring countries (Sōmushō 2017). There is little awareness of Japan's historical or contemporary ethnic heterogeneity: most Japanese would insist that one could either be Japanese or non-Japanese, but not both. The negation of social, cultural and ethnic differences would also mean that Japanese and non-Japanese

History of Japanese migration to Bolivia   25

are mutually exclusive categories; however, in a Bolivian and Latin American context, Okinawan Nikkei have continuously challenged such assumptions. Accordingly, Japan does not allow double citizenship – although it does exist.

Many scholars have criticised such notions as chauvinistic, ahistorical and static since they negate cultural influences from China, Korea, Europe and North America, quite prominent at different stages of Japanese history. Furthermore, by focusing on the central Kansai and Kantō regions, such discourses leave no space for existing regional cultural variations in mainland Japan and much less for ethnic minorities such as the Ainu, the indigenous inhabitants of Hokkaidō island (Befu 2009; Dale 1986; Lie 2001; Yoshino 1992). Much inconsistency exists between the "Japanese race" and the "Japanese culture" also for Korean and Chinese descendants, living for generations in Japan. Other examples of such ambiguities are Japanese of partly foreign origin or Nikkei. Finally, most Okinawans identify as part of the Japanese cultural sphere, but are conscious of cultural differences to mainland Japan. Some of them even consider themselves a distinct ethnic group.

In the Meiji era, Okinawans, like other minorities, were considered backward, lazy, unrefined, unreliable and barbarian; in short, a contrast to the "civilised" inhabitants of central Japan (Nakasone 2002). Nevertheless, mainland Japanese often depicted Okinawans in a mixture of envy and disdain as uncorrupted by progress and living a relaxed life in an exotic paradise. Cultural differences exist regarding alimentation, religious practices and social organisation; some people even state that Okinawans can be distinguished from mainland Japanese by their physiognomy. Whether this is true or not, most Okinawans have typical last names such as Taira, Higa, Yamashiro, Oshiro or Arakaki. After the annexation of the archipelago, the Japanese government decided to prohibit "typically Okinawan" haircuts and clothing since they challenged the cherished imaginaries of a homogeneous Japanese nation. The government of Okinawa Prefecture as well as most of its population, longing for modernity and equality with Japan, welcomed such policies (Amemiya 1998; Arakaki 2002b; Kerr 1964; Lie 2001; Nakasone 2002). The measures to make the Ryūkyū archipelago an integral part of Japan also aimed at eradicating *uchināguchi* [Okinawan language].[2] After the Second World War, the migrants' relation to mainland Japan did not become less complicated with the construction of U.S. military bases for both countries' regional security interests.

Even when abroad, fellow Japanese migrants generally regarded Okinawans as different; the latter were thus in the paradoxical situation to be considered Japanese by locals and non-Japanese by other Nikkei. Okinawans often tried to adapt to mainland Nikkei and avoided disclosing their origin – in contrast, the local population was usually not aware of differences between the two groups (Amemiya 1998; Arakaki 2002a; Mori 2003; Suzuki 2006).

After the Second World War, the relationship between Okinawans and mainland Japanese gradually changed. The distance to Japan grew while the relation to locals became more intense. This is true especially for the Nisei, for example in Hawai'i, as Arakaki (2002a: 132) points out: during the Second World War, both Okinawan and mainland Japanese descendants had been treated as foreigners

26 *History of Japanese migration to Bolivia*

and enemies, both had grown up in the same environment speaking English as their first language. For descendants growing up after the 1960s, the situation had changed again: on the one hand, reconnecting with one's Okinawan origin had become a positive asset; on the other hand, travelling to Okinawa was easier than before, not least because the Nikkei's economic situation had improved. Nowadays, Okinawan dance groups, Okinawan food specialities and Okinawan songs are an essential part of Nikkei festivals all over the Americas.

Also, in Okinawa Prefecture itself, inhabitants increasingly claim a special place in Japanese society, thereby challenging the assumption of a homogeneous Japan – although one has to bear in mind that Okinawa Prefecture is diverse with regard to culture, politics, language or history. The reaffirmation of Okinawan identity has resulted in a boom of local festivities and cultural practices. In contemporary Okinawa Prefecture, colourful *bingata* cloth, *beniimo* (purple sweet potato) cakes as well as *eisā* dance and *sanshin* music are ubiquitous symbols for Okinawan-ness, not least for tourists. The reconstructed Shuri Palace, destroyed once more by a fire in 2019, appears on the UNESCO World Heritage List and one of its entrance gates is depicted on the 2,000-yen banknote. In contrast to the present-day problems, Okinawan officials advocate a proud past with romanticised and essentialised imaginaries of the Ryūkyū kingdom as a peaceful country of traders bridging the world. The Second World War plays a substantive role in these initiatives: the prefecture has created a peace museum, issues a peace prize and celebrates peace day on 23 June.

Activities also point to Okinawan descendants overseas in order to envision a global community, supposedly inheriting an *uchinānchu* [Okinawan] spirit and embodying *yuimārū* [mutual help], *chimugukuru* [Okinawan spirit/heart], *chimuchurasa* [compassionate and beautiful in mind] and *ichariba chōdē* [once we meet and talk, we feel close]. To reconnect to overseas Okinawans, festivals like Uchinānchu Taikai are held on a regular basis, supported by associations such as WYUA (World Youth Uchinānchu Association) and WUB (World Uchinānchu Business Association) (Miyahira and Petrucci 2011). Overseas, Okinawan descendants themselves have created multiple networks and activities as well, as described in Chapter 7.

Emigration policies of the Japanese government

Emigrants have played an important role for modern Japan, already visible in the sheer amount of literature on overseas Nikkei communities. Japanese national and prefectural administrations played a key role in planning migration, making agreements with actors abroad as well as recruiting and training prospective migrants. Rather than focussing merely at the migrants' well-being, the different involved ministries pursued their own political projects (Gamlen 2008; Siu 2002). Japan continuously invested in overseas settlements and Nikkei, particularly via its official development assistance agency JICA (Japanese International Cooperation Agency), founded in 1963, and its predecessors, spending around 2.6 billion yen annually (Takenaka 2009b: 1330). In recent times, JICA also employed Latin

History of Japanese migration to Bolivia 27

American Nikkei, thanks to their local knowledge – and as a cost-effective alternative to Japanese employees (Manzenreiter 2014: 232).

In the beginning, national and prefectural governments hoped for remittances. In 1891, money transfers to Hiroshima Prefecture amounted to 54% of the entire prefectural budget (Endōh 2009: 61). With the migrants' assistance, the government of pre-war Japan tried to create international networks and links to foreign markets. It also hoped to diversify trade partners, trying to secure food supply for Japan's growing population and raw materials for its industrialisation. Consistent with this idea, the colonial ministry managed the relation to Nikkei before the war and opened overseas offices in Brazil, Peru and Mexico. Japanese business corporations purchased land in different regions of Brazil in order to import raw materials: in the late 1930s, Nikkei produced 57% of the country's silk, 75% of its tea and almost half of its cotton, although they constituted only 3% of Brazil's population (Azuma 2002a; Endōh 2009: 72ff., 170ff.). Migrants in Bolivia also supported the Japanese morally and materially during times of war and helped the Japanese authorities to negotiate with the local government to allow further migration.

At the same time, states all over the world have been regarding emigration as a kind of political safety valve in times of social unrest and harsh living conditions. Japan, too, has tried to send people overseas whom it regarded as potentially troublesome, such as poor peasants and urban labourers (Endōh 2009: 141). Emigration policies focused on families rather than on single migrants, considering them less likely to abandon the plantations. At the same time, Japan wanted to control whom it sent abroad. In the early years of mass immigration, Japanese government agencies also issued publications for emigrants on how to behave properly overseas (Dresner 2006). Their background was scrutinised, too: Hiraoka (1980: 59, 141ff.) notes that Japanese authorities controlled settlers bound for the Bolivian *colonia* of San Juan to discover if they belonged to political extremist groups or if they had criminal records. Especially Okinawans suffered restrictions when planning to emigrate since the authorities feared that they would disturb fellow migrants or that their supposedly inappropriate behaviour would shed an unfavourable light on Japan (Endōh 2009: 160ff.; Mori 2003). When abroad, education played an important role to mentally and spiritually strengthen migrants' minds. Before the Second World War, the Emperor's veneration and the Imperial Rescript on Education studied at school were important elements of this attempt to recreate Japanese society.

At the same time, Japan's wish to become equal with Europe and North America influenced emigration policies. The Meiji government thought that slave-like conditions for its subjects, comparable to those of Chinese indentured labourers, would hamper the country's ambition for power on a global level (Azuma 2002a: 32f.). Furthermore, it regarded migrants' prosperity and symbolic capital as a resource in international relations. Thus, not only the migrants themselves received support, but also their children and grandchildren.

Already during the period of isolation, Japanese intellectuals had heard of Latin America, but this part of the world seemed barbarian to them (Yanagida

28 *History of Japanese migration to Bolivia*

1998a) – thus, society regarded emigrants to this region with condescension. In turn, migrants' belief in Japanese superiority was reinforced by the nationalist education they received before the Second World War (Tsuda 2001b: 417). One explanation for the counterintuitive movement from Japan to Latin America is that mass migration to more popular destinations in North America was banned in 1923/24. Furthermore, advertisements exaggerated or distorted the actual circumstances, making prospective migrants believe in a sort of paradise with rich natural resources which allowed earning a living without major efforts; it also suggested that locals were overtly happy to welcome Japanese settlers. Moreover, Japanese authorities often inadequately or incorrectly informed outgoing migrants, while emigration projects were ill prepared. Nevertheless, Endōh (2009: 195) points out that the Japanese government was not very concerned about individual fate. Instead, migration to Latin America occupied a special place in the government's strategy to become equal to European and North American powers:

> In a nutshell, Japan took on its Latin America project as a way to exalt its national prestige and racial superiority in the international arena, specifically vis-à-vis the United States and Europe. Latin American nations undeniably belong to the Western World, with Spain and Portugal as their former rulers [...]. If Japan developed and prevailed over this poorer part of the Western world, it could feel triumphant. [...] Similar satisfaction might not be gained by mastering Asia, which belonged to the "inferior Orient." Ultimately, Japan's expanded statehood was directed at the greater West, via its weakest part, Latin America.

Japanese migration to the Americas

The Japanese were not the first Asians to travel to Latin America. Indications exist that the first were Filipinos on the Manila-Acapulco galleons in the late 16th century. During the 19th and early 20th centuries, many Chinese, Koreans and Indians arrived as indentured labourers to Latin America and the Caribbean, for example to work in railroad construction (Hu-DeHart 2002; Lien and Affigne 2002). In the last decades, thousands of Koreans and Indians migrated to Brazil, Argentina, Panama, Colombia, Paraguay, Bolivia and other countries (Park 2002; High Level Committee on the Indian Diaspora 2001). Several cities in Mexico, Argentina, Panama, Cuba and Peru host Chinatowns as a visible sign of the historical and recent migration from China and Taiwan (Siu 2002, 2007). For Asian migrants, Latin America was generally not their first choice; they preferred the economically more developed United States and Canada – some also hoped to move north, once they arrived in the southern part of the continent.

In contrast to most of these migrants, the majority of Japanese settlers in Latin America participated in official emigration programmes to establish permanent agricultural *colonias*. Since the male firstborn generally inherited his father's land in Japan, many second and third sons decided to emigrate (Staniford 2004: 5f.). Most emigrants originated from the southwestern prefectures of Hiroshima,

History of Japanese migration to Bolivia   29

Nagasaki, Fukuoka, Kagoshima, Kumamoto, Saga and Yamaguchi as well as from Okinawa (Endōh 2009: 102).[3]

The Japanese Ministry of Foreign Affairs (Gaimushō 2017b) estimates that 3.6 million Nikkei and Japanese reside overseas, mostly in the Americas, whereas the Association of Nikkei and Japanese Abroad (2017b) speaks of 3.8 million descendants all over the world. Ölschleger (2004: 545) estimates that about 340,000 Okinawans and their descendants live overseas – following his conservative assumption of 2.5 million Nikkei in the Americas, 14% of them would be of Okinawan origin. Okinawa Prefecture assumes that 400,000 Okinawan descendants live abroad (Dai-6 Sekai no Uchinānchu Taikai Jikkō Iinkai Jimukyoku 2016b) (Figure 2.3).

Japanese migrants' first destination in the Americas was Hawai'i with its sugar plantations in 1869. Today, Nikkei are the second largest ethnic group in the archipelago. Japanese migrants have also settled on the U.S. West Coast, where many went into small-scale farming; others worked in Canadian mines. Both Canada and the United States banned Japanese and Chinese immigration in 1923 and 1924, respectively. Shortly after the Japanese attack on Pearl Harbour, around 120,000 Japanese from the Pacific Coast were deported to internment camps. This number includes their children, U.S. citizens by birth, whereas the Issei were only allowed to naturalise after the war. Canadian Nikkei suffered a similar fate. In 1988, the redress movement in both countries achieved that the former internees received an apology and some compensation payments. Including those with partly non-Japanese ancestry, around 1.3 million Nikkei live currently in the United States, compared to 100,000 in Canada (Azuma 2002b; Kobayashi and Ayukawa 2002; Okihiro 2002).

Prior to the Second World War, 245,000 Japanese immigrated to Latin America. Brazil has by far received the largest share of Japanese migrants, both before and after the war. For the pre-war era, this corresponds to 189,000 individuals. In the same period, Peru received 33,000 legally sanctioned migrants, Mexico 14,700 and Argentina 5,400. Smaller numbers went to Bolivia and Paraguay as well as to Cuba, Chile and Colombia. After the Second World War, around 71,000 Japanese migrated to Brazil, 9,600 to Paraguay, 1,200 to Argentina, 6,400 to Bolivia and 1,400 to the Dominican Republic (Kikumura-Yano 2002a: 67).

Most immigrants were farmers or were categorised as such and underwent some training before going abroad. However, more than 50% of all post-war migrants did not stay in the often ill-prepared settlements, much to the annoyance of Japanese officials (Endōh 2009: 39ff.). Furthermore, many wanted to return to Japan, but could not do so because of ongoing contracts, lack of financial resources or intimidation by the governments of Japan and the country of destination. In some places such as the Dominican Republic, settlers filed lawsuits against JICA or government ministries (Endōh 2009: 158). Apart from these cases, the Nikkei have seldom criticised the Japanese government, perhaps because of ongoing dependencies. Although Latin American Nikkei enjoy a high socioeconomic status nowadays, Endōh's (2009: 39) final evaluation is devastating:

Figure 2.3 Current numbers of Japanese descendants in the Americas. Data is based on Gaimushō (2017a), Ibuki (2013), Peguero (2015), State of Hawai'i (2013), Statistics Canada (2016) and United States Census Bureau (2016).

History of Japanese migration to Bolivia   31

[P]ostwar Latin American migration was the distorted product of compromise between half-hearted and opportunistic Latin American host countries and the ineffective and injudicious migration planners of the sender state. In particular, the latter, which was weak-kneed in bilateral negotiations with the host states, accepted virtually any term proposed by the host governments [...] but had no contingency preparations in place when the migration-settlement plan went wrong.

With around 1.5 million Nikkei, Brazil with an estimated population of 210 million is home to the largest group of descendants in both relative and absolute terms. Migration to Brazil officially started in 1908 and increased after the entry ban to North America. Most settlers would work on temporary contracts in coffee plantations. They concentrated in the southeastern states of São Paulo and Paraná, but colonies have been founded even in the Amazonian state of Pará. Although the Brazilian government did not send Nikkei to internment camps during the Second World War, it forbade speaking and publishing in foreign languages and restricted foreigners' freedom of movement. This increased nationalist orientations among Japanese Brazilians who at that time lived relatively isolated, leading to violent conflicts among descendants over the question of whether Japan had won or lost the war. After the Second World War, many descendants migrated to urban centres like the city of São Paulo (Carvalho 2003; Ninomiya 2002). São Paulo's "Japantown," Liberdade neighbourhood with its Japanese-style shops and restaurants, has even become a tourist attraction. In 2017, the first of three planned "Japan Houses" worldwide, an initiative of Japan's Ministry of Foreign Affairs, was inaugurated on São Paulo's main avenue Avenida Paulista, illustrating Brazil's ongoing importance for Japan. The institution hosts a gallery and a restaurant and organises Japan-related events.

With around 50,000 people, Japanese Peruvians constitute the second largest Nikkei minority in Latin America. The first Japanese arrived in 1899. Unlike migrants in other countries, Peruvian Nikkei concentrated in urban areas from the start. Apart from Mexico, Peru is the only Latin American country that has experienced severe anti-Japanese violence and discrimination, in particular, the 1940 riots. State legislation was as well comparatively hostile to Japanese immigrants: already in 1937, Nikkei born in Peru were declared non-citizens, even though Peru, like most states in the Americas, applies jus soli. In the Second World War, around 1,800 Japanese Peruvians were deported to U.S. concentration camps, corresponding to approximately 80% of all Japanese Latin American deportees. At the same time, the perhaps most well-known Nikkei is Peruvian: in 1990, Alberto Fujimori was elected first Nikkei president in history (Masterson 2006; Morimoto 2002a).

The first Paraguayan Nikkei settlement La Colmena was already set up in 1936, but many more migrants arrived after the Second World War. From 1959 onwards, after agreements between both countries, more settlements were founded in the country's south and southeast. Like in Bolivia, Japanese migration to Paraguay was based on bilateral agreements. However, living conditions were difficult, transport and communication systems were underdeveloped and settlers had little experience in farming. Furthermore, locusts, malaria and political

32   *History of Japanese migration to Bolivia*

unrest led many settlers to quit the *colonias*. During the Second World War, the Paraguayan government closed Japanese schools and restricted community activities. Currently, apart from the six *colonias*, descendants also live in the cities of Asunción, Encarnación and Ciudad del Este. Similar to Bolivian Nikkei, the 6,000 Japanese Paraguayans are proud to be still fluent in Japanese (Kasamatsu 2002).

Other countries that received Japanese migrants before and after the Second World War are Argentina (Laumonier 2002), Mexico (Akachi et al. 2002; Melgar Tísoc 2012), the Dominican Republic (Horst and Asagiri 2000; Katz 2006; Riley 1999), Chile (Okihiro 2002; Takeda 2002), Cuba (Ropp and Chávez de Ropp 2002), Uruguay, Colombia, Venezuela and Guatemala.

Latin America's enthusiasm for Japanese migrants was limited. At a time when few migrants arrived from Europe, Latin American governments sent the Japanese to frontier lands to consolidate their territory. The Dominican Republic's authorities dispatched settlers to areas close to the Haitian border as a human shield against immigrants (Endōh 2009: 47f.). Japan became more acceptable for Brazil only after its increased economic development, its victories against China and Russia and its willingness to adopt European ways of life (Lesser 2002; Tsuda 2001b: 415). Few Europeans wanted to move to Bolivia, and I do not know any in-depth research on the country's motivation to accept Japanese settlers. However, Domenech and Magliano (2007) write that according to a law from 1926, Bolivia's government was racially selective in so far as it would have favoured European migrants to consolidate unpopulated territories and develop the economy. Also Endōh (2009: 27) writes on the Brazilian case that Japanese and other Asian migrants were not welcomed; however, they were preferred to Africans and indigenous people by those eager to "bleach" the country. In the 1930s, such anti-Japanese opinions among parts of the elites resulted in immigration quotas in Brazil and Peru. Nevertheless, apart from the Second World War, Japanese migrants in Latin America almost never suffered from a denial of civil rights. Except for Peru and Mexico, they have practically not become victims of racist attacks (Hu-DeHart 2002).

I will focus on Japanese descendants in Bolivia and sometimes compare them to Nikkei in other Latin American countries. Because of fundamentally different living conditions (Ropp 2002), I will not include much literature on Japanese descendants in North America. In the United States, where most research on ethnic minorities comes from, the state still supposes the existence of four mutually exclusive and tightly bounded races. For a long time, Asian immigrants were denied civil rights such as legal citizenship. Even today, although Asian descendants' educational achievements are above average, they complain about discrimination (Lien and Affigne 2002: 19).

However, ethnic groups in Latin America are less clearly defined and their boundaries more fluid. I do not intend to say that discrimination of individuals and groups on ethnic or racial terms does not occur (Graham 1990); but Latin Americans consider "racial mixing" a distinctive characteristic of their societies, sometimes even glorifying it. As a consequence, racial signifiers are often only one factor in the application of ethnic labels and individuals may more easily

History of Japanese migration to Bolivia 33

manipulate identities, as Sansone (1997: 280) observes. It is important to note that ethnic identity is strongly interwoven with class, Wade (2010: 39) writes: "[T]he Latin American material shows that, for example, the same individual dressed shabbily and smartly will be identified with different colour terms that locate the person on a scale between black and white." In a nutshell, an individual's acceptance does not solely depend on his or her ethnic identity, but on a combination of origin, habitus and class.

Roth (2003a) observes that Nikkei in Brazil were not forced to cut their ties to Japan to the same degree as Nikkei in the United States, resulting in a higher identification with Japan. Few Latin American Nikkei complain about the lack of opportunities as a consequence of their ethnic origin. Instead, they now enjoy a positive reputation, despite being regarded as foreigners. According to Park (2002: 169f.), for migrant minorities belonging to the Latin American middle class like Korean descendants – and I argue, also Nikkei – this means that they generally enjoy favourable treatment without becoming isolated from other ethnic groups, unlike what she observed in the United States and Canada.

Although the Nikkei may now enjoy a favourable reputation, this was not of much help in the 1980s and 1990s when the entire continent suffered from an economic crisis. At the same time, Japan was booming. Local labour force and technology could not supply the construction and manufacturing industries' needs any more. As a result, Japan started to recruit Latin American Nikkei. The migration of Nikkei to Japan is also known as *dekasegi* [working away from home]. Many Nikkei, even highly educated individuals, began to work on car assembly lines. Men typically found work as electricians or in construction sites, whereas women were often employed as geriatric nurses and golf caddies. These jobs are also known as the so-called 3K – *"kiken, kitsui, kitanai"* [dangerous, difficult, dirty]. Nevertheless, even in a 3K job one could earn about ten times more than in a qualified position in Latin America (Shōno and Sugiura 2013: 290).

Dekasegi became a mass phenomenon in the 1990s with the immigration law revision that allowed Nikkei of other nationalities to work in Japan. Visas were granted for up to three years and could be easily renewed. Furthermore, in 1985, the yen appreciated massively and made Japanese wages even more attractive. Agencies opened in Latin America to recruit workers for Japanese factories. Whereas in 1988, only around 4,000 Brazilian and 900 Peruvian nationals resided in Japan, their number increased to 210,000 and 530,000 until 2011. While 150 Bolivian citizens lived in Japan in 1988, their number rose to 1,800 in 1991 and 6,500 in 2008 (Shōno and Sugiura 2013: 313). After the Lehman Shock, the number has dropped to 5,400 Bolivian nationals (Sōmushō 2017). These statistics do not include those of double nationality; hence, 7,000 Bolivian Nikkei or more might be residing in Japan (Shōno and Sugiura 2013: 312). Latin American Nikkei are concentrated in some industrial towns of central Japan; in the case of Bolivian Nikkei, in Tsurumi ward in Yokohama, the city of Hiratsuka/Kanagawa Prefecture and Aichi Prefecture.

In 1990, Japan accepted unskilled labourers only if they had Japanese ancestry, demonstrated by a *koseki*.[4] One also needed an employer's or family member's

34 History of Japanese migration to Bolivia

invitation as well as a Japanese guarantor, but no test of language skills or cultural knowledge. Japanese authorities supposed that the Nikkei would adapt to living conditions easily and that the Japanese would accept descendants without problems since they shared the same "blood." Nevertheless, the Nikkei's arrival caused much more friction and debates than expected. Many Nikkei experienced downward social mobility and complained about discrimination on the job and housing markets, whereas the Japanese struggled with the unfamiliar presence of Japanese descendants who often did not speak Japanese and did not act like they expected a Japanese to behave, therefore being judged as culturally deficient (Takenaka 2003a).

In the meantime, after the end of the Japanese economic boom and with Latin America's economic revival, blue-collar jobs have lost attractiveness. Although some Nikkei still travel to Japan to work, they now usually do so after finishing their high school or university degree and not instead. Moreover, because of the 2008 financial crisis, about 100,000 Nikkei have returned to Latin America. Japanese authorities implemented a return programme, but participating meant renouncing the convenient Nikkei visa for the future (Manzenreiter 2013). Many Nikkei have stayed much longer than initially planned, especially those with school-age children. In the Bolivian case, too, a major part of the descendants' economically active population resides in Japan.

A sociohistorical portrait of Bolivia

With around 11 million inhabitants, Bolivia is a landlocked country in central South America, bordering Peru, Brazil, Paraguay, Argentina and Chile. On its surface of 1,100,000 km², it covers highly diverse landscapes and climate zones, a broad range of altitude differences and an extreme ecological diversity. The government seat La Paz is situated between 3,200 and 4,000 m above sea level, with 770,000 inhabitants in La Paz itself and 850,000 in the neighbouring city of El Alto, whereas the de jure capital is Sucre with 260,000 inhabitants (Instituto Nacional de Estadística 2012, 2017a, 2017c).

Bolivia is usually divided into the highlands in the west, sometimes with a further distinction between the valleys and the *altiplano* (high plateau), and the lowlands in the east. The southeastern Gran Chaco region is dominated by a hot and dry climate, whereas the eastern lowland regions are characterised by hills, plains and forests. The north hosts grassy floodplains and a part of the Amazon rainforest (Figure 2.4).

In Pre-Columbian times, different states existed in the Andes like the Tiwanaku civilisation or the Inka Empire. The Inkas did not conquer the lowlands, at that time populated by hunter-gatherers, despite the ongoing trade relations between highlands and lowlands. Ñuflo de Chávez, a conquistador arriving from Asunción, founded the settlement of Santa Cruz de la Sierra in 1561. In 1604, the town moved to its present location 220 km westwards and Jesuits founded missions for the regions' indigenous inhabitants. Even after independence in 1825, the lowland region, until today known as the *oriente* [east], remained virtually unknown to the

History of Japanese migration to Bolivia 35

rest of the country. According to Stearman (1985: 16), many urban dwellers in the highlands thought that "the *oriente* meant uninhabitable jungles filled with fierce animals, insect- and disease-ridden swamps and unknown territories with savages hiding behind every tree".

Although the indigenous population in northern Beni and Pando had been familiar with caoutchouc for a long time, it was commercially exploited only when automobiles became popular. At the turn of the century, the rubber boom attracted many foreign adventurers to Amazonia who hoped to become millionaires overnight. Among these were some Japanese as well. The town of Riberalta in northern Beni, formerly an insignificant hamlet, became the centre of this rubber

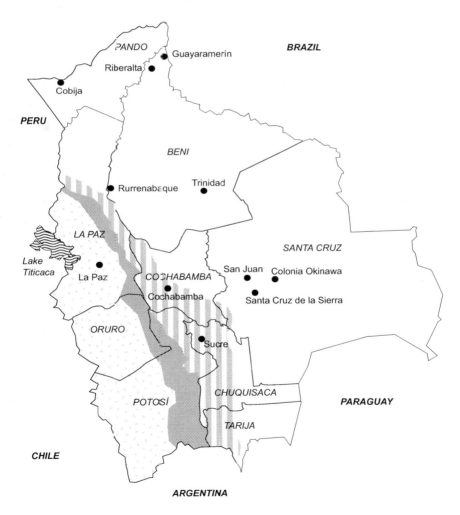

Figure 2.4 Map of Bolivia. The main climate zones from left to right: the altiplano, the central Andean range, the sub-Andean valleys and the lowlands.

36 History of Japanese migration to Bolivia

boom. In 1950, Santa Cruz Department hosted a population of only 286,000 on 370,000 km², most of them living in the town of Santa Cruz and surroundings. The Chaco War with Paraguay (1932–1935) resulted in massive territory losses for Bolivia, but with the side effect that Santa Cruz' contacts with the highlands intensified and that oil and gas resources were discovered in the department's south (Klein 2003: 173ff.; Sandoval 2003: 70ff.).

Bolivia's main export commodities have always been primary goods, but the generated incomes have seldom been used to improve general living conditions. Instead, Bolivia's history books are full of tin barons, petrol cartels and foreign companies engaged in the exploitation of silver, tin and saltpetre (Radhuber 2013) – the country has also been called a "beggar on a throne of gold." For much of Bolivia's history, military coups have been the rule rather than the exception and many presidents remained in office only for some months. Until the middle of the 20th century, the majority of Bolivia's population, especially its indigenous inhabitants, lived in rural areas with limited access to basic services and education, relying on subsistence farming. Santa Cruz Department's countryside was marked by semi-feudal circumstances and oligarchy, much land being under the control of a handful of landowners who cultivated but a tiny percentage of it. At the same time, the country was dependent on foreign aid (Klein 2003: 209ff.).

The revolution of 1952, led by the Movimiento Nacionalista Revolucionario (MNR), put an end to this land tenure system. Among other measures, the government under President Víctor Paz Estenssoro nationalised the mines as well as the oil and gas resources. Apart from agricultural mechanisation to reach self-sufficiency, his land reforms aimed at a more efficient use of the then scarcely populated lowlands – a strategy common to Latin America to postpone costly social reforms (Hiraoka 1980: 3). Subsequently, not only foreigners but also many highlanders settled in the lowland rural areas with or without the national government's assistance.

The lowlands' economy started to develop slowly. In 1959, Santa Cruz Department succeeded in obtaining 11% of its oil and gas revenues, resulting in a unique advantage as soon as new deposits were discovered. In 1954, a highway from Cochabamba to Santa Cruz, replacing the old mud road as a connection to the outside world; furthermore, a newly constructed railroad linked Santa Cruz to the Brazilian border (Monheim and Köster 1982; Sandoval 2003). National politics continued to be unstable: several military coups and frequent strikes marked the 1960s and 1970s. Especially during the dictatorship of Luis García Meza in the early 1980s, human rights abuses and corruption prevailed and cocaine dominated the economy. Return to democracy with three alternating parties in a relatively closed elitist system was accompanied by further economic decline and the collapse of tin prices, eventually resulting in hyperinflation (Sandoval 2003: 106ff.; Valdivia 2012). To solve these problems, the government under Gonzalo "Goni" Sánchez de Lozada implemented deregulations and privatisations, for instance, of the national gas and oil companies. However, parts of the population had come to see raw materials as an integral part of the country and strongly opposed such measures, leading to bloody protests. The so-called

History of Japanese migration to Bolivia 37

gas war culminated in the blockade of La Paz in October 2003, also known as "*octubre negro*" [black October], resulting in Sánchez de Lozada's escape to the United States.

Even today, ethnic, racial and class terms largely overlap in Bolivia. This is essential to understand the Nikkei case. The powerful strata are predominantly white, although the correlation between ethnic origin and power has become less important than it used to be. As Shakow (2014: 26) writes, terms that point to indigeneity are generally still understood to be equivalent to poverty. After the 1952 revolution, Bolivians should all identify as mestizos, and the new government officially de-ethnicised indigenous people as "*campesinos*" [peasants] (Shakow 2014: 80ff.). In the 1990s, neoliberal governments promoted indigenous cultures, but expressions of indigeneity were permitted only if they did not question existing power relations or the distribution of wealth. Despite daily racism, ethnic affiliation became a political factor only in the early 2000s. Promising an ethnically inclusive society, an alternative to neoliberalism, the alleviation of poverty and a more ecological way of life, Evo Morales, a former coca grower from Movimiento al Socialismo (MAS), was elected Bolivia's first indigenous president in 2005. Many unions, grassroots organisations and indigenous groups as well as parts of the urban middle class supported him; other voters, however, feared a return to the social disorder and the omnipresent drug trafficking of the 1980s.

At first glance, key economic figures for his term of office do not look bad. Between 2000 and 2014, Bolivia's economy grew at an annual rate of 4.2% on average. At the same time, poverty was reduced from 66% to 39.3%. Per-capita income almost doubled and access to secondary schooling and basic services improved significantly, although important differences remain between urban and rural areas (Banco Interamericano de Desarrollo 2016). Symbolically important for the Morales administration was the rise of the minimum wage, the nationalisation of oil and gas and the enforcement of laws against racial discrimination. Since 2009, a new constitution designates Bolivia as a "plurinational state" while recognising the rights of 36 ethnic groups.

Despite their leftist rhetoric, Morales and his administration turned more and more to neoliberalism and extractivism. Indigenous culture became a symbolic rather than a practical guideline.[5] Many voters were disappointed that the Morales administration failed to change the political environment marked by corruption. Even worse, some of his allies were accused of clientelism and theft of public funds. Social conflicts like the ones in Porvenir and Chaparina in 2008 and 2011 were "resolved" by force and persecution. In 2012, Morales lost more voter support during the protests against a planned road through the TIPNIS National Park in Cochabamba Department, opposed by local indigenous groups fearing ecological destruction and increased drug trafficking. In other words, social conflicts, often resulting in roadblocks, marches and strikes, remained as common as they were before Morales' presidency, producing significant costs for the entire country. Critical media came increasingly under pressure and finally, tensions emerged because Morales ran for president in October 2019, although a public referendum rejected his proposal and although the constitution originally prohibited

38 *History of Japanese migration to Bolivia*

more than two consecutive terms. After strong indications of electoral fraud and a three-week general strike, Morales escaped to Mexico.

Bolivia's economy is still far from diversified while the institutional capacity to deal with natural resources remains underdeveloped. Moreover, economy depends mostly on external market conditions. Gas and oil constitute almost half of Bolivia's exports; besides minerals and agricultural products such as soybeans (Instituto Nacional de Estadística 2017b). Productivity remains low and the temporary trade balance surplus resulted primarily from favourable prices on the world market and the growing demand from China. At the same time, the fiscal deficit and the foreign trade deficit have grown (La Razón 2018; Página Siete 2017). The distribution of financial incentives to poorer strata, financed by advantageous raw material prices, creates high expectations and new kinds of clientelism, while investment rates remain low not least because of legal insecurity.

Defining Santa Cruz' regional identity

Although differences between urban and rural areas remain significant, Santa Cruz Department has Bolivia's highest GDP, its highest standards of living and its highest economic growth rates (Instituto Boliviano de Comercio Exterior 2016). Soybeans constitute the most important crop, followed by sugar, cotton and corn; other economic activities comprise cattle farming, gas and oil extraction. The department's capital city hosts the Bolivian branch offices of several multinational agribusiness companies.

At the same time, the inhabitants' self-confidence has grown. In daily conversations, many *cruceñas* and *cruceños* try to differentiate themselves from highlanders. Lowlanders, also known as *cambas,* are regarded as open, hospitable and cheerful in contrast to *collas* from the highlands, said to be closed, stingy but hard-working.[6] Lowlanders claim to be of predominantly European origin in contrast to highlanders, often a reason for *cambas* to feel superior (Gustafson 2006; Plata Quispe 2008). Nevertheless, the construction of two seemingly racially and ethnically homogeneous groups – white *cambas* and indigenous *collas* – does not reflect reality.

Cultural differences between highlanders and lowlanders have received new meanings, and they have also been mixed with the triad of postponement, oblivion and centralism, as Seleme Antelo et al. (2005: 11) call it. Highlanders are often equated with the unpopular central hegemonic power. "*Colla*" has become a synonym for strikes, roadblocks and dependence on the national government; but they are also collectively held responsible for a broad range of social ills such as drug trafficking, deforestation and land occupations. Many *cambas* consider *colla* traders and street sellers to be an "invasion" of public space, contrasting the current situation with nostalgic imaginaries of a quiet old Santa Cruz (Kirshner 2011). At the same time, most *cruceñas* and *cruceños* do recognise the highlanders' contribution to local prosperity. The latter have indeed deeply changed the character of the city, Stearman (1985: 209f.) writes: "The industrious and ambitious highlander is beginning to spur the less competitive lowlander into fuller participation in the regional and national economies".

Especially between 2005 and 2010, the local autonomy movement gained popularity in the departments of Santa Cruz, Beni, Pando and Tarija. In Santa Cruz, this resulted in the approval of the autonomy referendum in 2008, while voters rejected the new constitution in early 2009. The *cruceño* autonomy movement is headed by Comité Cívico Pro Santa Cruz, an organisation founded in 1950 by representatives of elite families, large-scale landowners and members of right-wing parties. Consisting of more than 200 member organisations, it regards itself as a representative of civil society in an environment where political parties do not enjoy much trust. Comité Cívico's former president Rubén Costas was elected governor of the department in 2006 (Figure 2.5).

Actors such as Comité Cívico claim that *cambas* have never truly belonged to the Bolivian state since their ancestors came from Paraguay and, in contrast to highlanders, had nothing to do with the colonial Viceroyalty of Peru (Soruco 2008). Comité Cívico and more radical groups successfully use these notions to mobilise the population against the central government. Accordingly, whereas "Bolivian" represents centralism, poverty and failure, "*cruceño*" means modernity, productivity, urbanity and neoliberalism (Peña Claros 2009). Nevertheless, when using regionalist discourses to control tangible assets, Comité Cívico rather

Figure 2.5 Club Social ceremonial hall at the central plaza in 2007. The sentence on the building translates as: "Let us always be free cruceños," on the flag: "We are autonomous/Hold on cruceños/Let us continue making history."

acts for the interests of international agribusiness companies and the elites, despite its successful presentation as a lobby for all *cruceñas* and *cruceños* (Plata Quispe 2008). During the heyday of the autonomy movement, the media were dominated by discourses in favour of autonomy, whereas critical voices were largely absent even in the daily conversations of the city's population (Figure 2.6).

Although these tensions are frequently depicted as a clearly defined conflict between two ethnically distinct regions, the situation is much more complex and ambivalent on a closer look. Research lacks on non-elite supporters; it is even common to hear children of highlanders speaking in favour of autonomy with a distinct *camba* accent. Moreover, Goldstein (2004: 70) observes similar discourses in the highland city of Cochabamba where immigration from rural areas is framed as a racialised threat as well. Fernández Saavedra et al. (2014: 236) underline that despite the autonomy movement's aggressive regionalist rhetoric, *cruceño* elite circles still welcome *colla* entrepreneurs – they generally share a similar background and interests. Before Evo Morales' presidency, some prominent members used Comité Cívico as a stepping stone to national politics. Nevertheless, after MAS came into power, two different political projects confronted each other; thus, Santa Cruz' elites lost influence on the national level.

More contradictions appear when examining the supposedly successful "*cruceño* model." The autonomy movement glorifies private initiative, like the individual male pioneer subjecting nature. However, Santa Cruz' prosperity is mostly based on the availability of land and favourable tax agreements with other Latin

Figure 2.6 Residential areas Santa Cruz between Second and Third Ring Road.

History of Japanese migration to Bolivia   41

American countries. According to Instituto Boliviano de Comercio Exterior (2017), most soy is exported to only one country, Colombia. Soy production depends on imported seeds, access to foreign markets and international treaties: it hinges on factors beyond the farmers' control. Moreover, land use in Santa Cruz is marked by an extreme inequality. In short, regional agro-economy lacks modernisation, efficiency and competitiveness and is ecologically and socially unsustainable (Urioste 2011: 57ff., 2012: 446f.; Soruco 2008: 81f.).

The autonomy movement could not introduce its ideas of local autonomy in the new constitution and it lost power after Morales won the 2008 vote of confidence referendum. Some months later, a group supporting autonomy violently attacked public institutions in Santa Cruz, damaging the reputation of the entire movement's leadership that did not condemn these incidents. At the same time, the movement became divided: after a supposed coup attempt from Santa Cruz, the national government took legal action against some exponents, whereas others started cooperating with the national administration (Vegas and Cuéllar 2017).

Recent immigration to Bolivia

Many Bolivians have emigrated to Argentina, Brazil or Spain, countries with greater income possibilities. The International Organization for Migration (2018) estimates that around 1.6 million Bolivian nationals reside abroad. Immigration to Bolivia, however, has received less attention. Indeed, compared to some of its neighbours, the country has not attracted many immigrants since the late 19th century. According to a recent census (Delgado 2017), around 60,000 foreign nationals, mostly Brazilians and other Latin American nationals, reside in Bolivia, more than half of them in Santa Cruz Department.

Many German and Swiss adventurers arrived at Riberalta during the 20th-century rubber boom; German migrants founded some of the most famous rubber companies. Moreover, some Germans migrated to the Department of Santa Cruz after the Second World War to work as farmers, but they also founded companies in the department's capital, like the now defunct flag-carrier airline Lloyd Aéreo Boliviano. German, Italian and Croatian surnames are notorious among contemporary economic elites in Santa Cruz. Furthermore, some French left traces in architecture, mining and education (Bieber 2012: 188f.; Freddi 2003; Hollweg 1995; Prado 2007: 172f.; Seleme Antelo et al. 2005: 29; Wolff and Fröschle 1979). To my knowledge, the small minority of Russian farmers in Santa Cruz has not been studied.

During the Second World War, some German Jews fled to Bolivia. For these often highly qualified urban refugees, Bolivia was not an attractive destination, but they lacked better options. It comes as no surprise that their farming settlements were not successful. Consequently, many migrated to neighbouring countries after 1952. In 1975, around 1,400 German Jews lived in Bolivia, 1,000 of them in La Paz. They worked as physicians and in the mining industry; they founded bakeries and restaurants or small factories, thereby giving impulses to Bolivia's economy. The most well-known Bolivian of German Jewish background was

42 History of Japanese migration to Bolivia

probably Moritz (Mauricio) Hochschild, who arrived penniless in the 1920s and became one of Bolivia's three "tin barons" (Bieber 2012; Osterweil 1998).

After the First World War, some male Arab immigrants – often called "*turcos*," since present-day Syria, Lebanon and Palestine were then part of the Osman Empire – arrived in Bolivia, soon attaining middle-class status. Most of them worked in small commerce as peddlers or shop owners. They imported foodstuff, paper products and cameras, founded movie theatres and textile factories (Osterweil 1998). Well known among contemporary *cruceñas* and *cruceños* is especially the Telchi pharmacy chain. Descendant Carlos Dabdoub is a former health minister and part of the region's elite, whereas Juan Lechín was a prominent union leader. Most of the Arab immigrants were Christians who later married Bolivian women and did not maintain many ties to their region of origin. Based on a group consciousness formed by historical and cultural factors, most descendants self-identify with an Arab rather than with a Syrian, Lebanese or Palestinian origin, if at all. Arab descendants are not regarded as foreigners in present-day Bolivia (Osterweil 1998: 159) – in contrast to the Nikkei.

This migration strongly contrasts with the Mennonites. Starting in 1954, groups of Mennonites from Paraguay, Mexico, Canada and Belize have been arriving at the lowlands. Kopp (2015: 54ff.) estimates that more than 57,000 Mennonites live in Bolivia nowadays. Like the Japanese, they have founded agricultural *colonias* in the wider environment of Santa Cruz that were much more successful than the poorly planned Bolivian ones (Monheim and Köster 1982: 16ff.; Sandoval 2003: 58ff.). Adhering to a rigorous interpretation of Protestantism, they remain relatively isolated from the surrounding population. They are strictly endogamous, speak a Low German dialect and renounce many technical facilities of modern life. Like Japanese descendants, they have a reputation of being hard-working; but most *cruceñas* and *cruceños*, Nikkei included, consider this group strange and anti-modern. Mennonites enjoy some state guaranteed privileges such as school autonomy and exemption from military service. At the same time, they are well integrated into the local economy. With their distinctive habits, they are highly visible in Santa Cruz' Los Pozos area where they sell cheese, buy seeds and attend health facilities (Hedberg 2007; Kopp 2015).

Furthermore, small numbers of Chinese, Taiwanese and Koreans have settled in Bolivia and the Santa Cruz areas, but no systematic research on these groups exists. The Chinese are famous for owning small shops and inexpensive chicken restaurants (*pollerías*). East Asian migrants have established the private UCEBOL University, churches and at least one temple. In recent years, some Brazilians and a few Argentineans bought land in Eastern Bolivia and also married into the local elites. These farmers are well regarded and even considered allies of the regional cause (Gimenez 2010). Furthermore, many Brazilian medical students find it easier to enter Bolivian universities than the Brazilian ones.

Recent migrants are often subsumed under the neutral term *extranjero* [foreigner]. The expression implies that they come from industrialised countries, have contacts abroad and are integrated into capitalist networks (Osterweil 1998: 151). The Morales government has accused "foreign imperialism" time and

History of Japanese migration to Bolivia   43

again. Popular discourse, too, may associate foreigners, notably Peruvians and Colombians, with delinquency. Nevertheless, the migration from other countries to Santa Cruz is altogether well regarded compared to the migration of highlanders to the city: the threat seems to come from the inside, not from the outside.

Overview of Japanese migration to Bolivia

Japanese migration is usually divided into two phases, the pre- and the post-Second World War migration, that differ in important aspects. The first Japanese migrants reached Peru in 1899, sent by the private Morioka Company. However, living conditions at the Peruvian plantations were difficult and conflicts arose with employers and locals. Thus, the Morioka representative decided to send 91 immigrants to Bolivia soon after. They crossed the Andes in an exhausting three-week journey and started to work as *siringueros* [rubber collectors] in the Amazonian region. Although the Japanese Ministry of Foreign Affairs registered 200 migrants before the Second World War, Kunimoto (2013a: 46) estimates that about 2,000 Japanese may have reached Beni and Pando in this period.

The work as rubber collector was arduous, lonely and poorly paid; alimentation and medical care were insufficient. When around 1912, Malaysian rubber became more competitive than Latin American one, many Japanese started to work as small-scale farmers, carpenters, barbers, tailors and restaurant owners or opened little shops called *bazares* (Mitre 2006: 26ff.). Many founded families with local women not least because they could not afford to bring a bride from Japan. Around 1910, the first Japanese reached Trinidad, the capital of Beni Department, others settled in the towns of Rurrenabaque, Cobija and Guayaramerín (Kunimoto 2013a). In 1942, Bolivia officially declared war on Germany and Japan, but unlike in the capital La Paz, Japanese nationals in the lowlands were not affected by anti-Japanese measures.

Many pre-war Nikkei have lost conscience about their Japanese ancestry. With incomplete secondary education, many descendants' economic situation is difficult, while work opportunities remain scarce. Japanese ancestry became important only during the *dekasegi* boom. Some returning migrants were able to construct "*dekasegi* palaces," but not everybody has been successful (Shioiri 2013: 122ff.). Only rough estimations exist regarding the absolute number of pre-war Nikkei. Referring to data from Bolivia's national Nikkei organisation ANBJ/FENABOJA, Amemiya (2001) records that 7,000 descendants live in Riberalta, 1,300 in Trinidad, 500 in Guayaramerín and 1,000 in Cobija.

The first Japanese arrived in the Andes at the beginning of the 20th century. In 1930, 136 Japanese resided in La Paz (Furuki 2013: 54ff.). Some came as merchants and held small businesses such as barbershops, restaurants, *bazares* or medium-sized import-export companies. Other migrants worked in railroad construction between La Paz and the city of Oruro. Small numbers of Japanese citizens were registered in Oruro as well as in the cities of Potosí, Sucre and Cochabamba. Because the Bolivian currency was devalued between 1933 and 1935, goods for everyday consumption from European and North American

44 *History of Japanese migration to Bolivia*

countries increased in price and the poorer strata found an alternative in inexpensive low-quality products from Japan (Mitre 2006: 63ff.). Bolivia and Japan had signed the first commerce treaty in 1914 and four years later, the first Bolivian representative was sent to Japan, although the relation was not important to either country (Mitre 2006: 41). Sociedad Japonesa de La Paz, the city's Japanese association, was founded in 1922 and served as an intermediary between the immigrants and the next consulate in Lima.

Japan stopped its tin, antimony, lead and wolfram imports from Bolivia when in 1942, the latter broke off diplomatic relationships under pressure from the United States. Shortly after, Bolivia declared war on the Axis powers and froze the accounts of Italians, Germans and Japanese, if not naturalised or born in Bolivia. Many migrant-owned companies were closed, liquidated or sold. Despite the fact that most Japanese in Bolivia were not very prosperous nor politically active (Mitre 2006: 13), the Bolivian government sent 29 Japanese plus their families to the United States in order to fulfil the number of prisoners required by the latter. Meetings between Japanese citizens being prohibited, Sociedad Japonesa suspended its activities until 1952 (Furuki 2013: 57ff.; Mitre 2006: 78ff.; Sociedad Japonesa de La Paz 2012: 59ff.). Consequently, many Nikkei in La Paz avoided identifying as Japanese descendants after the war. In 1953, Bolivia and Japan resumed their diplomatic ties. A short-lived Japanese school was founded in 1956, another school eventually opened in 1967 (Furuki 2013: 75ff.; Sociedad Japonesa de La Paz 2012: 106ff.).

The Japanese association's home is a five-storied building in the central district of Sopocachi, hosting classrooms, a ceremonial hall, an office, a library, a museum and a Japanese restaurant. Furuki (2013: 48) estimates a relatively high number of 800 Nikkei living in La Paz, probably referring to the turn of the millennium. Some are descendants of merchants or trainees in foreign commerce who immigrated directly to La Paz before or after the war, others arrived from Beni and Pando, the remaining Nikkei are post-war descendants from the Santa Cruz region. Finally, some recent Japanese migrants are married to Bolivians. Whereas Santa Cruz hosts a Japanese consulate, the embassy and JICA's office are now located in La Paz.

The second migration phase started after the 1952 Revolution when the Bolivian government tried to attract foreign settlers to the eastern lowlands. While in pre-war times, mainland descendants were in the majority, the idea to found Japanese settlements coincided with the initiative of some Okinawans in Riberalta who wanted to help fellow Okinawans after the war. The U.S. Civil Administration of the Ryūkyū Islands was also interested in a migration project to alleviate Okinawa's social problems and eventually signed a contract with the Bolivian government. On the 15th of August 1954, the first group of migrants arrived at the site where Colonia Uruma settlement would be constructed, soon followed by more groups. Each family received 50 hectares of land – an incredible amount for a Japanese farmer of that time – but contrary to the contractual agreements, the Bolivian government did not provide medical, educational or whatsoever facilities. Some months later, an unknown illness claimed fifteen

History of Japanese migration to Bolivia 45

victims and a flood caused huge damages; the settlers thus decided to move. After two translocations, Colonia Okinawa was established in 1956 at its definitive site about 100 km northeast of Santa Cruz. Colonia Okinawa consists of the main settlement Okinawa I (Okinawa Uno or Dai Ichi), the smaller village Okinawa II (Okinawa Dos or Dai Ni) and the hamlet Okinawa III (Okinawa Tres or Dai San) around 20 and 35 km further south, respectively (Higa 2013: 203ff.).

The contracts would have allowed 3,000 families to settle in Colonia Okinawa, but conditions in Japan improved rapidly and made the migration to the faraway Bolivian *colonia* less attractive. Okinawan Bolivians' Japanese nationality was restored in 1967. In the 1970s, JICA initiated the production of cotton. Nevertheless, the experiment failed and farmers accumulated huge debts in Bolivian currency. However, they were fortunate insofar as their debt diminished with hyperinflation while they still received assistance from Japan in U.S. dollars. The number of descendants diminished since many young Nikkei did not return from their *dekasegi* stay. Sometimes, of a family with seven or ten children all but one or two ended up in Japan, further contributing to the community's ageing (Higa 2013: 233ff.; Suzuki 2010: 42ff.). It is estimated that at the beginning of the millennium, only around 10% of all migrants remained in Colonia Okinawa (Koronia Okinawa Nyūshoku 50 Shūnen Kinenshi Hensan Iinkai 2005: 81). Many descendants have migrated to the city since jobs outside agriculture are scarce; furthermore, not all sons could inherit land.[7]

Colonia Okinawa eventually proved successful with soybeans, providing around 40% of the national production in the late 1980s. With this economic improvement, farmers were able to purchase land outside the *colonia*. Today, on an area of about 47,000 hectares (Higa 2013: 200), they concentrate on wheat, rice and soybeans, calling themselves "*la capital triguera de Bolivia*" [Bolivia's wheat capital]. Most farmers are organised in CAICO (Cooperativa Agropecuaria Industrial Colonia Okinawa), the *colonia's* agricultural cooperative. Colonia Okinawa has around 800 Nikkei inhabitants, corresponding to less than 10% of the entire municipality's population.[8] Nowadays, it is a comparatively prosperous town with a small hospital, primary schools, sports facilities, Nikkei association buildings and a museum. Apart from Japanese inscriptions, the architecture of some individual houses and the wooden *torii* gate on the main plaza, few things look distinctively Japanese.

San Juan, also known as San Juan de Yapacaní, is located 140 km northwest of Santa Cruz de la Sierra. It was officially founded in 1955 following an agreement between Japan and Bolivia. The project coincided with a private initiative: already in 1954, entrepreneur Toshimichi Nishikawa had planned a sugar plantation with a test group of 14 families. The history of both *colonias* bears many parallels: whereas each family in San Juan received 50 hectares, the settlement was ill-planned and lacked infrastructure. Because of adverse climatic conditions, many farmers abandoned the *colonias*, and several violent conflicts broke out with non-Nikkei Bolivians. In the late 1980s and early 1990s, many descendants left for Japan. Until the late 1980s, the *colonia* faced more than once the risk of disintegration as a result of fluctuating prices, administrative problems

46　History of Japanese migration to Bolivia

and internal conflicts, but living conditions improved slowly (Fukaura and Nagai 2013: 243ff.).

Around 750 Nikkei live in San Juan today, corresponding to less than 10% of the entire municipality's actual population. Most of them have originated from Nagasaki and other southwestern prefectures. San Juan is well known for the cultivation of rice and eggs. It spreads over 27,000 hectares, but unlike Colonia Okinawa where houses are located close to each other, the *colonia* comprises many scattered farms apart from the central settlement with schools, the town hall, the hospital, the cooperative CAISY and other facilities (Fukaura and Nagai 2013: 239ff.; Kunimoto 1990). Both *colonias* are now part of one of the most productive zones in the department characterised by the extensive agriculture of fruits, sugar cane, etc.; San Juan calls itself "Bolivia's rice capital."

Whereas the *colonias'* migration history is extensively recorded in museums and in books compiled by the Nikkei or external researchers, descendants in the city of Santa Cruz have been scarcely documented. The first Japanese may have reached Santa Cruz around 1914, and 13 Japanese resided in the town in 1937, most of them merchants. In 1956, 27 Japanese males, mostly pre-war Issei as well as some post-war Issei and Nisei who had come from the nearby *colonias*, founded the Nikkei association Centro Social Japonés. The first association home was built as late as 1966 near Avenida Beni/Second Ring Road. More and more Nikkei arrived mainly from Colonia Okinawa: until 1967, the number of association members had risen to 100 (Aniya 2013: 170ff.; Santa Kurusu Chūō Nihonjinkai Sōritsu 50 Shūnen Kinenshi 2006: 60ff.). Okinawan descendants created Okinawa Kenjinkai[9] Santa Cruz in 1975. Its headquarters are located at Calle Antonio Vaca Diez, also known as Calle Adán Gutiérrez, in Los Pozos area (Figure 2.7).

Today, between 700 and 800 post-war Nikkei live in the city of Santa Cruz, more than half of them of Okinawan ancestry. This number is based on estimations: approximately 600 descendants, mainly of post-war origin, are Centro Social Japonés members (Santa Kurusu Chūō Nihonjinkai Sōritsu 50 Shūnen Kinenshi 2006: 289ff.); plus around 100–200 who are not affiliated. The number is plausible compared to the 2,400 Japanese passport holders that the Japanese consulate counts for Santa Cruz Department: most post-war Nikkei hold Japanese nationality and few Japanese diplomats or businesspersons work here. It is unknown how many descendants of pre-war immigrants reside in the urban area; few of them are members of Nikkei associations and they generally do not hold Japanese passports. The Japanese Ministry of Foreign Affairs (Gaimushō 2016) writes that 2,970 Japanese nationals and 11,370 descendants without Japanese passport live in Bolivia, whereas Manzenreiter (2017a: 199), based on data collected by the national Nikkei organisation ANBJ/FENABOJA, estimates the number at 12,400 Nikkei for the whole country.

Unlike most descendants in Brazil and Peru, Bolivian post-war Nikkei are generally still able to speak Japanese, although they do not necessarily write it properly. Nikkei children can study in the Japanese schools of Santa Cruz, La Paz, San Juan, Okinawa I and Okinawa II. The *colonias'* schools offer classes in Spanish in the morning and facultative Japanese classes in the afternoon, but schools in Santa

History of Japanese migration to Bolivia 47

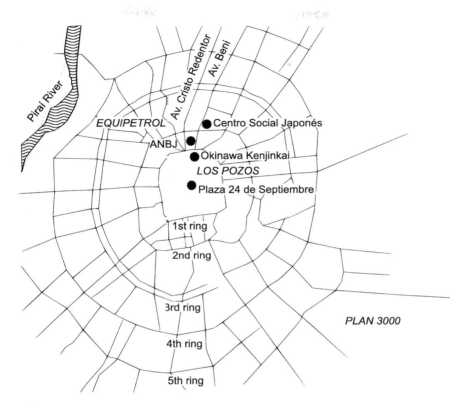

Figure 2.7 Map of Santa Cruz de la Sierra. CAISY, Fraternidad Fujii and the international airport are located next to Avenida Cristo Redentor more to the north; CAICO is situated at Avenida Cristo Redentor between Fourth and Fifth Ring Roads.

Cruz and La Paz open only on Saturdays. In Santa Cruz, a private school existed in the 1960s and early 1970s. The current institution was founded as a private initiative in 1965 and later incorporated into Centro Social (Aniya 2013: 176ff.). It has approximately 70 students between six and fifteen years, with a tuition fee of around USD 25 per month. Parents currently have to be members of Centro Social Japonés to send their children to class.

In the city, no quantitative data exist on descendants' socioeconomic situation compared to the local, regional or national average. However, it is unlikely to find post-war Nikkei who suffer from extreme poverty. As all interview partners agreed, the Nikkei enjoy a living standard above the national average, similar to descendants in other Latin American countries – and in contrast to many migrants from rural Bolivia (Takenaka 2003b; Tsuda 1999). This relative prosperity is reflected in their settlement patterns. No Japantown exists in Santa Cruz, but as data from Centro Social Japonés shows, its members live mostly within Fourth Ring Road and next to Avenida Cristo Redentor in the northern part of the city, for

48 History of Japanese migration to Bolivia

short, in areas associated with low poverty rates (see Figure 5.1 on p. 114). Some have also moved to one of the park-like gated communities in the Urubó region on the other side of the Piraí River. Several families, mainly from Colonia Okinawa, commute between the *colonia* and the city: typically, the husband works in agriculture, while his wife and children work or attend education facilities in Santa Cruz.

Conclusion

Whereas migration from a well-off country to a less developed place might seem counterintuitive, the historical summary has shown that both Japan and Bolivia had their economic and political agenda regarding the migration of Japanese citizens. Japan's wish to become equal with European and North American powers resulted in the government's strong engagement in emigration. It hoped to secure raw material imports and to show seemingly superior "Japanese values" abroad.

Latin American countries accepted Japanese migrants without much enthusiasm. After a first phase of unorganised migration, Bolivia aimed at consolidating its lowlands in the 1950s. Practically, the only foreigners who accepted to settle in the then undeveloped territory were the Japanese, hoping for a better future outside war-torn Japan. Post-Second World War descendants in Bolivia have reached considerable prosperity after a difficult start, not least because of the continuous Japanese assistance and *dekasegi* work migration to Japan. Many descendants have moved from the rural *colonias* to the cities of Santa Cruz and La Paz.

Regional dynamics will be important to understand the Nikkei's identity negotiations. At a time of rapid industrialisation and rural poverty in the late 19th and early 20th centuries, Japan tried to define its national identity with profound implications for one of the most important emigration regions, Okinawa Prefecture. As a formerly independent kingdom, it often challenged the prevalent idea of an ethnically homogeneous Japanese nation. At the same time, tensions between lowlanders and highlanders have been prominent in Santa Cruz, whereas the few foreigners have seldom attracted much attention. Instead, the Nikkei as well as other foreign descendants have been able to present themselves as a positive example.

Nevertheless, important differences exist between pre- and post-war migration from Japan: whereas the former was scarcely organised and not supported by Japan, the latter depended on international treaties and benefited from Japanese funds in a developing environment. These differences have not only consequences for descendants' socioeconomic well-being, but they also have profound implications for ethnic affiliations until today.

Notes

1 Carré (2009: 593) estimates that in 1620, around 700,000 Japanese had converted to Christianism, corresponding to 4–5% of the entire population. Since authorities feared that Christians would disturb the political order, they were persecuted or forced to aban-

History of Japanese migration to Bolivia 49

don their faith. From the 1870s onwards, the Christian religion was allowed, although not welcomed. Currently, less than 1% of Japan's population is Christian; they are especially numerous in Nagasaki Prefecture and other parts of Kyūshū (Gordon 2014).

2 Okinawan language, the only language proven to be related to Japanese, is better described as a group of sometimes mutually unintelligible dialects. Before 1879, the capital's dialect served as the kingdom's lingua franca. Few inhabitants were able to speak standard Japanese. After annexation, active efforts to substitute Okinawan by standard Japanese were made, e.g., in schools where children would be punished for speaking *uchināguchi*. While *uchināguchi* is not promoted in compulsory education and few parents speak to their children in one of the dialects, language programmes in the media and performing arts try to revitalise them. Okinawan standard Japanese has maintained a distinctive accent and some morphological and lexical characteristics, but is disappearing due to the influence of mass media, school and contact with other regions (Heinrich 2004; Majewicz 2006; Matsumori 1995; Osumi 2006).

3 The northeast offered perhaps even worse living conditions than the southwest, but never sent so many migrants to the Americas. Migration trends might be explained by cultural patterns like kinship ties and social networks. Another reason for the government to incite emigration might have been that before the Second World War, the southwest was an important industrial site where conflicts between the state and radicalised labourers and miners were common. No statistical data or specific literature exists about the emigration of *burakumin*, a stigmatised social minority (Aoki 2009; Neary 2009). Since many of them lived in the southwest, emigration might have been a strategy to escape discrimination (Endōh 2009: 4f., 112ff., 145ff.).

4 This family register records nuclear families with their children and serves as a proof of Japanese citizenship. It was established in 1872 for Japanese nationals, modelled after the upper classes' ideal with a male head of the family (Bryant 1991). Even today, the *koseki* records births, deaths, marriages, divorces, adoptions and the nuclear family's symbolic home.

5 The Morales administration's indigenist approach is marked by many inconsistencies, as Shakow (2014) and Pellegrini Calderón (2016) criticise. The Morales administration regularly idealised indigenous people as harmonious and static rural collectivities rather than depicting them as people with middle-class aspirations. Morales frequently refers to indigenous groups in his speeches, but many speakers of indigenous languages do not identify with such collectivities. Even though it is often repeated that indigenous people constitute the majority of Bolivians, only 31% self-declared as indigenous in the 2012 census (La Razón 2013).

6 "*Cruceño/cruceñc*" was formerly used to describe a person of Spanish origin, whereas "*camba*" meant an indigenous peasant tied to a plantation by debt (Stearman 1985; Waldmann 2008: 257f.). Today, "*camba*" is a common word for all people identifying as lowlanders, including the European descendant elites, implying more emotional attachment than the neutral "*cruceño/cruceña.*"

7 In Colonia Okinawa and San Juan, farming is a male occupation. Often, the eldest son is chosen as successor, although a younger son or a son-in-law may take over the farm as well.

8 Apart from Okinawa I with a mixed Nikkei/non-Nikkei population and Okinawa II and III dominated by Nikkei, the municipality comprises several other villages inhabited by non-Nikkei.

9 *Kenjinkai* are associations for descendants of a specific prefecture.

3 How ethnic identities justify symbolic capital

I sit on the sofa in Nataly Yonamine's hair salon "Salón Kaori," located in a small shopping arcade in Santa Cruz' expensive neighbourhood Equipetrol. It is the first time I meet her. A Nikkei client and neighbour had given me her phone number and I had called her just some hours before. It is a chilly afternoon in June, two months after my arrival. A few months ago, Nataly, in her late forties and of both pre- and post-war origin, returned from Japan where she had worked in a telephone company. She took over the salon named after her mother Kaori who passed away recently. Kaori was a well-known hairdresser, and together with other Nikkei women, she brought important innovations to Santa Cruz' hair salons, her daughter proudly tells me. Nataly now wants to continue her mother's successful business. She lives in a small house nearby and already seems to know each client, all of them wearing elegant dresses and fair in complexion.

While Nataly joins me on the sofa, her non-Nikkei employees, one of them her sister-in-law, attend to the clients. Nataly does not need my questions to tell the story of her life and to explain her views about Japanese migration to Bolivia. She proudly calls herself a "Japanese *camba*." Except for the green tea she serves me, few objects remind me of Japan. However, Nataly readily expresses her pride in the achievements of Bolivian Nikkei, more important for her than any monument. She praises the Japanese immigrants' "fighting spirit": they crossed the ocean to a foreign land where they eventually succeeded as pioneers under extremely difficult conditions. Nataly also alludes to Japan's economic boom, citing the slogan "Made in Japan" to evoke imaginaries of high-quality products. For her, prosperity is almost a natural outcome:

> "Made in Japan," for example, did not only take place in Japan, "Made in Japan" was created all over the world, as I heard from a journalist. The Japanese migrants followed the "Made in Japan" because their culture is like that. No matter if inside or outside the country, they acted in the same way and shaped the "Made in Japan." So they won the confidence of Bolivians, therefore everything Japanese is guaranteed.[1]

Like Nataly, most Nikkei consider themselves part of the Bolivian middle class, with its experiences, ambitions and specific forms of self-presentation. They share

DOI: 10.4324/9781003228295-3

consumption patterns with middle classes all over Latin America and associate themselves with modernity. The Nikkei work as doctors, engineers or in commerce, they send their children to private schools, travel to holiday resorts in the Caribbean, purchase late-model *camionetas* (SUVs) or acquire houses in gated communities (Liechty 2003; O'Dougherty 2002; Shakow 2014).

But the concrete example of Bolivian Nikkei also shows the manifold ambivalences of symbolic capital. With recourse to their history of immigration, the Nikkei present themselves as model citizens who have contributed to Bolivia's development, while non-Nikkei support this narrative. Nevertheless, explaining the Nikkei's symbolic and economic capital only with their efforts falls short: Japan's continuous assistance and the possibility to work as *dekasegi* has been even more important for their current socioeconomic wellbeing. Moreover, being a well-respected minority does not mean that the Nikkei are accepted as Bolivians: non-Nikkei generally consider them foreigners or "*chinos*" [Chinese]. But this is not necessarily bad, since ethnic identity is not simply the result of micro-level processes: Japan's soft power (Nye and Kim 2013) has helped descendants all over Latin America to attain a comfortable yet ambivalent position in society.

Hard-working, honest, reserved and on time – The pervasive discourse on "Japanese values"

Similar to Nataly's statement above, I would hear declarations connecting "Japanese values" and socioeconomic wellbeing time and again. Many Nikkei see their ancestors' cultural background as the best preparation for prosperity and non-Nikkei's acceptance. They often foreground that especially the first generation has worked hard to become part of the middle class: "*los Issei sufrieron harto*," "*hicieron muchos sacrificios*," "*cuando llegaron era puro monte*" – "the Issei suffered much," "they have made enormous sacrifices," "when they arrived, it was only jungle." Virtually all interview partners emphasised the importance of individual effort and related it to values (*valores*) and customs (*costumbres*). Rather than pointing to concrete practices, these "Japanese values" refer to ideal characteristics they designed as typically Japanese, such as discipline, thriftiness, modesty, loyalty, moral integrity, punctuality, cleanliness and solidarity – although it is not clear if everybody understands the same by each of these concepts. According to this narrative, a typical Japanese bears misfortune stoically and remains perseverant while maintaining honour and loyalty. Such values, most descendants acknowledge, may not be unique to the Nikkei. Nevertheless, many descendants claim to have demonstrated the benefits of such values in places where they mostly lack, regarding themselves as a role model for Bolivia, Latin America or even the whole world.

Respect is a key value, standing for consideration of the common good. Being respectful leads to mindfulness, honesty, responsibility and punctuality. A respectful individual does not touch other people's belongings, either. Setsuko Gushiken gives the example that whenever she breaks a glass, she wraps it in cardboard and binds it together in order not to injure the garbage collectors. Respect also

52 *How ethnic identities justify symbolic capital*

acquires the meaning of filial piety: most interview partners eventually underlined their gratitude to the Issei because the latter built up the *colonias.*

Some interview partners summarised these essentialised cultural traits under the term "Japanese spirit." This explanation figures prominently in the preface to the biography of Freddy Maemura, a Nisei from Beni who joined Ernesto Che Guevara's guerrilla (Hurtado and Solares Maemura 2006: 15f.); in 2017, his life was documented in the Japanese film "Erunesuto." Instead of describing the *guerrillero*'s individual character traits, his nephew explains Freddy's path of life with the discipline, the fighting spirit and the loyalty he had inherited from his ancestors: adopting a strict behavioural conduct similar to the samurai, he defended his honour up to death. His life might be a rather special example, but such interpretations reflect the supposed primordiality of ethnic affiliations already discussed, namely that "Japanese values" are transmitted quasi-genetically as an almost unchangeable canon of values to Nikkei anywhere, sometimes with the allusion to the racial marker of *sangre* [blood]. Compare to Ota Mishima's (1993: 191) pathetic statement when she describes the Mexican Nikkei's actual socioeconomic situation: "One can say that in these days, all Japanese, apart from exceptions, follow the samurai codex; therefore, their life is dedicated to working with mystical religiosity, without abandoning fine arts, culture and traditions, conserving in this way their identity" (my translation). In other words, most post-war descendants assume that in order to be Nikkei, one needs to have Japanese ancestry, but also a specific habitus.

Nevertheless, many Nikkei emphasise that one also has to cultivate and rec-reate these values through hard work and excellent education. In often similar words, many Nisei expressed thankfulness to their parents that the latter com-pelled them to study: thereby, one is able to improve oneself (*superarse*) and to move forward (*salir adelante*). The Nisei successfully graduated from high school (*salieron bachilleres*) and became university-educated professionals (*profesion-ales*). There may not be any typical occupation for Bolivian Nikkei except for those related to agriculture, but at second glance, many have chosen prestigious and well-paying jobs that require many years of study, such as medicine and engi-neering. Their career choices also coincide with the well-known stereotypes of Japanese and East Asians as overachievers in mathematics and natural sciences. Apart from that, Nikkei careers are diverse: one family has set up a watch shop, another one opened a hotel and several descendants own restaurants, pharmacies, travel agencies or garages. Some female Nikkei have become hairdressers like Nataly and her mother; other women sell food on demand (Taira 2005). Several Nikkei-owned businesses mainly serve Nikkei customers and almost exclusively employ Nikkei. They may or may not provide specific products and services related to Japan.

In short, most Bolivian Nikkei opt for professions that promise an attractive income. Those studying arts and humanities are rare – despite three relatively famous artists of Japanese origin, namely an actor, a painter and a poet. It was JICA's priority to train doctors and engineers; therefore, they offered scholar-ships for these careers (Aniya 2013: 189, 192). Some young Nikkei also reported

How ethnic identities justify symbolic capital   53

to be subtly advised what profession is adequate. These choices mirror practices of Sucre's elites (Barriga Dávalos 2016: 61ff.): here, the majority opts for more profitable professions like business administration, medicine and engineering, whereas only children of impoverished families, women – who are not supposed to support the family income substantially – or children of intellectuals chose careers in the humanities. Nikkei psychologist Michelle Nomura, however, thinks that many Nikkei do not become physicians because they are brilliant students. Like psychology, medicine means helping fellow human beings, but there is a subtle difference, she says smilingly: "Medicine is supposed to be a social service, but it's a lucrative service [laughs]. Social prestige." According to her, post-war Nikkei are overly materialistic and do not think so much in serving society – which would be the reputation they try to promote. At the same time, since they are busy making money, they forget to take care of the relationship with their friends and family, Michelle criticises.

Whenever I talked to non-Nikkei about my research, their discourses were strikingly similar. Many non-Nikkei support the view that descendants' economic capital is related to their "values." Some non-Nikkei even told me that they had learned from Nikkei how to work more efficiently, like the *paceño* (inhabitant of La Paz) Francisco Torrico. When I visited him through the arrangement of his long-time friend from high school, the well-known doctor Saburo Yamashita, he was full of admiration for his friend's ambitious family and the Nikkei in general, considering them a role model. Nevertheless, he acknowledges that also individual and not only cultural factors might have contributed to the Yamashita's success.

> The first time I went [to the Yamashita family home in San Juan], it was a very simple little house and quite a rustic life, very difficult because of the heat and other incommodities. But his father was a visionary. And it caught my attention how he was working, with a lot of enthusiasm, buying chicken, constructing the chicken cages or learning about incubators. And when I went there six years ago, the change was incredible [...] after 20 years. The road was paved, and they had a very nice construction just next to the old house [...]. [Saburo's father] started to produce rice, but he already knew that rice follows a cycle [...]. When rice production was booming, he was already studying poultry [...]. This mentality, always taking a step forward, always studying, that was very interesting for me.

Not only Francisco Torrico holds such a favourable opinion. Daniela Vargas, a non-Nikkei married to a descendant, declares to feel more secure when being with Nikkei, since they would not steal. A Nisei mother told me laughingly that as a "Japanese," the parent's council at her children's school would always elect her as treasurer: apart from a talent for numbers, a treasurer should also be entirely reliable. In other words, Japanese descendants enjoy much symbolic capital among non-Nikkei: they are considered both hard-working and honest. Nataly Yonamine's long-time friend, the Nisei Ritsuko Hashimoto, illustrates this

54 *How ethnic identities justify symbolic capital*

with an example. She is as eloquent on this subject as on other topics related to Japanese migration. Comfortably sitting in the armchair in her small living room full of Japanese souvenirs, she remembers her daughter's trip to São Paulo the year before, constantly intensifying her speech with the euphemistic interjection "*miércoles*" [Wednesday]:

> She went just with the necessary amount of money to São Paulo, but at the border when the bus should cost, let's say, 100 dollars, it was more than 100 dollars. And then she didn't know what to do and she calls me and says: "Mom, we don't have any money." And then a Bolivian lady who also went to Brazil for shopping asks her: "Do you need money?" She didn't know her. And [my daughter] says: "Yes, *miércoles*, I need, I don't know what to do." So the lady said to her: "I trust in the Japanese, so I will borrow you that money."

In contrast to most studies on minority–majority relations, non-Nikkei host few negative stereotypes on Japanese descendants. They may consider the Nikkei to be reserved, cold, difficult to understand, a little boring, unable to enjoy life and somewhat arrogant. One non-Nikkei acquaintance remembered a wedding she experienced as almost too organised to be enjoyable. A long-term non-Nikkei inhabitant of Colonia Okinawa, married to a descendant, remarked that the Nikkei worked too much, thereby endangering their health. Another non-Nikkei complained about a high number of meetings in Nikkei associations to decide on trivial issues.

But even the dislike for festivities can be turned into a supposed moral superiority. Non-Nikkei social scientist Fernando Prado observes that if "those Japanese" do not enjoy life, they will be dedicated to study and work, and consequently, they will be excellent professionals. But "shrewd" non-descendants may cheat the well-behaved, honest Nikkei who also suffer from their environment's general unreliability, Ritsuko explained to me. To my own surprise, I had found her house in a wealthy neighbourhood fast enough to ring the door precisely at 9 o'clock in the morning, as previously agreed on the phone. Ritsuko was excited about this "Japanese-style" punctuality, in contrast to what she regards as typically Bolivian practices.

> Therefore, I said, *miércoles*, how you're on time […], because this is what I really hate here and I say, *miércoles*, why am I not a *camba*, I'm not Bolivian because they taught us but almost with … [laughs]. And then like the *trámites*,[2] everything that's not complied […]. If I was Bolivian, I wouldn't suffer that much.

Time and again, I heard the anecdote that a Japanese descendant organised a birthday party, but at the agreed time only his or her Nikkei friends arrived. As a result, they had to wait with a growling stomach for hours for the other guests. Punctuality appears to be a quasi-inherited static value, becoming an explicit

How ethnic identities justify symbolic capital   55

boundary marker: Nikkei are on time, while non-Nikkei are not – because of their culture.

Even controversial behaviour can be framed in such a way to demonstrate distinction and moral superiority. I often discussed my research results with Mai Amuro, a post-war descendant in her early forties. She is a social scientist and works for an international N.G.O., quite an unusual career choice for a Japanese descendant, and generally takes a critical distance to other Nikkei. In the beginning, the social difference between the Japanese settlers and their non-Nikkei neighbours was small, she states. At the same time, the Issei claimed moral superiority with their comparatively higher educational level: "At least we knew how to read and write;" or with their diet: "At least we ate healthier food." The community would even explain thefts with adverse circumstances, Mai remembers:

> My parents say: "When we were small, we were so poor that we also stole. If somebody had an orange tree or a mandarin tree, we went and if we could, we stole because of hunger. But the code of conduct, the honour, not even in the worst poverty, they could take all this away from you […]." Even in the [Japanese] mafia, there is a code of conduct and there is respect between the criminals [laughs].

In addition, the positive stereotypes appear to be relatively robust against counter-evidence. Even a dishonest individual may not reduce the entire group's symbolic capital. My non-Nikkei house owner eventually found out that her only Nikkei acquaintance had cheated her and escaped abroad leaving behind major debts, a fact that was widely reported in the local media. Moreover, he had already served a sentence for another criminal offence. Even this incident did not change her generally positive opinion of Japanese descendants.

The narrative of "Japanese values lead to success" bears interesting similarities with what Yoshino (1992: 189) writes about Japan: "[T]he *nihonjinron* claims that Japan's 'economic success' is a cultural and moral victory of the Japanese, and this is all the more obvious when peculiar Japanese values are used to explain the apparent success." But the Nikkei's justifications also resemble the well-known "from rags to riches" narrative: immigrants arrive to a foreign land without resources, connections and language skills. They experience hardships and suffer from discrimination. Since they work restlessly, have a sound money management and contribute to their new home country's wellbeing, they eventually achieve socioeconomic upward mobility. This line of reasoning is not limited to contexts of international migration: in her research on middle-class identities in Cochabamba metropolitan area, Shakow's (2014) interview partners underlined that they had become prosperous by their own efforts, a reason for them to feel morally superior. In this context, it is useful to recall that already in the European Enlightenment, the bourgeoisie promoted hard work, thriftiness, orderliness, punctuality, etc., as a way to a stable economic existence and emancipation from the aristocracy, thereby distinguishing itself from the lower classes (Bahrdt 1790). In sum, the middle classes anywhere use seemingly unique values to justify their

56 *How ethnic identities justify symbolic capital*

status. Nevertheless, the narrative remains persuasive since it refers to a supposedly original character that was never lost despite all external influences.

Unreliable, lazy and funny – Stereotypes of non-Nikkei Bolivians

Stereotypes do not exist in empty space but need other stereotypes to contrast with. Nikkei frequently characterise non-Nikkei in a negative way: "those Bolivians" are said to be dirty,[3] undisciplined, wasteful, selfish, unpunctual, untrustworthy, immature and irresponsible, or, in sum, less civilised. Non-Nikkei are often characterised as rascals who lack respect and proper manners and who never repay their debts, but make countless demands without offering anything in exchange. Many Bolivians' risky driving style and their ruthless attitude towards pedestrians were as well mentioned as behaviours to avoid. As many descendants criticise, non-Nikkei only think of their own benefit, but not of the common good. Moreover, they are said to be potential thieves, as for example, Higa (2013: 229) describes for Colonia Okinawa, even though he attributes such controversial behaviour to social disparities. When, for example, a dance dress disappeared after an event at Centro Social, it was automatically supposed that a non-Nikkei Bolivian must have stolen it.

I have often heard that "Japanese values" should be complemented by some "Bolivian customs." The Nikkei generally consider non-Nikkei to be funny, entertaining and generous (Suzuki 2010: 122). Warm-heartedness expressed, for instance, when embracing a friend, was often cited as a behaviour worth imitating. Nevertheless, playing the clown might be useful at a party, but it does not qualify somebody to take on responsibilities at work. Therefore, these positive characterisations do not contest the generally negative stereotypes, but support the comfortable explanation for why the Nikkei's standard of living is above average.

Interestingly, non-Nikkei Bolivians often support these discourses. In Bolivia, foreigners have mainly been considered a model to follow – even though Japan is probably not the first country that comes to a non-Nikkei's mind when thinking of the so-called industrialised world. Eduardo Visentin, a non-Nikkei married to a Japanese descendant, observes:

> Bolivia is a country that generally wants to offer foreigners a pleasant life. Not only to the Japanese. If you're, let's say, German or Spaniard or another foreigner, the Bolivian practically retreats [...]. They think that the foreigner is better skilled [...]. It's difficult for us to acknowledge that we're also skilled.

The Morales administration repeatedly complained about supposed foreign imperialism; some laws were enacted to limit foreigners' economic possibilities. Despite this nationalist attitude, Bolivia is well aware of its low standards of living compared to the Latin American average. Instead of blaming foreigners, the middle and upper classes usually attribute this situation to the lower classes and the indigenous population, with obvious racist undertones. Many of its inhabitants

How ethnic identities justify symbolic capital 57

depict Bolivia as a place where everybody does whatever occurs to him or her, even if it means harming others, and they readily illustrate this opinion with concrete examples, followed by a resigned "*¡sólo en Bolivia!*"; "[This happens] only in Bolivia!" Santa Cruz' most important newspaper El Deber publishes a picture every day, handed in by readers, to accuse "uncivilised" behaviour such as throwing garbage in the street or driving inappropriately. Popular opinion holds that especially *cambas* prefer to circumvent the law to achieve their goals (Seleme Antelo 2007: 102; Waldmann 2008: 182f.). However, one has to bear in mind that the speaker generally does not present him- or herself as the wrongdoer, but as the positive exception who might at most be forced to break a rule by adverse circumstances. Instead, other Bolivians, especially those socially or culturally distant, are blamed for all social evils. In other words, non-Nikkei use Japanese descendants to criticise their own society.

Against the discourse of a disorderly Bolivia, Nikkei successfully present themselves as respectful model citizens, marking non-Nikkei implicitly or explicitly as rule-breakers. According to the 90th-anniversary book of Sociedad Japonesa de La Paz: "We are very proud of our parents' heritage because they have been Bolivia's best citizens with a blameless behaviour" (Sociedad Japonesa de La Paz 2012: 252); and: "We have strictly adhered to Bolivian laws" (ibid.: 253) (both my translation).

I will look at one of these negative stereotypes more in detail to demonstrate that they are not based on objective observation, but serve specific goals. *Cruceñas* and *cruceños*, in contradiction to the widely held perception of Santa Cruz as the country's economic motor, are said to dislike work and professional ambition. Already in the first half of the 19th century, the often-cited French traveller Alcides D'Orbigny (1945: 1100) wrote about Santa Cruz' inhabitants that they lived in abundance with much time to sleep and to visit friends. Images of a *camba* enjoying life in his hammock or playing the guitar under a tree are today celebrated and commercialised on T-Shirts, baseball caps and other souvenirs. One also hears this stereotype in daily conversations. One afternoon in Multimercado Okinawa, I was presented to Ramón Borja, a non-Nikkei Bolivian lawyer. When I explained my research, he commented that if non-Nikkei would have settled on the *colonias'* land, they would have burned it and hung up their hammocks – no wonder, according to Ramón, that Brazilians own nowadays so much land in lowland Bolivia, if Bolivians are so lazy.

Already in Greek antiquity, authors related climate and culture. Also, many Nikkei and non-Nikkei attribute the *cambas'* supposed laziness to the geographical environment. The tropical climate becomes a synonym for harmful influence on morals and values. According to this discourse, since the hot and humid climate in Santa Cruz favours plant growth all year round, nobody is in need to work hard nor has the energy to do so. Instead, many Nikkei refer to the harsher climate in Japan – which may nevertheless be doubtful in the case of Okinawa Prefecture – and the less fertile soils that, accordingly, made the Japanese more ingenious. The Nikkei had to struggle in order to survive; thus, they needed to be hard-working, disciplined and organised, they argue.

58   *How ethnic identities justify symbolic capital*

It is commonly believed that according to *cruceñas* and *cruceños,* work should be related to fun and talent, but not to discipline or sacrifice. Waldmann (2008: 238ff.), however, traces the *cambas'* supposed laziness back to the colonial feudalist society when the higher classes were taken as an ideal by the hard-working lower classes. Seleme Antelo (2007: 14) relativises the designation *flojo* (lazy) as an external value judgment: members of a pre-modern society do not need to stick to timetables. Nevertheless, in the era of urbanisation and globalisation with more competitive work models, different requirements and increasing living expenses, most parts of the population cannot afford to pass their day in a hammock. As Fechter (2010: 154ff.) observes in her research on expatriates in Indonesia, the myth of the lazy native reminds of colonial narratives and fulfils a specific function in an unequal society: it is used to exaggerate the expatriates' own importance and to justify their comparatively high salaries. Again, ethnic stereotypes become mixed with characterisations based on class.

Other than being interpreted as the moral failure of a whole group, such supposedly deficient behaviour could be attributed to a non-Nikkei's individual character or specific adverse circumstances, but it could also be regarded as an outcome of the unequal power distribution and economic inequalities. To give an example, while most Nikkei reside in the city's central areas and own comfortable vehicles, many lower-class non-Nikkei live in the outskirts and use the unreliable public transport system. Suzuki (2010: 69ff.) observed among non-Nikkei farmworkers in Colonia Okinawa a range of behaviours, such as theft, that can be interpreted as acts of everyday resistance (Scott 1985). Instead, many Nikkei attribute ethnic boundaries to the observable socioeconomic differences in Bolivia: those not able to attain prosperity were deemed too lazy or too unorganised.

"Barefoot but happy" – Staging Nikkei history

The Nikkei actively create and recreate their history at significant birthdays, in commemoration books and community museums, emphasising specific parts according to current needs. Recalling the history of Japanese migration, many interview partners presented a convincing story with the conclusion that their suffering eventually made sense. Keiko Taniguchi vividly remembered the settlers' disappointment when I interviewed her in the home of the Santa Cruz branch of Sōka Gakkai Buddhism, where she is today one of the leading figures. Keiko arrived as a child from Nagasaki Prefecture to San Juan and not least because of her faith, she declares to be happy today. Nevertheless, she remembers how she suffered because she did not speak Spanish whereas non-Nikkei turned out to be unreliable liars.

> The advertisement in Japan was very different. They said that they would give us 50 hectares of land to sow. "There's a paved road, there's a hospital, there's a school, there's electricity, water, telephone, everything" […]. But when we came here, it was very different. And once we were here, we couldn't leave any more […]. Many returned to Japan, many went to

Argentina, Brazil. But in the case of my family, we stayed because there was no money to return [...]. It was only true that they gave us 50 hectares of land, but it was a jungle with those trees with eight, ten meters in diameter [...]. And to chop a tree, they needed ten days or two weeks.

Typical occasions to remember such hardships are anniversaries of an ethnic association or of the first migrants' arrival to Bolivia. The programme of such events is generally almost identical in Bolivia and elsewhere. Not only are the Japanese ambassador, consul, JICA officials as well as Japanese prefectural and national government representatives invited, but also the Bolivian department's governor or other important politicians. Organisers are especially pleased if a member of the Japanese imperial family attends. Apart from banquets, dance and music performances, the anthems of Japan, Bolivia and the respective Bolivian department are obligatory. Nikkei representatives emphasise their indebtedness to the Issei in general and the contribution of distinguished descendants in particular, while underlining the locals' welcoming attitude and the ongoing harmony between Nikkei and non-Nikkei. Other official invitees from Bolivia and Japan praise the Nikkei as pioneers in Bolivian agriculture. Symbolic actions like planting friendship trees may be part of the programme as well. For the 120th immigration anniversary, a poster exhibition presented different Nikkei communities in Bolivia, immigration history, famous Japanese-Bolivian personalities etc. in different Bolivian cities; a film was produced as well (Embajada del Japón en Bolivia 2019c, 2019d). However, one should not forget that not everybody supports this official narrative and that the meaning of anniversaries is contested among descendants, for instance between different generations who have different ideas of what to celebrate and whom to invite (Amemiya 2001).

After the anniversary celebration, the association often compiles a book mainly for a Nikkei and Japanese audience, although nothing has been published for the most recent anniversaries in Santa Cruz Department. Such books include articles about the local country and its culture, historical overviews, memories of individual members and debates between association members on specific topics like the future of education or the relations with the majority society. A central motive is the first generations' suffering and their disillusion when they arrived at their new place of residence. As the Brazilian researcher Célia Sakurai (1993) notes, such books recount many anecdotes, emphasising their "typically Japanese" perseverance, "*o espírito do gambarê*" [the *ganbare* spirit], that enabled them to endure their destiny with resignation but without complaints.

Nikkei communities in Bolivia and elsewhere, often supported by Japanese volunteers, have been documenting their history in museums, staging a similar narrative as in books and during anniversary celebrations. Santa Cruz, in contrast to La Paz, Colonia Okinawa and San Juan, has no Nikkei museum, maybe because most descendants do not consider the city to have an independent past unlike the *colonias* as icons of Nikkei history.[4] Bolivia's Nikkei museums with up to three rooms each are small compared to the Museu Histórico da Imigração Japonesa in São Paulo that documents the Nikkei's presence in Brazil on three floors. Visiting

60 *How ethnic identities justify symbolic capital*

the *colonias'* museums is almost mandatory for any guest, but they are also a place for local children to learn about the settlements' history (Figure 3.1).

The museums mean a specific staging of history. Everybody could participate providing objects of daily use like plates, lunch boxes, teapots, saws, etc. San Juan's museum also exposes a samurai helmet and old Japanese swords as a proud reminiscence to the immigrants' warrior ancestors. Other exhibits include straw-made sandals or the skin of a giant snake. Pictures show the seven-day train trip from the Brazilian harbour to the Bolivian *colonia*, a group of settlers posing with saws next to the enormous trees, inundated mud roads and a small cinema presented as the settlers' only distraction. Sometimes, these memories are idealised in retrospect like a class of schoolchildren who, according to the caption in Spanish and Japanese, are "barefoot but happy." Moreover, photos also document marriages, important visits and festivities such as *undōkai* [sports festival]. Commemoration medals and anniversary certificates are displayed in a central location. Additional monuments in the *colonias* represent the individual male farmer pioneer, the pioneer family or initiators of the migration project. The guest books illustrate that visitors are deeply impressed by the contrast between the *colonias'* first years and the actual state of being. Apart from this celebratory

Figure 3.1 Migrants' suitcase at the museum of Japanese migration, La Paz. In front of the enormous picture of a ship, the vitrine shows several items that migrants brought with them to Bolivia: Japanese-style trousers and kimono, medicine, a passport, a dictionary, a pipe with tobacco, a pocket watch, a lunchbox, make-up utensils, a mirror, sandals, a sewing kit, a lucky charm for commercial enterprises and an umbrella.

How ethnic identities justify symbolic capital   61

pride, the museums also present nostalgic memories of a supposedly harmonious and united community with clearly circumscribed values and cultural practices untouched by the complications of modernity: they show the irretrievable loss of a kind of enchanted world that never existed in this form.

By celebrating how they built up the *colonias* out of nothing, Nikkei legitimise their presence in Bolivia as hard-working farmers but also as agents of development, demonstrating their rootedness in Bolivia. At the same time, one implicit message is that although they have lived in simple huts, they were able to overcome this situation thanks to their "Japanese values."

Rather than offering a scientific approach or a database for researchers, anniversaries, books and museums serve as a folkloristic self-enactment, telling an officially sanctioned story. Little historical context is shown, except for some important dates. Critical research lacks on the Bolivian government's reasons to accept Japanese migrants, and barely mentioned are the exodus of settlers, internal conflicts, JICA's support and the contribution of non-Nikkei employees. Self-critique is absent, too.

Younger Nikkei in particular may not be aware that migrants were not received with open arms. Akira Tokashiki arrived at Colonia Okinawa as a child. Apart from his work as an engineer, he collects information on Japanese migration to Bolivia, such as newspaper articles, and plans to write a book on Okinawan migration to Bolivia. After reading all these documents, he concludes:

> When in 1952 [president] Víctor Paz accepted the Okinawan migrants, I saw a note in [Santa Cruz' main newspaper] El Deber [...]. It was quite a strong critique because: "What benefits will these Asian immigrants bring?" Something like that. An interesting note [...]. The general public did not welcome them, not like the Japanese who write in their books that everything was rose-coloured [laughs] [...]. I think that Japan was not very well known to people here at that time, probably they didn't even know where the country was.

The most critical moment for Nikkei in La Paz was the Second World War. Even afterwards, many pre-war descendants in La Paz avoided contact with Japan and Japanese culture. They did not teach their children Japanese or refrained from registering them as Japanese nationals. Some changed the writing of their names to make them appear "less Japanese." Some elderly pre-war Nisei remembered from their childhood that even in the lowlands, the Nikkei's reputation was not as favourable as today. Anya (2013: 168) and Shioiri (2013: 108) report that shortly after the Second World War, pre-war Nisei suffered insults from non-Nikkei Bolivians in Santa Cruz – referring, for example, to their vegetable diet or their use of chopsticks – concluding that being a Japanese descendant was nothing to be proud of. Until after the Second World War, U.S. scholarship presented Japan as ahistorical and backwards and many U.S. films depicted the Japanese as treacherous (Befu 2009: 25) – a fact that certainly influenced Japan's perception in Latin America.

Nisei cattle breeder Ryoji Nakaima, too, remembers that in his childhood, the Nikkei suffered verbal harassment. He concludes that much has changed and he

62   *How ethnic identities justify symbolic capital*

draws a direct connection between the Nikkei's poverty and the insults: "It was because we were like people from Potosí, Oruro; all dirty we came from Colonia Okinawa on trucks. It took eight, ten hours." Although he remembers these negative aspects, Ryoji thinks that symbolic capital is an inevitable outcome, since the Nikkei will be respected because their "Japanese values" inevitably lead to economic and symbolic capital.

Rice, soybeans, fruits and vegetables – The Nikkei as agricultural pioneers?

As Nisei entrepreneur Setsuko Gushiken states, Nikkei should actively contribute to Bolivian society: "Like [the Latin American independence movement leader] Simón Bolívar said: you're not from where you were born, but from where you have fought." Many Nikkei use specific "fights" to legitimise their presence: they do not only claim to be emotionally attached to the lowlands, but they also state to be "pioneers" at the frontier of civilisation who have contributed to the country's wellbeing. Descendants emphasise that privilege is not a right, but an accomplishment, presenting themselves as experts who have introduced new crop varieties and taught local farmers specific techniques, for example, measures against poultry diseases. Such narratives are remarkably widespread in Latin America. A video on Santa Cruz Department's official website (Gobernación Autónoma de Santa Cruz 2009) celebrates the Japanese contribution to development, thanking the "*hermanos japoneses*" [Japanese brothers and sisters] who contributed to better living conditions. In Santa Cruz, the Japanese are said to have influenced the production and consumption of rice, soybeans, vegetables and fruits.

At first sight, Japanese influence on Bolivian rice production and consumption seems plausible. Despite being a globally popular staple food, the grain is central to Japanese culture, with rural life following rice cultivation. It is even said to contain divine energy, although it has not been Japan's exclusive staple food (Ishige 2009: 300f.; Ohnuki-Tierney 1993). At the same time, rice is widely consumed in present-day Bolivia – for example, in the Bolivian variant of the widely known *locro* soup, according to Iraola Mendizábal (2014) a consequence of Japanese migration.

However, Monheim and Köster (1982: 39ff.) as well as Ortiz and Soliz (2007: 17ff.) conclude that the Japanese contribution to Bolivian rice cultivation is marginal. Already in colonial times, Spanish missionaries and settlers introduced rice to the lowlands, but before the 1952 revolution, rice cultivation was costly, of low quality and not self-sufficient. Much rice was imported for around USD 1.8 million annually. The initial increase in cultivation after the revolution appears to be related to state support and large-scale landowners' fear of expropriations, but not to Japanese presence: rice was in demand and cultivators had the possibility to borrow machines at a low price. The newly arrived highlanders concentrated on rice as well, not least because it was easy to store in the isolated settlements during the rainy season. Indeed, the Japanese migrants have apparently introduced some wet rice varieties; but up to the present day, Santa Cruz'

How ethnic identities justify symbolic capital 63

growers focus on dry rice. Wet rice yields are twice as much, but its introduction is capital intensive and may be unaffordable for individual cultivators.

More evidence for the Nikkei's contribution exists in the case of soybeans, even though other factors than the Japanese presence enhanced its current popularity. According to Endōh (2009: 177f.), Nikkei settlers started soybean cultivation in Brazil as early as the 1920s. Pérez Luna (2007: 44f.) notes that the Japanese migrants – and the Mennonites – were the first to cultivate soybeans for subsistence in Bolivia. Soybeans, now the country's leading agricultural export product, became important only when the national government created specific market circumstances in the 1990s and when international monetary institutions started funding projects. Certainly, soybean cultivation would not be at its current level without the Brazilian expertise and capital (Gimenez 2010; Mackey 2011; Pérez Luna 2007; Valdivia 2010). Interestingly, even though it would relate the Nikkei to one of the department's sources of prosperity, they seldom claim its introduction. The reason might be that soy products do not belong to most *cruceñas'* and *cruceños'* diet, except for soy sauce.

Although it is difficult to find written sources, some evidence exists for a contribution in the case of fruits. Interview partners could name specific high-yield varieties introduced by Japanese settlers. Especially famous is the *ponkan* mandarine, introduced in 1961 (Fukaura and Nagai 2013: 251). It is popularly called "*mandarina japonesa.*" Other varieties include smooth cayenne pineapple, commonly known as *piña japonesa* [Japanese pineapple]; CAISY's general manager also mentions new species of mango, watermelon and banana. The Nikkei have ceased to cultivate them on a large scale; some non-Nikkei Bolivians have taken over the production. Furthermore, even though not a common fruit, persimmons are being sold on Santa Cruz' streets, possibly first cultivated by a Nikkei. Keisuke Sakata, a Nisei farmer from San Juan, has recently started growing coconuts. His friends jokingly predict that in some years, everybody will talk about the "Japanese coconuts" that will be as famous as the "Japanese pineapples" and the "Japanese watermelons." When presenting the Nikkei as agricultural pioneers, Keisuke proudly speaks of the "big mission" San Juan fulfilled for the region and asks rhetorically: "Who cultivates more mandarins? Now, it's certainly the people from here [non-Nikkei]. And who cultivates more lemons? Many people from here. Not to mention rice."

More than rice and soybean cultivation, Latin Americans relate Nikkei to the introduction of new vegetable varieties. Many *cruceñas* and *cruceños* say that before Japanese migration, only onions, carrots and tomatoes were known – since, in the lowlands, local diet was based on manioc, rice, chicken and beef meat. In Bolivia, this narrative can be traced back at least to 1923, when a newspaper article stated that thanks to the Japanese farmers, lettuce, pineapple, banana and rice became more accessible in Riberalta (La Gaceta del Norte 1923). Oshikawa (2013: 158), referring to Iyo Kunimoto's investigation in the 1970s, observes that Pando's population regarded vegetables as "something Japanese." Iraola Mendizábal (2014) writes that *cruceñas* and *cruceños* rejected the consumption of lettuce until the 1960s when the Japanese showed them the plant's benefits. Apart

64 *How ethnic identities justify symbolic capital*

from lettuce, one elderly non-Nikkei acquaintance attributed the introduction of parsley to the Japanese (Figure 3.2).

For many Nikkei, vegetable consumption has become a symbol of Japaneseness. Among post-war descendants, the narrative often goes that until recently, Japanese descendants were the only ones in Bolivia who would consume vegetables. Nisei Kentsu Hanashiro remembers that when his mother used to sell vegetables in the market around 30 years ago, she had only Nikkei, Korean and Chinese customers. According to some Nikkei, since climatic conditions in Japan were not as benign as in lowland Bolivia, each family relied on their garden. Migrants took the habit of vegetable cultivation and consumption to Bolivia, and in the late 1970s, the dooryard garden with carrots, cabbage, tomato, eggplant, radish and green onions was universal (Hiraoka 1980: 116). *Cruceñas* and *cruceños*,

Figure 3.2 Fresh fruits and vegetables from Colonia Okinawa, sold at "Okinawa Sunday Market" in front of Okinawa Kenjinkai.

How ethnic identities justify symbolic capital   65

according to this discourse, always had food in abundance, even meat, and did not need a garden like the sorely afflicted Japanese. CAICO general manager Mitsuo Ishimine resumes: "Eating vegetables is a habit of people who suffered." In informal conversations, many Nikkei underline the importance of vegetable consumption for a healthy lifestyle, criticising that the non-Nikkei still consume too much meat. Quantitative data is scarce, but the argument that Bolivians lack vegetables in their diet has an empirical basis. Moreover, with a growing sedentary lifestyle and a higher intake of fats and sugars, obesity and nutrition-related chronic diseases are on the rise (Agencia Boliviana de Información 2016; El Diario 2015; NotiBoliviaRural 2012). Meatless dishes or vegetarian restaurants are still hard to find even in a major city such as Santa Cruz.

As an everyday bodily practice, food is a central part of identity on an individual as well as on a collective level. Some descendants declared to have digestive problems when consuming meat, explaining that their bodies were not adapted to a carnivorous Bolivian diet. Chihiro Imanaka, a Nisei mother from San Juan, told me that she consciously accustomed her daughters to eat Bolivian food "so that they won't suffer later." Bolivian food was considered too heavy and leading to laziness and a long siesta, whereas Japanese food gave the energy to work and study, helping the Nikkei to achieve middle-class status.[5] Contrary to this narrative on "better Japanese food," many Nikkei consume a variety of items that can be considered "Bolivian" or at least non-Japanese: they buy *cruceño* snacks like *cuñapés*,[6] consume the omnipresent hot sauce *llajwa* and enjoy the – not necessarily healthy – *churrasco* [barbecue] on Sundays. Some Nisei parents furthermore complain that their children, much like their *cruceño* classmates, prefer to have *hamburguesas* [hamburgers] when meeting their friends. Even when they prepare a *churrasco* or visit a Bolivian-style restaurant, many Nikkei insist on vegetable side dishes that make the food symbolically palatable.

However, no systematic research has been done on a possible Japanese contribution to vegetable consumption in Santa Cruz. Instead, Stearman (1985: 66f.) notes that food items such as green beans, lettuce and tomatoes became available thanks to merchants from the highlands, while some non-Nikkei acquaintances attributed the increased production of vegetables to the Taiwanese or the Mennonites. Similarly, CAICO general manager Mitsuo Ishimine doubts that Japanese immigration had an effect on the cultivation of vegetables. He thinks that the lack of demand was due to a low level of education on the consumer side. According to him, changing patterns are due to TV programmes about healthy food. Furthermore, buying and eating vegetables appears to be highly class-related: vegetable consumption has become a habit of more affluent strata who consciously follow such nutrition trends. Food serves as an ethnic and social boundary marker, but also as a reason to feel morally superior. At the same time, many Nikkei are pleased to note these changing patterns: increased vegetable consumption makes non-Nikkei "more acceptable."

No matter if there is any proof for their contribution to local agriculture, Nikkei present themselves as agents of development and as forerunners of a modern, health-conscious lifestyle. This means propagating a win-win narrative of

66 *How ethnic identities justify symbolic capital*

productivity, job creation and quality of life. According to both descendants and non-descendants, the Nikkei have been sharing their knowledge, resources and installations instead of living off non-Nikkei Bolivians' expenses. Nevertheless, since knowledge and high-yield crops gave Nikkei an advantage, it is doubtful that teaching non-Nikkei neighbours occurred out of mere goodwill. As soon as locals broadly adopted new varieties, the Nikkei had to look for alternatives.

Yen and dollars – Japan's contribution to the Nikkei's prosperity

Without the intention to negate the immigrants' enormous efforts, explaining the post-war Nikkei's economic and symbolic capital only with hard work falls short. Most descendants nevertheless frame their current wellbeing as an almost natural consequence of their "Japanese values." But on a closer look, their connections to Japan have been decisive for their socioeconomic wellbeing, while they did not need to compete with non-Nikkei Bolivians. Whereas the Nikkei have used these opportunities quite effectively, I agree with the Nisei agronomist and programme insider Norio Miyaguni that the two *colonias* would probably not have survived without Japanese government assistance and *dekasegi*.

Manzenreiter (2017a: 208) summarises that while the Nikkei comprise less than 10% of the population in Latin America's Japanese *colonias*, they nevertheless control 90% of the settlements' assets, apart from enjoying a considerably higher life expectancy, lower child mortality rates and better access to basic services. As Amemiya (2001) notes: "By providing Japanese-Bolivians with benefits in the form of financial and technical aid to the Colonias and by their special treatment in immigration, the Japanese government is creating a special class in Bolivia."

In the beginning, the economic difference between immigrants and locals was small. Nisei farmer Seiichiro Takaki from San Juan remembers how this situation has changed, being one of the few interview partners who openly recognised the importance of external factors for the enormous socioeconomic gap: "Before, we lived at the same level, because we also lived in *motacú*[7] huts, we walked barefoot [...]. But we had a little more help than the Bolivians, so the economy grew, and the Bolivians stayed the same."

Indeed, whereas Bolivia offered land and not much more, especially the Japanese government has supported Nikkei in Latin America via JICA (Suzuki 2010: 50ff.). Several subnational actors such as Okinawa Prefecture have contributed as well, but to my knowledge, their role has not been studied systematically. Indeed, this assistance has perhaps been unique when compared to other emigration states. JICA has contributed in multiple ways: it offered trainee programs and scholarships for Nikkei to study in Japan to support their communities in Latin America. It funded schools, hospitals, administration and association buildings – in other words, all major constructions in the *colonias* – and Japanese volunteers still support some daily tasks (Embajada del Japón en Bolivia 2019a). JICA provided loans with attractive repayment terms,[8] donated machines and medical

How ethnic identities justify symbolic capital 67

equipment and sent books and videos to the library. It also funded several bridges between Santa Cruz and the *colonias* as part of its development assistance to Bolivia. With JICA's support, the Nikkei have been able to introduce new plant varieties and techniques. Suzuki (2010: 58ff.) notes that in 1998, ABJ, the hospital and the school still received up to 30% of their budget from Japan.

Hardships and failings were softened by Japanese assistance as well. After floods had devastated parts of Colonia Okinawa in 1992, JICA provided around USD 220,000 to reconstruct the damaged roads (Suzuki 2010: 59f.). During the hyperinflation of the 1980s, Nikkei farmers could erase their debts in Bolivian currency whereas they received support from Japan in U.S. dollars: JICA eventually paid for the currency devaluation, leading to the perception that the Nikkei were reliable debtors (Suzuki 2010: 47ff.). The Issei farmers initially focused on subsistence, but they started large-scale farming in the 1970s, supported by the Japanese government. However, cotton production failed in Colonia Okinawa and many farmers left to neighbouring countries or to Japan. The substitution of crops eventually turned out to be an excellent choice: growing soybeans became rentable in the late 1980s, and for the first time, Bolivian Nikkei enjoyed economic prosperity. Nevertheless, even JICA support might not have been of much use if the settlers' arrival had not coincided with a time of economic flourishing. After the 1952 revolution and the abolishment of feudalism, times were promising (Shakow 2014: 11f.).

All implicated governments have failed their promises or have committed serious mistakes. Whereas some Nikkei like Keiko Taniguchi mentioned Bolivia's

Figure 3.3 Mural at a ropeway station in La Paz, celebrating 40 years of Japanese cooperation in Bolivia.

68   How ethnic identities justify symbolic capital

broken promises, no interview partner ever alluded to failures on the Japanese side – perhaps because of ongoing dependencies. JICA closed its offices in the *colonias* in the 1990s and Nikkei now receive much less assistance than before the year 2000, a fact that most of them regretted but understood. JICA's assistance is shifting to projects for non-Nikkei.

JICA is generally regarded as honest and well organised in Santa Cruz. It is well known that it has financed important infrastructure projects in Santa Cruz such as the Hospital Japonés and Viru Viru as the city's international airport – to the benefit of the whole population. Nevertheless, as Mai Amuro points out, JICA's symbolic capital may also be related to the fact that it did not interfere in politics. Instead of discussing social problems, the sometimes precarious political situation in recipient countries, the degree of freedom or respect for human rights, Japan has rather focused on the technical aspects of development cooperation (Tsunekawa 1998) (Figure 3.3).

Apart from JICA's support, the possibility to work in Japan has proved essential to many Nikkei's prosperity. A high number of Bolivian Nikkei went for *dekasegi* from the late 1980s onwards, especially those who were not able to inherit land for a farm. *Dekasegi* was a reaction to growing mechanisation on the one hand and the Latin American economic crisis with few opportunities for upward mobility on the other hand. The departure of many settlers was indirectly beneficial to those who remained or returned from Japan: they could take over the land the leaving Nikkei sold them (Fukaura and Nagai 2013: 277ff.; Higa 2013: 233ff.; Suzuki 2010: 39f.). As in the case of many migratory movements, *dekasegi* migration had become such an essential factor of the *colonias'* socioeconomic system by the early 1990s that even when the bubble economy collapsed in 1991, the Nikkei still went to Japan (Suzuki 2010: 44ff.). Nowadays, few Nikkei move to Japan for work, and if they do, they usually leave after obtaining their university degree and not instead. In the meantime, not only has the demand for inexpensive labour in Japan decreased, but also Bolivia's economic situation makes it easier to pursue a successful professional career.

Some Nikkei had a clear strategy on what to do in Japan and how to use their savings in Bolivia, like Hakuo Tamanaha. He is an entrepreneur in his sixties from a farmer family in Colonia Okinawa. When still in Bolivia, he wanted to found his own export business for agricultural products but he did not even possess USD 10,000, so he decided to go for *dekasegi* and to build up contacts with future customers. Hakuo returned from Japan with USD 150,000, sufficient to realise his plan. Farmer Seiichiro Takaki from San Juan, too, has invested his *dekasegi* savings in land and machines. When he came back, the land was still cheap in the Santa Cruz Department after a time of economic crisis: "We have returned at a good time. Now it's more difficult because, in former times, land was worthless. It had value for those who worked on it. But now [...], you have to be an entrepreneur to start."

While Hakuo presents his stay as a strategic step in a successful career, for many Nikkei, going to Japan for *dekasegi* was an adventure or a kind of *rite de passage* to adulthood, an opportunity to broaden their horizon and to discover

How ethnic identities justify symbolic capital   69

the country of their ancestors, as I describe in Siemann (2018). Because so many young Nikkei have not returned, a whole generation is missing in Bolivia and Latin America: at the beginning of the new millennium, more than half of the young Bolivian-Okinawan population in Colonia Okinawa between 18 and 30 resided in Japan (Suzuki 2010: 43). Some of those who remain overseas have lost contact with descendants in Bolivia. Therefore, some Nikkei see *dekasegi* as unsustainable, accusing migrants of looking for quick money instead of studying and planning a professional career. As Seiichiro Takaki remembers, *dekasegi* was also a way to escape from economic problems. Minae Hara, a Nisei businesswoman from San Juan, is not sure either if *dekasegi* was beneficial to everybody.

> [I only know] about those who are above average […]. But one doesn't hear about those who are not well […]. Because there were families that out of pride didn't want their children to go for *dekasegi*, but other families because of necessity or because they couldn't give a part of the inheritance to their second or third child, they sent them [to Japan]. And normally it goes well.

Moreover, *dekasegi* was much easier for Bolivian post-war Nikkei than for other descendants not only because many are able to communicate in Japanese, but also because most of them maintain Japanese nationality – although double citizenship is not officially allowed. Some individual Issei have renounced Japanese citizenship to demonstrate their identification with Bolivia, whereas one family was not able to obtain Japanese nationality for their children following conflicts with consulate staff. Moreover, those with a non-Japanese father could not inherit Japanese nationality through their mother until 1985, and pre-war Nikkei generally do not hold Japanese passports because their ancestors did not have the possibility to register their children on time[9] or because they had considered the relation to Japan to be useless or dangerous.

Those without a Japanese passport generally regret this fact. Although a passport might stand for an affective identification with Japan, it is much more than that. Whereas Bolivian nationals need a visa for many countries, Japanese citizenship makes travelling much easier. Therefore, Mai Amuro is happy about her Japanese passport; but she does not feel comfortable among other Nikkei, prefers to speak Spanish, has never travelled to Japan and identifies first as Bolivian. She has observed differences in how she is treated at the border depending on which passport she uses. Mai concludes that border guards treat her better when she shows her Japanese passport since Japan occupies a higher place in the global hierarchy than Bolivia. Some Nikkei also take their Japanese nationality as insurance against economic and political problems in Bolivia. During my field research, Venezuela was going through a severe economic and political crisis until refugees begging for money became a common sight at traffic lights and in buses in Santa Cruz. There was a constant fear that something similar would occur in Bolivia, and in this case, a Japanese passport would be more useful than a Bolivian one in order to escape.

70 *How ethnic identities justify symbolic capital*

Can the *camba* be born anywhere? – Are the Nikkei accepted as *cruceñas* and *cruceños*?

When the Nikkei speak about co-ethnics as "*japoneses*," it may not mean that they negate their Bolivian-ness, but rather point to the situational nature of identity: they evoke their belonging to a common history and their differences to non-Nikkei. Nikkei regularly use "*boliviano/boliviana*" to refer to non-Nikkei Bolivians since their Japanese origin is in the foreground when in Bolivia – identifications will look different in a Japanese context. Alternative designations for non-Nikkei are "*la gente (de) acá*" [people (from) here] or simply "*ellos*" [they], if it is clear from the context.

As already stated above, North and Latin American countries have been considering themselves to be immigration destinations, allowing, for example, newcomers' children to acquire nationality via jus soli. The Bolivian state has never forced Nikkei to assimilate and Santa Cruz' society is famous for its extroversion and openness to foreigners. A wooden plaque with the often-cited sentence "*es ley del cruceño la hospitalidad*" [the *cruceño's* law is hospitality][10] greets incoming travellers at Santa Cruz international airport Viru Viru, possibly meant to console those who become desperate with the slowly moving queue in front of the passport control. Equally well known is "*el cruceño/camba nace donde quiere*" [the *cruceño/camba* can be born anywhere].

While many Nikkei emphasise their harmonious relations to non-Nikkei, even jus soli does not mean that all citizens receive equal treatment in daily life. Despite the fact that the Nikkei enjoy symbolic capital, the majority population can impose their vision and categorise them as "foreigners" – a categorisation that may or not be advantageous.

Remarks such as "you're really *camba*, but your face" or "without Japanese physiognomy, they would be like any *cruceño*" demonstrate that many non-Nikkei see an incompatibility between a *camba* or Bolivian identity and features interpreted as East Asian. Even well-educated non-Nikkei Bolivians who are more or less familiar with the history of Japanese immigration take part in excluding discourses, many times inadvertently. Also Eduardo Visentin, the fair-skinned son of an Italian migrant, observes that his Bolivian-ness is never questioned, unlike in the case of his Nisei wife Naoko. Naoko's sister from Colonia Okinawa told me with a mixture of annoyance and amusement how verbal exclusion may occur in a more indirect way. She has left Bolivia only for holidays but is sometimes asked why she speaks Spanish so well. Her husband, who grew up in the town of Vallegrande, famous in Santa Cruz Department for its distinctive accent, is regularly tested on specific words because many non-Nikkei cannot believe that he is able to speak like a *valluno*. Similarly, a large part of the Bolivian academic literature, for instance, on agricultural developments, refers to them simply as the "Japanese" – despite the fact that Nisei and Sansei are Bolivian citizens.

Most non-Nikkei take the Nikkei's body and especially their faces as a central reference for ethnic categorisations. It is therefore even worse for many Nikkei if they are called "*chinos*" [Chinese]: this means that Nikkei do not only look different

How ethnic identities justify symbolic capital 71

from Bolivians, but that all Asians look the same. A non-Nikkei teacher even remembered the expression "*los chinos de la colonia japonesa*" [the Chinese from the Japanese *colonia*]. Non-verbal references include gestures like pulling eyelids up with the fingers. One non-Nikkei acquaintance supposed that Micaela Tejada, the non-Nikkei spouse of a Nikkei, was of Japanese origin. She explained this with Micaela's body movements and her Japanese language skills – but with this line of reasoning, my acquaintance was clearly an exception. Nevertheless, within the category "Japanese" or "Nikkei," one can be classified as "more Japanese" or "more Bolivian," according to one's habitus, like "she is really Japanese, she is always on time." This also shows the limits of constructing ethnic identity: even a Nikkei who distantiates him- or herself from the family, the community and everything Japanese is still identified by non-Nikkei Bolivians as looking "foreign."

The Nikkei do not fit into the commonly held notion of who is Bolivian – in the national imaginary, Asian descendants do not appear. Similarly, the roughly 16,000 Afro-Bolivians, despite being part of the national folklore and recognised as an ethnic group in the new Bolivian constitution, may be categorised as Brazilians or citizens of another Latin American country with a significant African-descendant population (Busdiecker 2011: 15).[11]

Especially among close friends, it is common in Bolivia to use nicknames inspired by physical features, such as "*flaco/flaca*" or "*gordo/gorda*," referring to slender or corpulent persons. Such nicknames are often put into the diminutive form to show affection and to soften a designation that could otherwise be interpreted as an insult. Despite the government's attempts to abolish racialist thinking after 1952, skin colours are used as well. To give the reader an idea, "*negro/negra*" or "*choco/choca*" can refer to dark-skinned and light-skinned individuals, respectively, without necessarily implicating exclusion or depreciation. Persons with facial features interpreted as similar to those of Chinese may be called "*chino/china*" which does not always mean that somebody has Asian ancestry. However, most Nikkei understand the term as excluding.

Many remember that they started to notice being different when someone called them "*chino cochino*" [dirty Chinese] at school. As a result, Sansei Mayumi Iwamatsu observes that adolescent Nikkei do not know where they belong to since they feel excluded in both Bolivia and Japan. Most adult Nikkei have come to see "*chino/china*" as something inevitable, shrugging their shoulders resignedly. The definition of what means discrimination differs between individuals: some take "*chino/china*" as a kind of joke or as a normal part of life. Young Nikkei may even use the term or its diminutive "*chinito/chinita*" to jokingly refer to themselves or other Nikkei. Few, however, self-designate as "*chino/china*" in public like the Peruvian ex-president Alberto Fujimori during his election campaign. Other descendants consider the term to be a clear sign of inequality. Rafael Cho, a Sansei graphic designer of Japanese-Korean ancestry, criticises that calling a stranger "*chino/china*" means denying that person the right to an individual identity:

It's not that I hate the word "*chino*" because there are Japanese, Koreans who really have these resentments against Chinese [...]. Because of wars,

72   *How ethnic identities justify symbolic capital*

problems etc. But not me. That's not the point. It's the form how they say it. A friend comes, says to you: "Hey, *chinito*, how are you?" [But] once it happened to me in a pharmacy and I was waiting for my turn. And the pharmacist looks at me and says: "Hey you, *chinito*, what do you want?" Like that. You can't treat people like that. And in the end, everybody has a name, is a human being, we're all equal. But yes, it seems that people don't understand that. What can we do? I have to live with it. I get very angry, but... [laughs].

Interview partners adopted different strategies when trying to assert their Bolivianness. Ritsuko Hashimoto defends herself with her marked lowlander accent; and, according to her, the concrete benefit is that she pays less when bargaining in the market. Many Nikkei spoke about their department of origin as their preferred place to live within Bolivia. For interview partners, Bolivian identity encompassed a *cruceño* or *camba* identity, but regional identity gained importance at specific moments, especially when explaining their emotional attachment to a place that they called "home." For example, Nataly Yonamine proudly identified as "Japanese *camba*," emphasising with this emotionally connoted term her belonging to the lowlands. But, like many interview partners, she referred to herself as "*boliviana*" a few minutes later, before stating that "I don't know if I am Bolivian or Japanese."

Other Nikkei try to resist the categorisation as foreigners, explaining, for example, the history of Japanese migration to interlocutors in order to legitimise their belonging to Bolivia. Other descendants point to innovations in agriculture (see above). Others, however, relativise the importance of ethnic boundaries and identify with the middle class as another type of category encompassing both Nikkei and non-Nikkei. Only Naoji Ganaha, president of Okinawa Kenjinkai Santa Cruz, tried to redefine the whole group. After emphasising that he has served the Bolivian military, he referred to the genetic relation between Asians and American indigenous groups in an attempt to add legitimacy by this mythic-historical connection (Lesser 2008).

"*¡Chino!*" – Drawing boundaries to other East Asian descendants

"*Chino*" means Chinese – in other words, many non-Nikkei *cruceñas* and *cruceños* regard East Asian descendants as looking equally foreign. Even though they are all called "*chinos*," it does not mean the same to be identified as Chinese, Korean and Japanese descendants in Santa Cruz and Bolivia.

Around 3,000 mainland Chinese live in Santa Cruz Department and this number has been increasing in recent years, according to the Chinese consulate. At the same time, the number of Koreans and Taiwanese fell to around 250 and 50 individuals, respectively, as individual migrants estimated. The Chinese migrants are famous for owning *pollerías*, inexpensive chicken restaurants, others have opened small supermarkets, whereas several Koreans have arrived as missionaries. No official contacts are maintained between Nikkei associations and other

How ethnic identities justify symbolic capital   73

communities of East Asian origin. Exchange occurs mainly on a commercial base; they purchase vegetables, rice and other food items from each other. In Calle Antonio Vaca Diez and surroundings, several Chinese and Korean shops have opened next to Nikkei businesses. A Korean supermarket offers a large choice of vegetables, produced by Nikkei and other farmers, and has customers of different origins.

One young Nikkei remembered frowningly discussions with his teachers who called him "*chino*" despite knowing that he is of Japanese origin – he concluded that his teachers were simply ignorant. Even though non-Nikkei Bolivians may not always distinguish Japanese descendants from those of Korean and Chinese origin since they supposedly "look all the same," many Nikkei claim to have a better reputation than Chinese and Korean descendants if clearly emphasising their Japanese ancestry. Yoshiko Imai, a Japanese artist married to a non-Nikkei, alternatively presents herself as Japanese and Chinese to taxi drivers to see what will happen, experiencing friendlier reactions in the first scenario. As Ritsuko Hashimoto puts it, non-Nikkei Bolivians may confuse Japanese, Koreans and Chinese in the beginning; but in the long run, for example, in a job interview, the Nikkei clearly have an advantage because of their distinctive "Japanese values." Nisei Ryoji Nakaima relativises that only some poorer *cruceñas* and *cruceños* with a low educational level are not aware of the difference between Japanese and Chinese. "In general, the Japanese likes to work hard, and now the level of the Japanese is above average. [They] don't call you [*chino cochino*] [...]. The status of the Japanese has risen."

Many Nikkei depict Chinese and Koreans migrants as smart and skillful at making money, but also as shrewd, ruthless and egoistic businesspersons (Takenaka 1999: 115f.). Furthermore, they consider them to be dishonest and greedy troublemakers involved in dubious activities, implicitly or explicitly contrasting them to the supposedly morally superior Nikkei. They refer to media reports about some Chinese falsifying visas, engaging in human trafficking and running unhygienic restaurants, or they mention news about Koreans escaping with the money of rotating credit associations, murdering fellow migrants and mistreating domestic employees. Chinese products, in general, are ubiquitous in Bolivia, but they are usually equated with low quality. Though China is investing in Bolivia's infrastructure, Bolivians have many times been unsatisfied with the result. Projects are not always well done, following contracts full of inconsistent clauses, and they are realised by Chinese workers. This has resulted in several conflicts with locals (Correo del Sur 2016; Los Tiempos 2016; Montero 2018; Página Siete 2016). Nevertheless, when cases of morally questionable behaviour occurred among Nikkei, they did not challenge their symbolic capital.

Many Nikkei may be reluctant to interact with other East Asian descendants because they perceive that the latter enjoy less symbolic capital (Tsuda 1999: 215ff.). Another reason may be the increasing ethnic competition since the Koreans and Chinese migrants are becoming more and more successful in their economic activities. Mirroring the Nikkei's attempts for differentiation, Wimmer (2013: 121) observes that established migrants are many times hostile to newcomers.

74 *How ethnic identities justify symbolic capital*

Historically, Japan has considered itself superior to the "inferior Asia" and the cruelties the Japanese army committed in the Second World War against Taiwanese, Chinese and Korean civilians are not forgotten. This might have a repercussion in Latin America: an elderly Taiwanese living in Santa Cruz remembered being treated as inferior by the Japanese in the Second World War. Rafael Cho, of Korean-Japanese origin, has witnessed tensions between Korean and Japanese descendants in Santa Cruz that he traces back to these historical events.

As a further justification for the ethnic boundary, many Nikkei say that Korean and Chinese migrants see Bolivia and other Latin American countries as a natural stopover on their way to the U.S. or Canada, "their golden dream" in the words of Nisei travel agency owner Daiki Kaneshiro. According to him, the Chinese and Koreans have not developed the same emotional attachment to Bolivia as the Nikkei have; therefore, they cannot claim the same legitimacy. Daiki says that when their business fails, they simply migrate to Asunción, Buenos Aires, São Paulo or North America. He holds that the Nikkei are different since they arrived penniless and voluntarily chose Bolivia in search of a better life – their suffering and their contributions to the economy and society make them Bolivian. Following the same line of reasoning, Sociedad Japonesa de La Paz' (2012: 42) anniversary book emphasises how Japanese migrants donated food and goods of daily use to Bolivian soldiers during the Chaco War; and Furuki (2013: 55) mentions Sociedad Japonesa's participation in Bolivia's 100th anniversary on 6 August 1925. Agronomist Norio Miyaguni comments:

> This is JICA's philosophy, also of the Japanese government. In Japanese, this is called *ijūsha teichaku* or staying there, living there, dying there. Not like the Chinese, Koreans, business, they earn money and *pang*, they go to the United States. It means developing yourself there, contributing there, having children there. Therefore, the Bolivians respect us because we have not just come to sell chicken, earn money and *pang*, go away […], but we contribute to the country's well-being.

However, the reality is more complex than presented in retrospect. Rafael Cho recalls laughingly that his family originally wanted to apply for Brazil, but took the wrong queue. Also, Hiraoka (1980: 70f.) observes that Bolivia was generally not their destination of choice – some did not even know where the country was located. Many pre-war migrants planned to stay only temporarily, hoping to return to Japan or to re-migrate to North America, and many post-war Nikkei have not stayed where they were supposed to remain for the rest of their lives.

But things are changing slowly. Bolivian small-scale traders' business with China has been growing, leading to increased interest in Chinese classes (Stefanoni 2010: 126ff.); and especially the symbolic capital of Korea seems to be on the rise. The country is investing in roads and bridges through its official development agency KOICA, but is regarded as a more trustworthy partner than the Chinese. Korean pop culture has been gaining popularity all over the world (Kim 2013) and also among the Bolivian youth. Pirated Korean soap operas and

How ethnic identities justify symbolic capital   75

music can be easily found on DVD in Bolivian markets, and they are also popular among Nikkei. In La Paz, a Korean language school has opened to respond to this interest (Ramírez 2013). It remains an open question which implications such developments will have and how the Nikkei's boundary-making strategies will change with regard to other East Asian descendants.

"They are a very different culture from the *cruceño* culture" – Discourses on "integration"

Although the Nikkei do have frequent contact with non-Nikkei *cruceñas* and *cruceños*, I sometimes came across the statement that the Nikkei were "not really integrated" into *cruceño* society. Nevertheless, nobody offered a clear definition of "integration," for example, if it meant a specific degree of cultural similarity or the willingness to interact with non-Nikkei. Moreover, not everybody agreed if the Nikkei could be regarded as "integrated" or not.

While it is common for Nikkei to be categorised as foreigners or as "*chinos*," another question is whether non-Nikkei *cruceñas* and *cruceños* are willing to interact with them: admiring a descendant may not mean making friends with him or her. At least, this is the hypothesis of social scientist Fernando Prado.

> The *cruceño* is talkative, informal, likes parties, is irresponsible, has much energy and just does things. And if it goes wrong, then it went wrong, what can you do […]. He doesn't do any study if it's possible or not, he just does it. He loves spending money, he loves showing what he has; so all these characteristics are not like in Japanese culture. The Japanese culture is sober […], they use few words. When they say something, it's like that […]. So the Japanese said: "My God, you really can't work with these *cruceños*, they are so informal and lazy." And the *cruceños*: "These Japanese are strange, they don't talk. You don't know what they think."

Fernando notes that Japanese descendants are not as accepted as other immigrants were. Arguing that it is maybe too early for conclusions since the history of Japanese migration is comparatively short, he is sure that they were simply too different to be readily accepted: "There is a cultural difference that didn't exist with the Arabs. Because the Arabs, although they came here speaking Arab, they rapidly learned Spanish. They were the same in character, in culture […]. A very extroverted culture."

In other words, interview partners frequently explained interaction patterns with cultural factors. Nevertheless, the situation is more complex: especially the *colonias'* organisation prevented intensive contact with non-Nikkei in the first years. Post-war Issei arriving as adults did not frequent Bolivian schools or universities; instead, they worked on their own land and were able to recreate a community with distinct social norms.

But no matter if *cruceñas* and *cruceños* have been open to any newcomer in former times, Nisei Takatoshi Morishima from La Paz doubts that they continue

76 *How ethnic identities justify symbolic capital*

to do so. He has observed the emergence of *paceño* groups in Santa Cruz who feel rejected by locals. Similarly, Nisei Hiroshi Shindo, who has recently moved back to Santa Cruz from Japan, thinks that the "typically" easy-going attitude might be a thing of the past. His neighbours complained about his children making noise, something he had never experienced in Japan. Furthermore, the urban space becomes increasingly anonymous: neighbours born and raised in the city tend not to have much contact with each other. Whereas the lower classes once observed the higher classes' festivities from the side, the increasing privatisation of urban space impedes interaction between different strata – be it at school, in the neighbourhood, during leisure time activities or at work (Schoop 2008; Waldmann 2008: 202ff.).

Nevertheless, almost all descendants argued that a possible lack of interaction with non-Nikkei was a consequence of the Nikkei's attitude. Also, Takatoshi shook his head when talking about the Nikkei-run bar in Santa Cruz, regarding its existence as proof for the descendants' unwillingness to interact with other parts of society. Similarly, Nisei translator Kaede Itokazu is convinced that the Nikkei are not discriminated against but that their arrogance prevents them from entering in contact with others.

> They are so proud; they think that they are above everything. But it's so small, the Japanese society. If Bolivia is this [shows her little finger], then the Japanese society is that [points to the nail], and we have the nose so high.

According to her, the Nikkei should be more grateful since locals once received the Japanese with open arms. However, gratefulness is expected first of all of guests and foreigners, not of those who can claim their "natural belonging" to a place. To mention but two examples, this attitude is reflected in the countless statements during association anniversaries; and in ceremonies involving flag rising, the Bolivian flag always goes up first.

Without negating the importance of ethnic boundaries, other Nikkei put forward that Japanese descendants do interact with non-Nikkei much more than in former times, especially in the city. Whereas no Japanese neighbourhood exists, those Nikkei born and raised in Bolivia automatically create networks with non-Nikkei at kindergarten, school, university and work. As a result, social scientist Mai Amuro, despite being critical towards the Nikkei community, diagnoses that much has changed since the Issei's arrival.

> Until about 10 years ago, [they] were a society very much looking at itself, having high demands at itself [...], maintaining the conditions, the values, the principles and the practices, a bit like commemorating Japanese society in Japan, [...] much discipline and little motivation to open itself [...]. [But] this new generation [...] also does things without the backing of the Japanese community [...]. They have been to Japan [...], they know Japanese culture well. But at the same time, they have this confidence and therefore, they interact a little more.

How ethnic identities justify symbolic capital 77

Personal networks across ethnic boundaries may also have a practical function: they become a crucial resource for survival (Schubert 2017: 112ff.). In a country like Bolivia marked by a weak public welfare system, life is characterised by permanent insecurity and unpredictability, creating significant stress for the inhabitants. By way of illustration, organisational failure of public and private institutions results in a deficient public health system and troublesome *trámites* taking an unforeseeable amount of time. Apart from relying on privatised services, Nikkei and non-Nikkei alike seek alternative strategies, like using informal networks and trying to personalise relations with those in strategic positions. Tsuyoshi Kato, lecturer at one of the city's most important universities, resumes: "Friendship is more in the foreground than competence [...]. So it's good to be everybody's friend [...]. It's better to have a friend at the bank than the bank as a friend."

However, ethnic boundaries become mixed with class identifications once again. One elderly descendant, for example, complained extensively that non-Nikkei artisans were sly and sluggish; furthermore, they would work one day in order to get too drunk to appear the following day – the best Bolivian artisans were abroad, she concluded, while I never heard a bad word from her about her non-Nikkei son-in-law, a doctor. Like her, the Nikkei make friends among the non-Nikkei middle class while trying to create a contrast to the lower classes. Rather than to their non-Nikkei friends of similar social background, the Nikkei point to the lower classes' seeming disorderliness when characterising non-Nikkei as dangerous, disorganised, dirty, poor, selfish and giving birth to too many children. Also, Mai Amuro observes a strong sense of superiority especially among the Issei towards their non-Nikkei employees and co-workers: "They think they are better, only because of money or because of the power of their organisations!" All these derogative stereotypes are also regularly used to denote Indian-ness – see Nishida (2009) and Tsuda (1999) for very similar identification patterns among Nikkei in Brazil.

However, the social environment of Colonia Okinawa and San Juan differs substantially from the urban area, and descendants in the city consider Nikkei in the countryside to be "less integrated" into Bolivian society. The Nikkei constitute the *colonias'* most powerful group; most non-Nikkei are considerably poorer. In other words, it is a hierarchic relationship. Consequently, a Nisei in Colonia Okinawa who had grown up in the city says that one could not trust non-Nikkei in the *colonia*, who would always steal or ask for money, while non-Nikkei in the city were different. This relationship pattern is also reflected in Tadao Hikawa's statement. The young Sansei from San Juan acknowledges the social hierarchy when laconically stating that Nikkei have few non-Nikkei friends in the *colonia*, since "most people who live here are employees of Japanese descendants, so, you know, the boss and the employee don't get along with each other." Suzuki (2010: 73, 155) describes how Nikkei in Colonia Okinawa perceived their non-Nikkei workers as dependent, childlike, culturally distant and even as a potentially dangerous mass. Nevertheless, descendants may also feel responsible for their workers, for instance, paying for their medical treatment.

78 *How ethnic identities justify symbolic capital*

The Nikkei's identification with the *cruceño* elites or the so-called "traditional families" is complex as well. The elites encompass several families of Spanish, Lebanese, German, Belgian and Croatian descent but none with a Japanese surname (Prado 2007: 172ff.). Their way of living, shown every day on the "Sociales" party pictures in El Deber and other newspapers, is aspired by many *cruceñas* and *cruceños* who wish to possess the same consumer goods (Waldmann 2008: 218ff.). Nikkei hardly ever appear on the "Sociales" pages. As one Nikkei remarked, it is almost impossible to enter such influential and affluent circles. Descendants shook their heads in disbelief when mentioning that a non-Nikkei investor is able to construct a private bridge over the Piraí River to his enormous gated community. Consequently, Nikkei interview partners complained to Suzuki (2010: 80) that these circles were not only greedy and selfish but also racist towards Japanese descendants and cruel towards their employees. They thereby associated themselves with a social stratum they depicted for once as innocent and good-natured.

At the same time, the narrative of the poor migrants who have achieved economic wealth by their own efforts fits the regional elites' neoliberal ideas. To my own surprise, I was invited to a study circle of some Comité Cívico Pro Santa Cruz members to present my research. After the presentation, they unanimously praised the Nikkei's commitment to hard work that made them succeed, considering them a kind of "honorary *cambas*" despite being "different" – probably because the Nikkei have not tried to undermine the elites' power. They thereby implicitly and explicitly contrasted them to "those *collas*" or even "those Indians" as a racialised threat who supposedly only rely on the generosity of the state. Although I did mention the financial and material assistance from the Japanese government, the round failed to take note of it.

At the same time, it may not have any negative consequences for Nikkei if they are not "integrated." Urioste (2012: 450) concludes that a group does not encounter hostilities as long as it does not oppose the hegemonic ideas on regional *cruceño* identity. As a result, many Nikkei in Santa Cruz do not only explicitly identify as *cruceñas* and *cruceños* and/or *cambas* because they feel an affinity to Santa Cruz, but probably also to protect themselves. *Collas* are recognised to be hard-working and thrifty as well, but most Nikkei do not associate with the unpopular highlanders, declaring that they are smart but untrustworthy (Stearman 1985: 208; Suzuki 2010: 41f.). Similar to many other inhabitants of Santa Cruz, some Nikkei even make derogatory remarks about *collas*.

The national immigration law (Gaceta Oficial de Bolivia 1976) wants foreigners to "integrate," requiring them to learn the official language and to acquire knowledge of the country, with expulsion as the ultimate sanction in case of noncompliance. To my knowledge, this law was never enforced. Even the Mennonites rarely encounter hostilities, although the majority population does not consider them to be integrated at all. I never heard anybody criticising that the strictly endogamous Mennonites are exempt from attending Bolivian schools and performing military service. In other words, such a perceived ethnic closure is seldom considered a major problem by any side. Even though non-Nikkei appreciate when the Nikkei interact with the majority society, they do not formulate this

How ethnic identities justify symbolic capital   79

wish as an obligation. While the Nikkei did not need to adapt to *cruceño* society for upward mobility, many presented frequent interaction with non-Nikkei as desirable as well. When they emphasise that they "have integrated," mainly in comparison to the Mennonites, this is not the outcome of a detailed analysis. Instead, it means that they select a specific way to present themselves, knowing that non-Nikkei will be delighted. And if *cruceñas* and *cruceños* are able to "integrate" even the "closed Japanese," they see their self-identification as open and hospitable *cambas* confirmed.

Toyota trucks, anime and kimono – Macro-level influences on Nikkei identities in Bolivia

So far, I have predominantly discussed the micro-level. In addition, factors on the macro-level have significantly contributed to the Nikkei's symbolic capital in Bolivia: Japan's rise as an economic power with its globally available products has had a huge impact on the Nikkei.

With obvious parallels to Bourdieu's symbolic capital, political scientist Joseph Nye developed the concept of soft power, defining it as a power arising from "intangible, immaterial resources such as the country's culture, political ideas and ideologies" (Nye 2011: 31). Soft power is based on general perceptions of benignity, beauty, competence and credibility and can be used for persuasion. Fashion, food and other cultural practices may nevertheless be understood in a different way than in the country of origin (Nye 2011: 92ff.).

Although the Nikkei have not contributed much to Japan's popularity, they enjoy its benefits. Japan may not be the non-Nikkei's principal place of longing but nevertheless counts as attractive at a time when the world becomes less centred on the "West" and focuses increasingly on Asia. It is en vogue to learn about Japanese culture and to consume sushi. Technical items bearing the label "Made in Japan" such as televisions, cars, robots and the Shinkansen high-speed train promise high quality and reliability. Brands like Casio, Sony, Toyota, Panasonic and Nintendo are globally omnipresent. Other examples include karaoke, Sudoku games, the Kumon teaching method or martial arts like judo, karate and aikido (Frühstück and Manzenreiter 2002). Some young people in Santa Cruz and La Paz dress up as anime characters, watch Naruto and Sailor Moon. Pokémon and Hello Kitty products are sold at Bolivian street stalls. In order to actively support these trends, Japan's government has implemented the "Cool Japan" initiative to promote positive imaginaries at home and abroad (Daliot-Bul 2009; Naikaku-fu 2016; Valaskivi 2013). This also means a conscious or unconscious selection: *udon* and *soba* noodles are not as popular abroad as *ramen*, nor are controversial goods such as violent manga or whale meat. Few non-Japanese love *pachinko* [pinball] parlours, sumo wrestling or *nattō* [fermented sticky soy beans] (Sugimoto 2009: 14f.) (Figure 3.4).

In Bolivia, these imaginaries also stand for modernity. It is beyond the scope of this book to discuss the multiple meanings of modernity and its relation to tradition, but essential for my argument is that it is associated, among others,

80 *How ethnic identities justify symbolic capital*

Figure 3.4 Automobile advertisement in the streets of Santa Cruz: "Crown: The Japanese technology you know."

with positive imaginaries of urbanisation, consumerism, industrial production, technology and material comfort (Taylor 2002). With its ingenious products, high standard of living, good governance practices, political stability and a well-functioning social security system, Japan is regarded as a model. In the present case, it means that many Bolivians long to be part of this modernity they locate abroad, often uncritically considering foreign practices and goods to be superior to Bolivian ones. Thus, Japan's sharp rise from a war-torn country to a leading technology hub has increased its attractiveness. Being identified as Japanese descendants may mean being excluded as foreigners, but it can also stand for their association with modernity.

Therefore, in advertisements in the local newspaper El Deber, some Nikkei doctors emphasise that they have studied in Japan, aiming at additional credibility: attending university in a place of modern knowledge with high-quality equipment enabled them to become experts in Bolivia. This may be one reason that according to Centro Social's secretary, about 90% of the Policonsultorio Nikkei's patients are non-Nikkei.

While in post-Second World War Japan, technology export has contributed to national pride (Comaroff and Comaroff 2009; Iwabuchi 2002), many Nikkei and non-Nikkei forget that Japanese products were not always held in high esteem. Manufactured goods had been sold abroad since the late Meiji period, but they were usually of poor quality. Since they were much less expensive than other foreign goods, the poorer strata preferred Japanese textiles, toys, combs and buttons

How ethnic identities justify symbolic capital   81

(Mitre 2006: 67f.). Eduardo Visentin, a non-Nikkei married to an Okinawan descendant and around 50 years old, sees a straight connection between Japan's technology and its soft power. He dates back the change to the 1980s.

> When I was a child [...], all televisions were RCA, not Sony, and the fridges were Frigidaire, the toothpaste was Kolynos [...]. And I remember when the first Toyota trucks appeared. It was like: "Oh, who will buy that?" But little by little, Japan asserted itself through quality and technology and first of all through price. That means, an American truck cost 100, a Japanese one cost 50. And furthermore, they were good products.

Most Bolivians would not question the quality of a Japanese product, and the now high price of Japanese commodities make them even more desirable. Mai Amuro speaks of subconscious neuro-linguistic programming: "They told you that 'all Japanese products have a seal and a quality standard, they are durable and reliable' [...]. They always told me that I should look for a Japanese product, if possible." The role Japanese products played in the 1930s for the less affluent strata is now taken over by inexpensive Chinese goods. Consequently, the middle class generally relates these goods to poor taste (Tassi et al. 2013: 200f.), while Korean cars and other commodities have become acceptable. Eduardo Visentin estimates that the same will happen when Chinese high-quality goods reach Bolivia, if their country of origin will then be relevant for customers at all.

In sum, global influences have been important for Nikkei on the micro-level, although ethnic identity has usually been analysed in an exclusively local context. Tsuda (2007: 233), one of the few to recognise these influences on ethnic identity, also indicates that non-Nikkei Latin Americans may automatically apply positive imaginaries to Japan: "In fact, when specific knowledge about Japan is lacking, generalised and rather idealistic imaginaries about the First World are quickly substituted as if they were synonymous with Japan." But, also, most Nikkei seem to admire Japan because of its technological and economic development and the opportunities it offers them. Hence, their identification as Japanese descendants is strongly related to Japan's economic boom. The rapid spread of technical products enhances also the popularity of Japanese cultural practices (Sugimoto 2009: 14). Similarly, Takenaka (2009b: 1338) notes that the pride in "Japanese values" emerged only after Japan and the Nikkei all over the Americas had achieved economic stability.

Sugimoto (ibid.) divides the Japanese cultural elements consumed abroad into three layers: apart from the technological goods as described above, he identifies a pre-modern layer and the newest layer, Japanese pop culture. To start with the latter, some young non-Nikkei regularly organise anime festivals in La Paz and Santa Cruz. They download anime from the internet and translate it into Spanish. In La Paz, one may see groups of adolescents dancing to Japanese – and Korean – pop songs in public parks. One reason for this popularity may be that anime, manga, cosplay[12] and J-Pop lack clearly identifiable Japanese national and ethnic markers and are easily adaptable to other cultural contexts, Mouer and Norris (2009: 361f.) argue while referring to Koichi Iwabuchi's studies.

82　*How ethnic identities justify symbolic capital*

Japanese pop culture leads some non-Nikkei Bolivians, mostly young adults, to learn Japanese – even though the language is not of immediate use in Bolivia and has the reputation of being extremely difficult. Classes are much less expensive than French or German classes in the respective cultural institutions. During my fieldwork, approximately 30 students learned Japanese in Centro Social, plus some at a private language centre. The interest is much higher in La Paz where around 180 students study the language at Sociedad Japonesa – a high number association members are proud of, without being able to explain it. While events in Centro Social are mostly carried out by the Nikkei themselves and presented to a Nikkei audience, Sociedad Japonesa de La Paz is able to host cultural events such as presentations by a Japanese puppet theatre group touring through South America. These events, generally supported by the embassy or JICA, attract mostly non-Nikkei. While enrolment has decreased in recent years, long-time Japanese teacher Ruy Villanueva remembers that during the heydays of the anime boom, the first student arrived at 4 a.m. at Sociedad Japonesa de La Paz to sign up in the afternoon. According to Ruy, however, many students do not finish the course since they start out of a superficial curiosity and lack authentic interest. I experienced during my time as a Japanese student in Centro Social that few of my classmates entered in contact with Nikkei beyond their language classes. Therefore, I doubt that this fascination for Japanese pop culture necessarily increases interest in other elements of Japanese culture.

As the puppet theater presentation shows, Sugimoto's "traditional layer" is present in Bolivia as well. While non-Nikkei generally do not adopt these practices, "modern" technical appliances have contributed to make them popular. Apart from events featuring dances, songs and garments regarded as traditional, one finds homogenising, romanticised and ahistoric imaginaries that convey a sense of nostalgia for an idealised homeland. Japanese characters, temples, paper lanterns, cherry blossoms, autumn leaves, bamboo, Mt. Fuji and paper cranes are abundant on festival advertisements, on calendars and as decoration for community celebrations. Many Issei have large cupboards full of multi-part origami figures as a standard present for *keirōkai* [Respect for the Aged Festival] (Figure 3.5).

The traditional layer is also promoted at festivals where non-Nikkei are officially invited. Many of them appreciate that "those Japanese" appear to have a fascinating yet exotic and incomprehensible culture. I observed this attractiveness at the Kimono Fashion Show in July 2013, organised by the Japanese consulate in Santa Cruz and supported by Centro Social Japonés. It attracted about 300 visibly impressed spectators, overwhelmingly non-Nikkei. After presenting a film on robots, J-Pop, Japanese food and a ceramics factory, some descendants showed and explained different kinds of kimono. With laughter and applause from the audience, the president of Centro Social concluded: "As a good Japanese *camba*, I can tell you that sushi and manioc are a good match!" Similarly successful was Feria de Comunidades Extranjeras [Festival of foreign communities], organised some months later by the municipal government of Santa Cruz behind the central plaza. The invited Peruvian and Paraguayan groups became almost invisible whereas crowds of non-Nikkei Bolivians clustered around a Nikkei volunteer

How ethnic identities justify symbolic capital 83

Figure 3.5 Kimono Fashion Show.

teaching them how to fold an origami crane. Others took part in *soranbushi* dance under the guidance of San Juan's *seinenkai* [youth group]. Three elderly Nikkei women were busy writing the visitors' names in calligraphy. Wearing kimono, the women became even more exotic, but their garment also demonstrated their belonging to Japan and their authority to teach Japanese culture. For visitors, this staging expressed the "typically Japanese" delicacy, beauty, gracefulness and attentiveness to details. Food is always part of such festivals – Japanese cuisine is probably the most popular cultural element, as I will describe in Chapter 8. Nevertheless, it is questionable that all descendants, especially the younger ones, are in fact experts in these "typically Japanese customs."

Rocha (1999) states that for non-Nikkei Brazilians, practising tea ceremony means participating in an exotic and trendy culture that is nevertheless different from already known "Western" models. In a consumption society continuously searching for difference, non-Nikkei can find new stimuli when attending Japanese-style festivals and activities. The Nikkei themselves can promote otherness while at the same time reanimating collective self-awareness. However, this occurs on a small scale and without financial gains since admission fees, if any, only cover expenditures.

Apart from Sugimoto's three layers focused on material goods, one could also have a look at the power of media images. As an example, TV transmissions showed the entire world that after the 2011 tsunami, disaster victims waited

84 *How ethnic identities justify symbolic capital*

patiently for their food ration instead of looting supermarkets, whereas some citizens even volunteered in the destroyed nuclear power plant, putting their life at risk for the benefit of the whole society. Some interview partners stated that this demonstration of "Japanese values" would leave a deep impression. Although media images may lead to misconceptions – for example, that all Japanese women wear kimono in daily life, that the Japanese always have a camera at hand or that present-day Japan is full of samurai and ninja – they generally support Japan's good reputation in Bolivia.

Nevertheless, it is questionable if all these consumption practices mean that the described "traditional" cultural practices or media images have any measurable effect on recipients. Still, for Mai Amuro, Japan's popularity means that as a Nikkei, "You have an advantage and you can use it positively [...]. One feels comfortable everywhere now, at least me. Before, it was not that much but now that everybody discovers [Japanese culture]. I have an advantage because it's part of my identity."

Conclusion

While post-war Nikkei have become part of Santa Cruz' middle class, they skilfully apply specific narratives to justify this situation according to present needs. The dominant narrative on unique "Japanese values," found in daily conversations as well as in anniversary books and museums, foregrounds specific values and a particular interpretation of the past. Accordingly, punctuality, honesty, discipline and hard work invariably lead to socioeconomic success. Ethnic stereotypes explain cultural differences and justify hierarchies, presenting the Nikkei and Japan as prosperous, modern and morally superior. Interestingly, this narrative is widespread not only among descendants, but also among non-Nikkei who frequently present their country as a banana republic inhabited by an uncivilised people.

At second glance, the picture becomes more ambivalent. The Nikkei's current prosperity would not have been possible without Japanese assistance via JICA and the possibility to work in Japan as *dekasegi* migrants. Setbacks and the emigration of many settlers to neighbouring countries or Japan are seldom mentioned in historic retrospection. Moreover, similar "from rags to riches" narratives are widespread not only among migrants anywhere, but also among the middle class in general who need to explain social upward mobility.

Moreover, being regarded as foreigners or *"chinos"* means that their physiognomy seems incompatible with a Bolivian identity. In the country's national imaginary, its inhabitants are descendants of indigenous people and whites. Therefore, the Nikkei use several strategies to assert themselves, such as insisting on their blameless behaviour and their being different from other, less well-reputed Asian migrants. Although only partly based on historical facts, the narrative on their being agricultural pioneers is nevertheless persuasive. Nevertheless, ethnic boundaries do not mean impermeability, but contact between different groups even justifies their permanent recreation.

How ethnic identities justify symbolic capital 85

However, when non-Nikkei place Japanese descendants into the "foreigner" category, it means that on a macro-level, the latter can claim links to an industrialised country that are greatly appreciated in Bolivia. Following Japan's rise to an international power, not only its technology but also its culture have become popular among non-Nikkei. Hence, belonging to an ethnic minority means symbolic capital rather than stigma – Japanese descendants are presented and present themselves as model immigrants. Thereby, the Nikkei in Bolivia have rather taken advantage of already existing discourses than imposing their own moral standards.

Notes

1 She is alluding to the Brazilian expression "*japonês garantido*", referring to Japanese traders' trustworthiness.
2 "A tramite is translatable into English as a bureaucratic procedure or business transaction, but such a simple rendering omits the arduousness of the experience, the sense of an ordeal undertaken at great personal cost. [It is] a necessary, unavoidable bureaucratic hassle that you have to face if you want to function as a legal and legitimate member of society, but nonetheless an enormous drain on your time, energy, and resources" (Goldstein 2004: 90). Nevertheless, one should not forget that social and economic capital helps to solve the problem, e.g., by bribing, hiring somebody with experience in *trámites* or by accelerating the process via one's kin and acquaintances in important positions.
3 This is not without irony, because many Nikkei employ non-Nikkei Bolivian domestic workers to clean their homes.
4 This is illustrated by the fact that many non-Nikkei *cruceños* to whom I spoke about my research were not aware that a considerable number of descendants live nowadays in the city – and that even in the *colonias*, non-Nikkei outnumber descendants.
5 Interestingly, meat already served as a social and ethnic marker in Japan before the Meiji era: the *burakumin*, a discriminated social minority, were characterised as carnivorous (Lie 2001: 79). In the Meiji era, from a Japanese perspective, the difference between European and Japanese cuisine was made equivalent to meat versus rice, fish and vegetables (Ohnuki-Tierney 1993: 106).
6 Little rolls made of manioc flour and cheese considered a speciality of the lowlands.
7 A palm tree typical to the Bolivian lowlands (*Attalea princeps*).
8 Suzuki (2010: 207) writes that experienced farmers could obtain loans of USD 80,000, beginners up to 50,000.
9 In remote areas, for example in Brazil, many children were not registered as Japanese nationals since this was possible only until 14 days after birth. The period was lengthened to three months in 1985 (Yamanaka) 2000:132, 148).
10 It is part of Rómulo Gómez Vaca's ([1928]) poem "Desde mi umbral".
11 When I discussed this with social scientist Fernando Prado, he noted an interesting detail: in a city like Santa Cruz, famous for its countless beauty contests, models are mostly white. No beauty queens of Asian origin have won such a contest in Santa Cruz except for one of partly Chinese descent. In Brazil, Nikkei are not depicted as physically attractive, either: Nishida (2009: 435) notes that Nikkei are regarded as "ugly" but acceptable marriage partners, see also Ischida (2010: 110ff.). In this respect, it is interesting that they are generally also absent in *cruceño* carnival, another major social event in the city.
12 A performative practice where participants dress up as a specific anime or video game characters.

4 The daily creation of ethnic boundaries

One day in February 2014 after a visit to the Okinawa Kenjinkai office, I met travel agency owner Daiki Kaneshiro on the stairway. After exchanging courtesies, he called me back, asking if I would like to participate in the next *tanomoshi* [rotating credit association] meeting. "So that you can see how this is like," he added. The next Wednesday at dawn, he waits with some friends at Multimercado Okinawa to guide me to the next street. In the middle of the busy market atmosphere, they stop at an inconspicuous wooden door that only mentions the name of the bar. Although I have heard about this place before, I have passed several times without noticing it. After a long corridor, we arrive in a room with a spacious bar, several black leather sofas and a small scene with a microphone. Everything looks elegant and clean – and somehow Japanese, even though I could not say why. Two brothers in their thirties run the bar as their hobby, employing several Nikkei students as bartenders. It opens on Thursdays, Fridays and Saturdays and on demand. Since it is Wednesday, we are the only guests.

Today, the group consists of twelve men, all around 50 years old. All but Ramón Borja are of Okinawan origin. Some of these long-time friends are Nisei farmers from Colonia Okinawa, whereas others like Daiki and entrepreneur Taku Shimoji own a business in the city. All of them, except for Ramón, are members of Okinawa Kenjinkai and some are even association board members. While we are talking, mostly in Spanish, delicacies like pork with star anise are served on small dishes – "please serve yourself, you're invited!" As the cook Shota Murakami would tell me some days later, this food combines Japanese, Chinese and Bolivian cuisine. To those who do not know me, Daiki presents me as an anthropologist writing specifically about Okinawan immigration, until I correct him.

As Daiki explains, each participant will talk about something he thinks is interesting, important, pleasant or preoccupying. The topics are manifold but, in most cases, related to the Nikkei's future in Santa Cruz and Bolivia. I choose to speak about my impressions of Confra, as some of them have been on the organising committee. They do not comment much on it, but they seem pleased. Ramón speaks about the Japanese 5S[1] management philosophy, recently introduced in his company. Apparently, this process has encountered several cultural barriers. "But better now than never"; the others nod their head in approval. Farmer Koki Takamine thinks aloud about the pros and cons of genetically modified

DOI: 10.4324/9781003228295-4

The daily creation of ethnic boundaries   87

corn, whereas Daiki is preoccupied with the political situation in Venezuela with increasing repression, bloody protests and a middle class that is losing everything. The round becomes quiet when being reminded of the possibility that something similar might also occur in Bolivia. Only entrepreneur Taku Shimoji says aloud that he invests in foreign countries since, in Bolivia, one never knows. The round becomes more animated when Taku's brother Kenta speaks about the recent inundations in Beni. Everybody is excited when he proposes to send relief goods via the Japanese association of Riberalta. As Kenta explains, "we must be grateful" to the descendants of these first immigrants, some of which have lost their belongings in the floods.

The discussion becomes even more lively when Tatsuo Shiroma, a farmer from Colonia Okinawa who has remained quiet until then, expresses his preoccupation with education in Colonia Okinawa and the lack of employment. As a result, he fears the disintegration of the *colonia* and the loss of values. Suddenly, they all start talking and proposing ideas. Cattle breeder Ryoji Nakaima suggests developing Cetabol[2] station into a kind of technical university. Others mention Liceo Mexicano Japonés in the Mexican capital as a model for the promotion of "Japanese values." The consensus is that values like cleanliness are normal for Japanese descendants, but not for non-Nikkei Bolivians. Tatsuo has observed differences between the Japanese school and the other schools in Colonia Okinawa, stating that children from the Japanese school help more at home and hold their classrooms cleaner, even compared to Nikkei children from the city. Implicitly, Tatsuo warns of "corrupting Bolivian habits." The idea comes up to send a local TV channel to Colonia Okinawa to film *undōkai* and the habits of cleanliness to promote these behaviours. Moreover, the circle is also convinced that sport is a helpful means to ensure discipline among the younger generation. Koki urges everyone to start preparing for the 2016 Confra in Mexico.

After the round has finished and after some more drinks, they start talking about a lawsuit between two Nikkei and complain about the representative of a Japanese state entity who has disparaged Bolivia. Although this is not new to me, I am surprised since I am an outsider and interview partners seldom comment on such sensitive issues. Ryoji says, almost as if he wanted to excuse himself, that "in the end, we're also Bolivians," and proposes jokingly to send the representative back to Japan. Shortly before leaving around midnight, they come to the financial part of the *tanomoshi* meeting. Every participant hands in USD 200. Since nobody says anything, Daiki and Koki open a notebook to see whose turn it is. Winning a round of *jankenpon* [rock, paper, scissors] against Tatsuo, Koki leaves with USD 2,400.

Some days later, I interview Shota Murakami who cooked for the *tanomoshi* meeting. Shota is from San Juan, in his early thirties and has studied with the Japanese embassy's chef in Brazil. He explains to me that the previously mentioned bar is necessary for the Nikkei. In the *colonia*, one can still spontaneously meet at each other's house, but not in an urban environment where descendants do not live close to each other. Bars run by non-Nikkei are not suitable as a meeting point due to cultural differences, he says, and all other formerly existing Nikkei

88 *The daily creation of ethnic boundaries*

bars have closed. Because of such cultural differences, it seems logical to restrict entry. No advertisement is made except for a Facebook group; access is only granted to Nikkei and a few non-Nikkei friends, Shota explains.

> We as Japanese maybe don't like so much to dance and the custom here – in a bar, they dance a lot. So my cousin, when he thought about this, he founded the Japanese karaoke where the Nikkei can meet. And it's going well because all the Japanese come to meet there. They like to sing. There is the moment when the Japanese start dancing, but that's a different moment because it's after they started drinking [...]. So I don't know if it's a custom, but maybe the Japanese are a little shy in this respect.

The anecdote shows very ambivalent identifications: while all but Ramón were Nikkei of Okinawan origin, they identified with both Japan and Bolivia, depending on the context, and sometimes also with Okinawa. "We" and "them" were always defined differently depending on the context. The anecdote also demonstrates that boundaries are not impermeable: access may be allowed to selected non-Nikkei friends like Ramón, without questioning their status as non-Nikkei.

Therefore, the existence of such a community seems natural at first glance, but it is an outcome of specific more or less conscious boundary-making practices, and these practices receive specific meaning in daily life (Cohen 1992). Also, Roos und Lombard (2003) underline that it is essential for a community to have a narrative to create a collective character and a sense of belonging, although individual versions of this narrative may differ. This narrative marks the boundary between those who are part of the community and those who are not. It is important to note that contacts which are more or less voluntarily chosen, such as friendships and love relations, also serve to recreate and define the group.

A large family – Where the *comunidad japonesa* is created

In the city, most Nikkei have non-Nikkei friends; but while they become culturally similar to non-Nikkei Bolivians, they often point to specific differences as a reason for creating networks among co-ethnics. For many descendants, Nikkei are their primary group of reference. Practically all interviewees identified the existence of a *comunidad japonesa* [Japanese community] or *sociedad japonesa* [Japanese society] in Santa Cruz. This community also includes institutions and networks like the associations described in Chapter 6. Nikkei and non-Nikkei often regard the supposed closeness of the community, attributed to a shared set of norms and values, as typically Japanese. The mere existence of the once isolated Japanese *colonias* has certainly fostered these perceptions. The *comunidad* is sometimes described as if it was clearly definable and socioeconomically homogeneous, united by a common origin, universally shared values and Japanese language. However, I claim that such a community is not only heterogeneous but also consciously and unconsciously created (Cohen 1992).

The daily creation of ethnic boundaries   89

Interview partners frequently compare the *comunidad* to a quasi-biological large family. They are generally able to identify another Nikkei as a close friend of X or as a relative of Y. Several Nikkei also expressed to "feel at home" in this *comunidad*. Indeed, most descendants share similar living conditions, apart from their ethnic background, leading to similar tastes and habits: they prefer to socialise with other descendants as children and adolescents and marry within the group, later sending their offspring to Japanese school. This "community as family" metaphor also relates to the fact that Japanese migration to Bolivia was based on families rather than individuals. Nevertheless, this supposed homogeneity is questionable on a closer look and the margins of the *comunidad* are fuzzy: while seldom explicitly stated, most post-war descendants do not include the pre-war Nikkei in their definition of community.

It is striking that even though the *comunidad* is sometimes presented as natural, it is reinforced at specific moments like birthdays, weddings, funerals and different kinds of informal gatherings with few non-Nikkei present. As Shota describes, the bar described above is one location where ethnic identity is constructed. Apart from the nuclear family, the *comunidad japonesa* is an important place for children to become acquainted with culture and adequate social behaviour: they learn about "Japanese values" such as hierarchy, discipline and respect for the group and hear about the history of immigration. In addition, many Nikkei from Santa Cruz meet as children and adolescents in ethnically defined institutions such as *nihongogakkō* [Japanese school], *seinenkai* [youth group] or the Nikkei volleyball team. Young adults from the *colonias* may live together in the Okinawa Kenjinkai building and ANBJ during their high school years and university. Grown-ups meet in association activities, Fraternidad Fujii and when dropping off or taking home their children from Japanese school. The elderly come together at Day Service activities.

Tanomoshi have social functions like conviviality and the exchange of news. In former times, they meant an economic strategy based on trust and solidarity, especially in the first years of migration when there was little help from the Japanese government for the penniless migrants who were not fluent in Spanish. Until today, it is vital to trust other *tanomoshi* members; therefore, they are carefully selected. Despite the narrative on the "trustworthy Japanese," members who did not pay their fees or who escaped with the money of one or more *tanomoshi* have been a recurring problem (Tsujimoto 2012).

While institutional will or discrimination by real estate agencies may lead to the emergence of separate ethnic enclaves, such settlement patterns are no prerequisite for the social, cultural, political and/or religious self-organisation of minorities. The infrastructure of such an ethnic community may include places of worship, schools, restaurants and libraries, but also import-export businesses, banks and travel agencies (for a general discussion of such migrant businesses see, e.g., Zhou 2004). Such sites may become a place of socialisation and information exchange as well as a possibility to find work. In Santa Cruz, no separate Nikkei neighbourhood exists.

Nevertheless, Multimercado Okinawa is a place to meet acquaintances and to reproduce the feeling of belonging to an ethnic community. It hosts a fish seller, a

90 *The daily creation of ethnic boundaries*

shop with imported Japanese products, a stationery shop and a business with everyday products – most shop owners are Nikkei. A small restaurant offering sushi, *majadito*[3] and several kinds of vegetables and meat makes the place lively around noon. Multimercado lost importance since different supermarkets have opened all over the city. Especially on Saturdays, one can observe elderly Nikkei with enormous bags full of vegetables from the nearby Korean supermarket who wait for their taxi within Multimercado. Others have a weekly meeting with friends at the restaurant. In addition, some students from the *colonias* living on the second floor come for their groceries. Descendants may pay their membership fees in the Okinawa Kenjinkai offices on the first floor, visit one of the Nikkei hairdressers nearby or go to the Nikkei-owned travel agency around the corner.

Consequently, it is not surprising that friendships and love relations emerge between those who see each other regularly, rather than constituting an act of conscious boundary making in each case. Although I describe many cases where ethnic identity proves beneficial, it has an affective dimension as well and is not necessarily used for specific objectives.

"Don't stain your family's name" – How social norms are enforced

Many Nikkei consider behaviour privileging the collective to be "typically Japanese" and also "typically Nikkei." Whereas giving priority to building social ties with co-ethnics may also occur elsewhere, much has been published on the "groupish" Japanese, not least by themselves, often with reference to communal life in the rural village. Sugimoto (1997: 3) notes that according to popular discourse, the Japanese prefer the group's wellbeing over the expression of any individual intention. Furthermore, Japanese culture is not only famous for the avoidance of open conflicts but also for the distinction between "inside" and "outside the group" as well as for its emphasis on respect, hierarchy and seniority, reflected in the different honorific expressions and levels of politeness of Japanese language. Harmony is thereby regarded as a sign of maturity: one must not cause trouble, claim privileges or seek too much attention (Nakane 1973). Social cohesion and group harmony are believed to create a "consensus society," enabling the economic and political stability of the country as a whole.

Indeed, Nikkei association leaders have generally tried to maintain conformity and to avoid open conflict, especially in the formerly relatively closed *colonias* with its collective work model – a presentation that may eventually also make them feel more united. At the same time, being perceived as a supportive, harmonious and homogeneous community was certainly helpful for their relations with non-Nikkei and Japanese institutions. Therefore, the *comunidad* is marked by many unwritten rules, mutual obligations as well as rewards and punishments, in order to regulate members' behaviour (Takenaka 2003b: 476ff.). Sugimoto (1997: 245f.) notes that such behaviour towards the group is rewarded: for example, an enormous wooden plate in ABJ Okinawa's major community-building demonstrates these efforts. It covers almost the entire wall next to the entrance to the

The daily creation of ethnic boundaries   91

ceremonial hall, rewarding donors with their names in a prominent place, including the sum they donated for the construction of the building.

However, Sugimoto's reference to possible sanctions for reluctant individuals illustrates that such orientedness seems not to occur automatically, and this is also true for the Nikkei. Open competition and rivalry, questioning norms or acting out of purely individual motives, is discouraged and may be regarded as a sign of undesirable "bolivianisation." Instead of overt aggression, many Nikkei put a high value on restraint, preferring subtle clues to express tensions. One Nikkei explained that she greets everybody since she is well educated, while she avoids talking to those she does not like. Rather than open punishments, social pressure causes embarrassment and shame (Sugimoto 1997: 254f.).

Gossip is an important means to enforce social norms. People comment, often negatively, on third parties' flaws, failures, relations, hostilities, illicit business practices, extramarital affairs or on more trivial issues like a bride who is undecided on how to decorate her marriage party. Gossip is essential to stay informed, but rumours on unacceptable behaviour also support notions of morality, constructing boundaries. Furthermore, gossip may mean engaging in a competitive struggle, expressing envy towards successful individuals and leaders, thereby undermining those in powerful positions (Bourdillon und Shambare 2002; Gluckman 1963; Paine 1967).

Many Nikkei assume that the *comunidad japonesa* is especially prone to gossip, pointing to Japan's insular character. While the role of gossip in the construction of ethnic identity has been scarcely studied, evaluating the behaviour of absent thirds occurs in other small and closely related groups as well, notably in contexts where open confrontation is strongly discouraged (Amster 2004). Notwithstanding, many Nikkei, especially females, criticise this practice as a waste of time, like Ritsuko Hashimoto. She regards gossip as untrue talk of idle people that is destructive for the collective. According to Ritsuko, most descendants are simply "hypocrites":

> All the time when you go to Los Pozos, *miércoles*, there are people everywhere looking around, that one came to buy things, she bought this or that, I saw her smoking, I saw whatever. That's the Japanese circle. They don't tell you straight what they think. All the time they are gossiping. And later when you hear it, *uuuh*, they have already put tail and wings to it.

Other descendants declare to be more at ease with these rules: trying to avoid rumours in advance, they consciously or unconsciously restrict themselves to show the expected behaviour in anticipatory obedience (Foucault 1975). They believe that it is of utter importance what others think about the individual. Nevertheless, whereas criticising the group from within or breaking out of the scheme attracts gossip, it is much worse when acts considered gross infringements are made public. The consequence is that such individuals are shunned or distance themselves from other Nikkei. Descendants generally avoid mentioning incidents to outsiders, like the case of a Nikkei entrepreneur who sued two other

92 *The daily creation of ethnic boundaries*

descendants, causing embarrassment among co-ethnics. This recalls the often-cited Japanese concept of saving face to the outside: the correct and acceptable aspects (*tatemae*) are shown to the outside, while one's true feelings and opinions (*honne*) are not revealed (Sugimoto 1997: 26f.).

Behaving inappropriately can also have negative consequences for the family's and the ethnic group's honour, leading to even more pressure on the individual. As one association representative notes especially for the first generation: "They carried the Japanese flag on their back," meaning that controversial behaviour could even harm Japan's reputation in Bolivia. Cattle farmer Ryoji Nakaima tells his children: "You must never stain your family's name. It was so difficult for your parents and grandparents to establish that, so you must maintain it. If [my children] keep this mentality, I think they will be successful in their business." While rumours have much power in the *colonias* where inhabitants share a high number of acquaintances, they become less effective in the city. As university lecturer Tsuyoshi Kato remarks laughingly, norms are less strict than in the times of the samurai when an infringement might have led to ritualised suicide. However, outsiders seldom hear about controversial behaviour among Nikkei.

"There is more understanding" – Nikkei marriage practices

The nuclear family has been the migrants' basic unit and this idealised model[4] implied ethnical homogeneity. Although endogamy is presented as "natural," drawing an ethnic boundary through marriage is the outcome of specific social and historical processes as well, while exogamy and especially "mixed" children (see Chapter 5) mean that the boundary becomes fuzzy.

For Bolivian Nikkei, no law prohibited "mixed" marriages as compared for example to Namibia during Apartheid (Schmidt-Lauber 1998: 366ff.). But for merchants and employees in La Paz in the 1930s, it was common to arrange marriages with the so-called "picture brides," women from Japan they had never seen before. Such practices were unusual in Bolivian Amazonia, not least because farmers lacked the financial resources (Furuki 2013: 60; Thompson 1977). In the early years of San Juan and Colonia Okinawa, the Nikkei were strongly discouraged to marry outside the *comunidad* and settlement patterns encouraged endogamy. According to Centro Social's member list (Santa Kurusu Chūō Nihonjinkai Sōritsu 50 Shūnen Kinenshi 2006: 289ff.), one-third of 142 married couples are now composed of a Nikkei and a non-Nikkei – this number does not include widowed members. Slightly more men than women have married out and Suzuki (2010: 158) notes that in Colonia Okinawa, marriages of Nikkei men with non-Nikkei women are more accepted than of female Japanese descendants with non-Nikkei – nevertheless, also many of these couples have disengaged from the *comunidad*. As a comparison, Furuki (2013: 82), probably referring to the year 1999 and without specifying the proportion of males and females, states that of 63 couples in Sociedad Japonesa de La Paz, almost half were composed of a descendant and a non-descendant. Nevertheless, at any community celebration, few of these couples are visible, or often only the Nikkei spouse.

The daily creation of ethnic boundaries   93

The dependence on and the responsibility for the collective extends to marriage relations: rather than merely expressing sentiments, marriage is also a means to maintain group boundaries. Nevertheless, for lawyer Masutaro Higaonna, a Nisei, such social practices do not correspond to modern ideals of egalitarianism and individual achievement. He thinks that endogamy is "somehow immoral and illogical" in the age of globalisation, but says that parents all over the world prefer a marriage partner from the same group for their children to maintain a "unified culture" and "defend the nation." Like several other descendants, Masutaro says that it is simply natural to marry "within one's own race."

> It's not that we're racists [...], but we want our children to marry other [association] members' children [...]. At the moment, our children marry *collas*, *cambas* or other people of another origin. But in general, we hope that a certain level of culture and other things will be maintained.

Although interview partners like Masutaro underlined that they would not oppose their children's marriage choices, several Sansei did report that their parents told them to seek a Nikkei partner, preferably before the age of 30. At the same time, I have not heard of non-Nikkei *cruceñas and cruceños* objecting to their children's marriage with a Nikkei.

As Schmidt-Lauber (1998: 348ff.) states, endogamy as a boundary-making practice is the result of specific historical and social processes. Hatugai (2018) writes that arranged marriages were not only a common practice in pre-war Japan but they also used to reflect the respect for the Issei and the community's hierarchy in Brazil. Marrying inside an ethnic group stood for stability and confidence as well as for a possibility to strategically enhance one's family's influence in the community. Choosing one's partner by oneself or marrying a non-Nikkei was equivalent to selfishness and egoism and hence to an infringement of core values. Consequently, such marriages often meant a break with the family. Even if one is free to select one's partner, marriage is not only based on love but also on pragmatism. Also, many Bolivian Nikkei argue that the non-Nikkei's "customs" may be incompatible with their own (Suzuki 2010: 157ff.). They assert that between descendants, more understanding and confidence is possible, making marriage more "secure" and "more reasonable." Hence, they send their children to association activities or urge them to socialise with other Nikkei as one strategy to ensure that they marry a Nikkei later. Pointing to moral corruption rather than to a lack of understanding, one Nikkei explained his marriage with a descendant with the *cruceñas'* supposed infidelity. Setsuko Gushiken, an entrepreneur in the food sector, doubts that a Nikkei/non-Nikkei couple will be stable, pointing to food as a symbol for cultural understanding:

> A Bolivian spouse will never like the Japanese food that much. One of my brothers is not yet married, so I say: "When [...] you become married, you have to look for a Japanese descendant because you love Japanese food." And food can be a reason for dispute. Because if the wife can only cook

94   *The daily creation of ethnic boundaries*

meat, beef, he won't like that, he will look for somewhere else to eat. So my father said that [...] if there is much difference at the cultural level, there will be a shock. And he's right. And now my brother has a girlfriend, a Japanese descendant born here, so there is more understanding.

Similarly, a Nikkei father asserted that he could not imagine a daughter-in-law who would not know the most basic "Japanese values" like *ryoshiki* [common sense] and especially *enryo*, referring to the concept of self-restraint in order not to harm others. Nevertheless, his children would eventually take their own decisions, he added, shrugging his shoulders. Somebody who lacks "typically Japanese" filial piety and mindfulness may bring conflict into the family – but through endogamy, the *comunidad* is believed to maintain their "Japanese values" and avoid "bolivianisation" (Suzuki 2010: 157ff.).

However, the degree of tolerance towards exogamy varies from one family to the other and may also change over time. In some Nikkei families, marriage with non-Nikkei is strongly discouraged until today. Michelle Nomura and her mother Aurora Nakashima, Nikkei from a neighbouring country, vividly remember a conflict over such a marriage. Some years ago, a befriended Bolivian Issei couple was disappointed that their daughter wanted to marry a Nikkei of partly non-Japanese ancestry from another Latin American country; thus, they were reluctant to attend the wedding celebration. This was something Michelle and Aurora considered not only painful for the fiancés, but they also called the couple's attitude "backward," presenting exogamy as a desirable sign of identification with *cruceño* society. At least, the Issei couple eventually accepted the "mixed" marriage, Aurora and Michelle added. In another case, a young non-Nikkei friend supposed that her ex-boyfriend's Nikkei family rejected her not only because of her ethnic origin but also because she as a woman holds a university degree.

Many interview partners are conscious that the wider society sees exogamy as a positive asset. I heard many descendants uttering sentences like "The Nikkei are more integrated than in former times, the proof being increasing intermarriage." Nevertheless, even those descendants who criticise the *comunidad japonesa* as "too closed" have not necessarily married a non-Nikkei themselves. Douglass (1992: 165), too, has observed contradictory justification patterns among the Jamaican elite, concluding that endogamy has to be justified to the outside: "Openness serves an important ideological function as well: It maintains a situation of stable ambiguity that masks the marriage system's consistent patterns."

Marriage choices are also mixed with socioeconomic categories, although interview partners acknowledged this rather indirectly. It was striking that all Nikkei who had married a non-descendant had chosen a partner of similar socioeconomic background and of comparatively fair complexion – at least those who had officially presented their spouse to me. Nisei university lecturer Tsuyoshi Kato believes that descendants perceive differences between non-Nikkei of various national origins: according to him, marrying a U.S. citizen might mean additional symbolic capital in Bolivia since the United States are considered of higher status in the international hierarchy. Similarly, Nishida (2009: 433) notes that for Brazilian Nikkei in the 1960s, exogamy still stood for marrying down in socioeconomic terms, while Tsuda (1999: 218) writes that Japanese descendants in southern Brazil preferred to marry Italian and German descendants whom they supposed to have a higher socioeconomic status than other Brazilians. In a nutshell, an individual's acceptance does not solely depend on his or her ethnic identity, but on a combination of origin, habitus and class (Barriga Dávalos 2016: 67f.). To be considered acceptable, a non-Nikkei's education and profession can become more important than his or her ethnic background.

While personal attitudes on all sides continue to play an important role, marriages between Nikkei and non-Nikkei are more accepted than before, at least if they occur between individuals of a similar socioeconomic background. However, several descendants argue that the non-Nikkei spouse must adapt to the descendant and his or her values and practices, not vice-versa. In this context, it is interesting to note that two non-Nikkei spouses of Nikkei women told me again and again how hard they used to work, thereby referring to "typically Japanese" characteristics.

Several Bolivian Nikkei are married to former JICA volunteers; others found a Japanese partner while working or studying in Japan. However, many interview partners thought that during *dekasegi* it was easier for a Nikkei to marry another descendant. Descendants in Japan share a common life situation and similar behavioural patterns whereas the Japanese were regarded as unapproachable and culturally different (Shōno und Sugiura 2013: 300; Suzuki 2010: 174ff.). Other Nikkei justified their doubts concerning such a couple's stability with the argument that the Japanese would not get accustomed to living in such a faraway country, mentioning unpunctuality, failing basic services and corruption as strongly opposed to organised and clean Japan. Especially women were said to be too attached to their family; hence, a couple might decide to stay in Japan to the detriment of Bolivia's descendant community. The Nikkei, however, were generally confident to be adaptable to both countries. Thus, contrary to what one might assume, dating a Japanese born in Japan is not necessarily regarded as positive – a new boundary emerges.

"After the party, they have nothing to eat" – When consumption becomes dangerous

Despite the discourse on the Nikkei's non-integration, most Japanese descendants clearly identify as part of the Bolivian middle class. According to Liechty (2003), tales about morality, moderation and taste are among the defining features of belonging to this social stratum, but also competition with other members. Hence, ethnic boundaries play a role even in their relation to non-Nikkei of a similar socioeconomic background.

Already the often-cited French visitor Alcides D'Orbigny (1945: 1112) was excited about the importance of social events, as he wrote after travelling to Santa Cruz in 1830/31. According to him, all kinds of occasions were a reason to celebrate: the better part of the year was filled with parties, visits and dances, usually

96   *The daily creation of ethnic boundaries*

divided between men and women and different social strata. Until today, social compromises and gatherings play an important role in Santa Cruz. Many *cruceñas* and *cruceños*, Nikkei included, meet regularly with their former classmates from high school and university. Such social events can have a practically obligatory character. Mai Amuro told me with a sigh that she could not find any credible pretext to be absent at her high school graduation anniversary. What disturbed her was that apart from the ceremony itself, the event implied prior preparation, for instance, taking a group picture and buying a dress for the respectable sum of 800 bolivianos that she would never wear again. Moreover, she does not share many interests with her former classmates. Nevertheless, Mai recognises that such networks can be supportive; the group helped for example a former classmate who had fallen into poverty.

Whereas many Nikkei see prosperity as an almost inevitable outcome of their "Japanese values," it is important to note that material wealth is not of itself honourable. Many Nikkei characterise themselves as humble and modest citizens who avoid showing wealth too openly. Thereby, they map immoralities onto other parts of the middle class, arguing that consumption can be dangerous and corrupting (Liechty 2003). Nisei Kaede Itokazu is aware of such risks. She explicitly identifies as a member of the city's middle class, but she has not forgotten that she grew up in Colonia Okinawa in a *motacú* palm hut with an earth floor. After returning from a *dekasegi* stay, she lives in a spacious house with a swimming pool in an affluent neighbourhood, together with her husband and her two pedigree cats. We are sitting in her kitchen on a winter afternoon with a cup of hot cocoa and watching the rain. On the wall, I see a calendar from a Nikkei shop, like in many Nikkei houses, and in the corner, a bag for golf clubs. Kaede is proud of the many non-Nikkei friends she knows from golfing. While thinking about moving to Japan to live close to her two children, she deplores that descendants still hold ethnic prejudices and are therefore reluctant to interact with non-Nikkei. Kaede, who, depending on the situation, identifies as *camba*, Nikkei, Japanese, Bolivian and as a member of the middle class, is nevertheless critical of *cruceñas* and *cruceños* from a similar socioeconomic background. She says that the Nikkei – and *collas* – think of the future, considering that they might make an investment or fall ill; *cambas*, however, are not able or willing to think ahead. Consumption, in Kaede's opinion, is corrupting. Bolivians often say that appearance is of utmost importance in Santa Cruz; this becomes visible in the countless beauty contests and in the omnipresent model industry (Waldmann 2008: 171ff., 209ff.). Kaede finds this extremely disturbing. She regrets that her non-Nikkei *cruceña* friends put too much emphasis on outer appearance and status symbols. Instead of caring for their inner values or at least investing in nurturing goods, non-Nikkei seem addicted to extravagant fashion. Instead, she mentions educational achievement, albeit another commodity to assert status, as more important than material consumption.

> [The non-Nikkei *cruceñas*] will never go to a party with the clothes they wore at the last party [...]. They go to a beauty salon for their haircut, to get

The daily creation of ethnic boundaries   97

make-up, to beautify their nails [...]. Among my friends, there are some who are married, their husbands have a good status, a good job, they earn well. So they have always a beautiful house, nice clothes, they have a housemaid and everything [...]. But in the end, they spend so much money that they can't pay the school fees [...]. And no matter if they have the money or not, they will have a birthday party. And not a small one, but a big one, so the next day they have nothing to eat.

Descendants may be able to afford status symbols, but they hold not to depend on such amenities thanks to their "Japanese values." Although Kaede, too, employs an *empleada* [domestic worker], she is convinced that non-Nikkei *cruceñas* and *cruceños* are dependent on this support. She emphasises that her *empleada* only cleans the rooms, while Kaede washes, irons, cooks and cares for her cats and her husband because she does not like "sitting around with crossed arms." Mai Amuro, too, consciously taught her children to sweep and to wipe despite employing an *empleada*, since she thinks that hygiene is related to dignity. Moreover, Mai told me how her family collects rainwater for their plants and tries to avoid plastic waste, designating this as a good habit of their poor migrant ancestors. Like Kaede and Mai, several Nikkei asserted that they could do all household chores by themselves. As pollution, laziness and dependency are regarded as moral wrongs to be avoided, knowing how to clean is an important boundary marker to the non-Nikkei middle-class members who are supposedly unable to do so. They claim to propose an alternative to excessive consumption as a social ill that affects modern society and the environment.

Despite the discourse on seemingly static "Japanese values," it becomes clear that the "right" socialisation is crucial. Behind practices such as cleaning stands the fear that such norms would become lost. Often mentioned in the same breath, contact with non-Nikkei Bolivians was held responsible for many negative developments. If a Nikkei loses his or her "Japanese values," he or she becomes "bolivianised," "latinised" or "tropicalised." This was not only a common criticism of older Nikkei on the younger generations. Also, some Sansei regretted that their generation and especially children were losing the fighting spirit that had allowed their grandparents to cross the ocean to a foreign land. Clearly questionable behaviour among Nikkei, such as quarrels in the *comunidad japonesa*, is seen to be a result of "bad Bolivian influence" as well.

The city of Santa Cruz is regarded as especially corrupting. Chihiro Imanaka, a Nisei mother from San Juan, chose a supposedly more suitable environment for her two daughters to attend high school. As she told me during lunch in Multimercado Okinawa in the presence of her grown-up daughters, they went to school in the same city Chihiro had studied herself since, in Santa Cruz, they would have gone astray.

The ambience in Santa Cruz is not suitable for studying. I think that if my daughters had studied here in Santa Cruz, they would not be the same girls as they are now. Because in Cochabamba [...], they didn't go to parties [...],

98 *The daily creation of ethnic boundaries*

> they didn't use these [beautiful] clothes, they went out in track pants and T-shirts [all of them laugh] [...]. It's said that it's better to study in Sucre or Cochabamba because the climate is better for studying [...]. Here in Santa Cruz, there are too many friendships, too many parties.

But after the interview, when her two daughters dawdled around instead of leaving with two friends, Chihiro remarked that the two were so slow that "they don't seem Japanese," shaking her head as if she wanted to say "there is still potential for improvement."

In striking contrast to their discourses on modesty, most descendants do not renounce the amenities of middle-class life. Taking the example of mobility, I know almost no Nikkei who uses public busses in Santa Cruz, considered uncomfortable, unhygienic, unreliable and dangerous: in short, a means of transport for the lower classes and students. Instead, the middle class generally relies on their own car or the ubiquitous taxis. Car owners in Santa Cruz frequently drive family members and friends from one place to the other, and especially children and adolescents are regularly taken to school and leisure time activities by car. Personal cars represent status, safety and the freedom to move wherever and whenever one wants. When it comes to travelling to other cities or abroad, they take a flight, not the *flota* [intercity bus].

One day, I visited Naoko Kanai and her husband Eduardo Visentin at home for an interview. They live in a gated community area relatively close to the city centre and adjacent to booming Avenida Cristo Redentor. Naoko picked me up at the gate in her large new looking car and drove me a short distance along perfectly paved roads and little gardens to her single-family house where she lives with her husband and her three children. As far as I could see, they are not only able to pay for their children's education,[5] but can also afford a trip to Japan for the whole family. When I carefully remarked that they do not belong to Santa Cruz' poorer social strata, both immediately protested: they claimed that they live off their salaries, working hard as employees of an international company, and that they would earn much more in Japan. Lawyer Masutaro Higaonna, too, insists that the Nikkei are part of the lower middle class and struggle to make a living – while he owns land in the *colonia*, apart from a spacious SUV. Masutaro, Naoko and Eduardo present themselves as morally superior because they do not live off their fortune, like other, wealthier strata.

Nikkei – and other middle-class *cruceñas* and *cruceños* – justify the purchase of such amenities with a need rather than with a craving for external recognition. They argue, for example, that they own cars to be more flexible in an increasingly hectic life. Public transport to the gated communities outside the city is indeed scarce and unreliable. Moreover, many middle-class *cruceñas* and *cruceños* refer to insecurity as a motive to use private cars. As a consequence, living without specific amenities becomes unthinkable: constructing the outside world as dangerous reinforces behavioural norms (Caldeira 2000).

Compared to some other Latin American cities, Santa Cruz still counts as a safe place. Nevertheless, while *cruceñas* and *cruceños* regularly idealise the "old

Santa Cruz" as an idyllic town, crime and insecurity have become a frequent topic in daily conversations. In addition, sensation-seeking media reports create an atmosphere of fear and suspicion. While some critical voices state that the number of *maleantes* [criminals] shows the problems of an unequal society, public opinion holds that they mostly do not struggle to survive but are seduced by consumption goods, preferring fast but illicit ways to obtain them – one frequently hears that *maleantes* nowadays kill somebody for a cell phone. One is constantly advised to be careful when going out since it is common knowledge that certain locations are especially *peligroso* [dangerous] mainly at night because of an anonymous mass of potential *maleantes,* supposedly identifiable by their social and ethnic background. Places that are associated with the lower class are often per se considered to be dangerous, like the Plan 3000 neighbourhood – such areas are far away from the middle class not only geographically but also in a figurative sense.

The population, not without any reason, regards Bolivian police as well as the whole justice system as weak, incapable and corrupt. Thus, the middle class has adopted behavioural patterns and strategies to cope with risk. As a privatised commodity, security has obtained economic value (Caldeira 2000); investments in private security forces and surveillance systems are on the rise. Middle-class houses – depending on the inhabitants' income and level of preoccupation – tend to have walls with barbed wire and sometimes a barking dog next to the door. Others have moved to gated communities, and drive-in banks and private security forces are a common part of the cityscape.

In contrast to what Melgar Tísoc (2012: 196) observes for Mexico City, I have not heard about crime in Santa Cruz directed specifically at Japanese descendants. Whereas Nikkei are a highly visible minority, it is also interesting that Nikkei institutions do not have any special protection, for example, security guards. This can be regarded as an indication that most members of the Japanese-descendant minority do not feel an explicit target of crime. To my knowledge, Nikkei associations or other cultural institutions in Santa Cruz have not suffered assaults, even though at least one Japanese restaurant was robbed during my fieldwork stay.

However, some *cruceñas* and *cruceños* label all streets, markets and other public areas as dangerous. I remember my surprise when I met a Nikkei university student at a barbecue, held at one of my Nikkei interview partner's home in a park-like gated community. The student explained, without any protest from his interlocutors, that owning a car in Santa Cruz was necessary. His justification followed a common pattern, namely that it was too dangerous to walk in the streets because of the *maleantes* – I as a regular pedestrian was often more afraid of car drivers, coughing in clouds of exhaust gas from the ubiquitous minibuses. In other words, perceptions of the actual danger vary considerably and may not be objectively justified. Although most Nikkei – and other members of the middle class – lack empirical experience regarding the risk of entering a specific area, they still may consider a trip too dangerous: prevention is better than cure.

100 *The daily creation of ethnic boundaries*

Sweeping is more important than *kanji* writing – How Japanese school helps to construct ethnic identity

One crucial site to prevent the loss of values is the Japanese school. While according to Aniya (2013: 176), Japanese language education continues to be a fundamental and indispensable issue for descendants, I claim that to most parents, language classes are only of secondary importance – ethnic identity stands in the foreground.

Japanese schools or *nihongogakkō* were among the first institutions that settlers established in Latin America, although not necessarily with a professional curriculum. Such institutions were also meant to make a difference to local peasants who lived in comparably precarious conditions (Sakurai 1993). Japanese migrants sometimes hoped that children would continue their education in Japan; others wanted to transmit Japanese culture and identity. Moreover, school is a political arena: before the Second World War, the ultranationalist Japanese government tried to teach overseas students a nationalist mindset (Mori 2011). After the Second World War, schools like the ones in Colonia Okinawa and San Juan started to adapt to national curricula, especially regarding Spanish classes.

Nowadays, Japanese schools in the *colonias* offer Japanese classes every day, in La Paz and Santa Cruz only on Saturdays. The mostly female teachers, in their majority Nisei and Sansei, do not necessarily have a teaching degree, but regularly attend courses on didactics-related topics in Bolivia or elsewhere. Japan

Figure 4.1 Callisthenics [*rajio taisō*] before Japanese class in Santa Cruz.

The daily creation of ethnic boundaries 101

gives high importance to these schools as part of its assistance: JICA sends young volunteers and senior teachers as coordinators. It also provides special teaching material designed explicitly for Nikkei children, whereas, in former times, they would use books for Japanese pupils. Students learn the two syllabaries *katakana* and *hiragana* and some basic *kanji* characters. Regular festivities at school include Mother's Day, sports festival (*undōkai*), graduation ceremony, speech contest and participation in the standardised Japanese Language Proficiency Test (JLPT). Children are also supposed to present once a topic of their choice in *o-hanashi taikai* (speech contest) (Figure 4.1).[6]

Schools serve a dual function: they provide knowledge and skills, acknowledged by certificates, but they are also a place of socialisation and identity formation. More than just teaching language, Japanese schools transmit specific norms. For most parents I talked to, Japanese language education was not an essential part of Nikkei identity – which is contradictory since Bolivian Nikkei repeat again and again how proud they are of their language proficiency. Mai Amuro, for example, points out that she prefers her children to study English and thinks that it will be sufficient if they know some greetings and the most symbolic phrases in Japanese. When Mai hopes that her children will socialise with other Nikkei and "discover their identity," education points to the creation of ethnic networks, but also to the fact that she and other parents define school as a place to learn "Japanese values" (Suzuki 2010: 132ff.). It becomes evident that, apart from Japanese ancestry, habitus, too, is essential to be considered Nikkei. Although it is not clear in how far a Nikkei has to lose his or her "Japanese values" to become "bolivianised," Manzenreiter (2017a: 205) states that "[the Nikkei] are worried about the loss of national virtues, cultural identity, and ultimately about the risk of downward assimilation if they entrust their children to local public schools only."

Examples of such "good behaviour" are punctuality, respect, hygiene and hard work. Consequently, children's certificates show if they know how to greet and bow properly and if they arrive at school on time. Classroom posters in Japanese tell children "let's wash our hands." Every Saturday before class, children and teachers perform the widely known *rajio taisō* [callisthenics] to raise the energy level, improve health and create unity. Teaching "Japanese values" is also central to festivals like *undōkai* that children prepare and celebrate with their schoolmates, parents and families (Manzenreiter 2017a: 204ff.). Often, parents want their offspring to attend physically demanding extracurricular activities such as volleyball or Ryūkyūkoku Matsuridaiko dance to enhance their self-discipline, regarded as necessary for socioeconomic success. Modes of behaviour become thereby instilled in the body. For children themselves, Japanese culture may be fascinating for a different reason: Norio Miyaguni remembers laughingly that his son started attending Japanese class after learning that Nintendo and the manga series Dragon Ball are Japanese.

After classes, children clean classrooms and bathrooms, as it is also common in Japan. In fact, some children run around to chase flying plastic bags and play with the brooms and especially in the windy months, I was not always sure to see a difference between before and after the procedure. However, remembering her

102   *The daily creation of ethnic boundaries*

school days, Setsuko Gushiken assures me that this practice does have a long-lasting effect. After a party, everybody stays to tidy up with the host instead of delegating this task to a domestic worker, she holds: "What I learned at school is that after class, everybody has to clean, sweep, tidy up. Even if children have a housemaid, they clean [...]. But here [among non-Nikkei], it's different, [they say:]: 'You do this, you do that.'" Some descendants claim that children in Japan help their parents automatically in the absence of a domestic worker – and Nikkei children should be able and willing to do so, too. Some Sansei argued that cleaning schools modified their attitude towards household chores, but it remains an open question how measurable the effects would be.

While education quality plays a minor role for Mai, other parents think that language is indeed an essential vehicle to transmit ethnic identity. Non-Nikkei Micaela Tejada, fluent in Japanese and married to a Nikkei, lays much emphasis on her children's ability to communicate in Japanese.

> When I was in Japan, I had many Nikkei friends who didn't speak Japanese and people said: "Japanese face, Japanese name – and you don't speak Japanese?" Therefore, I want my children to defend themselves in Japanese so that they are not discriminated. If they lose the language, they lose almost half of their culture.

But parents like Micaela do not expect their children to become proficient speakers with one school day per week, as has come out in informal surveys at school. To improve their skills, some children are sent to the *colonias* or Japan. Proficient speakers also have better access to scholarships and jobs in Japan, but parents are aware that Spanish is essential to survive in Bolivia.

Nevertheless, the interest in Japanese schools is in decline. Schools in the *colonias* offer only primary education and most adolescents continue their studies in Santa Cruz. However, parents increasingly decide to send them earlier to the city since they think that education quality is better in Santa Cruz. A mother may move with the children to the urban area whereas the father stays at the farm. In the city, enthusiasm for Japanese school is not overwhelming, either: around 750 Nikkei live in Santa Cruz, but only 70 children attend classes. Some parents like Setsuko Gushiken, even though insisting on teaching their children "Japanese values," consider Japanese useless compared to English that they believe to offer more possibilities – Setsuko's children no longer attend the Japanese school. Others like Reiko Yohena suppose that her son will eventually become interested in Japan on his own. Some parents argue that their kids are too busy with their regular school tasks, others drop out when they are old enough to manifest themselves. Moreover, the Japanese language might also have been more popular in the heyday of *dekasegi*.

Attracted by Japanese culture and economic opportunities, some non-Nikkei parents have become interested in sending their children to school. Around 2010, around five non-Nikkei children would study Japanese in Santa Cruz' *nihongogakkō*. Some Nikkei welcomed this as a sign that Japanese culture is attractive. But apparently, not everybody was at ease. Soon after, only Nikkei children were allowed to sign up, vaguely justified with some non-Nikkei students and parents' "unsuitable behaviour." Meanwhile, more and more non-Nikkei Bolivian children have been entering La Paz's Japanese school. At the beginning of 2020, of 32 school children, 17 were of Japanese origin; but the school has never conducted any survey on their reasons to study Japanese. Similar to Santa Cruz, Nikkei children and parents in La Paz show less interest in Japanese school than in former years, a development no interview partner could explain but that both Nikkei and non-Nikkei regretted.

JICA and the teachers have recognised that classes have to change in order to maintain schools attractive. Moreover, curricula need to be adapted since children will increasingly learn Japanese as a foreign language. JICA has initiated some exchange programmes for students to maintain an interest in Japan and Japanese culture. The official goal is now to emphasise behaviours such as punctuality and cleanliness, thus, on "Japanese values."

No whistling at work, please – Educating non-Nikkei Bolivians

Several descendants propose that they should not only teach Nikkei children "Japanese values" but also educate non-Nikkei Bolivians to the benefit of Bolivian society. Hence, the workplace is an interesting site to study these negotiations of boundaries. According to some Nikkei, showing reliability and punctuality makes a difference to the "typically Bolivian behaviour" that both Nikkei and non-Nikkei regard as unsuitable for business and public administration. Instead, being on time means a practice of the industrialised world, supposedly leading to economic progress and modernity. Nevertheless, the Nikkei acknowledged that some rare cases of unpunctual Nikkei exist.

University lecturer Tsuyoshi Kato also mentions singing while listening to music, whistling at work or speaking in a loud voice as concrete undesirable practices he tries to discourage. Nisei Kazuyuki Hamaoka, holding a leading position in one of Bolivia's most important food companies, has learned important working skills in Japan, such as attention to clients. He observes that compared to Japan, Bolivia lags behind in hygiene, discipline and punctuality. Interestingly, rather than fearing a "corrupting effect," Kazuyuki argues that individual Nikkei like him are able to influence a number of non-Nikkei for the progress of the company. He regrets that the latter are not necessarily willing to follow his advice. For Kazuyuki, this means "suffering," but he nevertheless thinks that his employees can change under good guidance. He wants to engage his co-workers, the company and the whole country on its way to modernity. Kazuyuki remembers how the Japanese 5S management method was implemented in his company – although not on his initiative, but because of a general fascination for the Japanese economical miracle. Having grown up in Bolivia, he finds this difficult:

> When [the] HR responsible came […], I told him that it's not impossible, but difficult […]: "To implement the 5S now, I assure you that we won't get any

104 *The daily creation of ethnic boundaries*

result, because people here don't like to change. They like to stay how they were raised." So I tell the employees: "That's not only for the company. It will also help you at home, to have order, cleanliness, so when I see how you work, I already imagine how your home is like [...]. It reflects in your work."

In other words, as the representative of a powerful industrialised nation, he supposes to know best what his employees and co-workers need.

In a well-intended paternalism, many Nikkei see themselves in a position to teach non-Nikkei Bolivians how to behave and how to work: the latter appear to be children one must guide, teach and control. An intervention following rational criteria seems necessary to increase the performance of the company as well as to improve law-abidingness, diet and hygiene among staff. This implicitly suggests that non-Nikkei make progress only because of an outside agency. The supposedly faulty behaviour of non-Nikkei, especially workers, naturalises and justifies existing hierarchies. These discourses strikingly resemble those justifying colonialism (Bhabha 2004; Scott 1998).

At the same time, the Nikkei become engaged because they possess cultural knowledge and build, by their own account, a bridge between Bolivia and Japan. Agronomist Norio Miyaguni emphasises that these experiences legitimise his authority as a development worker:

Having a Japanese face but understanding how the Bolivian thinks, I've benefitted much from that [...]. Because I'm just one more farmer, I've grown up like them [...]. I can talk to them about the problems they have, but also offer a solution from a Japanese point of view.

I have not heard any non-Nikkei Bolivians questioning such suggestions. *Tanomoshi* member Ramón even welcomes the introduction of the Japanese 5S method. Several other non-Nikkei claimed that their Nikkei co-workers and superiors had taught them how to work properly. I witnessed a talk the Mexican Japanese entrepreneur Carlos Kasuga held in early 2014 in Santa Cruz, earning much applause from the predominantly non-Nikkei audience. In his talks, he puts forward modern management ideas mixed with "Japanese" elements, but also some references to "typically" Latin American habits. For him, status is based on personal excellence. Therefore, it is important to focus on good time management, hard work and personal growth, while he underlines that it is essential to remain honest and to care for others. The audience seemed impressed by his management philosophy – "change your way of thinking to the Japanese style" – and considered these practices a model for Latin America. Despite this acclamation, it remains, of course, unclear if such inputs have any concrete result.[7]

Also, Jiro Kojima doubts that the efforts to educate non-Nikkei have any long-lasting effect. He is a Nisei engineer from San Juan who has collaborated with JICA on different projects and recently opened an engineering bureau with a non-Nikkei colleague. According to him, Japanese culture has proven useful in an economic context and could serve as a model for non-Nikkei. Jiro does not refer

The daily creation of ethnic boundaries   105

to "blood" as an unchangeable marker of ethnic difference; but non-Nikkei peasants are raised differently and their way of thinking is simply incompatible with progress and modernity, he claims:

> It's difficult to implement something the Japanese way that it can be applied in the Bolivian environment. It's utopic or, let's say, very cultural. Complicated [...]. It can be copied, but not the spirit of those who work with it [...]. We have tried that in communities where people are poor because they don't work. They don't have the custom to put more effort than for what they eat. They don't think about saving money. They don't think that you can store your food and eat the next day [...]. They don't think: "If I produce the double, I sell one part, I keep a little and I will grow."

While Jiro's statement again justifies ethnic and social boundaries, it would not be desirable for Nikkei, either, that the others adopt all these "good Japanese practices" since the Nikkei themselves would no longer be regarded as the positive exception.

"People there are like ants" – The Nikkei's ambivalent relations with Japan and the Japanese

As already demonstrated, Japan continues to be present in most Nikkei's life, for example as a topic in daily conversations. *Nihon* [Japan] is their ancestors' homeland, but also their cultural reference and the source of their current prosperity. Nevertheless, the definition of "home" is difficult. The Nikkei increasingly regard themselves as Bolivian citizens of Japanese ancestry and hence as different from the Japanese.

Even Nikkei who have never travelled to Japan know from their friends and family how the country must be like. Imaginaries have often recurring features that contrast with Bolivia, for instance, punctuality, clean streets and romanticised imaginaries of the four seasons in central Japan. Media transmit such imaginaries while they mean a connection to Japan, for example, via the Japanese NHK TV channel (Suzuki 2005). For one interview partner, it was so important not to miss his daily *dorama* [soap opera] on NHK that we interrupted the interview for 15 minutes to watch it.

Japanese government officials, family members and friends visit Bolivia from time to time, especially for the *colonias'* anniversaries. Bolivian Nikkei, too, travel to Japan, although regular journeys are not possible due to the enormous distance and costs: a trip takes 30 hours or more and exceeds USD 2,000. Of course, such journeys have become much more comfortable than in the 1950s and 1960s when trips by ship and train took between two and four months. The Nikkei may visit members and friends, taking advantage to see some tourist sites; others travel to Japan if they have a serious health problem: in this case, they trust Japanese doctors and clinics more than Bolivian ones. Younger Nikkei often go to Japan on a scholarship during high school or university from one week to

106 *The daily creation of ethnic boundaries*

several years. A visit to Japan is also an important experience to see the country of one's ancestors and to discover if one's notions correspond to reality. Fukaura und Nagai (2013: 278) also observe an educational effect of *dekasegi* stays: some young descendants learned proper manners and returned full of positive energy, they write. For many Nikkei, the trip is a valuable experience to become conscious of their origins.

Many Nikkei are impressed by the role technology plays in daily life, the high degree of organisation and the safety of public space. Visitors remember the considerable number of different products and the *konbini*, ubiquitous small retail shops with long opening hours. The Nikkei usually consider the Japanese as respectful and honest, and they are excited that shop sellers greet customers with a loud "*irasshaimase*" (welcome); when back in Bolivia, they miss the philosophy of "the customer is king." Japan appears to be a modern, desirable site, but also a place of institutional efficiency where the issuing of a passport takes some days and not months like in Bolivia.

The internet and improved flight connections facilitate contact with Japan and, in contrast to most Peruvian and Brazilian Nikkei, post-war Nikkei in Bolivia generally have the advantage to hold Japanese nationality and to be able to speak Japanese. In the dominant binary opposition between Japanese and foreigners, they may pass as the former, depending on individual factors such as language skills or cultural knowledge. This may bring some advantages like finding work outside the blue-collar sector and renting an apartment more easily (Suzuki 2010: 108f.).

Nevertheless, many Nikkei have an increasingly ambivalent identification with Japan. Subtle details tell them that they are different from the Japanese. Some Issei have difficulties in recognising the country they left shortly after the Second World War. Other descendants may note that their variety of Japanese includes Spanish words or expressions in disuse in Japan, becoming a source of amusement for the Japanese (Nakato 2012). One Nikkei artist, while attending an advanced training in Japan, remarked that she could pass as Japanese; but her teachers and peers were puzzled by her direct communication style and found her colourful, Latin-style clothes strange. CAISY president Hideo Iwamatsu resumes: "You go to Japan, and of course, you're a Latino for them. Even if you have a Japanese name and surname. That means that we're Latinos there and in Bolivia, we will never be considered [Bolivians]." Especially *dekasegi* migrants who do not enjoy much symbolic capital as manual labourers have negative impressions of Japan when they experience downward social mobility (Suzuki 2010: 83ff.). Many Nikkei have limited contact with the Japanese, for example, when they reside in neighbourhoods famous for their high percentage of descendants. When I was talking to a young Nikkei in his twenties who was about to leave for Japan, he already assumed that he would end up in a place like Tsurumi ward in Yokohama with a high percentage of Latinos and that he would mainly socialise with other Nikkei.

Although many Nikkei appreciate some aspects of Japan, the country is also presented as an example to avoid. Some descendants are disappointed since the Japan they heard of seems to have disappeared, if it ever existed. The Nikkei may

The daily creation of ethnic boundaries 107

even experience the ubiquitous technology as negative; especially in the enormous, densely populated metropolitan regions, everything seems anonymous. The high degree of organisation also leads to their impression that the Japanese, despite their supposedly exemplary behaviour, are cold and apathetic workaholics, closer to robots than to humans. Rafael Cho, who took a break from his studies to work as an electrician in Japan, experienced that Japan resembles an enormous, stressful factory: "People there are like ants, they come out of the train *woooum* and into the street *krrrrr*. It's incredible, there are rivers of people." Kentsu Hanashiro found it strange how his Japanese co-workers accepted orders without question.

> [In Bolivia,] I lived at my parents' house, so I didn't have the experience of working, *arubaito* as one says in Japan. Maybe I would have needed it here. I went there, I thought I was doing things well, but until now I remember the difference of "why". They told me "not like that, like this", but I didn't get why [...]. In contrast, a Japanese: "*Hai, wakarimasu, hai*" [yes, I understand, yes]; and I: "Why, *nande*"; and they get even angrier.

Another example some descendants mentioned is the high cost of living, as all Nikkei know who have tried to buy fruits or meat for a Latin-style *churrasco* (barbecue): both would be cheap and abundant in Bolivia. As a result, many descendants increasingly identify as Bolivians of Japanese ancestry and as different from the Japanese. While in Japan, they may express such feelings of estrangement by joining Bolivian- or Latin-style activities. Whereas in Bolivia, they might complain about the "slow and lazy Bolivians," the discourse changes in a Japanese context. Bolivia may then be presented as a sort of paradise untouched by the problems of modernity, where life is calm and relaxed and where people have time for friends and family. Thereby, Bolivia is not only associated with personal freedom and human warmth, but also with happiness. Consequently, after their return, many interview partners emphasised that their stay abroad made them appreciate life in Bolivia.

But not only do they declare to have adopted some supposedly better "customs" in Bolivia; some interview partners even claim that the Nikkei were more authentic than the Japanese themselves. Because of modern life, "Japanese values" such as diligence, responsibility, group-orientedness and filial piety are eroding in Japan, according to these Nikkei, who claim that life in the diaspora helped to preserve such values. They mentioned specific practices like joint cooking and dining after a funeral in Colonia Okinawa, interpreting this as a proof that solidarity and a sense of community still prevail in the diaspora.

As a result, even when in Bolivia, many Nikkei insist on being different from the Japanese. Especially the later generations increasingly claim to have adopted "good Bolivian customs." As an example, Daiki Kaneshiro considers the Japanese as cold. Even though he has never lived in Japan, he heard that while in a Bolivian apartment house, a new inhabitant soon becomes acquainted with everybody, the Japanese would not even greet their neighbours, but complain if somebody uses

108 *The daily creation of ethnic boundaries*

the toilet after 11 p.m. Therefore, Daiki considers Latin Americans an example of how to show affection towards others:

> I've been many times to the airport [...]. When a Latino leaves, although it's only for a week, for a month, for a year, two years, father and daughter hug each other tightly. It's a very affective physical contact. If a Japanese leaves [...], he may only shake hands with her [...]. Although the heart of this father is destroyed, even if the heart of this child is also destroyed. But they don't show it, there is no contact for cultural reasons [...]. When volunteers come from Japan for the first time and they live here and they see how people kiss [each other] on the cheeks to greet, they are happy to see that [laughs].

Such experiences give Nikkei in Bolivia self-consciousness vis-à-vis the Japanese: they are no longer the poor migrant farmers in the jungle dependent on foreign assistance. Instead, they have attained a life standard similar to the Japanese middle class and they know what is good or bad for them. Several Nikkei say that the Japanese are naïve and complicated, compared to the practical, smart and life-experienced Nikkei who, through their experiences in Bolivia, know how to deal with *maleantes* and *trámites*. Travel agency owner Daiki gives an example:

> I once received a group from Japan. There was one Japanese who had four wheels on his suitcase, and one was twisted, so three wheels worked, and the fourth didn't. "I have to go to the Varig [airline] office [...], I want to complain!" [...] "But [why], if it [still] works?" "No, no, I want Varig to issue a paper that this wheel arrived broken, during their flight, etc., and I want their general manager to sign that, and [...] I will talk to the insurance [...], and they have to replace that wheel or that suitcase!" [Covers the face with his hands] [...] People are raised like that [in Japan], but not here. What will I do with another suitcase; I tear off the wheel and put another one. But [...] they don't accept that, it's their education. It's extreme. Hopefully, we will never reach that.

Kaede Itokazu, who returned to Santa Cruz after many years in Japan, also underlines the advantages of living in urban Bolivia with the example that she has access to fresh vegetables, unlike in a Japanese city, and that she has much more time for her friends. She enjoys a high standard of living in Santa Cruz – admittedly, thanks to her savings in Japanese currency. "To live well in Japan is difficult for us. But in Bolivia, it's possible. With the pension we receive from Japan, we can live well here in Bolivia." After all, she has returned because Bolivia is her homeland, she says firmly.

Conclusion

Santa Cruz does not have a Nikkei neighbourhood, but descendants regard the existence of a *comunidad japonesa*, characterised by distinctive "Japanese values," as natural. Despite the discourse on the group-oriented and harmonious

The daily creation of ethnic boundaries 109

Japanese, social cohesion is not an automatic outcome but is ensured by regular interactions and specific norms. They are enforced by social pressure, for example, gossip, that nevertheless become less effective in a city where contact with other Nikkei can easily be avoided.

While many Nikkei present interaction with non-Nikkei as positive, it also bears the risk of losing "Japanese values" and eventually their status as a successful minority. Hence the importance of an institution like the Japanese school, where children learn Japanese norms and values rather than Japanese language. Many Nikkei also consider consumption as a risk for the maintenance of "Japanese values." Nevertheless, they seldom renounce middle-class amenities, also with the reference to increasing crime rates.

Hence, such discourses and practices are not without contradictions. The wish for interaction with non-Nikkei society contrasts with the attempt to distinguish themselves from the same society. One example in point is intermarriage with non-Nikkei: many parents argue that marrying another Nikkei is equivalent to harmony while presenting exogamy as positive sign of integration into *cruceño* society. At work, many Nikkei propose to guide their non-Nikkei employees in a paternalist attitude, while implicating that becoming too similar is neither possible nor desirable.

Finally, also their relation with Japan becomes increasingly ambivalent. Descendants often feel and are categorised as foreigners in Japan. Especially the *dekasegi* experience has led to a certain estrangement. Even in Bolivia, they increasingly claim to be different from the Japanese, adopting specific "positive" Bolivian habits and declaring their identification as Bolivians.

Notes

1 5S refers to a workplace organisation method based on *seiri, seiton, seisō, seiketsu* and *shitsuke*, which can be translated as "sorting unnecessary items out," "making workflow smooth," "keeping everything clean and safe," "standardising the best practices" and "training regularly" (Gapp et al. 2008).

2 Centro Tecnológico Agropecuario en Bolivia: a small agricultural technology institute administered by the two cooperatives.

3 A well-known lowland dish with rice, dried meat, chicken or duck, fried egg and plantain.

4 Among Nikkei, one seldom hears about divorce and children born out of wedlock in a country where seven out of ten marriages are divorced and where unwed mothers are common (Zapana 2014). Nevertheless, children born out of wedlock are seldom in Japan and suffer from stigmatisation and legal discrimination. At the same time, divorce was very common in the 19th century, a fact that is mostly forgotten in contemporary Japan where divorce rates are now comparable to Western Europe after an all-time low in the middle of the 20th century (Fuess 2004; Hertog 2009).

5 Since public schools are generally of low quality, those who can afford the high tuition fees send their children to private schools. Colegio Cambridge, the most expensive school in Santa Cruz, costs around 2,600 bolivianos per month. The minimum salary in Bolivia was 2,122 bolivianos in 2019 (Instituto Nacional de Estadística [2019]).

6 The *nihongogakkō* for children must not be confused with Japanese evening classes for adults ("*cursos de difusión*") at Centro Social and Sociedad Japonesa.

7 Several videos of Carlos Kasuga's talks can be found on youtube.com.

5 Dynamics of inclusion and exclusion in the *comunidad japonesa*

Via ANBJ's secretary, I had managed to obtain some phone numbers of pre-war Nikkei in Santa Cruz. One of them was reluctant to be interviewed but eventually said that her mother would be delighted to talk to me. I had already heard of Camila Nishioka, an association leader from Guayaramerín in Bolivian Amazonia, and I was lucky that she had just arrived in Santa Cruz for medical treatment.

It is a sunny morning in March. I ring at the door of a single-family house in the northern part of the city. Somebody, maybe an *empleada* (domestic worker), leads me into the front room, serves me some tea and lets me alone for the next half an hour. I listen to the singing birds outside, look at the cake models in a vitrine – this seems to be the daughter's business – and flip time and again through the cake catalogue, a folder made from pictures pasted on paper sheets. I ask myself if I would ever buy a cake with grey sugar icing and wonder if something more will happen this morning. Suddenly, a slim woman, clothed in a long skirt, runs in. Radiating energy, Camila sits down and straightforwardly talks to me about Japanese migration to Guayaramerín, bitterly and extensively complaining that the pre-war Nikkei have almost not received any help from Japan, be it scholarships, medical equipment or land. Camila is the daughter of Nicolás Suárez' Japanese cook and his non-Nikkei wife – Nicolás Suárez was a "rubber baron" who installed his company's headquarters in the village of Cachuela Esperanza near Guayaramerín. As Camila discovered after having his diary translated, her father had come to Latin America because he wanted to see the Southern Cross. She only knows some basic phrases in Japanese because the family language was Spanish, but she has travelled to Japan to visit her children. Camila herself studied in La Paz and found an administration job in her hometown, apart from engaging in different social causes. With more than 70 years, she is a well-known figure in Guayaramerín.

Like in the case of Camila's father, pre-war descendants' ancestors were mostly single males who migrated, for example, to the towns of Riberalta, Guayaramerín and Cobija and often founded families with non-Nikkei women. Not all of their grandchildren and great-grandchildren are nowadays aware of their Japanese ancestry and many descendants have not achieved upward social mobility: being a peasant in the Amazonian rainforests has been much less rewarding than in the surroundings of Santa Cruz. Northern Beni is more than 900 km and 1,500 km

DOI: 10.4324/9781003228295-5

Inclusion and exclusion in comunidad japonesa   111

away from the urban centres of La Paz and Santa Cruz, respectively, and is difficult to reach during the rainy season. Basic services often lack, making the region
economically unattractive. In the 1980s and 1990s, higher education was practically non-existent and inhabitants could seldom afford to send their children to
Santa Cruz or other cities to study.

Camila Nishioka vividly recalls the 100th anniversary of Japanese immigration as a motivation for her to improve living conditions in Guayaramerín with
the help of her Japanese ancestry. Back in 1999, she was dreaming of eradicating malaria – a disease unknown in present-day Santa Cruz – or of a library for
descendants and non-descendants alike. However, she did not obtain the financial
means neither from Japan nor from post-war Nikkei; and she concludes with bitter-
ness: "If [post-war descendants] want a hospital, they get a hospital!" For pre-war
descendants, even the opportunities to migrate to Japan are limited. Scholarships
for Japanese descendants are not of much use to them. They are generally not
eligible: nor have many in Beni and Pando had the opportunity to study Japanese,
nor may they be able to prove Japanese descent. Some cannot spend even modest
sums on *trámites* for *dekasegi*. As Camila remembers, many prospective migrants
became disappointed: "Not even 25% of all those who wanted to go could do so.
There is a boy who has sold his house once and his motorcycle twice, who drove
a taxi and didn't get the visa."

As a result, the younger generations have lost interest in Japan. Most Nikkei
association members are not able or willing to pay the modest membership fee.
This makes it difficult for Camila, president of the local association, to find a
suitable successor with the necessary cultural knowledge. She regrets that the
younger generations do not possess any idea of how to behave with Japanese visitors. It is difficult to stop Camila, but at the end of the interview, she once again
expresses her gratitude that I am interested in the pre-war Nikkei's fate. Finally,
she invites me to Guayaramerín, explaining that once I am there, I just have to tell
somebody on one of the ubiquitous motorcycles who I am looking for in order to
be taken to her house.

As the anecdote demonstrates, the binary distinction between "Japanese" and
"non-Japanese" has been continuously challenged in the diaspora. Hence, also
the *comunidad japonesa* is marked by tensions between a supposed homogeneity and a growing heterogeneity in ethnic, cultural and social terms. As a result,
opinions differ on what it means to be a "legitimate" Japanese descendant. The
gap between cultural meaning and ethnic identity (Eriksen 2013: 293) is the topic
of this chapter.

"Small village, big hell" – Heterogeneous
identifications among post-war Nikkei

Although Nikkei association leaders may try to present descendants as a united
group, individual post-war Nikkei's attitudes towards taking part or not in the
comunidad japonesa vary to a high degree. Notably, the urban setting makes different individual orientations possible. Whereas an inhabitant of Colonia Okinawa

112   *Inclusion and exclusion in* comunidad japonesa

or San Juan may be subject to social control to a comparatively large degree, a broad range of alternatives exists in the city: one may find work in different contexts and make friends of various ethnic origins. The confrontation with other models of life may mean self-reflection and the questioning of norms, possibly leading to increasingly dynamic ethnic identifications (Pardo and Prato 2012). This means that the *comunidad*'s standards of conduct may be less relevant for individual Nikkei and that its social sanctions become less effective.

However, even though interview partners sometimes contrast descendants in rural and urban areas, it is difficult to rigidly separate them since many commute on a regular basis between both places. Already around one-third of all Nikkei in Santa Cruz Department live in the capital, but the *colonias* play an important role as a visible symbol of Japanese history: over time, they have become a kind of nostalgic homeland (Creighton 2010: 147f.). They are frequently idealised as an idyllic place where life is comfortable and relaxed, where one has sufficient time for friends and where children can play outside without any security concerns.

Cultural differences between Nikkei in the city and the countryside, often framed as "more Japanese" and "less Japanese," are seldom explicitly addressed. While many descendants regard the urban Nikkei's lifestyle to be less authentic, they describe especially San Juan as united and "just like Japan." Some descendants claim that the *colonias'* Nikkei inhabitants have preserved the Issei's "Japanese spirit," they speak better Japanese and perhaps even *uchināguchi*. Thus, several Nikkei put forward that a researcher should definitely do research in the *colonias*, whereas the urban setting was presented as a potential threat to ethnic continuity. Sansei Ryoichi Sunagawa from Colonia Okinawa explains:

> The differences are the morals or the Japanese ethics [...], but there [in Colonia Okinawa], you learn the culture, everything they teach you at school in [Colonia] Okinawa [...]. Therefore, people [in Colonia Okinawa] know more, like *sanshin, eisā* [...]. But not here [in Santa Cruz], they don't know that unless maybe you enter *eisā*. But the people who are born here [in Santa Cruz], I see them more as Bolivians, like the way they behave [...], like their way of greeting or the respect towards the elderly, everything that's part of ethics and morals.

Whereas they recognise the *colonias'* claim to be more traditional, Nikkei living in the city do not necessarily see the *colonias* in a positive light, claiming that other characteristics are more important. Often, they frame the city and the countryside as "*abierto*" and "*cerrado*," respectively. Literally, this means "open" and "closed," but the terms are synonymous with "modern," "progressive" and "cosmopolitan" on the one hand and with "conservative," "reserved" and even "backward" on the other hand. According to many Nikkei in Santa Cruz, the *colonias'* inhabitants are unrefined, male chauvinist and fond of gossiping; they do not possess the same intellectual scope as city dwellers. Furthermore, urban Nikkei criticise the lack of possibilities for individual enterprise and leisure time activities in the *colonias*; assuring that hunting and fishing are the inhabitants'

Inclusion and exclusion in comunidad japonesa   113

exclusive pastimes. One non-Nikkei *paceña*, while shaking her head in disapproval, remarked that Nikkei in the countryside chew coca and drink like indigenous *campesinos* at the bottom of the social and ethnic hierarchy: she meant that they may possess economic capital, but definitively do not behave according to middle-class norms.

The topic of "being open" also emerged when urban Nisei and Sansei compared their individual attitudes with other descendants in the city, notably the Issei. Many consider themselves "the exception" and claim to be more "integrated" than other descendants. They were often critical of certain aspects of the *comunidad japonesa* but did take part in some activities and cultivated individual friendships. Nisei Kaede Itokazu explains: "Bolivians are more open, so I don't like to be with [Nikkei] in a group [...]. Because if you're all the time only with Japanese, what should that be for? [...] There would be no sense to live in Bolivia."

Whereas Kaede distances herself from the *comunidad japonesa* for specific reasons, she still identifies as Japanese descendant and as Bolivian. Mai Amuro identifies as descendant as well, but first as a social scientist, feminist and Bolivian. As her case illustrates, the engagement in the *comunidad* can also vary over time. Born and raised in Santa Cruz as daughter of a Centro Social president, she participated in activities as a child and adolescent but distanced herself as an adult from the *comunidad*. She and her Nikkei husband decided to send their children to Japanese school shortly before I met her for the first time in 2013, although, she explained, that decision was taken under family pressure. In this way, she came in contact with other Nikkei parents. Nevertheless, she is clear that she prefers not to socialise with descendants. Instead, Mai thinks that self-realisation is easier outside the *comunidad*. She rejects many of its unwritten rules that stand in conflict with her individual attitudes: "Being inside means a big commitment. Being outside, one sometimes would like to take part, but one can be free [...]. And when I analyse this, being inside means playing according to their rules and these rules are sometimes very strict."

These cases also show that many urban descendants appreciate having an individual choice regarding their participation in the *comunidad*. While both Mai and Kaede present themselves as "exception" and "different," their statements reflect what Lie (2001: 165) notes about social norms in Japan: many Japanese express difficulties to conform to strong social norms when saying that they are "atypical" Japanese. While Kaede and Mai consider themselves Nikkei and are considered Nikkei by others, they prefer to socialise with descendants only selectively: a gradual participation in Nikkei networks is possible, at least in the urban environment.

Some Nikkei, however, have almost completely lost touch with the *comunidad*, like Tsuyoshi Kato, born in San Juan. It was remarkable that almost no other interview partners had ever heard about this university lecturer. Tsuyoshi does not want to be part of Nikkei networks. He regards the *comunidad* as restrictive, controlling and too conservative, and during the interview, he several times used the saying "*¡Pueblo chico, infierno grande!*" [small village, big hell]. He prefers to socialise with non-Nikkei, but still identifies as descendant and emphasises that he is as fluent in Spanish as in Japanese.

Some descendants, moreover, do not identify as Nikkei at all. Yuriko Uehara, of both pre- and post-war origin and in her early thirties, has never had much contact with other descendants and does not speak Japanese. She remembers how she took part in *seijinshiki* [coming of age] celebration more than ten years ago since her parents are affiliated to Centro Social. For her, it was an awkward moment: she did not feel any connection to the participating Nikkei she considers "too closed." It is clear to her that she is a *camba* who happens to be the daughter and granddaughter of migrants.

Finally, some descendants have decided not to engage too much with other Nikkei for socioeconomic reasons. It is striking that one seldom hears about descendants who are financially less well-off. Indeed, compared to Brazil or Peru, where descendants are more numerous and more time has passed since the Issei's arrival, Bolivia's post-war Nikkei community is socioeconomically more homogeneous in both the city and the countryside. Although not everybody went to Japan for *dekasegi* and although only farmers directly received funds from JICA, most Nikkei in Santa Cruz live in affluent neighbourhoods within the Fourth Ring Road, in the north and in the gated communities on the other side of the Piraí River, according to data Centro Social has collected on its members' place of residence (Figure 5.1).

Figure 5.1 Place of residence of the members of Centro Social. The broad ring corresponds to the Third Ring Road.

Inclusion and exclusion in comunidad japonesa   115

However, these data exclude non-members and some Nikkei might not become affiliated because of financial difficulties. Although I doubt that any post-war Nikkei suffer from extreme poverty, socioeconomic diversity does exist and not everybody can afford an expensive car or a spacious house. To give the reader an idea, one Nikkei, once owner of a successful business, lost much money because of bad investments, another one was struck by illness and some farmers are indebted because of loans. In such a case, one may move to Japan for *dekasegi*. Family networks can soften hardships as well, as Mai Amuro explains with the example of her husband who helps a relative after bankruptcy. Friends and family may give support out of solidarity; but according to Mai, if somebody is not able to comply with the high demands, "it also means shame, the shame of the one who is disgraced, so you must help this person in order to avoid gossip." Those who are not able to live up to the standard often feel embarrassed because they consider it an individual failure. Consequently, as one interview partner explained, she had withdrawn from Centro Social in order to save money, but also because of gossip. In other words, a "good Nikkei" should be well-off; those who are less successful in socioeconomic terms are marginalised, despite the supposed solidarity of the *comunidad*.

For non-Nikkei Bolivians, prosperity seems to coincide with ethnic and racial features: the perception prevails that everybody with a Japanese face is wealthy, as Sumiko Aoyama observes, a post-war descendant in her thirties who has grown up in the *colonia*. She receives me in the small house where she lives with her family-in-law – but still in the expensive Equipetrol neighbourhood. Sumiko herself does not have much contact with other Nikkei in the city, and she states that she does not care for money, symbolic capital or a professional career.

> People think that because I've a Japanese face I throw away my money just like that. But I'm not like that because I don't even have money to throw away. But the Japanese descendants [...], when they have to do a *trámite*, they throw away their money like that to facilitate the process. Therefore, when we buy things, something without a fixed price, they ask for an exorbitant sum.

Sumiko considers herself smart and quick-witted compared to the average Nikkei since she is able to bargain with market sellers and taxi drivers. While she admits that she cannot compete with other Nikkei in socioeconomic terms, she does not discredit other Nikkei's prosperity, but she questions the importance of wealth. She still identifies as a Japanese descendant, but she emphasises that she possesses other and perhaps more important qualities to reach her goals.

Does Japanese face mean Japanese language? – Language as an ethnic marker

The Japanese language has always served as a marker of Japanese-ness – in contrast, non-Japanese are seldom supposed to speak it. Whereas the unequal

116 *Inclusion and exclusion in* comunidad japonesa

language competencies foster dynamics of exclusion, the meaning of Japanese language skills is increasingly contested among post-war Nikkei, especially among later generations.

Many post-war Nikkei are proud that they are fluent in Japanese – they claim that they are "more Japanese" compared to pre-war migrants in Bolivian Amazonia or neighbouring countries. Nisei Keisuke Sakata from San Juan resumes: "Japanese face – Japanese language; that should be normal." For him, language is directly connected to a specific ethnic identity and even to Japanese racial features. Sansei Ryoichi Sunagawa from Colonia Okinawa claims that he learned Spanish only after entering school. For Ryoichi, speaking Japanese is an essential feature of being Nikkei. In the future, he wants to use his skills to create business contacts. He feels privileged to speak Japanese but regrets that not everybody sees it this way.

It is important to differentiate between written and oral skills. Although most Nisei and Sansei may be able to communicate in colloquial Japanese, few can write it correctly, even if they have lived in Japan. Although any language has different levels of formality and complexity, written Japanese with its three writing systems poses specific difficulties: one needs constant repetition in daily life to retain *kanji* characters at least passively. Children in Santa Cruz' Japanese school are not supposed to write fluently in all three systems: since *hiragana* and *katakana* or even *rōmaji* [Japanese written in Latin letters] are sufficient for informal use, Nisei and Sansei may simply know the most emblematic *kanji*. Two Nisei remembered from their childhood that they learned *kanji* only when voluntarily reading manga and corresponding with pen pals in Japan. Another Nisei admitted to repeating the *kanji* of his own name when renewing his Japanese passport: not being able to properly sign the document would be shameful to him. In Nikkei-owned companies like the cooperatives, written Japanese is seldom needed and may be delegated to one employee with the necessary skills. As a result, Nisei lawyer Masutaro Higaonna calls his language skills with some understatement "deficient Japanese": "I have, for example, about 5% of grammar. And the Japanese writing has about 8,000 letters [...]. Of the 8,000, I don't reach even 5% [he takes out his pocket calculator]. 450. Maybe not even that."

Since most Nisei and especially Sansei are illiterate in *kanji*, they are unable to access much information that is available only in Japanese. In contrast to La Paz, where a team composed mostly by Nisei organised a bilingual publication for Sociedad Japonesa's 90th anniversary, in Santa Cruz Department, the Issei dominated the writing process for the last books in the first years of the millennium. That the books are in Japanese means the exclusion of younger generations, Masutaro criticises: "Because there are Japanese who came with their studies completed, who finished high school in Japan [...]. [The books] are for this social group [...]. That means, in other words, we're discriminated."

There is also a consensus that oral language skills have been decreasing, even in the *colonias*. Fewer children than before pass the highest level of the standardised Japanese Language Proficiency Test (JLPT). JICA's vice-director Ichiro Ninomiya has noticed as well that few Nikkei apply for the translator jobs the

Inclusion and exclusion in comunidad japonesa   117

organisation offers, be it because their language skills are decreasing or because the job is not attractive compared to other posts. Especially Nikkei in the city are not only considered "less Japanese" in general, but also less proficient speakers. Schools in Santa Cruz and La Paz only offer classes on Saturdays and sometimes during summer holidays, and urban Sansei generally communicate in Spanish with each other. Some descendants claim that women in the *colonias* speak better Japanese than men, and I could witness several informal *seinenkai* meetings in San Juan where Japanese was used almost exclusively. Moreover, children in Japanese-Bolivian schools in Okinawa I, II and San Juan can attend Japanese classes every afternoon. Nevertheless, even San Juan's *seinenkai* members regretted that children and adolescents would prefer to speak *castellano* [Spanish] nowadays.

However, the situation is diverse: some children communicate in Spanish with their parents but in Japanese with their grandparents who live in the same household; others have lived in Japan. Still, more and more children have their first contact with Japanese language in class – but not all children enter Japanese school. Therefore, they may have difficulties in communicating with elderly relatives fluent only in Japanese. For Ryoichi Sunagawa, economic change, in combination with interethnic contact, is an essential factor for the loss of Japanese language among the younger generation. Whereas his Issei grandfather spoke only *uchināguchi*, his father went for *dekasegi* to Japan and knew both *uchināguchi* and Japanese.

My father's generation [...] lived in those times when there was nothing. They had just cut the jungle to build houses without electricity, without water, without anything. There was hardly any school, there was no possibility to have a good Japanese education. And people younger than me hardly speak any Japanese again [...]. If you have a Bolivian wife or husband, there is less necessity to learn Japanese. If you live here, you don't need it [...]. Life has become better, there is more money, everything is easier. Therefore, parents tend to have an *empleada*, and kids grow up with the *empleada*. And therefore, they learn Spanish naturally and aren't used to speak Japanese [...]. We should be poor again.

Ryoichi's friend Natsuyo Makishi who is also from Colonia Okinawa holds a similar opinion. She has attended several Pan-American Nikkei meetings and experienced that Bolivian Nikkei still speak Japanese comparatively well. Natsuyo remembers how her father went to Miami to a Nikkei sports meeting, discovering that everything was in English: "Don't you find that strange? [laughs] [...] That can't be. Isn't it an anniversary of the Japanese?" However, language skills also decrease in Bolivia, she regrets: "It's our [...] strength and it shouldn't be lost, but obviously, it is getting lost." For Ryoichi and Natsuyo, losing Japanese language means losing identity since language proficiency would mean understanding Japanese culture. It is beyond the scope of this book to discuss if language skills are a prerequisite to understand cultural practices, but it is obvious that they help to access information on Japan.

118 *Inclusion and exclusion in* comunidad japonesa

According to Ryoichi and Natsuyo, not only prosperity and increased contact with non-Nikkei was harmful to Nikkei children's language proficiency, but especially Nikkei/non-Nikkei marriages. Several descendants like Ryoichi argue that children of such couples do not speak Japanese well; thereby, they implicitly reject such marriages. Following Ryoichi's argument, descendant children who do not speak their ancestors' language would be "less Japanese." Indeed, several post-war descendants feel ashamed since they are not as proficient as they want to be, feeling that a "good Japanese" would know the language. However, some Nikkei also relativise that if the mother – who is supposed to spend more time with her offspring than the father – speaks Japanese, children will maintain the language. As an example, a Japanese teacher mentioned the children of Japanese speaker and non-Nikkei Micaela Tejada and her Nikkei husband.

Other Nikkei do not attach the same meaning to language. It might be no coincidence that Ryoichi and Natsuyo who have grown up in the *colonia* put such an emphasis on the Japanese language – in the city, Spanish is becoming the Sansei's exclusive means of communication. Japanese language proficiency is increasingly associated with individual attitudes. For those Nikkei who consciously speak Spanish to their children, understanding Japanese culture is not necessarily related to language. Especially descendants who do not feel comfortable with Japanese language may argue that living specific "Japanese values" and culture is much more important for Nikkei identity. Moreover, these descendants frequently claim to be Bolivians of Japanese ancestry and not Japanese – considering this a virtue. Consequently, the Pan-American Nikkei events described in Chapter 7 focus more on Spanish, Portuguese or English to unite mainly younger Nikkei from different countries.

While the necessity to speak Japanese in daily life decreases, Japanese language proficiency continues to be symbolically important. Some Bolivian Nikkei without a high level of Japanese have held important positions in Bolivian Nikkei associations, but differences in fluency generally establish a kind of hierarchy between the "less Japanese" descendants and the "more Japanese" descendants who enjoy a higher legitimacy. Also, Michelle Nomura and her mother Aurora Nakashima have experienced subtle exclusion because of their low level of language proficiency. Being members of Centro Social, they are pre-war descendants who arrived from a neighbouring country in the 1990s. They do not consider themselves Japanese but clearly identify as descendants and Latin Americans while consciously maintaining some cultural practices. Aurora, now over 70 years old, remembers that at her arrival, she "suffered" because she did not speak any Japanese; "they looked at me with condescension" (*"me miraban feo"*). She learned some basic Japanese expressions only in Santa Cruz. Her daughter Michelle, in her forties, has had similar experiences, criticising post-war Nikkei as "too closed":

> I understand more or less what they say, but I can't really express myself and when they know that you don't speak *nihongo* [Japanese], they discriminate against you. I understand, but I feign not to understand [laughs]. Once in my

Inclusion and exclusion in comunidad japonesa 119

presence, some people [...] were talking, like "There are those who don't speak *nihongo*, they are useless." They knew who I was and I became so angry, I wanted to tell them that I don't speak it but I understand [...]. If you don't speak Japanese, you're like inferior or something [...]. Even if they are born in Bolivia, they identify more as Japanese than as Bolivians.

In the Spanish-language interview, Michelle used the words *nihongo* [Japanese language] as well as *nihon* [Japan]. Fixed expressions children learn at school at the latest include *ohayō (gozaimasu)* [good morning] and *gomen (nasai)* [sorry]. Specific concepts may be difficult to grasp in Spanish, such as *gochisōsama (deshita)* [said after finishing one's meal], *tadaima* [I'm back home] or *okaeri (nasai)* [welcome home]. In addition, one hears *onegai (shimasu)* [please], *mottainai* [wasteful, more than one deserves], *shitsureishimasu* [said when entering a room belonging to somebody else], *otsukaresama (deshita)* [said to one's colleagues after finishing that day's task], *ganbatte* [hold on, go for it] or *enryo* [diffidence, restraint, reserve]. Other terms include specific dishes and ingredients, sometimes without any equivalent in Spanish, like *ocha* [tea], *gohan* [rice], *shōyu* [soy sauce] and *onigiri* [rice balls]. *Ohashi* [chopsticks] and *butsudan* [Buddhist ancestor shrine] are related to Japanese culture as well. Japanese terms are also prominent when addressing somebody or talking about family relationships, like *obāchan/obāsan* [grandmother or senior woman] and *ojīchan/ojīsan* [grandfather or senior man], but also *nēnē* [older sister, also used symbolically].[1]

Different levels of proficiency, however, may disappear in the long term, with Spanish becoming the exclusive medium of communication. Nevertheless, even among those who only speak Spanish, specific words are maintained as signal words to resist "bolivianisation."

Issei, Nisei, Sansei – The negotiation of tensions along generational lines

As already indicated, identifying or being identified as member of a specific generation has been essential in the Japanese diaspora, also in Bolivia. The "Japanese value" of filial piety is especially celebrated in *keirōkai* [Respect for the Aged Festival] in September. Both Centro Social and Okinawa Kenjinkai organise an event with dance, speeches, food and a gift for each of the senior attendees. The regular Day Service activities for the elderly, too, originate in this idea of gratefulness as opposed to the supposedly "Bolivian-style" individualism and egoism.

However, conflicts have time and again emerged over the hierarchy between Issei as a superior elder (*senpai*) and Nisei as younger obeying *kōhai*. The Issei are sometimes referred to as "*japoneses netos* [true Japanese]" or "*japoneses nacidos en Japón* [Japanese born in Japan]". Nevertheless, the term "generation" is not clearly defined and often refers more to experiences than to biological succession. In most cases, "Issei" stands for those who arrived in Bolivia in the 1950s as young adults. But already those who came as children and mostly grew up in Bolivia tend to position themselves between the first and the second generation. "Issei"

120 *Inclusion and exclusion in* comunidad japonesa

generally does not include recent Japanese migrants, either, nor does it commonly refer to children born during their parents' *dekasegi* stay. It is also unclear if the child of an Issei and a Nisei counts as the second or third generation. Instead, "Nisei" normally refers to the age range somewhere between 40 and 60 whereas being identified as "Sansei" usually means that somebody is a young adult.

Among descendants in the Americas, tensions between generations have been persistent. Conflicts are generally framed as resulting from differences between a closed, conservative first generation and a flexible, relaxed, "tropicalised" second generation. Many Issei have been considering their children and grandchildren to be selfish, egoistic, careless, not Japanese enough and therefore potentially untrustworthy. Differences between a wartime generation and those grown up under more comfortable socioeconomic circumstances might increase these tensions (Sugimoto 1997: 65ff.). These different attitudes may lead to conflicts as Amemiya (2001) exemplifies for the two Bolivian *colonias*: many Issei considered the younger generations to be imprudent for expanding their cultivations with borrowed money, whereas junior Issei and Nisei thought that making debts was a part of the game. Differences of opinion became also evident regarding the general attitude towards life since many Issei insisted on hard physical work in the fields. The Nisei rather believed that they should enjoy leisure time already before they are retired while rejecting the idea to work alongside their non-Nikkei workers (ibid.).

The Japanese state, too, sees Japanese-ness being lost over time in the diaspora: the Nisei are regarded as culturally and ethnically closer to the Japanese than the Sansei, enjoying better visa conditions (Takenaka 2009a: 264f.). In many states, a proof that one's mother or even grandfather was a national is sufficient to apply for a passport, but Japan sets a time window to register children: descendants willing to naturalise as adults must fulfil the same criteria as other foreigners. Similarly, JICA's exchanges for Nikkei generally only include Nisei and Sansei (JICA 2018b, 2018c). According to the Japanese state, "blood" is essential to define somebody as Nikkei, but it is not enough to maintain Japanese-ness in the diaspora over time (Figure 5.2).

While Nisei and Sansei do recognise that to be "tropicalised," they do not consider this a flaw. Instead, they claim that the Issei are too inflexible and strict, they do not know Bolivia enough and try to comply with old-fashioned Japanese norms. One frequent point of critique is that the Issei are "cold." Daiki Kaneshiro concludes that the Nikkei should be open to adopt "positive" Bolivian behaviours, since "in the end, you have to learn these things and mix them and take the good ones." Being considered "in between" means a virtue and an advantage in life, says Nataly Yonamine full of self-confidence: "I know the good and the bad things of both [...]. [Therefore], if I want to be the best person, be that. I feel good because I know I can survive in Japan and everywhere".

Although they recognised that times are changing, some Nisei report that family relations remain hierarchical, making it difficult for Nisei and Sansei to assert themselves. The older ones often decide and the younger ones are supposed to obey and accept norms without discussion. Many younger descendants, even if they are objectively right, are reluctant to confront the Issei who may

Inclusion and exclusion in comunidad japonesa   121

Figure 5.2 Keirōkai (Respect for the Aged Festival) in Centro Social Japonés.

consider this a lack of respect. Kentsu Hanashiro, a Nisei in his 30s, gives an example:

> My father is 75 years old. There is much difference in age. It's another way of thinking, it's quite old [...]. He always wants to be the one who takes the decision. I have to go to inform him what I want to do and he will allow it [...]. For example in my business, I ask him if I can improve something: "Today I want to paint," [and he says:] "No, how can you do that?!" There is a discussion [...]. I want to have everything beautiful. [And he says:] "No, that means spending money. You won't have that money [for other expenses]." But I as an entrepreneur, I have another opinion: it's an investment, not an expense.

Nevertheless, Creighton (2010: 148f.) argues that when the Issei deplore the decline of filial piety, it does not necessarily mean that this value would be typically Japanese but that they demand a behaviour convenient to themselves.

At the same time, many emphasised during interviews how much they were indebted to the Issei, presenting the first generation as a role model. The younger Nikkei should learn from the elderly and listen to their advice, they explained. Despite criticism of the Issei, many Nisei and Sansei declare that it is essential to respect the elderly, justifying this with the former having sacrificed themselves for their children's upward social mobility.

"Okinawans are more Bolivian" – Constructing cultural and ethnic differences to mainland Nikkei

Throughout the Japanese diaspora, Okinawan descendants have been regarded as "different," as "less Japanese" or even as "non-Japanese." While national and

122 *Inclusion and exclusion in* comunidad japonesa

ethnic identities have often overlapped in the Japanese case, many Okinawans question this assumption, regarding themselves as culturally and/or ethnically different. In some instances, Okinawans have been discriminated against in the diaspora. Suzuki (2006), however, argues that the lack of contact with mainland immigrants enabled descendants in Bolivia to maintain an Okinawan cultural identity without their belonging to Japan being questioned.

In Santa Cruz, Okinawan descendants dominate numerically – no census exists, but about two-thirds of all Centro Social members are Okinawan Nikkei. One reason for this dominance may be that Okinawan descendants preferred to settle in Santa Cruz, whereas those from San Juan have tended to move to La Paz. Moreover, Colonia Okinawa is located closer to the city; as a result, inhabitants can easily commute.

When asked about differences between Okinawans and other Nikkei, interview partners from both parts came up with countless yet similar examples. They generally attributed differences to climate as well as to Okinawa's historical relations with the Chinese empire. Okinawan Nikkei are described as cheerful, direct, relaxed, hospitable, flexible, extroverted and funny, but also as unrefined and slow. Some descendants even observe physiognomic differences, stating that Okinawans have differently shaped eyes, more body hair, and a darker skin, and are shorter or more corpulent than other Nikkei. Travel agency owner Daiki Kaneshiro, he himself of Okinawan origin, says laughingly that Okinawan descendants love to organise Okinawa-related events: "The Okinawan makes much noise!" At the same time, Okinawan Nikkei are described as extremely solidary and proud. As Daiki says, all these characteristics are part of the "Okinawan spirit" that he observes even abroad:

> I have seen it many times here in the office. [An Okinawan comes,] he meets somebody and asks: "Where are you from? Ah, from Okinawa?" They start talking as if they would have known each other for their whole life. And they have just met. "And what part of Okinawa are you from?" […] That's very common, that's normal. It's part of the Okinawan spirit. […] The Okinawan always clings to other Okinawans. So, when he sees that somebody is from Okinawa and worse from his town … it's like they were friends or brothers. He invites him to lunch, to dinner, he takes him out for sightseeing…

According to interview partners, this "Okinawan spirit" is prominent in the diaspora as well. Reiko Yohena works at ABJ San Juan as an Okinawan Nikkei. While she declares not to have many friends in San Juan, she observes significant cultural differences between both *colonias*.

> There is a word in Okinawa: *nan kuru naisa* […]. It means that things will happen anyway, everything can be arranged, everything is possible. In San Juan, this word doesn't exist. In San Juan, they plan, they organise, they do things with anticipation [laughs][…]. In Okinawa, there exists another word: *ichariba chōdē*. You meet each other and you're already brothers and sisters,

Inclusion and exclusion in comunidad japonesa   123

although you don't know each other. In San Juan, that [expression] doesn't exist, either. They are very reserved, more conservative, more prudent. But that doesn't mean that they are bad people. Once you are friends with them, they are very good people.

Okinawan Nikkei implicitly or explicitly contrast themselves with mainland Nikkei, or *naichi* as Okinawans sometimes call them, who are considered to be formal, closed, conservative, reserved, traditional, hierarchical, shy, organised, ambitious and always on time. Some Okinawan Nikkei consider San Juan to be too closed even to newcomers from the mainland who would, therefore, prefer to move to Colonia Okinawa. Akira Tokashiki, who arrived to Colonia Okinawa as a child, mentioned wedding celebrations:

A wedding in San Juan is very reserved. The invited ones have their designated seat [...] and until the greeting ceremony hasn't finished, you can't even have the drop of a drink, and also [...] only those who received an invitation can come [...]. Instead, in [Colonia] Okinawa, they invite the whole family, so they bring their kids, and the kids are running around, the young people bring drinks and start drinking [laughs]. The food comes, and they start eating. But in San Juan, you have to finish the ceremony, then the toast, then they start drinking and eating [...]. That's the difference because they are more conservative in San Juan. Instead, in [Colonia] Okinawa, it may be a little disorganised.

While mainland Nikkei are said to be "more authentic Japanese," Okinawans are regarded as "bolivianised." By way of illustration, most Nikkei claim that mainland descendants are more fluent in Japanese and have intermarried less with non-Nikkei. Nevertheless, many Okinawan Nikkei declare this lack of "typical Japanese" characteristics as a virtue, considering themselves as "more Latin American" due to their supposedly more relaxed attitude (Lesser 2002; Mori 2003). Ryoji Nakaima, for example, remembers that when he moved with his parents to Okinawa Prefecture as a child, he perceived little difference to Santa Cruz, since climate and mentality were almost identical; but he experienced culture shock after moving to Tōkyō later. Consequently, many Okinawan Nikkei may over communicate similarities with *cruceñas* and *cruceños* and state to have more contact with non-Nikkei, presented in this case as a clear advantage and something to be proud of. This self-consciousness was also reflected in the fact that many Okinawan Bolivian interview partners automatically supposed that my research would exclusively deal with Okinawan descendants.

Many Okinawan Nikkei declare themselves to be different from the "normal Nikkei." Some claim to belong to a different ethnic group, such as young Yoshimi Matsumura, who returned with much enthusiasm from a year-long stay in Okinawa Prefecture, clearly distancing herself from mainland Japan: "I'm not into Japanese culture." Others, like Nisei Norio Miyaguni, hold that they belong to the same ethnic and national group, but with a slightly different cultural heritage,

124   *Inclusion and exclusion in* comunidad japonesa

since "we're the same blood." Daiki Kaneshiro emphasises: "It seems that the Okinawans want to [...] separate themselves from the Japanese community. But it's not like that, it happens everywhere, also in Brazil."

In former times, relations between Okinawan Nikkei and mainland descendants used to be tense. One interview partner remembered that Okinawan Nikkei in Santa Cruz consciously communicated in *uchināguchi* to exclude other Nikkei in Centro Social gatherings. Ritsuko Hashimoto from San Juan even speaks of discrimination against co-ethnics since descendants of non-Okinawan origin could not take part in Okinawa Kenjinkai's *ekiden* long-distance relay race or its *undōkai*. Okinawan Nikkei Norio Miyaguni, too, remembers frequent quarrels between different groups of descendants from his *seinenkai* times. In the meantime, open hostilities between descendants from the two *colonias* have disappeared. Descendants mostly think that their grandparents' resentments, generally attributed to the war, are outdated. San Juan's cooperative CAISY, for example, donated money for the construction of Colonia Okinawa's association building in the 1990s. Only one Okinawan Sansei called people from San Juan arrogant – ironically, her father originates from that *colonia*. However, a certain distance remains, often called "rivalry." Okinawan Nikkei seldom visit San Juan or vice versa, although individual relationships do exist. Nevertheless, despite noting some differences, several mainland Nikkei perceived no tensions, like mainland Nikkei Minae Hara from San Juan who declares that most of her friends in the city are Okinawans, concluding that they are all Japanese descendants like herself. Keiko Taniguchi from San Juan remembers that she even learned *uchināguchi* when she came to the city in the late 1960s.

At the same time, many Okinawan descendants emphasise that they are open also to non-Okinawans, alluding to a distinct Okinawan spirit born out of a mixture of cultures. On a closer look, it is difficult for them to attract mainland Nikkei: the latter are apparently reluctant to join Okinawan activities. One example is the Ryūkyūkoku Matsuridaiko dance group. Non-Nikkei Bolivians constitute half of the group of about 30 active and 30 passive members, but no more than two people of mainland origin have joined the chapter in recent years. Instead, young adults in San Juan have chosen to perform *soranbushi* dance at association events, explaining that they themselves liked its dynamic movements and that non-Nikkei would enjoy their presentations as well.

While some Okinawan descendants insist on a different ethnic identity emphasising specific markers, observable differences in daily life become lost, one example being language. Suzuki (2006) describes that *uchināguchi*, more precisely a variety similar to the main islands' dialects, was widespread in Colonia Okinawa around the year 2000. Some of my Okinawan Bolivian interview partners proudly mentioned Japanese scientists who had studied *uchināguchi* in Bolivia. Nevertheless, I heard it on very few occasions, especially not in the city. Only the elderly and the inhabitants of Okinawa II and III are said to be fluent speakers. Some Okinawan Nikkei state that it is not possible to maintain both; therefore, they pragmatically opt for Japanese language. Except for some young adults who participate in Okinawa-related activities such as Ryūkyūkoku Matsuridaiko,

Inclusion and exclusion in comunidad japonesa 125

sanshin rehearsals and Okinawan youth meetings, many consider *uchināguchi* to be too difficult, rude and not beautiful. Changes in language use were also attributed to TV consumption: media from mainland Japan are said to influence even the recognisable Okinawan accent in standard Japanese.

However, some words from *uchināguchi* may be used symbolically, such as concepts expressing "typically Okinawan" solidarity like *yuimārū* and *ichariba chōdē* or specific terms such as *neri* for the Japanese *okura* [okra]. A large street sign with the Okinawan formula *mensōre* greets incoming visitors at the *colonia* and Okinawa Kenjinkai's activities for the elderly bear the Okinawan name "*kari-yushikai*" [happiness meeting]. At festivities, Okinawan Nikkei proudly recommend goat meat soup as an Okinawan speciality and Okinawa Soba soup is also a self-evident part of the menu. From time to time, Okinawa sumo contests are held in Colonia Okinawa, some young descendants learn classical Okinawan court dance and senior Nikkei practice Okinawan folk songs. Several Okinawan Nikkei also offered pictures with idyllic Okinawan beaches to me, urging me to visit these sites, others had decorated parts of their house with lion-like *shīsā* figures or used colourful *bingata* cloth bags, both considered to be typically Okinawan. In other words, while they become culturally similar to other Nikkei, they insist on specific symbols to underline their ethnic difference.

Since Okinawan Nikkei dominate the central association Centro Social, Okinawa-related activities are prominent in Santa Cruz. Ryūkyūkoku Matsuridaiko is a self-evident part of any Centro Social festivity, similar to karate – a martial art that originally comes from Okinawa, although globally known as "Japanese." As a result, some Okinawan descendants supposed that mainlanders felt excluded. Nevertheless, no mainland Nikkei interview partner confirmed these assumptions. Only Keiko Taniguchi remarked with a mixture of mockery and amusement that Okinawans always have to be special. She noted that Okinawan Bolivians were mingling different traditions too much and were coming up with Okinawan dances in inappropriate settings. Sansei Mayumi Iwamatsu from San Juan even envied Okinawan descendants for being more present in wider society but stated that she would not join Ryūkyūkoku Matsuridaiko dance since "it's the other *colonia's* culture." At the same time, for non-Nikkei, Okinawa and Japan are generally synonymous (Siemann 2017) – Okinawa is for most of them equivalent to Colonia Okinawa, but not to a Japanese prefecture and a formerly independent kingdom.

When I asked her for an evaluation, Japanese researcher Kozy Amemiya argued that the attachment of Okinawan Bolivians to Japan might be stronger than in Okinawa Prefecture itself: when in 1997, the prefecture discussed independence from Japan, Okinawan descendants in Bolivia generally did not agree with that idea. Until today, they do not distance themselves from the Japanese flag or the Japanese anthem. Being identified with Japan means symbolic capital in Bolivia, and as Japanese citizens, Okinawan Nikkei have also benefited from JICA's financial, material and educational support. In interviews, many descendants identified also as Japanese, referring to Japan as a prosperous country and an example for Bolivia. In short, they adopt a pragmatic attitude and under communicate differences to mainland Nikkei in such cases, for example when non-Nikkei

126 *Inclusion and exclusion in* comunidad japonesa

categorised them as "exemplary Japanese." The difference between Okinawan and mainland Nikkei is emphasised as long as it is useful.

"We didn't receive anything" – Pre-war descendants' ambivalent identifications

Okinawan Nikkei, later generations and even post-war descendants who do not speak Japanese are still considered part of the *comunidad japonesa*, although they may sometimes be regarded as "less Japanese." But as Camila's example demonstrates, post-war Nikkei categorise pre-war descendants to be basically Bolivians with some Japanese ancestry, showing the boundaries of "Nikkei."

It is entirely unclear how many pre-war descendants live in Santa Cruz. Some of them are descendants of migrants who came to Santa Cruz before the *colonias* were established; others arrived from Beni and Pando more recently. They mostly remain invisible to post-war Nikkei, with the exception of prominent public personalities or those married to post-war descendants. One of these pre-war spouses even became president of Centro Social without speaking Japanese, another became CAICO's general manager. Nevertheless, whereas many pre-war descendants acknowledge their Japanese origin, the majority does not feel Japanese and does not have an interest in joining the *comunidad japonesa*. Some young descendants attend Japanese classes for adults or try to otherwise explore their origins but consider themselves Bolivians with remote Japanese ancestry. Consequently, the terms *"japoneses," "descendientes"* and *"comunidad japonesa,"* when used by post-war Nikkei, seldom include pre-war descendants. Most post-war Nikkei think that pre-war descendants have lost everything Japanese apart from their last name or some facial features. They may express that pre-war migrants are "too bolivianised," namely irresponsible and lazy, just like non-Nikkei Bolivian lowlanders are said to be; or, in short, as "an example to avoid" (Amemiya 2001). At the same time, non-Nikkei Bolivians regard pre-war descendants, especially the later generations, practically as Bolivians.

In Riberalta, the Bolivian town with the highest number of Japanese descendants, Japanese ancestry was not relevant for a long time. The Japanese government and JICA were mostly absent (Embajada del Japón en Bolivia 2019a). With the *dekasegi* boom, a *koseki* became the entry ticket to a better future. The *dekasegi* migration changed and revived Riberalta although inequality increased, as Amemiya (2001) writes, since two years were sufficient to earn an amount equivalent to a lifetime salary in northern Beni. *Dekasegi* may have revitalised links to Japan, but it seems not to have contributed to descendants' identification with that country. Since many descendants did not succeed in obtaining the visa, they lost interest in association activities. In Bolivian Amazonia, identifying as a Japanese descendant appears to be closely associated with possible material benefits.

Pre-war Nikkei do not hold Japanese passports because their ancestors did not have the possibility to register their children on time or because they considered

Inclusion and exclusion in comunidad japonesa   127

the relation to Japan too dangerous. Whereas Japanese nationality is not a requirement to apply for membership in Nikkei associations, it facilitates trips to Japan. Since a proof of Japanese ancestry was required for a Japanese visa, they obtained economic value: in the 1990s, *koseki* were sold for around USD 2,000 each, as some interview partners remembered. Other inhabitants of the Amazonian region sought Nikkei marriage partners. A further possibility was to falsify the *koseki*: Nisei Betty Moriyama from Riberalta, now in her 70s, remembers that her brother, who had died at the age of 12, suddenly had five children on paper. Other prospective migrants discovered that somebody had already gone to Japan in their name. Such occurrences were much to the anger of pre-war association leaders like Camila Nishioka who feared that all pre-war Nikkei would be suspected to be "false." Others had problems being recognised as descendants because their last names had changed at one point of time, like the last name "Sacka," derived from "Sakaguchi" or "Sakamoto." Moreover, many documents were lost or burned in Japan during the Second World War, especially in Okinawa Prefecture (Takenaka 2009a: 269). In short, Japanese authorities eventually decided over the legitimacy of descendants' ancestry and hence over their chances for socioeconomic upward mobility.

Álvaro Taguchi, a teacher and law student from Beni's capital Trinidad and around 30 years younger than Camila, can talk for hours about the pre-war Nikkei being neglected. Álvaro, Camila and some others have tried to make a census in Beni. After this experience, he concludes that few Nikkei have achieved social mobility through *dekasegi*. Many have not finished school since they had to start working early in life. It would have been more sustainable to support their studies instead of giving them a Japanese work visa, he argues. Álvaro himself, from a middle-class background, was able to visit Japan on a scholarship. Once there, he interviewed several *dekasegi* migrants. As he told me, half disappointed and half angry, he felt injustice. But he nevertheless distances himself from his interview partners as socially different:

> They dedicated themselves to having children, to work and to waste their money [...]. But one day, they would get tired. Bolivians are lazy and easily get tired. And they don't want to come here because here, they have nothing [...]. They couldn't make use of that time and that's why they don't want to come back, they don't have where to go, they don't have a house, the family lives like before. The Japanese who has made progress is rare, because they stick together with other uneducated people and don't think like we do.

Álvaro concludes that their ethnic origin and their ancestors' merit should stand in the foreground. He does not challenge the definition of Nikkei by ancestry, but he relativises the importance of cultural knowledge and accuses post-war Nikkei and Japan of being morally wrong. According to Álvaro, descendants in Beni and Pando are economically uninteresting for the Japanese government that does not consider them "really Japanese": it is, therefore, not the pre-war descendants' fault if they lack education cultural knowledge and financial stability. Instead, post-war migrants obtained much financial and material support from Japan, he

128 *Inclusion and exclusion in* comunidad japonesa

adds; furthermore, they received land from the Bolivian state. Álvaro accuses Japan of ingratitude, since after the Second World War, the pre-war Nikkei even not only sent money to the suffering Japanese population, but also supported post-war migrants at their arrival in Bolivia. But: "The pre-war migrants were those who helped Japan, and they didn't receive anything in return. And the [post-war migrants] received everything and gave nothing back."

Similar to Álvaro, Japanese researcher Yumi Shioiri (2013: 123) observes that most Japanese migrants in Amazonia married illiterate women from lower social strata; many had to support large families and were not able to send all children to school, especially when living far from town. Except for some engaged association members like Camila and Álvaro, usually well-educated and of middle-class background, few descendants identify as descendants: Nikkei identity in Beni and Pando seems to be highly class-related.

Moreover, pre-war migrants in the Amazonian region have never formed tight-knit settlements like the post-war *colonias* with their strong institutions. The possibilities to travel to Japan were much more limited than today, and Japanese books or other media did not reach them. When I ask her what remains of Japanese culture in Pando's capital Cobija, association president Inés Oshima smiles and answers with a single word: "*Nada* [nothing]."

Thinking of her advanced age, Camila Nishioka still has some plans. She wants to compile a publication on the Japanese presence in Cachuela Esperanza, since she feels the need to record some events as long as there are living witnesses. No self-written anniversary books exist so far in Bolivian Amazonia. At the same time, she has difficulties in finding a new president for Guayaramerín's small ethnic association since descendants lack even the most basic cultural knowledge:

> It has to be somebody educated, who behaves well. When the [Japanese] princess came [for the 100th anniversary of Japanese immigration] – you know, in Japan nobody can get close to the princess, touch her, shake her hand, or, even worse, kiss her on the cheeks [...]. But sometimes, these people [from Guayaramerín] have not had a good education and don't know what to say or they do something embarrassing [...]. Our people were born and grew up in the forest, they don't know about [Japanese] customs [...]. Because one lady who wanted to be the president, when we received the princess [...], she went to the princess, shook her hand and kissed her and embraced her. I wanted to die on the spot!

The socioeconomic circumstances for pre-war descendants in Santa Cruz have been much more comfortable, but important parallels exist regarding their lack of identification as Nikkei and their low degree of organisation. A relatively well-known pre-war descendant is Carlos Wada, an artist in his 70s. He grew up in the city of Santa Cruz and describes himself as "*camba neto*" [a true *camba*]. Sitting in his atelier, he extensively remembers his immigrant fathers' stories. The journey to the Bolivian lowlands was arduous, as were the first years: tree felling, long workdays, snakes, caimans and insects as a constant annoyance

Inclusion and exclusion in comunidad japonesa   129

figure prominently in these accounts. However, his father told Carlos much less about Japan. As he remembers, only in the 1950s did some Japanese newspapers from São Paulo arrive in Santa Cruz, and before the foundation of Centro Social Japonés in 1956, joint activities were limited to informal tea parties. Carlos inherited some objects from his father that make him curious, but he acknowledges that what he knows about Japanese art and history comes from books:

> My father never mentioned his country, but maybe he taught some traditions to my older brother, his eldest son. Some words in Japanese. But to the others, he didn't teach us anything because he left early in the morning to go to work. And when we woke up and had breakfast, he was already away, and he returned at night, so we didn't have the time.

Off the record, a senior Okinawan post-war descendant told me that pre-war descendants were "too mixed with Bolivians". However, most post-war Nikkei avoid stating that children of Nikkei/non-Nikkei ancestry are "less Nikkei"; instead, they refer to a different habitus. As previously mentioned, women are regarded as carriers of culture because they are the principal caregivers according to the dominant social model. In the case of Carlos Wada and many others, the mother was not able to teach them anything about Japanese culture. Daiki Kaneshiro believes that even a prolonged *dekasegi* stay in Japan does not make a change. Of pre-war and post-war origin, he has grown up in Santa Cruz' *comunidad japonesa*. Some pre-war descendants may try to recuperate "Japanese values," insisting for example on punctuality, but in his opinion, without much effect.

> They simply didn't have the opportunity to live in an environment where father and mother were Japanese. But today, many of them are in Japan, they went to work there, and they learn many things over there. But when they come back to Bolivia, one realises that many things are very difficult to learn as an adult, if you don't learn them well as a child.[2]

Post-war Nikkei are able to define who counts as a legitimate descendant, marginalising pre-war descendants in Santa Cruz' *comunidad*. At the same time, many post-war descendants use the first migrants to demonstrate the continuing importance of Japanese migration in Bolivian history. They are likely to mention hamlets like Japón, Tokyo, Mukden[3] and Yokohama as vestiges of Japanese presence in Bolivian Amazonia. Nevertheless, it was the post-war Nikkei who organised the celebration for the 100th anniversary of Japanese migration in Santa Cruz.

Many pre-war Nikkei criticise, in turn, that they are generally not even invited to anniversaries and that Japanese officials have generally given them the cold shoulder. Nevertheless, pre-war Nikkei do not have any large organisations, strong networks or economic power to assert these claims (Amemiya 2001). Many pre-war Nikkei representatives underline the contributions of their ancestors to Bolivia's wellbeing, for example, see an essay in Santa Cruz' major newspaper *El Deber* by Pedro Shimose (2012). Still, most post-war Nikkei do

130 *Inclusion and exclusion in* comunidad japonesa

not identify with this well-known poet from Riberalta or with Carlos Wada, and Pedro Shimose identifies even less with post-war descendants than the painter does.

Like Carlos, some pre-war migrants join Japanese events but do not feel accepted because they are "mestizos"[4]: "They respect me, they know that I'm a well-known artist, and they invite me to celebrations, but they have never invited me to become a member of [Centro Social], for example. That's a clear signal." Indeed, pre-war Nikkei's marginalisation is reproduced in ethnic associations. Although it were the pre-war migrants who founded Centro Social and although they are in principle free to apply for membership, no more than three pre-war descendant families can be found on the list, plus some pre-war Nikkei married to post-war descendants. Many are not interested in applying for membership in Nikkei institutions, even those who have lived in Japan; and some might not be able to afford membership fees. Centro Social's former secretary states, in turn, that it is difficult to integrate pre-war Nikkei, even though I do not know of any systematic attempt to do so. Instead, post-war Nikkei seem mostly not willing to financially or otherwise support pre-war Nikkei. JICA's vice-director Ichiro Ninomiya, too, notes that communication is more difficult with Nikkei in Bolivian Amazonia than with the *colonias*.

Some loose relations have emerged on a personal level, especially between Okinawan Nikkei of pre- and post-war origin. Some post-war Nikkei from Santa Cruz have travelled to Riberalta for anniversaries and donated goods at the time of the 2014 floods, as mentioned in the *tanomoshi* meeting. Nevertheless, this engagement does not necessarily mean redefining ethnic boundaries. Being of Okinawan origin, they express their wish to connect to other Okinawan Nikkei, expressing that they should be grateful to the first immigrants. Pre-war descendants were also explicitly invited to participate in Confra sports meetings, but few of them actually participated. Some pre-war Nikkei eventually expressed their satisfaction that, in 2015, the Japanese ambassador attended the 100th anniversary of Riberalta's Japanese association as a symbolic gesture.

On the margins? – Nikkei from other countries, "mestizos," Japanese and non-Nikkei

An unknown number of Nikkei from other countries, "mestizos," recent Japanese immigrants and non-Nikkei spouses, friends and association employees have been participating in the *comunidad japonesa*. Since many Peruvian and Brazilian Nikkei are also partly of non-Nikkei origin and/or of pre-war ancestry, categorisations may overlap (Takenaka 2005; Tsuda 2001a). Apart from the word "mestizos," the Nikkei use no specific denomination for these people and rarely refer to them as collectivities. While they seem to be an anomaly in the *comunidad* that is seldom explicitly mentioned; research on their role remains scarce. Hence, this subchapter can merely offer a short overview.

Except for JICA volunteers and diplomats, the latter only numerous in La Paz, most newcomers from Japan are permanent residents, such as ex-volunteers

Inclusion and exclusion in comunidad japonesa   131

married to Nikkei or non-Nkkei Bolivians. If ethnic ancestry, cultural knowledge and habitus are essential to be accepted in the *comunidad*, one might assume that recent migrants from Japan of exclusively Japanese origin will be welcomed with open arms. However, this is not the case. While some long-time Japanese residents have been engaged in Nikkei associations and even in Centro Social's association board, others distance themselves. Japanese artist Yoshiko Imai is married to a non-Nikkei *cruceño* and has been living in Santa Cruz for many years. She feels awkward in the *comunidad* she considers too conservative, supposing that it might be easier to interact with Nikkei if she had children in the Japanese school. Therefore, Yoshiko prefers to take part only in Centro Social's tea ceremony club, avoiding further involvement. Miyu Shirai, a Japanese immigrant in her thirties, is married to a non-Nikkei *cruceño* who lived in Japan and speaks Japanese fluently. She moved to Santa Cruz during my fieldwork. Despite her extrovert character, she found it difficult to apply for membership in Centro Social due to the newly implemented guarantor system. Notwithstanding the discourse relating "Japanese" and "reserved," Miyu concludes, shaking her head, that instead, the Nikkei community is "too closed." Their experiences contrast with my observations at Sociedad Japonesa de La Paz where the association's representatives proudly state that they integrate not only Okinawan descendants, mainland Nikkei and pre-war descendants, but also a number of recent migrants.

Similar to pre-war Nikkei, I conclude that especially those not married to post-war Nikkei find it difficult to feel at home in the *comunidad*. This shows that newcomers are often identified as members of a specific family rather than as individuals. Despite their undisputed cultural knowledge of Japan, they have to conform to the Bolivian Nikkei's notions of Japanese culture. Similarly, Siu (2002: 198) argues in her research on Chinese migration to Panama that being of Chinese origin does not mean being accepted as a community member, since behavioural norms are set by the Chinese Panamanians.

Nikkei from other countries such as Brazil and Peru might or might not enter in contact with the *comunidad japonesa* as well, not least depending on whether they have family ties to post-war Nikkei. Similar to recent Japanese migrants, Nikkei from other countries show individually different patterns of participation in the *comunidad*, but they seldom occupy central positions in associations. Centro Social's secretary knew of several pre- and post-war Nikkei from neighbouring countries who never attend association activities and have not applied for membership. Many Bolivian Nikkei distance themselves from Peruvian and Brazilian Nikkei and claim that "they already lie and steal," having lost their "Japanese values" since their ancestors' arrival before the Second World War. Some Bolivian descendants also suspect that many Peruvians could not prove their Japanese ancestry. They may not face open rejection, but they often find it difficult to be accepted as newcomers – if they are interested in closer interaction.

Aurora Nakashima and her daughter Michelle Nomura are pre-war descendants of exclusively Japanese ancestry who arrived from a neighbouring country in the 1990s and who speak only rudimentary Japanese. While being affiliated to Centro Social, they perceive the *comunidad* as "too closed" and too oriented in Japan.

132 *Inclusion and exclusion in* comunidad japonesa

Aurora and Michelle emphasise that in their family, they consume Japanese food, but they appreciate that Nikkei in neighbouring countries "integrate much more."

Similar to the discourse on exogamy, while emphasising in interviews that more and more "mestizos" were born, several descendants used them as a proof of the Nikkei's openness. Some of these Nikkei with non-Nikkei ancestry have held key positions in the cooperatives or as teachers. However, it is striking that while Centro Social's member list shows a number of "mestizos," they are mostly invisible in association activities – a possible conclusion is that they feel rejected. Nevertheless, unlike what Salverda (2015: 111ff.) observes for whites in Mauritius, "mixed" Nikkei are not denied membership in ethnic associations.

Little research exists on Japanese of partly non-Japanese ancestry apart from Fish (2009) and even less has been published on "mestizos" in the Japanese diaspora. Hatugai (2018) notes that Japanese Brazilian "mestizos" are considered to be "more" or "less Japanese" according to markers such as their name, physical features, habitus, cultural knowledge or their "percentage of Japanese blood" – this fluidity makes their acceptance by other Nikkei less predictable. Moromisato Miasato (2002: 200) writes that "mestizos" are disturbing the well-defined binary categories of "Japanese" and "Latin American" since it is not clear which category they belong to: "The truth is that racial intermixing is an uncomfortable and bothersome issue because it upsets accepted meanings and alters the idea of a unitary and cohesive community [...]."

Some pre-war descendants confirm that they feel discriminated because of their "mixed" ancestry, like Narumi Montaño, a teacher at Santa Cruz' Japanese school in her early thirties. Her family comes from Riberalta and she grew up in Japan where she was harassed for being "mestiza." Although she has a broader cultural knowledge about Japan than many post-war Nikkei, she thinks that the latter look down on her. She attributes this to the fact that she is not related to them and does not have a Japanese surname. According to Carlos Wada, other Nikkei discriminate against him because he lacks cultural knowledge. He thinks that "the Japanese are racists still today," claiming that they only marry among themselves and do not want to give him as "mestizo" Japanese nationality. Moreover, he cannot forget his meeting with a Japanese entrepreneur around 40 years ago. Carlos had previously asked him to finance his exhibition, pointing to a common ethnic origin. The entrepreneur's condescending attitude hit the temperamental painter's pride; Carlos became so angry that he was about to slap the interlocutor. For Carlos, it is clear that his non-Nikkei mother was the reason for the latter's behaviour.

For post-war Nikkei of partly non-Japanese ancestry, the situation is perhaps even more complex. Suzuki (2010: 160ff.) interviewed some Nikkei/non-Nikkei couples in Colonia Okinawa who reported that their children were discriminated against by Nikkei classmates. However, at least in Santa Cruz, I have observed a high degree of variation regarding their identification and participation in association activities, as the examples of Kimi Ayala and Mariana Yabu demonstrate. Both are of non-Nikkei Bolivian and post-war Okinawan origin – in Mariana's case, her father is Nikkei, in Kimi's case, her mother. Rather than considering themselves to be half – the commonly used Japanese word *hāfu* [half] for people of Japanese/

Inclusion and exclusion in comunidad japonesa 133

non-Japanese origin suggests that they are "not really Japanese" – Kimi and Mariana understand themselves to be both but with entirely different outcomes. Psychology student Kimi and her two younger siblings regularly take part in Okinawan activities such as Ryūkyūkoku Matsuridaiko and classical court dance, taking over leading roles and socialising with Nikkei and non-Nikkei alike. Her mother has been a member of Centro Social s board of directors. Some years ago, Kimi went to Okinawa Prefecture on scholarship to learn about the archipelago's culture and to improve her Japanese skills since she is not a very proficient speaker. She found the trip fascinating and was excited to meet her extended family. Mariana's relation to the *comunidad japonesa*, however, is completely different. She is ten years older than Kimi, married to a non-Nikkei and working as a Japanese teacher. Mariana has grown up in Japan, remembering some harassment because of her light brown hair, while her Spanish still has a slight Japanese accent. She generally does not socialise with Nikkei and, like her family, she shows no interest in association activities.

Only one "mestizo" interview partner of post-war origin mentioned ethnic discrimination as a reason not to join other Nikkei. Rafael Cho is in his thirties and of Japanese-Korean origin. He did not have much contact with other Japanese descendants during childhood and does not speak Japanese. Rafael went on *dekasegi* some years ago, an experience he describes as almost traumatic. When he was in his early twenties, he was invited by his cousin to join *seinenkai* but he felt the legitimacy of his Japanese origin being questioned, pointing to the long-time discrimination of Korean descendants in Japan.

> That year, the princess Sayako came from Japan [for the 100th anniversary of Japanese immigration]. So, the Japanese community would organise all the food, the reception, etc. But they excluded me [laughs][...]. Because my father is Korean and although my uncle was president of Centro Social Japonés [...]. They asked everybody for a photo, we had to fill out a form, etc. I did all that, and in the end, they told me: "No, you can't take part [...]". They called my cousin to tell her that I wouldn't take part, but all others would [...]. [Later,] I participated in trips, barbecues or the festivities in Centro Social Japonés, when they had a karaoke contest. And I always felt a little excluded because of my double origin, and in the Korean community, I felt the same. I didn't only feel it; they treated me differently [laughs].

Interview partners never stated explicitly that "mestizos" were different from other Nikkei because of their "mixed" ancestry; instead, some remarked that children of partly non-Asian origin were especially cute, saying proudly that such children would always have visible Asian features. Others subtly argued that children of partly non-Nikkei origin would be less exposed to Japanese culture, since the transmittance of supposedly shared ethnic values and behavioural patterns occurs first in the family. Especially if the mother is non-Nikkei, children would be "more Bolivian," since fathers are supposed to have less contact with their children. More research would be needed on subtle practices to include or exclude these Nikkei, but I suggest that not just their ethnic origin but a bundle of

134 *Inclusion and exclusion in* comunidad japonesa

factors play a role to determine if or not a "mestizo" is regarded as Nikkei, self-identifies as Japanese descendant, takes part in association activities or otherwise enters in contact with Japanese culture. I conclude from the three described cases that "mestizos" are much more likely to be considered part of the *comunidad* if their parents are engaged in associations and consciously introduce them into the *comunidad*.

Non-Nikkei often call children of post-war descendants and non-Nikkei "*chinos*" as well, meaning that they are still visibly different. Even though some Latin American intellectuals mystified marriage between different "races," this does not mean that Nikkei "mestizos" form part of this "new Latin race." As Hatugai (2018) concludes, such Nikkei come to signify a new difference and not a synthesis of differences.

Finally, Japanese descendants' definition of "Nikkei" does not encompass Bolivians without Japanese ancestry, even those recognised to embody "Japanese values." Some of these non-Nikkei have created meaningful ties to the *comunidad* and contribute to its construction. To my knowledge, no research has studied the non-Nikkei's role in Latin American Nikkei communities. Some of them are interested in Japanese culture in general, in Japanese or Okinawan dance or are fond of baseball. Some have Nikkei friends, are married to Nikkei or work for Nikkei institutions. They cannot apply for regular membership in most ethnic associations – unless they are married to a Nikkei –, but they may attend association events just like any member. The inclusion of these individuals points to inconsistencies and contradictions: they are often considered to be an exception, without stereotypes as such being questioned. In other words, such non-Nikkei may take part in descendants' activities if they accept the rules and norms of the *comunidad*, but it does not make them Nikkei. None of the non-Nikkei interviewees claimed to be Japanese, although they spoke Japanese, had broad cultural knowledge or had lived there for years.

Some of the non-Nikkei regularly present in descendants' circles are spouses of Nikkei, like Daniela Vargas. For some years, she took part in Day Service and the women's section (*fujinbu*) where she even served a one-year term as president. She does not speak Japanese but is fascinated by Japanese culture after living in Japan for some time. Micaela Tejada, married to a Nikkei, speaks Japanese fluently and has been president of *fujinbu* as well. Other non-Nikkei spouses who do not speak Japanese might still hope that their children will become interested in Japan and the *comunidad japonesa*, trying to motivate them to take part in Nikkei activities with more or less success. Sometimes, these spouses also adopt specific customs, such as a Catholic non-Nikkei mother showing her children how to put incense for her parents-in-law on the *butsudan* ancestor shrine. Nevertheless, the same woman feels awkward when joining association events. Like many recent Japanese migrants and Nikkei from other countries, non-Nikkei partners often consider the *comunidad* "too closed." Although they are members of Santa Cruz' Nikkei associations through their husband or wife, no attempt is made to actively include them.

Ryūkyūkoku Matsuridaiko dance has become popular among non-Nikkei Bolivians, too: around half of the participants are non-Nikkei. Some members

Figure 5.3 Ryūkyūkoku Matsuridaiko at Feria de Comunidades Extranjeras.

of the informal group even try to embody Japanese – or Okinawan – culture, whereas others are more interested in the dance itself. My Nikkei interview partners appreciated the growing number of non-Nikkei members, although they hoped that more Nikkei would join. The group has been invited to Japan-related events such as associations' celebrations, birthday celebrations, marriages as well as the inauguration of a Honda subsidiary and an Asian-style restaurant – but also to school festivals and pre-Carnival parades. Like the karate club that has as well many non-Nikkei members, the group represents the Nikkei community to the outside – while the dance is considered to be typically Okinawan in Japan. Some interview partners used the participation of non-Nikkei to demonstrate the Nikkei's supposed openness. However, it is interesting that the advertising posters for events generally feature only individual Nikkei dancers and that members disagreed if a non-Nikkei could become group leader (Siemann 2017). Hence, there seem to be limits to the propagated universalism. Several non-Nikkei members felt disadvantaged not least because of their origin, and around 2018, some decided to found their own little *eisā* group. Another long-time non-Nikkei member criticised that not all non-Nikkei had the same financial possibilities, e.g., to visit chapters abroad, whereas the Nikkei members would not even notice such differences, always repeating that "we are a big family and all equal" (Figure 5.3).

At the same time, non-Nikkei seem to be more readily accepted in Sociedad Japonesa de La Paz. Adult non-Nikkei language students' participation in major

136   *Inclusion and exclusion in* comunidad japonesa

associations has become self-evident, while more non-Nikkei than Nikkei children study Japanese. Some non-Nikkei have been working for ethnic associations and have even taken over strategic positions, like Adela Prieto and Ruy Villanueva. Adela is Sociedad Japonesa's long-time secretary, knowing the association like few others. She once received a JICA scholarship, her son-in-law is a recent Japanese immigrant and she has organised several exhibitions with the many origami figures she has folded over the years. Adela remembers that she was initially considered inferior to Japanese descendants, but does not feel that difference any more. Ruy has become a Japanese teacher for non-Nikkei adults after studying in the same school in the 1980s. Only in the beginning, he felt resistance from one person in charge. He has become the school manager and some association members even present him as a positive example. Ruy became a teacher for association members' children only in 2010, although there was nothing written prohibiting a non-Nikkei's employment in this strategic position. Nowadays, he feels that association members and fellow teachers do not treat him any different: they talk to him in Japanese without trying to simplify their speech. At the same time, he has assumed the informal role to explain "Bolivian" behaviour to Nikkei association leaders, telling them, for example, that a non-Nikkei defaulter would not repay his debts. He concludes:

> In La Paz, the Japanese community has become more open, because the Japanese as such are very closed to foreigners [...]. This has obviously historical reasons [...]. So, I could become a teacher here [...]. However, I'm proud that many students take me as a role model and want to do something similar to what I do.

It is difficult to conclude in how far and in what ways these non-Nikkei are accepted or excluded from the *comunidad japonesa*. Similar to the cases of foreign Nikkei, "mestizos" and recent Japanese migrants, individual attitudes on both sides – that may also change over time – are essential. Furthermore, one has to take into account that extremely few non-Nikkei have been playing a role in the *comunidad*; it remains an open question if reactions would change if a much higher number of non-Nikkei would join activities.

Conclusion

In Japan, ethnic and national origin is often correlated with culture (Yoshino 1992), and post-war Nikkei in Santa Cruz may present themselves as a culturally homogeneous group to the outside. However, especially in the urban setting, a combination of different factors such as ancestry, habitus, class, personal contacts and individual attitudes decides how far one participates in the *comunidad*, identifies as Nikkei and is identified as such. Boundaries sometimes overlap and receive specific meanings, such as "more Japanese" and "less Japanese." This also means that instead of binary distinctions between Japanese and non-Japanese, degrees of Japanese-ness are possible in the diaspora.

Inclusion and exclusion in comunidad japonesa 137

Whereas the rural colonies are still marked by a high degree of social conformity, the city offers a variety of possible lifestyles. On an individual level, several descendants distance themselves from other Nikkei, expanding their network beyond the *comunidad's* behavioural norms. Others stay away from the small Nikkei community because of socioeconomic reasons, and some do not identify at all as Nikkei. This also means that many do not send their children to Japanese school and speak mainly Spanish with them, despite the fact that many Bolivian Nikkei are proud to be "more Japanese" than Nikkei elsewhere because of their language skills. Nevertheless, many younger Nikkei only know some symbolic expressions in Japanese, arguing that Japanese language is not important for Nikkei identity.

Whereas the first generation often claims legitimacy as "authentic Japanese," the latter generations argue that they are adapted to living in both Bolivia and Japan. Tensions also exist between Okinawan and mainland Nikkei. Interestingly, while Okinawans have been discriminated against in other places in the Japanese diaspora, they are numerically dominant in Santa Cruz. Hence, many non-Nikkei have come to regard Okinawan-style activities as typically Japanese. Nevertheless, while many Okinawan Nikkei insist on being culturally or ethnically different from the mainland Japanese, they enjoy the possibilities their Japanese passport offers them.

The borders of Nikkei-ness become evident in the case of pre-war descendants, whom post-war Nikkei and the Japanese state regard as non-Nikkei. Contact between the mostly male descendants in Amazonia and Japan stopped even before the Second World War and was never re-established. While some pre-war leaders insist on being descendants of the first migrants, most of them are not interested in their origin abroad or do not have the means to become familiar with Japanese culture, making ethnic identification a class-related phenomenon.

The situation is also highly ambiguous for recent Japanese migrants, Nikkei of partly non-Japanese ancestry, Nikkei from other countries and non-Nikkei who take part in the *comunidad,* showing that newcomers are primarily identified as members of a specific family rather than as individuals. But a complex bundle of different factors, such as upbringing in the community or marriage with a Bolivian post-war Nikkei, decide on their acceptance. Nevertheless, more research would be needed on the fuzzy boundaries of Nikkei-ness in Bolivia and abroad.

Notes

1 Research lacks for the Bolivian case; for a list of Japanese words used in Peru, see Watanabe (2010).
2 One might also speculate if the fact that pre-war descendants generally do not have Japanese nationality plays a role in the *comunidad,* but this is beyond the scope of this study.
3 The former capital of Manchuria, until 1945 a Japanese-controlled puppet state, is today known by its Chinese name Shenyang.
4 Children of Nikkei and non-Nikkei parents are popularly called "mestizos". This stands in contrast to the general use of this term in Bolivia, referring to descendants of Europeans and indigenous people.

6 Nikkei ethnic associations' rise and decline

The third Saturday of each month is Day Service, the meeting for Centro Social's elderly members. It is a warm, cloudy morning in March 2014. I arrive at the main entrance that normally remains closed except for special events. I pass the explanatory plaque thanking JICA and other donors who made the building possible, but once more, I remark that it needs some renovations. Daniela Vargas and six other adult volunteers, clothed in red aprons, are preparing the ceremonial hall on the first floor. Apart from one boy and the doctor, all volunteers are female. Like Daniela, some are members of the actual *fujinbu* [women's section] board and practically obliged to help, one is a JICA volunteer and others just want to show their gratitude to the elderly association members. Two women brought their adolescent children who give a hand as well. I help them to put chairs and tables and revise the material they will need for the activities. The nurse and the doctor install the balance and the blood pressure monitor. Around 10 o'clock, the first *obāchan* [senior women] and *ojīchan* [senior men] appear at the door, many of them with the red shirt bearing the Centro Social logo with a plum flower and the inscription "Day Service." As far as I know, all of them are long-time members and predominantly post-war Issei. We greet them friendly with much bowing and ask for their health. The doctor and the nurse start the medical check-up, noting the results of all fifteen on the respective health cards. Some participants sit down in a circle to exchange the latest news.

After the examination, the moment has come for the well-known warm-up callisthenics or *rajio taisō*, performed since the late 1920s in schools and workplaces all over Japan to the same piano melody. Probably none of those present would need the screen the volunteers have installed to see what comes next. The following exercises include bowling with a plastic ball and some wooden blocks. Not all *obāchan* and *ojīchan* hit the blocks – but fun is definitely more important than winning. In the meantime, some other volunteers and I cover the tables with newspapers. One participant brought small potted trees, garden scissors and twigs in order to demonstrate how to refine plants. Everybody listens with interest, at least in the beginning, and one of the adolescents takes pictures with her cell phone. Issei dance teacher Sadako Mori presents the next exercise: dancing with two red and white sticks. She shows the dance figures on stage and the mostly female participants try to follow her, some much more successfully than others.

DOI: 10.4324/9781003228295-6

It is almost 12 o'clock. In an adjacent room, we put the last seaweed strips on the already prepared plastic plates with noodles and vegetables, distribute the chopsticks on the table and start serving tea. Everybody sits down, but before we start eating, the Issei repeat the song they will present at the elderly citizens' meeting in the *colonia*. Finally, with much chatting and laughing, everybody grabs his or her chopsticks to enjoy the meal. Some relatives appear at the door to take the Issei home, while the volunteers start cleaning and tidying up, highly satisfied with the joyful morning and with the happy faces of the *obāchan* and *ojīchan*.

"A mania for associations" – Nikkei associations in Santa Cruz

"When two Koreans meet, they found a church. When two Chinese meet, they found a business. When two Japanese meet, they found an association," the saying goes. Maeyama (1979: 589) starts his article on ethnicity, secret societies and associations among Nikkei Brazilians with the sentence "The Japanese in Brazil may be called 'an associational people in an unorganizational society'", concluding that Brazilian Nikkei have "a mania for associations". It is striking that few scholars have looked at the role of ethnic associations in general and the Japanese diaspora in particular, except for Maeyama (1979), Staniford (2004) and Takenaka (2003b).

Many migrants found a central cultural association with several subgroups where members can spend their free time and take part in social activities. They may create parent councils, regional associations, sports clubs, political interest groups and religious associations (Heckmann 1992: 104ff.). Such institutions provide mutual support and represent migrants' rights and interests, they organise social events and ensure the younger generations' cultural socialisation.

In the Nikkei case, *nihonjinkai* (or *nikkai*) fulfil this role as an umbrella organisation for different subgroups. Such organisations are, at least in principle, open for all Nikkei or Japanese regardless of their or their ancestors' prefecture of origin. Their size and structure vary, as does the range of activities they organise. Such *nihonjinkai* have emerged as mutual help organisations to ease hardships and join forces in a foreign country, but they also serve as points of contact for Japanese administration.

Contemporary *nihonjinkai* fulfil first of all cultural functions by providing space for regular leisure time activities and festivals. They are also a means to channel funds from Japan, acting as an interface between Japan, Bolivia and the Nikkei community: they help incoming Japanese and non-Nikkei visitors who want to learn more about Japanese migration. On Centro Social's notice board, one finds job advertisements, the address of a fish importer as well as information on how to register for the upcoming elections in Japan or on how to apply for support as a victim of the Hiroshima atomic bomb.

In 1915, the Japanese Association of Riberalta was founded as the first Bolivian *nihonjinkai*. In the absence of a consulate, the association with 160 members acted as a representation of the Japanese state. It aimed at establishing a harmonious relationship with the local population while uniting descendants through cultural activities (Kunimoto 2013a; Oshikawa 2013). In Santa Cruz, a group consisting mainly of pre-war migrants founded Centro Social Japonés in 1956. Similar organisations exist in La Paz as Sociedad Japonesa de La Paz as well as in the *colonias* as Asociación Boliviano-Japonesa, namely ABJ Okinawa and ABJ San Juan. The latter two are also called Nichibo, the short form of their Japanese name.[1] During some time, the ABJ took over public administrative functions like infrastructure management.

Centro Social Japonés is a registered association according to Bolivian law and a non-profit organisation exempt from taxation. Approximately 120 families are affiliated, corresponding to around 700 individuals. The association owns a two-storied building near Avenida Beni/Second Ring Road with an administration office, clubrooms, a kitchen and a courtyard. The ceremonial hall provides space for Nikkei events but is also rented out to non-members. Regular rehearsals for tea ceremony, karaoke, karate and Ryūkyūkoku Matsuridaiko dance take place within its premises. Furthermore, the same building hosts the Japanese school, a Japanese restaurant and the joint medical practice Policonsultorio. Like most *nihonjinkai*, Centro Social Japonés organises Day Service activities for the elderly; it hosts a *fujinbu* group for married women and a *seinenkai* club for adolescents and young adults, both being essential to carry out association activities. Centro Social also organises regular cultural events like the annual Bon Odori festival or *undōkai* [sports festival]. Finally, the association administrates a mausoleum for members at the central municipal cemetery (Figure 6.1).

Regional associations have played an important but scarcely researched role in Japanese migration. *Kenjinkai* as organisations for descendants from a specific

Figure 6.1 Centro Social Japonés with Policonsultorio Nikkei.

prefecture maintain the connection to the respective region of origin. When the prefecture offers scholarships to descendants, *kenjinkai* serve as an intermediary in the application process. With around 120 associated families in both Santa Cruz and Colonia Okinawa, Okinawa Kenjinkai Bolivia is the only Bolivian *kenjinkai* to form a registered association. Okinawa Kenjinkai Bolivia serves thereby as the umbrella organisation for both Okinawa Kenjinkai Santa Cruz and ABJ Okinawa in Colonia Okinawa. I will not take into account other, informally organised *kenjinkai*.

Whereas Centro Social Japonés' courtyard looks deserted during daytime, Okinawa Kenjinkai is located in busy Calle Antonio Vaca Diez close to other Nikkei businesses and Los Pozos market. The building's ground floor hosts Multimercado Okinawa with several shops offering Japanese products and/or owned by Nikkei. On the first floor, one finds the offices of Okinawa Kenjinkai Bolivia and Okinawa Kenjinkai Santa Cruz, a conference room, a Nikkei-owned company as well as a Nikkei accountant and a Nikkei lawyer. Students from the *colonia* live on the second floor. *Kenjinkai* members can use a kitchen, a meeting room and a sports ground for regular activities such as volleyball training, *sanshin* lessons and folk song rehearsals. One *kenjinkai* leader and member of Centro Social estimated that around three-quarters of Okinawa Kenjinkai members are also members of the *nihonjinkai* (Figure 6.2).

Since 1988, Bolivia's *nihonjinkai* are organised in the national umbrella organisation. It changed its original name Federación Nacional de Asociaciones Boliviano-Japoneses (FENABOJA) to ANBJ (Asociación Nikkei Boliviano-Japonesa) for administrative reasons. It has five active members by 2019: Santa

Figure 6.2 Okinawa Kenjinkai building.

Cruz, La Paz, Colonia Okinawa, San Juan and Cochabamba. Associations from Beni and Pando have passive status, although Riberalta's Asociación Boliviano-Japonesa plans to become an active member. Informal Nikkei circles exist in Sucre and Porvenir. ANBJ's office is located in a quiet side street of busy Avenida Monseñor Rivero within walking distance of Okinawa Kenjinkai and Centro Social Japonés. Students from San Juan rent the remaining rooms (Figure 6.3).

Furthermore, Heckmann's typology of migrant associations mentions ethnic sports clubs. Such groups, sometimes administered by *nihonjinkai*, have been common among Nikkei in the Americas. In the case of Santa Cruz, Fraternidad Fujii was founded in the late 1980s in the outskirts of Santa Cruz as an independent association. Several sports facilities and a clubhouse are at roughly 40 active members' disposal. Moreover, Mapaizo Golf Club has a high proportion of Nikkei members. A further example of a Nikkei-founded sports club is the baseball association Equipo Cóndor in La Paz. Such leisure time facilities are small compared to the enormous Nikkei club Asociación Estadio La Unión (AELU) in Lima or even the Centro Nikkei Paraguayo outside Asunción, constructed with a Japanese donation on an area of 15 hectares (Kasamatsu 2005: 154).

Unlike many other migrant groups, Japanese descendants have not established associations with an explicit interest in Japanese politics; neither are there groups seeking representation on a local, regional or national level in Latin America. Moreover, religious associations are rare. Specific Nisei groups have emerged in opposition to the Issei-dominated *nihonjinkai*, but they have disappeared over time. Furthermore, a recurring form of collective organisation are the previously rotating credit associations (*tanomoshi*) and Japanese schools. Descendants from

Figure 6.3 ANBJ building.

Nikkei ethnic associations' rise and decline   143

the same village or town may form a *sonjinkai*, but in Bolivia, such groups are not formally organised. In some other countries, *kenjinkai* have joined in national *kenjinkai* federations. Further associations or informal circles comprise groups of Issei who arrived on the same ship, neighbourhood associations, student groups, professional associations, cultural activity clubs and of course the farmers' cooperatives, described in Chapter 8.

Nikkei associations were founded in the absence of other pre-existing relations, like kinship ties beyond the nuclear family (Maeyama 1979). One can also regard the *nihonjinkai* as an expression of respect for institutionality. The Meiji state was constructed as a "family state" (*kazoku kokka*) superior to the nuclear family, thereby establishing a fixed hierarchy requiring loyalty, obedience and the fulfilment of one's individual duty. This means that the migrants were already used to neighbourhood associations, including the internal differentiation into age-based subgroups, as a form of organisation and control since premodern times. However, Reichl (1995: 52) observes that the love for associations is more intense in Brazil than in Japan, concluding that such an organisation is one way to express ethnic identity: "As they migrate from what is for most an ethnically homogeneous social environment to one that is heterogeneous, they must identify themselves as Japanese in relation to others."[2]

The meaning of putting incense – On the absence of religious associations

Bolivia's population is mostly Roman Catholic – at least by name – with a growing number of Protestants. In major cities such as Santa Cruz, one finds Korean Protestant churches, Chinese temples, Arab mosques and a Sikh worship place. Nevertheless, no exclusive Nikkei religious group exists in Santa Cruz: compared to migrant groups in other settings, religion has not played a decisive role in Nikkei identity formation. This lack of religiosity seems rare at a time when for instance in Europe, popular discourse often connects migration with religion or even religious extremism. The Nikkei's apparent lack of religiosity is also interesting because it is common in Bolivia to display religious symbols or to refer to divine will with the expression "*si Dios quiere.*" Although the Bolivian state is secular according to its new constitution, few people publicly identify as atheists.

Interestingly, those non-Nikkei who talk about the supposedly "non-integrated Japanese" generally overlook the fact that practically all Nikkei have converted to the dominant religion, Christianity. Most of them are officially Catholics, apart from some individual members of Protestant churches and several Buddhists. One Catholic priest from Japan frequently appears in the media and enjoys much popularity among non-Nikkei Bolivians. A group of nuns from the Miyazaki congregation runs schools and children homes; furthermore, a few individual Protestant priests of Japanese origin work in the region. During association anniversaries, different religious authorities participate in interreligious ceremonies, for example, to honour the deceased. To my knowledge, no statistical data on the Nikkei's religious affiliation have been gathered in Santa Cruz, and it was striking that

144   *Nikkei ethnic associations' rise and decline*

few Nikkei referred to religion as a source of values during interviews. They often seemed indifferent or even reluctant to discuss religion-related questions and seldom came up with the topic by themselves. As Gaudioso und Soares (2010) and Morimoto (2007) describe for Brazil and Peru, one finds Buddhist ancestor shrines with incense burners in Catholic homes of Bolivian Nikkei as well, other religious objects being seldom. In their statutes, Nikkei associations declare their neutrality in religious matters. This apparent lack of religiosity is not a recent phenomenon: although freedom of religion was officially guaranteed, no self-proclaimed Shintoists and no Buddhist priests lived in San Juan in the 1960s (Thompson 1968).

Some Nikkei Protestant churches exist in Brazil, but in Santa Cruz, Sōka Gakkai[3] is the only visible religious group related to Japan, founded by some Nikkei families in the 1970s. They own a major association building, Centro Cultural SGI Bolivia, next to Avenida Cristo Redentor/Third Ring Road. Currently, less than ten Nikkei families in Santa Cruz are affiliated, still occupying the highest leading positions. Most members, however, are non-Nikkei Bolivians. SGI seems to focus on Bolivian converts: they set up temples in other major Bolivian cities without Japanese presence, and their external communication is exclusively in Spanish. This is consistent with Ionescu's (2002) view: she claims that SGI sees its potential for expansion abroad rather than among Japanese or Nikkei. In Brazil, where one can observe a steady growth of evangelical churches, some middle-class non-Nikkei Brazilians join groups like SGI, looking for spiritual orientation and enjoying cultural activities like sports, choirs and the Japanese flower arrangement *ikebana* (Clarke und Somers 1994; Gaudioso und Soares 2010; Matsue 2002; Nakamaki 2003; Tomita 2004).

Conflicts among Nikkei of different religious affiliations are rare. In her account of the first years of San Juan, Kunimoto (1990: 149f.) mentions aggressive proselytising of some Sōka Gakkai members. Japan's overseas migration office feared that SGI would gain too much influence; thus, it assigned education to the Jesuits. Apparently, there are no controversies between Centro Social Japonés and Sōka Gakkai members at the moment. The latter even contributed to the construction of the new Centro Social building several years ago (El Deber 2006). However, the secretaries of ANBJ and Centro Social were somehow suspicious of SGI, supposing that the group had a hidden agenda. This mirrors the discussion in Japan: Sōka Gakkai is a controversial denomination, criticised for a diffuse but accentuated ambition for political power (Davis 1992; Höhe 2011).

One reason for this pragmatic approach to religious creed is that Japanese religions do not claim to be mutually exclusive.[4] In modern Japan, religion is seldom highly visible, or, as Lie (2001: 127) writes: "Religion became a marginal social phenomenon." Shintoist *kami* spirits are closely associated with the Japanese territory and difficult to take abroad. Nevertheless, until the end of the Second World War, migrants venerated the emperor as a symbol of Japanese-ness, together with the Imperial Rescript on Education that was supposed to embody important "Japanese values" such as loyalty, filial piety, benevolence, modesty, harmony and moral integrity, but also the willingness to sacrifice one's life to the emperor.

Nikkei ethnic associations' rise and decline 145

After Japan's defeat in the Second World War, this practice was abandoned. Another reason to give up religious practices was the migrant populations' specific composition: the performance of ancestor worshipping is the right of the eldest son who seldom went abroad. In the 1970s, the community used to improvise funeral rites based on partly remembered sutras. Ancestor worship was revitalised when the Nikkei felt they would stay in Brazil (Maeyama 1972).

Even the Japanese government was reluctant to allow religious practices abroad, as the case of Brazil demonstrates: they denied exit papers to religious personnel and discouraged the construction of shrines and temples. Already before the Second World War, they urged migrants to convert to Catholicism for harmonious relations to locals, economic advantages, the possibility to benefit from non-Nikkei godparents or the right to be buried in a local cemetery (Carvalho 2003: 16; Gaudioso und Soares 2010; Maeyama 1972: 162). In the Bolivian *colonia* of San Juan, according to Kunimoto (1990: 146ff.) and Thompson (1968: 204f.), most converts had practical rather than faith-based reasons. Moreover, some Nikkei from Kyūshū and especially from Nagasaki already arrived as Catholics.

This pragmatic approach is striking to non-Nikkei like Eduardo Visentin. He is married to Okinawan Nikkei Naoko Kanai. Eduardo has observed over the years that the Nikkei perform some religious rites, particularly those associated with ancestor worshipping, without perceiving any conflict with Christian religion:

> At Naoko's mother's home, they celebrate more New Year than Christmas. Or, when somebody passes away, they follow the custom to put incense [...]. They go and put incense, they kneel down. They do the same as the old Japanese.

He concludes that religion is not fundamentally important to the Nikkei: "There is a religious transference to the Nisei, but they did not transfer them the whole part. They do everything by imitation only [...], they don't know the background." Therefore, I agree with the Peruvian researcher Morimoto (2007) who sees Buddhist funeral rites as an attempt to preserve some cultural elements rather than manifestations of a specific creed.

"To be a good Japanese" – Membership in ethnic associations

Through membership regulations, associations have been trying to recreate and perpetuate the group and to define who is a "legitimate" Japanese descendant. Many Nikkei thought that setting up ethnic associations was a "natural Japanese behaviour" since "in a foreign country, one needs to be close" and "everywhere in the world, the Japanese live close to each other."

In the beginning, associations served as support groups. They could give advice to newcomers and serve as a link between migrants and Japan. Demonstrating unity has been an additional reason to found associations, entrepreneur and former Centro Social president Hakuo Tamanaha argues: their physical presence with an impressive building means a gain of symbolic capital and security. In

146 *Nikkei ethnic associations' rise and decline*

the event of problems with non-Nikkei Bolivians, a collective entity can better defend and protect its members and seek support, lawyer Masutaro Higaonna says: "If you're a single natural person, you're not important to the consulate and the embassy". However, few descendants think that they need such a protection nowadays.

Agustín Okita, a long-time board member of Sociedad Japonesa de La Paz in his late thirties, emphasises the principle of reciprocity: he declares that he wants to give something back to the association he knows since childhood while declaring that he is not interested in material benefits.

> Even if Sociedad Japonesa wouldn't offer anything to me, I would stay affiliated [laughs], I would pay [...]. The identification I have with that group, I eventually consider many of them to be my family [...]. In order that this organisation stays alive, even if we only meet there, I support it without expecting that they will give me a swimming pool one day.

But association membership can also mean expanding one's networks, and the commitment to a non-profit cause may increase individual symbolic capital. Helping, for example, in Day Service may not only express gratitude to the Issei, but also the wish for self-affirmation and fellow members' recognition.

Providing space for socialising and cultural activities is among the associations' primary functions: through joint activities, a sense of community is created beyond the family, individual friendships and random encounters. During activities, members meet friends and acquaintances, exchanging news and rumours. Ethnic identity is created through shared space and activities, be it ritualised meals, *mājan* [mah-jong] games or singing. When urging their children to participate in events and activities, some parents hope that they will later marry another member. The mere existence of such ethnic associations could be interpreted as a sign of undesirable closure, but I have never heard such statements among non-Nikkei.

When being asked about their motivation for joining an ethnic association, most members said that they felt obliged because of their ethnic identity: "To be a good Japanese" and "to increase the Japanese spirit," as Issei Sadako Mori resumes. Applying for membership is still an unquestioned act for some children and grandchildren of association members. However, especially in a context like La Paz where the Nikkei population is smaller and where some members lost their relation to Japan in the Second World War, interview partners stated that joining Sociedad Japonesa was an act of conscious identity affirmation. Association president Fanny Yoshikawa underlines the importance of festivities and regular activities for pre-war descendants like herself and her family:

> I remember that one day, my son looks at himself in the mirror and asks: "Why am I Japanese?" How can I explain this to him? [...] If my son is asking me like that, imagine how it is for families who didn't have relations [to other Nikkei], so it's our responsibility to work about identity.

Nikkei ethnic associations' rise and decline 147

Association membership means defining ethnic boundaries. As Maeyama (1979: 594) states, *nihonjinkai* membership was almost mandatory for Japanese settlers in the Brazilian *colonias* before the Second World War, being also a means to enforce social norms. Anyone who terminated membership or was for some reason rejected by others suffered subtle exclusion as "non-Japanese," being urged to leave. One could, for example, be removed from the list when opening a business without permission, since this meant bringing discord and disturbance into the community (Endōh 2009: 185f.). For pre-war Bolivia, Mitre (2006: 92) describes that one member was excluded from Sociedad Japonesa de La Paz after criticising Japanese totalitarianism. For the Nikkei today, however, affiliation is often a matter of individual choice, especially in the urban area. In Colonia Okinawa and San Juan, the vast majority still figures on the respective ABJ's membership list – in the environment of the *colonias*, not complying with the norms can lead to social pressure and the *nihonjinkai* may also be the only institution to offer specific facilities, like Colonia Okinawa I's large swimming pool.

Nowadays, anybody of good repute can apply for Centro Social membership, according to its statutes – as long as the association board agrees. In practice, associations only accept applicants who can prove Japanese ancestry. *Nihonjinkai* membership in Santa Cruz also includes the spouse, regardless of his or her origin, their children and potentially other family members. Association membership is a condition for some scholarships; the same is true if one wants to send one's children to Santa Cruz' Japanese school. In Sociedad Japonesa with its individual affiliation system, non-Nikkei Bolivians can apply for passive or "honorary membership," but cannot join the association board.

Takenaka (2003b: 473) observes for the socially more diverse Peruvian Nikkei community that the participation in associations is mainly a middle-class phenomenon for descendants of exclusively Japanese ancestry: owners of major corporations, as well as Nikkei who cannot or do not want to afford membership fees, seldom join Nikkei associations; neither do intellectuals, artists, Japanese businesspersons or diplomats. Although Bolivia's Nikkei population is much smaller and socioeconomically more homogeneous, several descendants do not join Nikkei networks in general because they reject specific norms and practices, as described in the previous chapter. Moreover, especially pre-war descendants are marginalised in Santa Cruz' associations. While anybody of Japanese ancestry may join, associations claim the authority to define who is a legitimate descendant.

Why cleaning the festival ground is as important as the festival itself – Association activities and events

Some Nikkei fold origami, practice tea ceremony or participate in Ryūkyūkoku Matsuridaiko dance to feel close to their origins. Many more attend events like Karaoke Contest or the annual Bon Odori festival. Through such activities and events, associations reproduce ethnic identity. They try to define, promote and control Japanese culture, thereby emphasising specific norms and values and presenting the community to the outside. Even though they are not congruent, associations act as reification of the *comunidad*. Following Gans (1979), the more the Nikkei become culturally similar to mainstream society, the more meaning is attached to such activities. Interestingly, many Nikkei regard the number of events as an indicator for the preservation of identity: the more, the better. Through such activities and events, one is supposed to learn and understand Japanese and Okinawan culture (Figure 6.4).

However, experts may not always be available. In the tea ceremony group, participants mutually correct each other and look up the proper movements in books while the dance group relies on videos. Whereas activities and events are related to the narrative on "Japanese values," participation does not necessarily mean acquiring concrete knowledge. It is not guaranteed that everybody has an idea of the origin of their hobbies or even considers such detailed knowledge to be important. For example, many members of Ryūkyūkoku Matsuridaiko dance group are not familiar with the deeper historical and religious background of this dance. When I asked a young Okinawan descendant about the picture behind the scene of Colonia Okinawa's event hall, she had no idea what it represented – in fact, it was one of the most famous sites of the prefecture and the former seat of the Ryūkyū kingdom, Shuri palace.

At a time when Japanese descendants become culturally similar to the non-Nikkei population, Nikkei associations have often been choosing specific symbolic representations according to the community's needs and possibilities (Gans 1979). Since a common understanding of Japanese culture may lack, such representations are ambiguous and imprecise enough to accept various meanings

Figure 6.4 Origami shown at Sociedad Japonesa de La Paz. The designs represent an indigenous Bolivian woman and carnival figures.

Nikkei ethnic associations' rise and decline 149

(Cohen 1992: 18ff.). Symbols are selected among uncontroversial cultural practices such as music, dress, food, dance, etc., to present an essentialised version of Japan as an imagined homeland. These practices may change over time. Choosing cultural symbols also means manipulation: as Takenaka (2003b: 475) states, the selection silences potentially controversial practices like violence, pornography, political issues or other controversial topics because, in leaders' eyes, they might cast a negative light on their construction of "Japan."

At the same time, seemingly typically Japanese festivals have changed their meaning abroad or are even an invention of the local Nikkei community – while still serving to show ethnic boundaries. Belonging is enacted in front of members and non-members, showing staged authenticity in a spectacular and highly choreographed synthesis of culturally decontextualised elements. One example is the Bon Odori festival in Santa Cruz. It originates in Obon, the joyous festival to honour the ancestors' spirits held in July/August. During Obon, families visit their ancestors' graves to make food offerings; it is also popular to set lanterns on water to guide the souls of the deceased to the other world; eventually, everybody joins in Bon Odori dance (Ashikaga 1950; Smith 1962). The festival is substantially different in the Bolivian setting. In Santa Cruz, the Bon Odori festival is the annual celebration of Centro Social held in late October. Some women wear a colourful *yukata* [casual kimono] and each association member contributes to the event, for example, selling small handicrafts, sushi, *mochi*,[5] *okonomiyaki*,[6] *anticuchos*,[7] among others. An integral part of the programme are karate and Ryūkyūkoku Matsuridaiko presentations. Finally, both Nikkei and non-Nikkei join in Bon Odori dance.

Most Nikkei may have at least an idea about Obon in Japan. However, few non-Nikkei know about the practically invisible religious origins of Bon Odori festival. Therefore, Keiko Taniguchi from San Juan told me that Ryūkyūkoku Matsuridaiko should not be part of the celebration since it does not represent the whole of Japan and is not meant for everybody to participate – although in a Bolivian setting, mixture might be okay, she added smilingly. Notwithstanding, Bon Odori is culturally distinctive and looks Japanese in a Bolivian context. For non-Nikkei in Santa Cruz, visiting Bon Odori means an imaginary trip to Japan by taking part in a colourful festival and enjoying "exotic" food. Similarly, Colonia Okinawa's harvest festival Hōnensai (Festival de la Buena Cosecha), celebrated in mid-August, has become a tourist attraction for non-Nikkei with its food specialities, Bolivian dances, *sanshin* music, *shishimai* lion dance and Ryūkyūkoku Matsuridaiko (Figure 6.5).

Non-members are generally not denied access during such events, in contrast to what Takenaka (2003b: 473) observed in Lima's Nikkei association where those racialised as non-Nikkei may be stopped at the gate. At the same time, discussions have emerged about the participation of non-paying outsiders. It becomes clear that opening festivities to a broad public potentially means loss of control. In the case of Hōnensai, ABJ employee Keita Itosu complains about the drunken non-Nikkei in the central plaza after the festival and about the garbage lying around everywhere, giving a poor example to children and endangering the *colonias'*

Figure 6.5 The shishimai or lion dance at Hōnensai, observed by the non-Nikkei public.

symbolic capital among non-Nikkei. However, he regrets his powerlessness. Closure might not be desirable, either, since such events mean positive publicity.

With such activities, Centro Social Japonés and other associations take over the responsibility for cultural diffusion. Occasionally, with support of the consulate, the community organises events such as Kimono Fashion Show and Festival de Comunidades Extranjeras where specific emphasis is laid on demonstrating Japanese culture to non-descendants. During such events, the Nikkei claim the authority over Japanese culture, trying to control its diffusion in Bolivia. Even non-Nikkei support this notion: Sociedad Japonesa's secretary Adela Prieto thinks that the *nihonjinkai* is able to teach more authentic origami than the existing commercial courses.

Consequently, one generally observes a clear role division: the Nikkei show non-Nikkei Bolivians how "authentic Japanese culture" is like, and "Bolivian activities" and "Japanese activities" are strictly separated. For the Karaoke festival in Santa Cruz, only Japanese songs can be chosen. During *undōkai* in San Juan, if a non-Nikkei dance group or school children perform Bolivian dances, they are shown before or after Japanese dances. The non-Nikkei teachers prepare Bolivian-style *majadito* [lowland dish with rice, dried meat and plantain] for lunch, while the Nikkei association sells Japanese-style *obentō* [lunchboxes]. Presenting Japanese culture means responsibility for Sociedad Japonesa, since it must not be confounded with other East Asian cultures, association president Fanny Yoshikawa argues. In her opinion, maintaining 'purity' means preserving the popular brand of Japanese-ness.

Nikkei ethnic associations' rise and decline 151

We have the responsibility [...], for example with the kimono. There are kimono for festivals, there are other kimono, *yukata* [casual kimono] [...]. So these things, I think they are important to promote. And now there are many Koreans, there are many Chinese, so they get confused. We have to look at the difference. Everybody has his or her own culture and customs.

The separation between "Japanese" and "Bolivian" is also evident in the use of space. Even if the event is officially meant to bring Nikkei and non-Nikkei together, spectators often remain separate. Some non-Nikkei join descendants, but never vice-versa. Hōnensai is organised almost exclusively by Nikkei, recognisable by their colourful *happi* coats. After the end of the official programme, the Nikkei, accompanied by some non-Nikkei friends, continue celebrating in private spaces, whereas exclusively non-Nikkei Bolivians visit food stalls, games and other attractions behind the plaza.

Associations do not only present Japanese cultural practices, but they also want to demonstrate and transmit "Japanese values" after, before and during activities. Helping, for example, in Day Service, means demonstrating "Japanese values" like cooperation, solidarity and filial piety. The transmission of values is also central to sports events such as *undōkai*. It started under the Meiji government at schools and other social institutions to form robust, disciplined and healthy imperial subjects (Guttmann und Thompson 2001: 92). Similarly, Ryūkyūkoku Matsuridaiko was initiated as a meaningful activity for bored adolescents, its origin being *eisā*, an Okinawan dance for Obon (Siemann 2017). As a result, several descendants believe that such sports activities have an important function beyond the acquisition of cultural knowledge. As Suzuki (2010: 144) states, through physical exercises and self-discipline, children are supposed to become successful citizens unaffected by "negative Bolivian habits."

Such exercises receive particular emphasis in a rural environment like Colonia Okinawa and San Juan. Accordingly, *undōkai* in the *colonias* is more competitive than in the cities. In the countryside, many Nikkei hold training sessions beforehand to succeed in the fierce competition that usually means running over different distances. In contrast, Santa Cruz' and La Paz' *undōkai* are a moment for young and old to have fun in different games. One can observe that the more playful the activities, the more the boundary between members and non-members becomes blurred. As a reward, participants receive laundry detergent, soy sauce, toilet paper, towels, pencils, small sweets, etc., donated by individual members (Figure 6.6).

At the same time, activities are meant to present a harmonious and collaborative community able to organise a major event. Many interview partners declared that everybody gives a hand, implicitly or explicitly comparing this behaviour to non-Nikkei. Cleaning the ground after the event by picking up even the smallest paper shreds is an integral part of the programme. Futoshi Sakihara, former secretary of Centro Social Japonés, remembers a Japanese festival at Manzana 1, an open space behind Santa Cruz' central plaza used for performances. He emphasises that cleaning means demonstrating respect towards other *cruceñas*

152 *Nikkei ethnic associations' rise and decline*

Figure 6.6 Cleaning the sports ground after undōkai in La Paz.

and *cruceños:* "If there is a festival, there is always much garbage, so we went [...] to pick up the garbage [...]. That's our work, I mean, to comply with our obligations, so they evaluate us well in the city of Santa Cruz." While pollution is declared ethically wrong, the symbolic act of cleaning the ground does not only represent the enactment of "Japanese values," but also means justifying their symbolic capital and their status as model citizens.

Organisers are extremely proud if they manage to follow the plan and to be on time "like in Japan". As Futoshi emphasises, the festival mentioned above did not only finish early in order not to disturb the neighbours. Even the small delay – by Bolivian standards – was on purpose.

> We planned to start at 7 p.m., but we started at 7:15. We also could have started at 7, but we didn't because next to it is the cathedral and we know that at 7, they have their church service. We didn't want to disturb them, so we waited for 15 minutes. But we complied with the rest, so the representative of the city government evaluated us positively [...]. At 10:15, 10:30, everything finished.

Futoshi Sakihara and other organisers apparently reach their aim to present Nikkei in a favourable light: while witnessing association members cleaning the ground after *undōkai* in Santa Cruz, a non-Nikkei mother told me in an admiring tone

Nikkei ethnic associations' rise and decline   153

that everybody should take them as an example. After activities in her children's school, she complained, garbage lies around everywhere.

A greeting card from the Imperial family – Why relations with Japan are beneficial to both sides

Nikkei associations also serve as a communication channel between the Nikkei and Japan. Centro Social Japonés, for example, received USD 300,000 from JICA for the construction of its new building completed in 1997; this is equivalent to almost 40% of the total cost, according to Okinawa Kenjinkai president Naoji Ganaha.[8] At the same time, certificates from the Japanese government are prominently displayed in association offices and several association leaders proudly showed me greeting cards from the Imperial family.

Nikkei associations have in turn donated money in the case of natural disasters in Japan – of course, these are symbolic donations, considering the small number of descendants in Bolivia. Already after the Kantō earthquake in 1923 as well as during and after the Second World War, Latin American Nikkei communities collected funds to send them overseas (Endōh 2009: 182f.; Sociedad Japonesa de La Paz 2012: 42f.). They also donated money after the Kōbe earthquake in 1995: ABJ San Juan sent USD 5,000 and CAISY USD 3,000 (Fukaura und Nagai 2013: 276). Also after the Tōhoku disaster in 2011, Bolivian Nikkei sent 6 million yen to Japan according to (Fukui 2017: 6). Nevertheless, the relationship remains, of course, unequal.

Relations may be beneficial to descendants in particular, but the Japanese government follows its own agenda when investing in Nikkei institutions. It collaborated with Nikkei brokers for their migration projects, using Nikkei associations as an extended arm of Japan. Since being "between" two countries does not mean that descendants' identity is simply given, a state like Japan may want to ensure loyalty. Therefore, Japanese national and prefectural government officials regularly visit association anniversaries.

Nikkei associations have been organising cultural and educational activities together with the Japanese consulate. Examples are the previously mentioned festivals Kimono Fashion Show and Festival de Comunidades Extranjeras, organised by the consulate and supported by Nikkei association members. This is convenient for Japan: associations have a network on the local level, mobilise volunteers and possess their own infrastructure; there is no need to maintain expensive cultural representation offices. The Nikkei can thereby help to promote Japanese culture and convey a positive perception of Japan. But, as Takenaka (2003b: 477) notes, if the Nikkei try to follow a Japanese cultural model, they will always be considered as "not Japanese enough" by the Japanese.

"These people lack the Nikkei spirit" – How Nikkei explain the lack of interest in associations

Since identifying as Nikkei is a positive asset in Bolivia, it should be attractive to participate in ethnic associations. However, some urban Nikkei do not join

154   *Nikkei ethnic associations' rise and decline*

association activities and an unknown number has even cancelled its membership in the *nihonjinkai*, despite identifying as descendants. Ethnic identity, symbolic capital and prosperity seem not related to association membership.[9] As a result, during my research in 2013, even the general assembly of Centro Social Japonés to elect a new board had to be postponed, because it was without the necessary quorum.

The interviewed former members did not complain about Centro Social's comparatively high membership fee of USD 15 per month, but they were often unsatisfied with the price-performance ratio. Some families remembered that they left Centro Social in times of financial difficulties and did not return after their situation had improved – although associations should serve as a mutual support group. Others were critical of associations in general. Furthermore, several families left after disputes with other members, and many who arrive from the *colonias*, especially those from San Juan, do not apply for membership in Centro Social Japonés, while remaining members of ABJ Okinawa or ABJ San Juan. Moreover, some Okinawan Nikkei said that they did not have time for two associations at once, opting for Okinawa Kenjinkai that seemed more harmonious and united – a fact they attributed to the "Okinawan spirit."

Many Nikkei regret that the associations' character has changed and that nothing is as it used to be. According to their diagnosis, moral decline, selfishness, apathy and individualism are the main reasons for members' absence. They complained about the supposedly growing importance of individual pleasure and material benefit, generally pointing to other, unnamed members. As Nisei Masutaro Higaonna resumes, many only appear when food is served. Okinawa Kenjinkai Santa Cruz president Naoji Ganaha thinks that members should be more grateful to the institutions as guarantors of symbolic capital:

> These people lack [...] the Nikkei spirit [...]. Without paying anything, when there is Bon Odori, why do they participate? When there is Karaoke Festival, they go to Centro Social [...]. What a shame [...]. One must contribute. Therefore, everybody lives well.

Many descendants mentioned an idealised spirit of cooperation against which they measure the actual state of affairs with nostalgia. In retrospect, former times may be romanticised since membership was almost mandatory and migrants struggling to survive might not have had time or energy for leisure time activities (Staniford 2004: 85). Whereas some Nikkei attributed the supposed loss of values to prosperity, others thought that it was due to "bolivianisation." According to Nisei Hiroshi Shindo, the Japanese spirit vanishes in the second generation.

> The Nikkei [refers to Nisei], when they present a paper [...], they don't look at the contracts to rent out the hall, they don't put attention to such things. The most important thing is to have fun. In the case of the *japoneses netos* [true Japanese], it's not like that; they have to look well at these details: "My God, one boliviano was lost [...], or 50 centavos."

Nikkei ethnic associations' rise and decline 155

He thinks that community feeling and ethnic identity had declined mainly in the urban environment; even the Issei now use the facilities without respect for others. Hiroshi remembers perplexed how he crossed some Issei playing gateball[10] in Centro Social's ceremonial hall: "It can't be, I mean, the Japanese blood ... It can't be". According to Hiroshi, associations work better in the "really Japanese" *colonias.*

The distance between leaders and members seems to grow. Since leadership is not ascribed, in principle, able and interested individuals are elected, generally for terms of two years. Nevertheless, as also Takenaka (2003b: 473f.) describes for the Japanese-Peruvian Association, they are mostly chosen on informal consent among a small circle constituted by trust. In Santa Cruz, association leaders are usually male post-war descendants of exclusively Japanese origin, over 40 years and economically stable.

Some Nikkei consider leaders incompetent and incautious, complaining like Hiroshi that board members are not as careful "as the Japanese should be" and that data management does not work. Especially when conflicts between the board and some members arose, several Nikkei spoke about Centro Social leaders as a greedy, egoistic and closed group that destroys associations rather than bringing them forward. Some descendants even used the word *"camarilla"* [clique], equating leaders with a hostile criminal group. According to young entrepreneur Ayaka Shimoji, many leaders lack a vision for the entire community. Paralleling the discourse on the loss of "Japanese values", she thinks that they use facilities for their own purposes, instead of representing all members' interests: "We have reached a period of commodity, of personal opportunities, so everybody only sees their own personal benefit [...]. Sometimes they take it as a title."

At the same time, one has to acknowledge that leadership positions are not very attractive. Some interview partners argued that the Japanese per se do not like prominent public functions, but association leaders obtain few rewards – positions are without pay – for sometimes considerable stress. Furthermore, leading a small Bolivian association does not imply an increase in immaterial resources, unlike what Takenaka (2009b: 477f.) describes for the enormous and powerful Japanese-Peruvian Association (APJ). Thus, Naoji Ganaha, president of Okinawa Kenjinkai Santa Cruz, has experienced that it is difficult to find candidates:

> Here [...], everything is very small, there are few inhabitants [...]. In Argentina, there are big entrepreneurs who represent the country. Here in Bolivia, Santa Cruz, there are no big entrepreneurs [...]. So the Okinawan association in Peru, they make an election campaign, that's something big. They say that the president of the Okinawan association in Peru is like a hero.

Despite the discourse on moral decline, many Nikkei lack interest in associations rather because they are not attractive any more: they can afford to give them up, although ironically, they may deplore this development. Ethnic associations have mostly lost their original function as mutual support groups: most Nisei and Sansei are prosperous Bolivian citizens and do not see themselves as victims of

156 *Nikkei ethnic associations' rise and decline*

discrimination needing protection. I already demonstrated that several Nikkei voluntarily distance themselves from the *comunidad*, relying on non-Nikkei friends. Moreover, many descendants maintain relations with Japan on a personal level via relatives and friends, they speak Japanese or have close friends who do so. They do not need a *nihonjinkai* to obtain scholarships, to do translations or to create networks, although they may use them for such purposes. Furthermore, the small Bolivian *nihonjinkai* have not been able to become attractive leisure clubs for an ethnically defined group from the upper middle class. Manzenreiter (2017a: 208) resumes:

> [I]n light of the current advanced division of labor between different agencies in charge of public administration (provided by the state), business management (representing the farmers' interests), and cultural life (more and more privatized), the benefits of (mandatory) membership are increasingly questioned.

"We could do many more things that we don't do now" – Is it possible to reform the *nihonjinkai*?

While the *nihonjinkai* have become less attractive for contemporary Japanese descendants, practices of exclusion and inclusion as well as different definitions of Nikkei-ness result in ongoing tensions. Central are disagreements between the first and the subsequent generations: many interview partners equated them with a division between "more Bolivian" and progressive members on the one hand and "more Japanese" and conservative ones on the other hand. This means, of course, an oversimplification: not all Nisei or Sansei are enthusiastic about changing current structures, and some Issei are desperate about their contemporaries they consider too conservative. Notwithstanding, asymmetrical role expectations and hierarchies were not questioned for a long time since the interest in being part of a community prevailed: social control was stronger and descendants were less conscious about alternative ways of life.

As in any other collectivity, conflicts among members have always occurred; however, they have seldom resulted in open disputes. But around the year 2016, such quarrels led to the closure of Policonsultorio and the exclusion of some Centro Social member families, among them a former president. Many Nikkei talked about these incidents in open disbelief, like teacher Narumi Montaño who witnessed how two members shouted at each other in the schoolyard, fearing the negative influence on her pupils. Like Narumi, several Nikkei stated that they felt ashamed since such occurrences contradicted the "typically Japanese" solidarity and harmony as a supposedly inherent cultural trait. Others like Masutaro Higaonna stated that it was not "elegant" to discuss the situation. In turn, association leaders reacted by closing Centro Social to outsiders. A trust-based guarantor system was implemented in order to reinforce homogeneity and avoid conflicts. Events would still be organised since everybody expected them to be carried out, but attendance declined further. It was striking that only a handful of parents and

Nikkei ethnic associations' rise and decline   157

teachers stayed after the official part of Mother's Day celebration, and at *undōkai*, it became obvious that some groups did not mix with each other. After a change of directory, the situation seems to have calmed down; Policonsultorio has reopened in the meantime.

Nevertheless, I argue that these conflicts are related to different expectations rather than to moral decline. Formal membership rules have often excluded Nisei and Sansei from decision-making, but also women (see below). In most Nikkei organisations, the father is automatically designated as head of the family and therefore allowed to vote in elections, following the *koseki* system. In 1872, this family register was modelled after the upper classes' family ideal with a male head (Bryant 1991). Daughters usually remain on their father's register until they marry and enter their husband's *koseki*.

Nikkei history books are full of stories like the one above where the second generation built their own associations since their parents considered them not Japanese enough. Kasamatsu (2007a) cites the saying "*nisei no jidai ni nattara dame desu ne*", meaning that associations collapse when the Nisei manage them. Sociedad Japonesa's chronicle mentions the foundation of a separate Nisei group in the 1950s. In the late 1980s, disputes between first and second-generation women resulted in the entire association board's renouncement (Sociedad Japonesa de La Paz 2012: 86ff., 130). Such intergenerational conflicts have been solved on an organisational level – the fusion of both organisation types – but differences of opinion remain.

While many Nisei hold that respecting the elderly is an inherent part of Japanese culture and should be maintained, they still consider the Issei leaders to be old-fashioned and observe that seniority is more important than ability. Many Nisei deplore that the first generation is not dynamic enough to attract younger descendants, but rather focuses on the elderly's needs. To give an example, Shuji Ando, himself a senior Paraguayan association leader, regrets that few Issei show interest in modernising associations. Moreover, he observes that many Issei refuse to give up power, a behaviour he explains with Japanese culture:

> The Japanese have this mentality to perpetuate a position [...]. They are not interested in the formation of others who might follow. We [in Asunción] do it very differently. Seldom will somebody be president again. We always look for a new one [...]. I think that in the long run, this will bear fruit. [Because] among the Japanese association presidents, some of them are 20 years in their position, so there is no renewal.

Circumstances may have changed since Amemiya's (2001) article on power struggles over the 100th anniversary of Japanese immigration to Bolivia, and many Nisei have taken over leadership positions. However, they denounce that some conservative Issei still try to influence decisions behind the scenes.

At the same time, several Nisei and Sansei recognised that some small long-awaited changes have taken place. For example, the associations' ways of communication are modernising slowly: e-mail is increasingly used for the associations'

158   *Nikkei ethnic associations' rise and decline*

newsletters, not least for financial reasons. But association homepages, if existing, are out of date or have even been closed. Mayumi Iwamatsu from San Juan and her *seinenkai* colleagues think that attitudes have also been changing. They vividly remember how the older members used to regard any of their ideas to modify procedures, for example, when planning an event, as a lack of respect. However, Mayumi and her friends recognise that bringing in their opinion became easier over time. Moreover, the fact that associations have been inviting non-Nikkei to specific festivals, occasionally held even in public space, may be regarded as a significant change. In contrast to Sociedad Japonesa de La Paz, Centro Social leaders have not yet addressed structural issues such as gender inequalities or the inclusion of pre-war descendants, Nikkei/non-Nikkei families and recent Japanese immigrants, for example through individual membership.

Those Nikkei who are interested in joining Japan-related activities increasingly prefer small single-focus groups with flat hierarchies (Moya 2005). Instead of participating in multi-function associations, especially younger Nikkei may join such groups to express Japanese-ness and Okinawan-ness in a more flexible way. It is not necessary to be affiliated to an association in order to join groups like Ryūkyūkoku Matsuridaiko dance. These groups require small contribution fees, if at all, and do not require much commitment beyond their rehearsals.

Nisei Daiki Kaneshiro is unhappy with the current developments. He is a travel agency owner who through his job and his participation in Pan-American Nikkei events has known descendants from different countries. Whereas he acted as president of Centro Social around 15 years ago, he is now disappointed with the organisation, preferring to engage for Okinawa Kenjinkai and Confra. His office in the travel agency's rear section is coated with wood panels in light shades with a grimly looking figure from Japanese theatre, a gift from some Nikkei ladies made from cloth. On the shelf, two *shīsā* guardion lions from Okinawa dominate, apart from a colourful little bus, apparently coming from the Columbian city of Cartagena, a beckoning *manekineko* cat figurine and a doll in rose-coloured kimono with a golden fan. Between answering phone calls regarding flight connections, Daiki deplores a lack of participative policies in associations. But he is not nostalgic for the past. Instead, he proposes that institutions should try to bring similar interests together to the benefit of the entire community. When he was president of Centro Social, he invited a group of Nikkei hobby artists from a neighbouring country to exhibit in Colonia Okinawa as well as in a public cultural institution in the city. But he observes that several informal groups dedicated to Japan-related activities, like a Japanese drum group in Okinawa III, function independently from each other. Since Daiki has taken part in many Pan-American events, he compares the current state of affairs with Nikkei associations abroad, concluding that

> The institutions should work for all these [Japan-related cultural] groups [...], supporting them, giving them space, giving them incentives [...]. Many times we fail in this. We fail at the institutional level. We could do many more things that we don't do now. And there are small groups that manage

Nikkei ethnic associations' rise and decline 159

themselves on their own, and they finance themselves out of their own pocket. We could bring them all together, reduce costs, give them a space where they could practice what they like.

Daiki points to ANBJ as a key actor on the national level. Nevertheless, dissatisfaction with ANBJ leadership is widespread: accordingly, ANBJ lacks a vision, does not take any risks and is too formalistic, incompetent and slow. As a result, few nation-wide activities have been carried out so far and ANBJ did not support a recent national Nikkei meeting organised by the newly founded Nikkei Association of Cochabamba. The national Nikkei organisation remains largely invisible and its Issei president declined my interview request, claiming that the organisation has merely an administrative role. He lives in the *colonia* and only comes to Santa Cruz from time to time. In general, Bolivian Nikkei have been much less united on a personal and institutional level between the two *colonias*, Santa Cruz, La Paz, Beni and Pando. Daiki and his friends compare ANBJ to Peru's and Paraguay's national organisations that organise different cultural and sportive activities to bring Nikkei from different places together. They conclude that Nikkei in other countries have "another spirit" and are "more open." While in Brazil and Peru, associations have also found pragmatic and inclusive responses to manage diversity, this spirit could theoretically also emerge in Bolivia, Daiki states:

> If the people from FENABOJA [i.e., ANBJ] don't go abroad and see what is done there [...], they will never understand. And unfortunately, they never travel. Because one doesn't invent these things, one goes to the neighbouring countries to see what they are doing. And there, you see these things and say: "Hey, if we could do that in Bolivia, for our elderly, for the children, the adolescents..."

However, Daiki concludes that it is not only the association leaders' fault:

> And [the ones of ANBJ] can do it. But they simply don't do it, and the rest of the society like us who are affiliated, we stay there with crossed arms and wait that things happen and that one day somebody does something. So if you look for the ones to blame, in inverted commas, that's all of us because we don't put them under pressure so that they start doing activities.

Nevertheless, it is unlikely that drastic changes will occur soon. In 2017, four years after the first interview, different *nihonjinkai* delegates re-elected ANBJ's president. Although some Nisei like Daiki had planned to promote a well-known Nisei candidate, the latter did not receive the necessary support. Daiki seems resigned that his initiatives have not brought significant changes and that interest in associations is further decreasing.

The result is institutional fragmentation. A conflict broke out already in the mid-1990s when members were divided over Centro Social's new association

160 *Nikkei ethnic associations' rise and decline*

home. The question was if the new building should be constructed at the old location at Avenida Beni/Second Ring Road. A well-known picture from the 1950s shows only the savannah north of the Second Ring Road, but because of the city's enormous growth, Centro Social is now located almost in the centre of Santa Cruz. Consequently, the association has no possibility to expand into the densely populated neighbourhood. Or should the building be constructed outside the city, with sufficient space for sports facilities? Nisei Reiko Yohena vividly remembers the discussion:

> The older ones didn't want to. "How will we sell an association home that has cost us so much, and go so far away?", for example. Instead, the younger ones: "This association home in the centre is not useful anymore, we need a place where to do *undōkai* [...]. When we want to do *undōkai,* we have to lend other peoples' sports grounds. We have no place where the children can go for a weekend."

After the decision in favour of the city centre, Reiko and some other Nisei, mostly of Okinawan origin, decided to found Fraternidad Fujii as sports club, and Reiko, former secretary of Centro Social, declares to feel happy that she is no longer affiliated to the latter association. Interestingly, when the Japanese consulate organised the already mentioned Kimono Fashion Show, two young "mestizos" acted as moderators, one of them being a well-known actor in Santa Cruz – both have a distanced relationship with the *comunidad.* It seems to be easier to bring in new ideas outside established associations.

Something similar occurred in recent years with Daiki and several of his friends, some of them former members of Centro Social's directory board. They prefer to participate in Pan American events or to become engaged for Okinawa Kenjinkai. Okinawan descendants underline the more intimate yet open and inclusive atmosphere. Ayaka Shimoji, once Bolivia's youngest and first female Okinawa Kenjinkai president, explains her commitment to this specific environment:

> I don't share the ideas of those people who are now in leadership positions [in Centro Social], their way of thinking, their policies, I wouldn't do it like that. I wouldn't be a help for them, maybe one more member on their list [...]. I prefer not to be a passive member. I prefer to be in a place where I can really contribute.

However, Okinawan Nikkei represent around 60% of all Centro Social members – one may put a question mark behind this explanation and ask how far leaders' individual attitudes play a role. Okinawa Kenjinkai has become more active in attracting Okinawan descendants to cultivate a specific Okinawan identity. Several events like *keirōkai* [Respect for the Aged Festival] and *seijinshiki* [Coming of Age Day] are now held twice: once in Centro Social, once in Okinawa Kenjinkai – although almost the same participants attend them. Some years ago, Okinawa Kenjinkai established *kariyushikai*, an activity equivalent to Day Service. Naoji

Nikkei ethnic associations' rise and decline 161

Ganaha, president of Santa Cruz Okinawa Kenjinkai, was bursting with ideas to animate the association. He explained that he created these events because some *kenjinkai* members are not affiliated to Centro Social Japonés and that they might feel excluded.

Nevertheless, Reiko Yohena, co-founder of Fraternidad Fujii and now responsible for ABJ San Juan's office in Santa Cruz, detects, first of all, a waste of resources:

> Members are the same everywhere [...], and we have to contribute [financially] to each association. If everything would be the same, like in Peru for example, or in Brazil ... In Peru, there is the APJ, the Asociación Peruano-Japonesa, and everything is included, like the *kenjinkai* [...]. It should be like that, but unfortunately, it's not possible here, because we're geographically separated, also historically. If we would put together everything, economically or socially, we would be very strong. But everything is dispersed. A huge ceremonial hall in Okinawa I, a swimming pool, everything is there, but only those from Okinawa I benefit. We also have a huge multipurpose hall in San Juan [...]. If we would put everything together, I think we would be the delegation number one of all foreigners here.

"We're the official cooks of Centro Social" – Gender roles

When examining Nikkei identities from a gender perspective, women, too, are marginalised in decision-making processes in associations. Many unwritten norms restrict women's choices in the *comunidad japonesa*, notably in the *colonias*. Women generally do not adopt leading roles in public and semi-public space, like the ABJ or the cooperatives, and they are not supposed to take over the family's farm (Suzuki 2010: 148ff.). Few jobs exist outside agriculture; many married women stay at home with their children, even those with higher education and working experience in the city.

Whereas women have not played a visible role in association activities, their work has been essential behind the scenes. Especially in the *colonias*, women carry out much unpaid work for association events. They organise Day Service activities for the elderly or run San Juan's library. Through such activities, women fulfil an essential role in defining Japanese-ness, having for instance the authority over what is cooked (Omori 2017). Mai Amuro underlines that this supporting role is essential to the stability of the entire *comunidad* and the male Nikkei's individual success. She also acknowledges that women are crucial for maintaining the equilibrium since they hold much power in the domestic sphere, mainly over financial issues:

> "They are the basis", my mother-in-law said [...]. "Here, we as women are still in the kitchen, but without us, all this wouldn't be possible, this stability, this equilibrium." And she is right. Because if you have one compact group that does all the difficult work, the other group can go outside, appear in public, do business, position itself, advance. If there would be a disequilibrium or

162 *Nikkei ethnic associations' rise and decline*

> if women would start a struggle for power, much energy would be lost. The Japanese are organised even in that [laughs].

Although cooking for events means self-affirmation and recognition from male association members, *fujinbu* member Daniela Vargas remarks in an ironic tone: "We're the official cooks of Centro Social." She would prefer more explicit appreciation and she would also like to discuss other issues rather than "just food." However, Daniela acknowledges that some changes do have taken place. *Fujinbu* members reduced their workload at festivals contracting external help, despite resistance by several male and female members who argued that the ideal women's section should do everything by itself according to "tradition." Accordingly, "good Japanese women" do not spend valuable resources on external services.

Daniela alludes to the fact that the membership system practically excludes females from voting in elections: women are designated as head of a family only if married to non-Nikkei. While I have met female Nikkei entrepreneurs, doctors and other university graduates with high responsibilities, few women have been in charge of an association, except, of course, for *fujinbu*. There have been no female Centro Social or ABJ presidents so far, but the already mentioned entrepreneur Ayaka Shimoji served one term as Okinawa Kenjinkai Santa Cruz' first female president. Sociedad Japonesa de La Paz with its individual membership system had a female head during my field research, similar to the newly founded Nikkei association of Cochabamba. Interestingly, various women have served as association presidents in Beni and Pando; however, as those *nihonjinkai* are practically defunct, such positions do not imply symbolic capital.

For social scientist Mai Amuro, such a role model is terrible for associations and the entire *comunidad*: it seems as if women were not capable of intelligent decisions. When alluding to the tensions between Centro Social members, she says:

> I think the institutional process would be very different if women would say a little more, would participate more. For example, if they would express their vision in meetings. Because they are more mature, they think in the common good, not in personal power, in leadership power over this or that group.

Also in Japan, while women and men are equal before the law, gender roles are nevertheless restrictive. Whereas many women are college graduates, they generally earn much less than males, fulfil mostly auxiliary positions at work and are supposed to stay at home after having children, although they may significantly influence family decisions behind the scenes (Imamura 2009). Like Bolivia and Latin America in general, *cruceño* society has the reputation of being male chauvinist as well: reinforced by a conservative Catholic ideology, women have comparatively less influence in many parts of society and are often supposed to remain in the private or semi-private sphere (Waldmann 2008: 70ff.). Nevertheless, several Nikkei and non-Nikkei interview partners regarded urban *cruceño* society as offering much more freedom to women than the *comunidad japonesa*. For

Nikkei ethnic associations' rise and decline 163

example, Naoko Kanai chose to marry a non-Nikkei, thinking that Nikkei men expected her to be subservient. Despite cherishing some elements of Japanese culture, Mai Amuro, too, prefers to socialise with non-Nikkei instead of taking part in association activities. She considers social norms in the *comunidad* to be a relic from pre-war times and as psychological violence against women and children. In contrast to Japanese conventions, Mai as a self-declared feminist insists on using her maiden name instead of her husband's name. She told me that she feels strange in the *comunidad*, especially when visiting Colonia Okinawa, for her a place of gendered limitations where her behaviour is closely monitored. Mai points to a different canon of values that is more important for her than any obligation towards the community.

Santa Cruz' Nikkei associations have recently made some efforts to include more women in association boards and organising committees. It is an open question if individual board members mean a substantial change; or, as a male member of Sociedad Japonesa commented on this development in Centro Social in an ironic tone: "This is to keep the ladies quiet." Also Mai is disillusioned with the result. She thinks that these changes are rather symbolic and do not show any real will for innovation. Mai remembers how she created a small scandal when proposing an Okinawa sumo contest also for females. At the same time, she criticises that many women do not question being relegated to the domestic sphere. For an anniversary of Okinawa Kenjinkai some years ago, she took part in the organising board with nine other females and ten males. She was deeply disappointed that the women would only raise their voice when it came to food preparation. Akiyoshi Chiba, a male second-generation association leader from Asunción, came up with a similar example without my question. No more than two Paraguayan association presidents have been women because of a lack of candidates, he told me:

> We wanted to have a gender balance, 50 – 50. So first a man, then a woman [...] to break it up. [...] And there are no women, imagine, there are no female candidates. Not that we don't want them, but there are none.

Those who object to the association's gender norms mostly stay away instead of trying to cause a change. Mai holds: "But what should I tell them, and me entering there? No, I really don't have the motivation or the energy, and it's not the moment, people are comfortable". The current socioeconomic stability is responsible for the "hyper-archaic mentality" that wants to maintain gender roles from a Japan of the past, Mai argues. Too much energy would be wasted if open conflicts broke out, she says laughingly: "Even in this the Japanese are organised – they know how to keep the pressure low!" She concludes with an ironic remark, thinking of the NGO sector where she works: "Sometimes I want to say that they should rather organise these programmes and talks on women's capacitation for Nikkei women!"

Mai had joined Centro Social only because she wanted to send her children to Japanese school. In 2017, to my great surprise since I know her critical attitude, she served a one-year term as *fujinbu* board member since she thought that

164 *Nikkei ethnic associations' rise and decline*

the board's composition gave her the chance to change something from within. Together with non-Nikkei *fujinbu* president Micaela Tejada, Centro Social directory member and businesswoman Minae Hara and some others, she achieved that new female *nihonjinkai* members are no longer obliged to join *fujinbu*. Moreover, they no longer need a letter from their husband to vote in his absence. Changes are small, but Mai was satisfied since this meant a step towards gender equality, she said: "They were violating my constitutional rights!"

Holes in the roof – How Nikkei imagine the associations' future

As Reiko Yohena's statement above implied, disagreements between members may also lead to financial fragmentation. Therefore, many Nikkei are increasingly worried about the associations' financial sustainability. Because of the decreasing number of paying members, alternative sources of income have to be found. Compared to Asociación Peruano-Japonesa in Lima as an exclusive club with a huge cultural centre, schools, a theatre and a hospital (Asociación Peruano-Japonesa [2017]), Bolivia's Nikkei associations are small and much less attractive. Centro Social members receive deductions in Policonsultorio Nikkei and elderly members can attend Day Service. They have the right to be buried in the Japanese mausoleum in the city's main cemetery, and Japanese school is a unique offer.

Japanese schools, mostly financed by Nikkei entities and JICA, are one case in point. The popularity of language classes depends on the country's attractiveness, for instance, if working in Japan is economically interesting. In this context, it is not helpful that financial support from Japan decreases. At the same time, the number of students declines in the *colonias'* schools because of low birth rates and a general lack of interest. Santa Cruz' complementary school shows a similar picture and the situation may be further aggravated by the fact that it currently does not accept non-Nikkei students. Around 50 children, mostly Nikkei, are enrolled in Okinawa I's Japanese school and kindergarten; but they would need perhaps double that to pay off, ABJ employee Keita Itosu says. Okinawa II's school has a different organisation structure: half of the day, it is financed by the Bolivian government and follows the normal curriculum. Around 120 children are enrolled – but only 20 children attend Japanese afternoon classes that require an extra tuition fee. The small JICA-supported hospital in Colonia Okinawa is not self-sustaining, either. Ichiro Ninomiya from Bolivia's JICA office explains that many non-Nikkei patients cannot afford high fees, while salaries are a significant cost factor. At the same time, several competing hospitals have opened in the neighbouring city of Montero.

The *nihonjinkai* themselves face difficulties as well. To give an example, half of Sociedad Japonesa's revenues comes from renting out the association's ceremonial hall – but competition is growing (Sociedad Japonesa de La Paz 2012: 250). Additional issues with tax authorities might emerge if the associations' non-profit status is questioned, a problem Sociedad Japonesa already had to face. Moreover, boards have been careless with membership fees, relying on members'

Nikkei ethnic associations' rise and decline 165

or language students' promises to pay. Finally, Nikkei associations undergo rapid ageing not least because many younger descendants cancelled their membership or moved to Japan. The consequences of all these developments are already visible in Centro Social: for some time, rainwater has been entering through holes in the roof.

One key question is how associations will define membership in the future and what this will mean for the Nikkei's ethnic identity. Non-Nikkei members might become essential for the associations' survival – Sociedad Japonesa already relies financially on its growing number of non-voting, "honorary" non-Nikkei members. Therefore, San Juan's former mayor Katsumi Bani proposes to transform Nikkei associations into something similar to Centro Paraguayo Japonés in Asunción. This cultural institution is now administered by the city while the building has been financed by Japan. Interested non-Nikkei can become affiliated, too, but it hosts only some activities related to Japanese culture. Since the Bolivian *nihonjinkai* do not offer many attractive facilities, it is unlikely that non-Nikkei members will claim for equality. However, Tomoji Yamashita, Nisei lawyer and former president of Sociedad Japonesa de La Paz, wonders if it might face similar issues as the local German club one day. He joined the club without being of German origin, simply because members can use a variety of sports facilities. German-speaking members once had a preferential status; but when the club grew, other members filed a suit for discrimination and won.

When I visit Sociedad Japonesa de La Paz one afternoon in August 2017, the noise of hammer blows and drills echoes in the windowless but spacious office with sofas and exhibits like a Japanese sword. Secretary Adela Prieto and her young Japanese assistant check reservations for the ceremonial hall, process membership applications, answer occasional phone calls and discuss *undōkai* preparations. Adela still has time for two of her favourite activities, chatting with visitors like me and folding origami papers. Apart from an impressive number of Japanese books covering a major part of the walls, Adela's highly elaborated origami figures occupy an entire shelf and a glass cabinet. Some combine the Japanese technique with Bolivian motives such as condors, Bolivian Carnival characters and women in distinctive indigenous habits. I sit down at the black, upholstered rotating chair next to the radiator and Adela, clothed in a wool poncho, prepares some green tea for me. In the meantime, she reflects aloud on the changes that have taken place during the many years that she has been working in Sociedad Japonesa. She greatly appreciated the Issei presidents who only left office after all the work was done and who even contributed with their personal funds, while she considers the second generation to be less careful, thinking that they do not know the statutes and lack a vision for the future. She also worries about the decreasing number of members, now around 140, and consequently, about the declining amount of membership fees. Still, the board decided to carry out some renovations. Adela is also worried that the younger generations will increasingly stay away, except for the JICA volunteers and some recent migrants from Japan who are a source of hope for her. She finishes her monologue thoughtfully remembering that for the 90th anniversary in 2012, an association leader predicted that Sociedad Japonesa

166 *Nikkei ethnic associations' rise and decline*

will cease to function on its 100th birthday. "This was some years ago ... so I don't know for how much time this will still exist."

Conclusion

Ethnic associations are an important aspect of identity construction among Nikkei, but are seldom discussed in literature. They were once founded as mutual help organisations, maintaining contact with Japan. Nowadays, they try to define who is a "legitimate" descendant. Activities are central to creating the *comunidad japonesa* as well as specific cultural values and unwritten codes of conduct. Whereas they also present an officially sanctioned form of Japanese culture, it becomes clear that such representations serve first descendants' needs rather than showing "authentic" Japanese culture. Interestingly, religion and religious associations play a negligible role in the Nikkei's identity negotiations.

However, the *comunidad* is no longer equal to Nikkei associations. They lose significance at a moment when urbanisation and economic diversification weaken the necessity of membership. On a closer look, it becomes clear that despite the supposed equality of all members, most associations are not based on individual interests but on household representation, implicitly reproducing traditional structures of inequality. This is the case for younger generations who see that their attempts for reform fail, but it is also true for female members who are underrepresented in leading functions. In sum, associations have seldom been able to integrate members with different expectations or different origins. While Bolivia's Nikkei associations are too small to become a leisure time club for an ethnically defined part of the middle class, they are increasingly challenged to maintain financial stability.

Notes

1 To be exact, Comité de Fomento or *chiiki* as a separate association is responsible for the organisation of festivities in the *colonias*. Its members overlap to a large degree with those of the respective ABJ.
2 However, at a closer look, this fondness for associations is not unique to Nikkei. Moya (2005: 837f.) proposes that migrants' different ethnic identity in general favours the foundation of such collective entities. In Santa Cruz, other foreign migrants and their descendants have their associations as well, for example, the "Swiss Circle," although they might not have the same size and infrastructure as the *nihonjinkai*.
3 The Buddhist group Sōka Gakkai [value creating society] was founded as Sōka Kyōiku Gakkai in 1930. Sōka Gakkai International (SGI) has around 12 million practitioners worldwide according to its homepage (Soka Gakkai International 2015). Proselytising is an important part of their activities.
4 Covell (2009: 147f.) observes: "Studies on modern Japanese religions frequently note that in surveys of Japanese religion the number of believers of the various religions is generally twice the actual population of Japan." Japanese religion consists of five strains that have influenced each other and that fulfil different "tasks" in people's life: Shinto, Buddhism, folk religion, religious Taoism and Confucianism. Okinawan belief systems have again distinct characteristics (Lebra 1966), and the Japanese have

also incorporated elements coming from other creeds, like Christian-style weddings. Japanese religious beliefs are marked by an emphasis on harmony between humans, gods and nature; as well as individual ceremonies and ancestor veneration (Earhart 1982; Nakamaki 2003).

5 Japanese glutinous rice cakes.
6 A kind of Japanese pancakes combined with vegetables, meat or fish.
7 Latin American roasted beef sticks.
8 However, associations have also been founded in settings where individual migrants did not receive much support, for example, in Beni and Pando. Another example is Santiago de Chile's Sociedad Japonesa de Beneficiencia (Takeda 2002). Although Japanese Chileans have never received much support from Japan, the small group has organised, for instance, the Pan American events COPANI and Confra.
9 However, this situation is not unique to Bolivia, see for example Brazil (personal communication by Érica Hatugai).
10 An outdoor activity for the elderly, similar to croquet.

7 Nikkei networks in Latin America and beyond

Sanshin sounds fill the air at the closing ceremony of the 2014 World Youth Uchinānchu Festival (Wakamono Taikai) in Düsseldorf, Germany. Clothed in a grey-blue *yukata* [casual kimono] and *geta* sandals, the president of Okinawa Kenjinkai Germany turns out to be a professional player of his instrument. Around 30 young participants, all wearing T-shirts with the slogan I LOVE OKINAWA, react with almost frenetic applause to this performance of Okinawan-ness. To close the programme, everybody joins in a joyous and chaotic Okinawan-style *kachaashi* dance with waving hands and stamping feet – the message is that everybody is Okinawan at this very moment.

After meetings in Brazil and the United States, and before going to the Philippines in 2015, the 2014 event takes place in Germany. Finally, in the course of the 2016 World Uchinānchu Taikai, the meeting will be held in Okinawa Prefecture. The Okinawa-based WYUA (World Youth Uchinānchu Association) chose Düsseldorf since it hosts around 380 Japanese companies, shops, temples and a Japanese school and holds regular events featuring Japanese culture (Japan-Tag Düsseldorf/NRW e.V. 2018). Most participants are around 20 years old. Two-thirds come directly from Okinawa Prefecture; one organiser is a Korean living in the archipelago. The remaining attendees are Okinawans who reside in central Europe, two non-Okinawan students from the local university and a mainland Japanese lecturer living in Germany. Organisers had expected more participants, but Okinawa seems not to be well known in Europe.

Sponsored by a number of Okinawan companies, the programme booklet presents WYUA, Okinawa Prefecture, some famous tourist sites and *sanshin* music. It tells attendants that networks along ethnic lines are essential to Okinawans worldwide. It also features a greeting message from the prefecture's governor and an overview of the worldwide diaspora with portraits of Okinawans living in Germany, Great Britain and France. According to the governor, making new friends is essential for such a meeting. He hopes for the enrichment of Okinawa's networks and the development of human resources to pass down *uchinā* [Okinawan] spirit, emphasising that Okinawa is an archipelago of peaceful co-existence and interaction with other cultures. Indeed, I will later visit some participants in Okinawa Prefecture.

After a city tour by bus to Düsseldorf's most important sights and a stop at a restaurant serving sauerkraut, the next two days are filled with workshops,

DOI: 10.4324/9781003228295-7

Nikkei networks in Latin America and beyond 169

presentations and meals in a local community centre. Since peace education is an important part of Okinawa Prefecture's cultural policies, the slightly improvised programme includes the workshop "Pass the baton: memories of war and peace." Small groups thoroughly discuss – mostly in Japanese – their experiences with peace education at school and visits to the Second World War sites in Okinawa Prefecture, before creating a poster in English and presenting it to the others. Afterwards, participants fold paper cranes, a well-known Japanese peace symbol. Following the serious discussion, the atmosphere becomes joyful with *obentō* lunch boxes and Japanese sweets, including Okinawan-style *beniimo* purple yam cakes. Other programme items centre on topics such as "How can we coexist with nature, but live a convenient life?", "What culture do you want to pass down?" and "Younger generations don't speak *uchināguchi.*" One Okinawan Brazilian participant, around 30, tells me that he finds the group discussions somehow cute since they show that participants are still young, full of idealism and a little naïve. Some participants give short presentations, for example on the history of Okinawan migration to Brazil. The *seinenkai* president of Bolivia's Colonia Okinawa sends greetings via video message and we watch an anime about Okinawan migration to the *colonia*, produced by some *seinenkai* members. Not everybody is fluent in Japanese, English or German; a student from the local university's Japanese studies institute translates complex issues. However, most of the time, participants get along by themselves without problems.

Now, in the joyous atmosphere of the farewell party, the flags of Great Britain, Okinawa, Brazil, Peru, the United States, Bolivia, Germany and Argentina are taken off the wall for some group pictures. In a corner, I record a video message with the Okinawan youth association president who will travel to Colonia Okinawa's 60th birthday shortly after. My – not very professional – presentation of Miruku Munari, the most emblematic Ryūkyūkoku Matsuridaiko song I had learned in Bolivia, causes great enthusiasm among the young Okinawans who had learned to dance the same song at school. While the other attendees will visit Paris before flying back to Japan, I leave for the train station to return home. As a farewell present, three of the organisers give me the picture of an Okinawan beach in a seashell-decorated frame: "Please visit Okinawa!"

The term "Nikkei," used for Japanese descendants in different countries, already points to common characteristics, experiences and interests. Whereas Bolivian Nikkei associations are losing members, Pan-American Nikkei events as well as events for Okinawan descendants become increasingly popular. Indeed, in contrast to what I wrote about many Nikkei's lack of interest in ethnic associations, the same interview partners were usually enthusiastic about these events, implicitly or explicitly arguing that the more Pan-American events there were, the better for the maintenance of "Japanese values." The core referent for these descendants is no longer Japan, but their country of residence and Latin America as a whole. However, only Creighton (2010), Kasamatsu (2005) and Takenaka (2009b) have published on these networks.

Several factors increase the popularity of such activities and events. The Nikkei experience a growing figurative distance to Japan, a country that they may not even know personally. While they become more self-confident as Japanese descendants in the Americas, they can afford to travel and new communication channels facilitate contacts. Taking these trends into account, international exchanges and meetings are popular not least because their event character does not imply long-term involvement for participants, unlike membership in community associations. Moreover, Pan-American Nikkei events are an opportunity for Nisei and Sansei to implement their own ideas.

Confra, COPANI, Fénix, etc. – Pan-American Nikkei events

Many Bolivian Nikkei have maintained relations with descendants in other Latin American countries as a result of remigration, marriage or studies abroad. Based on such networks, some Nisei started to organise meetings between descendants from different countries in the 1960s and 1970s, such as occasional sports tournaments or beauty contests. The creation of COPANI and Confra intensified such contacts in the early 1980s.

Already in the introduction, I presented the biannually held Confra tournament. During this meeting, national teams compete against each other in athletics, baseball, futsal, volleyball, table tennis, golf, judo, etc. In early 2014, the 21st Confra was held for the first time in Bolivia: around 500 participants from all over Latin America attended the four-day-event in Santa Cruz and Colonia Okinawa, among them more than 150 Bolivian Nikkei from Santa Cruz Department, La Paz and Beni. At least in Bolivia, Confra is more popular than COPANI (Figure 7.1).

Figure 7.1 Volleyball players from different countries at Confra 2014.

COPANI (Convención/Convenção Panamericana Nikkei, also called PANA convention) is organised biannually by APN, the Asociación/Associação Panamericana Nikkei or Pan-American Nikkei Association, officially established in Mexico City in 1981. Nikkei from all over the Americas meet for several days to discuss Nikkei-related issues and to socialise. With the 2003 meeting in Santa Cruz, it was held for the first time in Bolivia. APN and COPANI want to enhance the exchange of information and the diffusion of Japanese culture, while creating ties among different Nikkei communities. Workshop topics include discussions on the term "Nikkei" as well as fundamental questions such as how to position as Nisei, Sansei, Yonsei, etc., in the respective country of residence. Participants debate on the future of Japanese language education and the situation of Human Rights in the Americas. Some workshops address more practical issues such as problems in agriculture or how to organise health facilities. Furthermore, panels discuss the Nikkei's role as entrepreneurs, their positioning in industry and commerce as well as their experiences in politics. While participants tend to be older than Confra attendees, COPANI also includes a youth programme. Around 300 participants attended the meeting in Santa Cruz in 2003, but other events have received up to 500 attendees (Takenaka 2009b: 1338).

Specific exchanges are organised for young Nikkei, such as Fénix (Paraguay), Dale! (Argentina), Lidercambio (Peru), Vibra Joven (Mexico) or Movi-Mente (Brazil). Bolivian Nikkei have not created such a youth festival, but they have already hosted Niseta Tours for Okinawan descendants that have been held in different South American countries.[1]

Furthermore, apart from small initiatives between Japan and different Latin American countries, the Kaigai Nikkeijin Kyōkai (Association of Nikkei & Japanese Abroad), located in JICA's headquarter in Yokohama, emerged from a festival on the initiative of Japan's National Diet in 1957. Apart from organising annual conventions in Japan, it has been engaging for Nikkei in Japan with language classes, internship programmes and seminars (Association of Nikkei and Japanese Abroad 2017a). Whereas Japan is in the centre of these conventions, Pan-American Nikkei events can be interpreted as an attempt to emancipate from the country of their ancestors.

"Emotional patrimony" – How to transmit "Japanese values" on a Pan-American level

With the definition of an overarching identity, the above-described Pan-American Nikkei events aim at perpetuating "Japanese values" while uniting Nikkei from different countries. Acting together and joining forces, organisers hope that they will maintain a distinct identity as Latin Americans of Japanese origin.

For Ryota Kurihara, such events are essential to maintain "Japanese values" in the face of cultural loss as an imminent danger. He is a Paraguayan Nikkei in his early twenties who studies in Asunción, but was raised in Paraguay's second-largest city, Ciudad del Este; and, according to the car he is driving, his

172   *Nikkei networks in Latin America and beyond*

family is prosperous. He has already visited some Pan-American Nikkei events in Paraguay and elsewhere and is extremely enthusiastic about the idea of bringing together Nikkei from different countries. When I interview him in August 2015 in a Japanese restaurant in Asunción, he, as the national *seinenkai* president, is preparing the next Fénix [Phoenix] youth festival in December. They expect between 30 and 40 attendants at the national Nikkei federation's country house. Ryota and his friends want the movement to grow not only in the cities but also in the Paraguayan *colonias*. Therefore, they make a two-day-trip to the major cities and the *colonias* to present the event. Ryota regrets that many young Nikkei "are in their own world" and "don't integrate much" into Nikkei groups. Instead, according to Ryota, taking part in such events is an indicator of ethnic consciousness. Like anniversaries, Fénix, COPANI, Confra etc. are regarded as key moments to engage with a long-term perspective against "latinisation." Events like Fénix are a moment to become aware or to reconnect to one's ancestors' country of origin. Hence, Ryota and his friends invite some Issei to accompany them on field trips or to teach them Japanese dances.

Many Nikkei interview partners who had participated in such events said that they had all felt like brothers and sisters, a "unique experience." While we enjoy a large plate of sushi, Ryota explains to me that during such an event in Argentina, he became aware that he belongs to something bigger than just the Paraguayan Nikkei community. Whereas he has never been to Japan, taking part in such an event means for him to experience a sense of belonging to a Pan-American community. He also speaks about the reinforcement of his identity as Nikkei, while he interestingly refers to "feeling Argentinean":

> I got to know more young people. It was like we were all from Argentina at that moment. [We were] all from different countries, but we were in the same place and had fun at the same time. And it's very interesting because, in these meetings, ideas emerge on an international level. It's a very good event because it supports a lot everything that's Nikkei, that many people don't know or they forgot about their roots.

In other words, more than giving rational reasons for participation, Ryota attaches an emotional value to these events: organisers like him hope that positive emotions will create a sense of community. Akiyoshi Chiba, a Paraguayan Nisei involved in Pan-American events for many years, foregrounds that the participants develop the consciousness to be part of something bigger:

> They should have a concept of emotional patrimony. They have to have something, it's like the concept of the sense of belonging, that's mine or I have taken part. They have to feel part, if not, they don't give value to it.

As a result, social activities such as eating together or playing outdoor games are important to make the programme more attractive and to maintain the threshold low. Karaoke contests, golf tournaments and group trips to local tourist sites are

Nikkei networks in Latin America and beyond 173

an important part of COPANI and Confra as well: indeed, some Nikkei participate only in leisure activities and do not join discussion sessions. The importance of positive collective emotions becomes also evident in the Fénix promotion video (Unión de Jóvenes Nikkei del Paraguay 2012), centring on concepts such as "feeling," "magic," "dream," "friendship" and "sharing."

Nevertheless, activities during Fénix are also meant to transmit "Japanese values" like honesty, loyalty and respect for the elderly. At a time when individualism is thought to be on the rise on a global level, the goal is to strengthen solidarity in order to ensure the continuity of a Pan-American Nikkei community. Moreover, sport is seen as an excellent means to maintain such a spirit. One Bolivian Nisei expressed his expectation that his nephew whom he characterised as a former lazy drunkard will become motivated to continue playing football after Confra since sports had already helped him to become a better and hard-working person. Hence, the name of the Argentinean festival "Dale!" [Go for it!] originates in the well-known Japanese expression "*ganbatte*," referring to animating oneself, making efforts and moving forward (Asato 2012). The Fénix promotion videos mention concepts such as "advancement," "energy," "learning" and "future" – even though such concepts are not unique to the Japanese or Nikkei, but could come from any manual for self-improvement.

Daiki Kaneshiro, member of the 2014 Confra organisation board, has been visiting such events for decades. According to him, such activities are essential to increase awareness of one's origins and to become more self-confident. He emphasises that connecting with other descendants, adopting "Japanese values" and becoming emotionally involved does not only strengthen participants' ethnic identity, but also enables them to become leaders. This is reflected in the name of the Peruvian youth meeting "Lidercambio" [leader change] – although it is unclear what "leadership" might mean. Daiki admits that such activities may rather point to a general moral education: "Maybe not all become leaders, but it gives them much moral strength. They teach them morals, ethics, how they must behave in the world and things like that." While not everybody is present in these events, Daiki and other participants believe that such ideas will be disseminated in their respective networks.

During workshops and informal encounters, participants discuss similarities and differences. Daiki foregrounds that one may adopt ideas from other descendants who have gone through similar experiences. He and other participants are deeply impressed by the association activities they witnessed abroad. Nevertheless, while referring to "traditional values" and trying to connect to descendants from other countries, long-term participants like Daiki and Katsumi Bani also feel part of Bolivian society. The latter served two terms as mayor of San Juan – in other words, taking part in such events may be even correlated to an increased commitment to the respective society. Daiki concludes that identifying as a Japanese descendant means connecting to other cultures in a globalised world. He is pleased that since the beginning of the millennium, more and more young Bolivian Nikkei have been following the example of Nisei like him:

174 *Nikkei networks in Latin America and beyond*

Today, thanks to all these types of experience and because of the internet, we have a network where nobody feels alone. All Nikkei in Bolivia now have friends in Peru, in Buenos Aires, in Paraguay, in all parts of the world and vice-versa. So this in a certain way strengthens them and makes them think that Bolivia is not the world. The world is much bigger and if you have a bigger mind, a broader mind, you have higher aspirations. And I think that's good for everybody. It makes them grow.

However, the Fénix promotion video mentioned above gives the impression that systematic knowledge transmission about Japan or Nikkei history is once again not in the foreground. While the performance of songs and dances plays an essential role during such events, their use is first of all symbolic.

"Your accent is different, but you feel like a family" – Negotiating a Pan-American Nikkei identity

Complex and layered identities play a central role in Pan-American Nikkei events: participants refer simultaneously to various sources of identity, with different aims and outcomes. Nevertheless, after Confra, psychology student Kimi Ayala from Santa Cruz points to a common origin as a uniting feature:

It's nice to have this kind of fraternisation, where you can get to know other people. And there you feel that although your accent is different, your culture is different to mine, there is something that unites you. You feel like a family.

They may express the wish to improve their Japanese skills, but the language is not central to a Pan-American Nikkei identity. Interestingly, in a personal essay on her experiences at the 2017 COPANI in Lima, one participant from the United States declared that taking part made her more motivated to study Spanish in order to be able to create friendships with Latin American Nikkei (Nagase 2017).

Participants often emphasise that "Japanese values" are most important to form a united diaspora, like Daiki Kaneshiro:

The topic of the Pan-American Nikkei community strengthens you as Nikkei, but they somehow instil in you the Nikkei values that don't exist in other cultures. So one tries to take all the good things of being Nikkei and the best of Japanese culture as well as from the country where one lives and one makes that symbiosis to take out the best.

During these events, the term "Nikkei" is used on purpose to express interrelatedness. Participants say that the Japanese have arrived at different destinations, but their descendants have maintained many similarities, a distinct ethnic consciousness and links with Japan. For years, defining a Pan-American Nikkei identity has been central to COPANI meetings: questions such as "who is Nikkei" or "what does it mean being Nikkei" are debated at length to discover what unites

Nikkei networks in Latin America and beyond 175

descendants from different countries. Such debates on identity also promote a sense of belonging to a diasporic community with common ancestry.

At the same time, discussions on the term "Nikkei" are also a consequence of growing diversity (Takenaka 2009b: 1340). Whereas Confra participants all identified as Japanese descendants, they also referred to their country of residence; see for instance the different sports suits in national colours and the omnipresent flags. Furthermore, although it was implicitly assumed that Nikkei face similar living conditions wherever they reside, they discovered as many differences as similarities and found stereotypes confirmed. One of the organisers considered an Argentinean Nikkei player "more Argentinean than the real Argentineans," because he was unwilling to congratulate the winners after his team had lost against Bolivia in the finals. Most Bolivian Nikkei interview partners acknowledged other participants' Japanese ancestry but considered them "less Japanese" compared to themselves. Nikkei from those countries, as stated before, are mostly pre-war descendants and many have non-Nikkei ancestry. Instead, many Bolivian Nikkei, along with the Paraguayan participants, claimed to be the "most Japanese," often citing their language capabilities but also a specific habitus. Daiki proudly remembers that some foreign Nikkei were impressed by locals during dinner at Colonia Okinawa: they waited until the guests had taken their food before they served themselves. He sees this as an expression of *enryo* [respect towards others]. Whereas their "Japanese-ness" was a reason for many Bolivians to feel proud, some of them also pointed out that they should learn from Brazilian and Peruvian Nikkei. They claimed that descendants in these countries engaged more for their respective society and that they organised a greater number of Japan-related events.

Bolivian Nikkei regularly compare themselves with other Latin American descendants, but they almost never refer to North Americans with whom they lack personal contacts, a common language[2] and comparable experiences. Kasamatsu (2005: 93) observes that the first COPANI was held in Mexico to present successful Latin American Nisei to North Americans who did not know much about descendants in the south. While no North Americans were present at the 2014 Confra, Takenaka (2009b: 1332) writes that language and cultural barriers between Anglophones and Latin Americans impeded socialising at the COPANI meetings she attended. Whereas this observation points to the limits of a Pan-American Nikkei identity, more studies would be needed to draw further conclusions.

While many Bolivian Nikkei claim to be culturally close to Japan, the latter plays a decisive yet ambivalent role in these conventions – a role that has changed over time. In the 1950s, Japan started to hold regular conferences for Nikkei in Japan with the participation of high-ranking Japanese politicians and members of the Imperial Family. When the Nisei began organising Pan-American meetings, it meant an attempt to distance themselves not only from the Issei but also from Japan.[3] Consequently, the Nikkei's focus was not so much on the creation of ties to Japan, but on common topics in the Americas. Tensions between Nikkei and Japan have faded away, while the emphasis is shifting from American identities

176 *Nikkei networks in Latin America and beyond*

to including more Japan-related issues. While they claim to be different from the Japanese, there is less need to distance themselves from Japan.

Organisers regularly invite Japanese diplomats and display well-known positive symbols of Japanese-ness such as origami, calligraphy, etc. Creighton (2010: 136) observes that such symbols connect the Nikkei to Japanese culture, whereas they also stand for being different. By way of illustration, the song *Furusato* [homeland] suggests nostalgia for one's childhood home and a traditional way of life. When it is sung at COPANI, it acquires an additional meaning since it is performed to express Japanese heritage, but also their belonging to the Latin American *colonias* (Creighton 2010: 147f.). Organisers sometimes invent new symbols that do not directly relate to their Japanese origin, suggesting that the Nikkei constitute an own ethnic group. An example is the floral friendship tree at the 1999 COPANI in Santiago de Chile (Creighton 2010: 152). Participants try to create a common history, thereby justifying their goal to construct a Pan-American community (Takenaka 2009b: 1337). When honouring personalities who have made outstanding contributions to COPANI or Confra, organisers emphasise the shift from a Japanese past to a Nikkei past.

At the same time, when the Japanese government sends representatives or writes greeting messages, Japan is indirectly acknowledging that there exists something between "Japanese" and "non-Japanese." However, relating to Japan does not mean the same for everybody. Latin American Nikkei are more comfortable with playing the Japanese national anthem *Kimigayo* or showing the Japanese flag than North Americans are. The latter have fought hard for their rights as U.S. and Canadian citizens and fear that expressing too much attachment to their ancestors' homeland will reinforce old stereotypes of being a disloyal fifth column. For Latin American Nikkei, the relation between their home countries and Japan has obviously been different (Creighton 2010: 149f.; Takenaka 2009b: 139f.).

Japan sees these conventions as a means to maintain diasporic connections. Hirabayashi und Kikumura-Yano (2002: 156) underline that the Nikkei as Latin American citizens are supposed to assume a special role: they should be a "bridge" between Latin America and Japan, embodying "Japanese values" and speak Japanese, at best. It remains unclear if these goals can be reached and how much gain there is for either side. However, class plays an important role to define who counts as "bridge": the notion of equal partnership seems not to extend to *dekasegi* workers in Japan who "return" to Japan as blue-collar workers (Manzenreiter 2014).

While all these events are focused on a global scale, they are rooted locally. Consequently, the first COPANI organisers hoped to transmit "Mexican cheerfulness" to foreign participants (Kasamatsu 2005: 93). Other examples are tours to local sites as well as the local show master and the "typically Bolivian" *caporales* dancers at the Confra inauguration. A Bolivian Nikkei child in a "traditional" Bolivian dress headed each delegation that entered the sports ground. With such elements, organisers tried to demonstrate their expert status in Bolivian culture.

Nikkei networks in Latin America and beyond 177

It is important for organisers to invite prominent non-Nikkei guests to gain legitimacy in their country cf residence. Welcoming speeches and messages from local, regional or even national government representatives are always part of the programme. At Confra, an official representative presented messages from the mayor and the governor of the department. The consuls of Paraguay and Peru, too, attended the inauguration ceremony. For the 2014 Confra, instead of relying solely on Nikkei associations, they received funds from Santa Cruz Prefecture; moreover, a Nikkei-owned fashion company, local car sellers and a bank, apart from CAICO and ABJ Okinawa, sponsored them. Moreover, the inauguration ceremony was held at the city's main stadium Estadio Ramón Tahuichi Aguilera. Organisers thereby wanted to present the community to non-Nikkei Bolivians, demonstrating their status as prosperous and cosmopolitan Bolivian citizens, able to carry out a large, costly and harmonious event. Nevertheless, a conflict emerged between ABJ Okinawa and the non-Nikkei mayor of Colonia Okinawa about the ambulant sellers on the main street because ABJ feared that they would create a negative impression among visiting foreigners.

Therefore, as Takenaka (2009b: 1336f.) writes, speeches on how the Nikkei have contributed to society thanks to their "Japanese values" and despite all hardships are an integral part of such events. Organisers emphasise that some Nikkei have attained important positions in society, economy and politics, including the former Peruvian president Alberto Fujimori[4]: "In every country where the Nikkei were present, stories would go, Nikkei per capita income was above the national average and, on a per capita basis, there were more Nikkei professionals than professionals from any other ethnic group." These achievements all over the Americas were then explained with the supposedly unique values.

At the same time, Takenaka (2009b: 1343) notes that the Nikkei could create such events because they enjoy comfortable socioeonomic status rather than being poor and marginalised: it is not an automatic consequence of shared ancestry, but a result of their own changing living conditions. Nevertheless, being ethnicised as foreigners in their counties of residence, an experience mainly regarded as negative, may have been an additional reason to develop a feeling of belonging together.

While Confra organisers invited some non-Nikkei speakers, their participation was restricted within certain limits. Organisers put advertising posters on the street and in shops to invite non-Nikkei spectators to the 2014 Confra – posters for community events can generally be found in ethnic associations, but seldom elsewhere in the city. There was no entrance fee, either. While one non-Nikkei was involved in the organisation as a coach, all athletes were of Japanese ancestry since Confra requires those participants whithout a Japanese surname to prove their origin (Confra XXIII 2018). Non-Nikkei sympathisers can take part at COPANI (Takenaka 2009b: 1339), but I have not heard that they occupy leading roles. In sum, while these events may be partly accessible for non-Nikkei, ethnic boundaries are not questioned as such.

Nevertheless, the Nikkei are not the only ones who wish to create a supranational diasporic identity referring to a common ancestry, culture and history with

178 *Nikkei networks in Latin America and beyond*

values formulated broad enough for everybody to feel included – see for example the Global Organisation of People of Indian Origin, the World Lebanese Cultural Union, the World Jewish Congress or the World Armenian Congress. Takenaka (2009b: 1339) cites an association leader who is convinced that "Japanese values" are important to the entire world: "The essence of Japanese values is good for all humanity: respect for the elderly, respect for the authority and no violation of the law." It was no coincidence that the background track of the Fénix promotion video (Unión de Jóvenes Nikkei del Paraguay 2014) was "Save the world" by the group Swedish House Mafia. Fénix participants' commitment to an orphanage perfectly suited that idea: contributing with food and playing with children, they make a positive contribution to Paraguay as model citizens of Japanese ancestry.

"Bolivia needs to open her mind" – Taking the Pan-American Nikkei identity home

Among Bolivian Nikkei, it is still common to speak about themselves as "*japone-ses.*" Nevertheless, especially Confra and COPANI participants emphasise that they are different from "*japoneses.*" They underline that they were born and raised in the Americas and therefore identify as citizens of these countries, in addition to their Japanese origin. Accordingly, the 2014 Confra organising team called itself "Nikkei Bolivia." The term's increasing prominence is perhaps also a reaction to the growing salience of ethnic difference in Bolivian politics.

Drawing to such a Pan-American Nikkei identity is not so much a matter of generation or length of stay, but of orientation, Shuji Ando from Paraguay underlines.

> This COPANI [in 2003], we almost took it to Bolivia by force, because […] for many years, Bolivia was at the margin of Nikkei activities [...]. I don't know why. I think it's also a problem of the head because [the then president of ANBJ] said "I am Nikkei", but I told him, "you're not Nikkei, you're pure Japanese". I always told him like that, and I argued with him.

Whereas such events have been organised for more than 30 years, few Bolivians have participated compared to descendants from other countries. Okinawan descendants from both the city and the *colonia* take part to a larger degree than other Nikkei. But adhering to new identities may mean challenging old ones. Therefore, Ayaka and her co-organisers deplore that many descendants in Bolivia do not have that consciousness yet or are even reluctant to embrace a Pan-American Nikkei identity: many Japanese Bolivians still call themselves "*japoneses.*"

Although Daiki presents such events as highly attractive, Confra organis-ers experienced that many Bolivian Nikkei do not support them. Reiko Yohena remembers how reluctant many Nikkei were when asked to contribute. Many told her that there was no need for the event, that Bolivia's Nikkei community was not prepared for Confra or that Reiko and her co-organisers would put funds into their own pockets. Interestingly, Koki Takamine, a Nisei farmer and involved in

Nikkei networks in Latin America and beyond   179

Pan-American Nikkei activities for many years, argues that this attitude is "typically Bolivian": according to him, Bolivians are too submissive, introverted and shy – and Bolivian Nikkei, too. Co-organiser Ayaka Shimoji, too, emphasises that this lack of interest is not related to an unstable financial situation. While she has participated in Pan-American Nikkei events since she was fourteen, she deplores the "closed mentality" of many post-war Nikkei in Bolivia who do not understand the importance of such events.

> If you tell them that they should invest in their children that they travel to a competition like the one in January [refers to Confra] or to a leadership exchange or something like that, they find it stupid, it's a waste of money or time for them.

Therefore, Ayaka hoped that the 2014 Confra would not only help to maintain "Japanese values," but would also bring new initiatives she sees as necessary for Santa Cruz' Nikkei community:

> In this kind of events, one feels the pride of being Nikkei, of getting to know so many people, of having this community, of opening one's world. And I think that Bolivia lacks to open more her mind. In Bolivia, we have somehow been stagnating in how we think, in how we see things.

Of course, the attainment of such goals is difficult to prove; but in retrospect, Reiko Yohena expresses her satisfaction that several participants from Bolivia travelled to the 2016 Confra in Mexico: "This means that it was worth the effort."

Through Confra. the organising board hoped to unite Bolivian Nikkei. While it is difficult to measure this objective, many post-war Nikkei and non-Nikkei from Santa Cruz who used not to attend Nikkei community events were indeed present as spectators. Among the athletes were also some "mestizos" and pre-war descendants. However, most Bolivian competitors were post-war descendants of exclusively Japanese ancestry from Santa Cruz and Colonia Okinawa, thereby partly reproducing patterns already known from Nikkei associations – although, contrary to what occurs in associations, they were mostly Nisei and Sansei. Sometimes, specific prerequisites may make it difficult for everybody to attend: Confra organisers invited all descendants to take part, but Fénix organisers wanted participants to be members of an invited Nikkei organisation.

Building up a Pan-American Nikkei identity is also related to class; in other words: participation is costly and therefore, only a specific selection attends (Takenaka 2009a: 1338f.). Adults paid a fee of USD 300 at the 2017 COPANI in Lima and, in addition, they had to afford accommodation and travel, while the Confra participation fee in Santiago de Chile one year later amounted to USD 200, hotel included (Confra XXIII 2018; COPANI 2017b). As a result, pre-war Nikkei without financial means were mostly absent at Confra in Santa Cruz. Unlike for most post-war Nikkei with a middle-class socioeconomic background who may easily book a flight to Peru, Chile or Mexico, even the trip to Santa Cruz was too

180 *Nikkei networks in Latin America and beyond*

expensive for many descendants from Beni and Pando. Individual solutions were found for some participants, enabling them to stay with a host family during the event.

In the case of Confra in Bolivia, Nikkei associations were not directly involved in planning, either: Ayaka Shimoji from the organising board declares that it would have been impossible to organise such an event from within established organisations. As also Kasamatsu (2005: 94) writes about the emergence of Pan-American events, one reason to organise the first COPANI was that the Nisei were excluded from association activities. Instead, organisers criticise that the invitations to La Paz were delayed on their way through Nikkei institutions. Daiki Kaneshiro is not surprised since he remembers that already in the past, associations never supported him or other participants when travelling to Pan-American events. In the case of Confra in Santa Cruz, the local *nihonjinkai* president and the ANBJ chairman were eventually invited to hold a speech in order not to enhance tensions between different subgroups. Daiki and his co-organisers were much more delighted about Confra initiator Carlos Kasuga's presence.

A worldwide *uchinānchu* network – Okinawa-related events

Especially Okinawan descendants have developed strong networks at the Pan-American level and beyond. However, research lacks on participants' motivations; neither did I find in-depth studies on the goals of Okinawa Prefecture and its inhabitants to organise such events. Although they share similarities with events such as Confra or COPANI, some particularities exist.

Several Japanese prefectures maintain contact with overseas descendants, but not to the same degree as Okinawa Prefecture. Moreover, Okinawan descendants visit each other for *kenjinkai* anniversaries, they meet at WUB (World Uchinanchu Business Association) or WYUA events and organise the Niseta Tours youth meeting. Other young descendants have joined Ryūkyūkoku Matsuridaiko dance and visited chapters abroad (Siemann 2017). Okinawan descendants explain the high number of events and descendants' enthusiasm to participate with the interconnectedness that would naturally emerge among Okinawan descendants. However, even in the Okinawan case, ties between the ancestral homeland and descendants do not emerge automatically (Figure 7.2).

To strengthen a Pan-Okinawan identity different from a Japanese one, Okinawa Prefecture has been much more active than the national government. Their efforts demonstrate the importance of subnational actors in diasporic relations, although so far not discussed in the literature on Nikkei. Okinawan teachers give *sanshin* classes abroad and the prefecture awards scholarships to young Okinawan Bolivian descendants to visit the archipelago, meet their extended family and receive some professional training – also *sanshin* and *eisā* lessons are included in the programme. Finally, a group of "Uchina Goodwill Ambassadors" is supposed to create and maintain links between Okinawa Prefecture and Bolivia or other countries of residence.

Nikkei networks in Latin America and beyond 181

Figure 7.2 Kachaashi at Wakamono Taikai in Düsseldorf.

The most important Okinawa-related cultural activity is Uchinānchu Taikai festival, organised every five years in the prefecture's capital Naha. It points especially to overseas descendants who are welcomed "back home." In 2016, around 415,000 people attended the sixth Uchinānchu Taikai, taking part in networking activities, cultural performances and the large parade on Naha's main street Kokusai Dōri [International Avenue]. In Bolivia, too, the enthusiasm to travel to Okinawa Prefecture for Uchinanchu Taikai was remarkable despite the distance and the costs – elderly descendants, though, may be funded by their village of origin. 15,400 people were eventually present at the closing ceremony, where October 30 was declared as World Uchinānchu Day (Dai-6 Sekai no Uchinānchu Taikai Jikkō Iinkai Jimukyoku 2016a; Mitchell 2016; Ryūkyū shinpō 2016). In order to pass down *uchinānchu* values and to create networks among subsequent generations, WYUA concurrently held activities for young Okinawans and descendants (Dai-6 Sekai no Uchinānchu Taikai Jikkō Iinkai Jimukyoku 2016c).

Events such as Uchinanchu Taikai differ from other Nikkei-related events in so far as the prefecture emphasises exchange between descendants and Okinawans rather than only among Nikkei. Younger attendants could for instance stay with local host families. The prefecture envisions a global community with a common *uchinānchu* [Okinawan] spirit, based on shared ancestry and culture. This spirit is expressed in the already mentioned slogans of solidarity and understanding. At

182 *Nikkei networks in Latin America and beyond*

the same time, I have not witnessed that Okinawan descendants try to distance themselves from the prefecture.

Attending Uchinanchu Taikai was a valuable experience for Natsuyo Makishi, a young descendant from Colonia Okinawa. She was excited by the amount of hospitality she experienced, by the great importance locals attach to the event and by the feeling of belonging to a large family. This experience motivates her to maintain Okinawan culture in Bolivia since she thinks that the *colonia* resembles Okinawa Prefecture in former times. Similar to mainland descendant Ryota, Natsuyo thinks that cultural loss is an imminent risk. She regrets that many young descendants are not interested in Okinawan culture. Thus, she and her friends have organised karaoke events.

> We want Okinawan music to be played in 100 years [...] [in Colonia Okinawa]. But there are people who [just] come and watch and eat [...]. Sometimes it makes me angry [...]. We try to stimulate them [...], but it's very difficult [...]. They [always] have excuses and more excuses.

Natsuyo has also been active in Bolivia's Ryūkyūkoku Matsuridaiko chapter and Okinawa-related discussion groups for young descendants. She sees her commitment at the regional and international level as a means to strengthen Okinawan descendants' identity in Bolivia. However, after taking part in some meetings, young descendant Yoshimi is a little disappointed that, according to her, these groups often do not come to concrete results.

The discussion group is at least theoretically open to non-Okinawans, similar to Wakamono Taikai in Düsseldorf, and the slogan of the 2016 Uchinanchu Taikai was "Let the whole world move to the Uchina beat," relating directly to non-descendants. Nisei lawyer Masutaro Higaonna emphasises: "[Okinawan] culture is not only for Okinawans, but it's for everybody [...]. And it's good when everybody takes part." Such discourses may also be a strategy to differentiate Okinawa-related events from mainland Japanese ones, where access is more restricted. Nevertheless, more research would be needed on the dynamics of inclusion and exclusion and on how ethnic boundaries are negotiated.

Whereas mainland and Okinawan events remain separate, some descendants such as Daiki Kaneshiro, Koki Takamine and Kimi Ayala have been taking part in both types. They understand Okinawa-related festivals as a subtype of Pan-American Nikkei events: a Pan-American Nikkei identity can thereby encompass a Pan-Okinawan identity. As it also occurs in the archipelago, Okinawan events abroad creatively relate elements regarded as typically Okinawan with others that are considered to be Japanese. Wakamono Taikai participants in Düsseldorf folded paper cranes, a classical Japanese origami figure and peace symbol; peace being a major issue for Okinawa Prefecture. At the same time, well-known practices regarded as Okinawan such as *sanshin* and *eisā* were a self-evident part of the programme. The Okinawan flag was displayed among the flags of countries with major descendant populations – the Japanese flag, however, was absent. Okinawa's controversial relation to Japan was not explicitly discussed, either.

Nikkei networks in Latin America and beyond 183

Okinawa Prefecture has specific goals when supporting such events. It emphasises its ethnic heterogeneity and its openness to a globalised world compared to Japan, understood to be more closed to foreign influences. Apart from enabling everybody to have a pleasant time on the islands during Uchinanchu Taikai, Okinawa Prefecture tries to present itself as a unique place in Japan, in contrast to its actual social and economic problems and its dependency on Japanese financial support (Allen 2009). Not least to gain power vis-à-vis the central government, it supports its diasporic networks to gain support in the controversy around the US military bases.

Despite the discourse on the unifying *uchinānchu* spirit, both sides' goals and understandings may not be identical. I already mentioned different symbolic uses of food in Okinawa Prefecture and Colonia Okinawa. Moreover, Okinawan Bolivians practically never refer to the military bases or peace-related activities. For most Okinawan Bolivians, a Pan-Okinawan identity is depoliticised: building networks and preventing cultural loss stand in the foreground. Therefore, further research would be needed to determine if such networks are useful for Okinawa Prefecture to achieve its goals.

Further studies would also be required to determine how far Okinawa Prefecture's authority is diminishing when it comes to defining Okinawan culture and to control Okinawa-related events. Some events are even disconnected from Okinawa Prefecture: the Niseta Tours youth meeting focuses solely on young descendants in the Americas – although their Okinawan origin serves as a reason to come together. Similar to events such as COPANI, importance is shifting to Okinawan communities in Latin America as the imagined homeland.

Conclusion

Transnational organisations and their activities provide a new ethnic identity for individual Nikkei from different places yet with a similar ambivalence towards Japan as culture of origin. They hope to create an overarching Nikkei identity with a central place for Latin America, instead of a "deficient" Japanese identity.

Sporadic events such as the Pan-American Nikkei Convention COPANI or the sports festival Confra are used to maintain symbolic "Japanese values" in order to resist negative cultural assimilation and maintain a sense of cultural identity as Japanese, while appealing to positive emotions. At the same time, it becomes clear that despite similarities, many differences exist between descendants from different countries.

Events are also a means for emancipation for later generations who are unsatisfied with ethnic associations. Descendants also use meetings to present themselves as a successful minority to a Latin American and Japanese audience. Nevertheless, as the example of Confra has shown, it is difficult to conceal existing tensions among local Nikkei communities in the course of events.

At the same time, Okinawa-related events have been successful in appealing to a worldwide Okinawan community, based on an "Okinawan spirit," which, at least at first sight, also integrates non-Okinawans. Nevertheless, Okinawa

184 *Nikkei networks in Latin America and beyond*

Prefecture and descendants abroad have their own agendas. Hence, it is unclear if Okinawa Prefecture will reach its political goals through such events.

Notes

1 Another example of a Pan-American Nikkei initiative is the web portal *Discover Nikkei* (www.discovernikkei.org) with Nikkei-related articles in Spanish, Portuguese, English and Japanese. The website traces back to the International Nikkei Research Project of the Japanese American National Museum in Los Angeles. This project resulted in several publications such as Kikumura-Yano (2002a) and Hirabayashi et al. (2002), both also available in Japanese, and fostered the idea of a common identity by assuming that Nikkei communities with similar experiences exist.
2 Portuguese and Spanish are, at least with some practice, mutually understandable. One can often witness that Portuguese and Spanish speakers stick to a mixture of both languages known as *portunhol/portuñol* for communication.
3 In the 1990s, the redress agreements in the United States and Canada resulted in the consciousness of being connected, Creighton (2010: 140f.) writes, concluding that this was essential to the emergence of Pan-American Nikkei events. I agree only partially since these agreements were not relevant for Latin America.
4 It should be noted, however, that Alberto Fujimori is a highly controversial personality, as I will discuss in Chapter 9. While COPANI and Confra declare to be politically neutral, he was for a long time considered a model to follow and named honorary APN president soon after his election. He even held a speech at the 1995 COPANI in Lima – despite showing clearly authoritarian traits, he still enjoyed much popularity at that time (Kasamatsu 2005: 124ff.,141ff.). His daughter Keiko, an equally controversial politician, was invited to speak at the 2017 COPANI in Lima (COPANI 2017a).

8 Searching for an economic basis

Maybe Ayaka Shimoji sees herself as a born entrepreneur. After some insistence with the staff, I obtain permission to interview her at the headquarters of her family's fashion company in central Santa Cruz. One afternoon in August 2013, she awaits me in her simple office radiating optimism. In her late twenties, she has recently become the managing director of the company. Ayaka and her siblings have practically grown up in the company that has remained a family business: whereas her father Taku acts as president, her mother develops new products, her sister is responsible for the commercial strategy and her brother is about to expand into other areas, since "we already know how to create a company."

Ayaka is proud to tell me about their several subsidiaries all over Santa Cruz and their imminent expansion to Cochabamba. She remembers that the company started with USD 10,000 of her father's *dekasegi* stay. He had used the funds to purchase machines in order to produce T-shirts and school uniforms. The Bolivian textile industry suffered especially in the first years of the millennium because of imported second-hand clothes and because a trade agreement with the United States was cancelled in 2008. Consequently, the company focuses now on Bolivia. It produces more than 60,000 garments per month and has a capital of around USD 3 million, probably being the largest Nikkei-owned private company in Bolivia. In 2013, after more than 20 years of existence, it had 180 regular employees and worked with around 20 independent manufacturing places (Rojas Jordán 2013). Their simple, high-quality garments, sold in bright and spacious shops, are explicitly directed at the Bolivian urban middle class. Neither the garments nor the models on their website appear to have any connection to Japan; practically all employees are non-Nikkei. The company insists on serving a Bolivian clientele as a Bolivian company. It sponsors events for a broad public like a marathon or a golf tournament, it is present in social media and sells via e-commerce.

When I mention JICA's support for the *colonias*, Ayaka just shakes her head. She emphasises once more that her family, based in the city for a long time, has relied on their own effort and taken advantage of Bolivia's economic growth without receiving any subsidiaries. Full of self-confidence, Ayaka is straightforward, and without taking much time to breathe, she claims that everybody who works hard will succeed:

DOI: 10.4324/9781003228295-8

186 *Searching for an economic basis*

> We as a family have opened three new companies of completely different branches [...]. We have already understood how to establish a company, how to create a brand, how to commercialise, so we think that we can make any product successful [...].We want to compete at the national level, to be a prominent company.

For her, it is simply natural for a woman to become an entrepreneur, arguing that any woman can succeed if she wants, even in a male-dominated society like Santa Cruz or the *comunidad japonesa*. When not at work, Ayaka engages for Okinawa Kenjinkai: she was the association's youngest and first female president, but she emphasises how indebted she feels to the Issei. Moreover, she is part of the Confra organising team since she regards her experiences at Pan-American Nikkei events as an inspiration.

In a full-page interview published in the business pages of Santa Cruz' major newspaper El Deber some weeks later, Ayaka's father Taku Shimoji emphasises his faith in Bolivia's economic future and his entrepreneurial spirit, despite several drawbacks. He also underlines that his company attaches much importance to quality: if a garment does not comply with quality standards, it will not be sold. According to Taku, the Japanese values he had learned while working in Japan, such as organisation, respect and punctuality, are key factors for success. These values are displayed on the wall of Ayaka's office, too, to serve as an inspiration: modernity and cleanliness, among others, are crucial – although, when reading the poster, I think they could come from any management handbook. When I ask her about the poster, she answers:

> This paper reflects how a Japanese is like. Maybe in countries like Bolivia, it's not yet like that, it's not essential to be an honest person, to be a responsible person. So I think all these things, for us, the opportunity to get to know Japan, to have Japanese roots has been of much worth, and this is also an inspiration for us.

The Nikkei's socioeconomic status is tightly related to their ethnic identity and their symbolic capital. Like Ayaka, several Nisei and Sansei feel confident to assert themselves in Bolivian society without having to rely on Japanese support. Especially during my fieldwork in 2013/2014, it was noticeable that Bolivia's macroeconomic strength had grown and that the economy was developing like never before. Everywhere in Santa Cruz, one could find construction sites for high-rise buildings. New bridges and underpasses on Av. Cristo Redentor made it easier to reach the airport and real estate prices were increasing. Whereas the U.S. dollar has been a parallel currency for years, it became common to make loans in the national currency bolivianos.

However, Ayaka's case may not be typical for the Nikkei's involvement in the Bolivian economy. Although they have attained an advantageous position, they are nevertheless challenged to maintain their prosperity above average. The Nikkei are relatively prosperous in the two *colonias*, but agriculture

Searching for an economic basis   187

needs less workforce than before and, of course, not everybody wants to become a farmer. At the same time despite Ayaka's optimism, the urban environment still offers comparatively few jobs for the middle class and competition grows. Suzuki (2010: 62f.) notes that the second generation could therefore not maintain their privileges in the city: "The socioeconomic privileges Okinawan-Bolivians enjoyed in Colonia Okinawa, in short, failed to translate into socioeconomic success in the larger Bolivian society." Bolivia's and Santa Cruz' economic situation has certainly changed since the late 1990s when Suzuki realised his research. Nevertheless, he certainly has a point when indicating that urban Nikkei do not enjoy any privileges. Instead, many descendants start to feel the vulnerability Liechty (2003) identifies as central to the middle class.

"This stability won't be forever" – Are the Nikkei prepared for the Bolivian labour market?

Few scientific studies on ethnic minorities argue that they have comparatively better chances in the labour market – except for the so-called highly skilled migrants (Favell et al. 2008). In contrast, many Nisei and Sansei are convinced that they would always find a job, explaining their possible advantage with their "typically Japanese" honesty and reliability and with their excellent education, the latter presented as a matter of fact. Most descendants in Santa Cruz do not believe in a "glass ceiling" and do not observe any discrimination towards foreigners or persons regarded as such in the Bolivian labour market. Nisei businesswoman Minae Hara: "We know that we will be in a good position because we always have this culture of responsibility." Ryoji Nakaima, too, claims that his ethnic identity was helpful to attain a leadership position in Santa Cruz' cattle breeder association FEGASACRUZ: "I thought that it would be uncomfortable with this face among all the *choquitos*,[1] but it was rather positive for me." Mai Amuro states laughing that the only job out of the Nikkei's reach would be drug trafficking.

Many Latin Americans still think that all Japanese descendants are educational overachievers and that parents force them to study hard. This notion is reflected in the macabre joke that in order to enter Brazil's most prestigious university, Universidade de São Paulo, one has to kill a *japonês*. Indeed, many immigrants considered education to be necessary for upward social mobility, trying to send their children to good schools and universities. Furuki (2013: 83), referring to a study by Iyo Kunimoto, claims that of those born in the 1970s, almost three quarters had studied at university. To my knowledge, no recent surveys exist.

After their studies, many Nikkei decide to enter Nikkei companies, including the cooperatives. Others work at Nikkei institutions like Kenjinkai, Centro Social, ABJ or Japanese schools. Of course, this tendency cannot be generalised to all Nikkei. Young graphic designer Yoshimi Matsumura prefers not to work in such a company, as she declares firmly; she would feel too controlled.

As it is common all over the world, social capital is essential to find a job. Thanks to such networks, there is hardly any unemployment among Nikkei. Qualifications become of secondary importance when Nikkei business owners

188 *Searching for an economic basis*

employ descendants due to their origin, regardless of their skills (Barriga Dávalos 2016: 64f.; Salverda 2015: 145ff.). This is especially visible in sensitive positions: in a Nikkei-owned business, the treasurer is usually a Japanese descendant as well. Hiroshi Shindo, for example, was looking for a cashier through an announcement he put on Centro Social's notice board. It did not mention that only Nikkei were eligible – this could result in legal trouble for discrimination – but it was written in Japanese.[2] Although conflicts over control and succession might also emerge inside families or ethnic groups, for Hiroshi, these practices are related to a question of trust. Nevertheless, he emphasises that he might employ a non-Nikkei if he knew him or her personally.

> When it comes to managing the cash register, the management of money, I don't know why we have more confidence in our race. It's discrimination [laughs][...]. Like I told you, [I came back from Japan] only one year ago [...]. One doesn't have much contact. Therefore, it's faster [to put a job advertisement on the notice board]. But why should I lie? We have a little more confidence in our blood.

Nevertheless, many Nikkei employers seem to prefer Nikkei employees even in less sensitive positions: ethnic homogeneity in the company stands for economic stability. Some descendants explained the preference for Nikkei employees with different communication styles, arguing that Nikkei communicate more indirectly in order not to upset the other. Consequently, Sansei Shota Murakami, a cook working on demand, thinks that it is better to maintain the ethnic boundary in work life:

> The Japanese are on time, reliable, all this. The Bolivians are not reliable, they lie, they promise [without keeping their promises]. When they see that the Japanese works for two or three people, the Bolivian, instead of helping him, takes advantage of him and even exploits him.

In contrast, some descendants like Nisei Kaede Itokazu believe that the Nikkei tend to work in Nikkei companies because they are not willing to compete in the Bolivian labour market – although engaging for a Bolivian company and eventually Bolivian society would be desirable, she thinks. According to Kaede, the Nikkei are simply ill-prepared and unwilling to interact with the broader society. Therefore, they lack important connections with possible employers and business partners. Kaede blames the parents: instead of joining golf clubs, *fraternidades* or Carnival *comparsas*, she observes that they only rely on their Nikkei network; hence, their children will not enter a prestigious non-Nikkei company. Working with descendants may be more comfortable, but they should be more ambitious, she thinks.

> Here [...], we have very big companies. The Japanese [...] lose a good opportunity to have a good desk in any company [...]. The doctors are fine because

Searching for an economic basis 189

they come out of university, they go and put their practice, and that's it [...]. But people who study administration and all that, do you think that in a bank there is a Japanese, in CRE[3] there is a Japanese, in COTAS?[4] [...] I don't see a single Japanese in a good company, because they can't enter, they can't compete because the parents themselves don't have contact with Bolivian society, so their children eventually finish university, and they don't have work [...]. They go to Japan to work, and their studies here in Bolivia are useless in Japan!

According to Kaede, the Nikkei are not the representatives of a prosperous minority, but overly dependent on Japanese assistance and unable to adapt to the Bolivian environment even in the third generation. Kazuyuki Hamaoka, too, mentions the example of a young Nikkei who does not work in his profession after finishing his degree but helps his father on the farm. He thinks that this means a deplorable waste of resources since the Nikkei should engage in Bolivian society, although he knows that many are reluctant to enter a non-Nikkei company, attributing this to a deep-seated cultural fear of conflicts:

We all have this fear in the beginning, if it will go well, if I will do it well, if not what will my superiors tell me, what will my boss tell me? But all this is an experience that one learns [...]. So you improve. So I always tell [my daughter]: "If it suits you, keep it, if not, ignore it." But if you work with your father, he won't challenge you.

However, social scientist Mai Amuro is more pessimistic: she thinks that the Nikkei are simply unable to compete with non-Nikkei, criticising that descendants look only for the accumulation of material goods and pleasure. She does not observe any cultural incompatibilities or a loss of values, but according to her, life is becoming too stable and convenient to be creative and innovative. As she says, overprotectiveness is a typical phenomenon within the Bolivian upper middle class that lives in "bubbles." Mai remembers laughing that after graduating from a Catholic high school for girls, it was a shock for her to enter public university: only then did she learn about the existence of indigenous groups in Santa Cruz Department. The danger of this "bubble" is to lose curiosity, Mai explains in a more serious tone: there is no necessity to move forward against obstacles, "*superarse,*" as the immigrants themselves had to do.

[The Issei] were generations who survived the war, people who suffered many difficulties, but who moved forward. They took the decision to come to a different world because obviously, they had nothing to lose [...]. But these people were so perseverant, so brave that they didn't let the new generations to be equally perseverant and brave and auto-sufficient and free [...].

For this reason, she observes that the younger generations have lost the migrants' strength of character because, for a long time, education was not necessary to

190 *Searching for an economic basis*

guarantee financial stability. In other words, the stereotype of well-educated descendants is more of an illusion than reality, Mai holds.

> Many young people, my friends, my contemporaries [...] have not studied at university. And it's not because they didn't have the economic conditions, but it's because they were not interested, not motivated, because they had a secured life and they still have a secured life.

In a country like Bolivia, where the state provides little support for upward social mobility, social capital is often more important than formal education and diploma. Many Bolivians do not work in the careers they have studied or frequently change jobs. Narumi Montaño, while thinking aloud about migrating to Japan, complained to me that she knew even doctors and engineers who preferred to run a copy shop or to sell fried chicken in order to earn more money and to have less trouble with bureaucracy. The Bolivian economy offers few middle-class jobs and highly specialised professions are seldom needed. Moreover, notably in the 1980s, universities were frequently on strike and finishing a degree in Bolivia was difficult. Later, carrying on the family farm, built up with JICA loans, was more promising. In addition, going for *dekasegi* was easier – and more profitable – than joining a Bolivian company.

Consequently, Mai and Ichiro Ninomiya, JICA's vice-director in Bolivia, observe that many Nikkei have not focused on education to anticipate future challenges. They are economically well because of external factors, but this has not resulted in a sustainable socioeconomic situation. Consequently, if the Nikkei continue to search for employment only in Nikkei companies, they may eventually lose their status as upper middle class, Mai warns: "This stability won't be forever [...]. The young ones will have to educate themselves and compete on an equal level in the market."

The head of a mouse or the tail of a lion –
Nikkei entrepreneurs in Bolivia

In the introductory anecdote, Ayaka Shimoji presents the success of her company as an almost natural outcome of "Japanese values." Especially in the United States, the Japanese have been called "economic animals" (Yamagata 2009); however, the term also implies an exaggerated focus on money. At the first COPANI in 1981, participants were preoccupied that the aggressive behaviour of some Japanese companies in the United States, notably in the automobile sector, would have a negative influence on the Nikkei's symbolic capital (Kasamatsu 2005: 96).

Nevertheless, while many descendants own businesses, it is striking that except for the Shimoji family, few prominent Nikkei-owned companies with more than 30 employees have emerged. The Nikkei are not known for start-ups with new products and innovative processes, either. Their companies never appear in rankings on the country's largest and most lucrative enterprises. Several interview partners, be they descendants or not, expressed their surprise that Nikkei companies

Searching for an economic basis 191

are also virtually unknown to non-Nikkei consumers, in contrast for example to the widely known Telchi pharmacy chain, founded by an Arab descendant.

For cattle farmer Ryoji Nakaima, however, it is "the idiosyncrasy of the Japanese" to be self-employed. Some Nikkei claim that this is a result of the Issei's pioneering work: migration and entrepreneurship are per se risky. Apart from avoiding problems with one's superior, one benefits financially, Ryoji holds: "It means looking for independence and getting a little more. For sure it's because of this small spirit of entrepreneurship that they put into your head." He argues that starting a business in Bolivia is the best way to prosperity since competition is not yet as intense as elsewhere. He tells his children:

> Here in Bolivia, if you're an employee, you die from hunger. You have to start a business. And even if it's small, *más vale ser cabeza de ratón que cola de león* [it's better to be the head of a mouse than the tail of a lion] [...]. It's still a country where you can bring some ideas from the outside, do some business and [...] each business might be interesting. You earn much better than if you're an employee, and if it's only selling *anticuchos* [beef chunks on a stick].

Ryoji presents his decision to start cattle farming as a way to follow the most promising path and as a natural step for a Nikkei. Migration literature, usually focusing on North America, often supposes the contrary, i.e., that migrants start a business because it is their only possibility rather than because they want to realise their ideals (for an overview see Zhou 2004).

While Ryoji thinks that the typical Nikkei is self-employed, micro-businesses are nevertheless common in Bolivia. Seleme Antelo et al. (2005: 114) cite a non-Nikkei interview partner who sees self-employment as a typical *cruceño* characteristic. Furthermore, Bolivia's streets are full of self-employed vendors who sell virtually everything from clothes, books and pirated DVDs to soft drinks, fruits and bread. In August 2016, Bolivia's informal sector counted for more than 70% of the total economy (El Deber 2016). Although they may indeed make more – sometimes even substantially more – money than employees in the formal sector, micro-entrepreneurship is generally equivalent to endless workdays and a lack of social protection. In other words, becoming an *anticucho* seller in the street may result in self-exploitation.

While several Nikkei like Ryoji own small businesses today, a look at the past shows several examples of Nikkei entrepreneurs of medium and large companies. One case was the Komori family in La Paz that once employed up to 1,200 people in textile manufacturing and mining. Their company Casa Comercial Komori even survived the Second World War, but the macroeconomic conditions worsened after the 1952 revolution, leading to its closure in 1956. The owner then founded Toyota Boliviana in La Paz in 1957. At a time when the brand was still unknown in Bolivia, the company imported not only cars but also motorcycles and construction machines. During its best times between the 1960s and 1980s, it employed around 60 people in its central office, garage and spare parts warehouse.

192 *Searching for an economic basis*

Its long-time president, José Tatsuo Kawai, was born in Lima and grew up in Japan. He employed young adults from the *colonias* and created a scholarship; moreover, he contributed financially to community facilities in La Paz and Santa Cruz, headed several immigration anniversary committees and acted as first president of ANBJ/FENABOJA (Sociedad Japonesa de La Paz 2012: 156ff.; Furuki 2013). However, the company went bankrupt after his son had taken over. Three well-known contemporary Nikkei entrepreneurs are the Paraguayan Víctor Maehara, owner of an egg company, the Peruvian Enrique Miyasato who has built up a glass and aluminium factory and the Mexican Carlos Kasuga, founder and director of the Mexican division of a Japanese yoghurt company.

Ichiro Ninomiya, the Japanese vice-director of JICA in Bolivia, thinks that founding companies may become an alternative to agriculture. Nevertheless, the lack of "big" entrepreneurs does not surprise him. Instead of looking for cultural reasons, he sees envy as a characteristic of small communities, resulting in harmful gossip and impeding economic initiatives. I have indeed heard allegations against one Nikkei entrepreneur, accusing him of being selfish and greedy, since, for example, he went to court against a Nikkei couple. Moreover, other descendants accused him of bringing discord into the *comunidad japonesa* while leading an association. Such allegations also show deeper anxieties, as Shakow (2014: 36) notes, and may be a means to express tensions between the ethics of equality on the one hand and individual enterprise and upward mobility on the other. Takenaka (2003b: 473) observes that wealthy businesspersons distance themselves from the *comunidad* in Lima. Nevertheless, I did not hear such accusations against other Nikkei entrepreneurs in Santa Cruz, which suggests that individual attitudes, for example towards norms of reciprocity, play an important role to determine acceptance.

While the lack of entrepreneurs might be interpreted as a handicap, it might also be presented as a moral advantage. During a visit to San Juan with Saburo Yamashita, a well-known doctor born in the *colonia*, and his non-Nikkei wife Micaela Tejada, we visited Keisuke Sakata. His contemporary Seiichiro Takaki, a farmer like Keisuke, joined us for an interview. Sitting in the Sakata's living room and enjoying some coffee and fruit jelly made by Keisuke's wife, the four soon started a vivid discussion on the topic, concluding that it is difficult not to become corrupted by the Bolivian environment. They were convinced that for cultural reasons, the Nikkei prefer to maintain a low profile: they are too honest and prefer harmonious interpersonal relations.

Saburo: There are many problems with bribes and all this at work. And generally, when we have a company, we have to pay *coimas* [bribes] in order that it survives.

Keisuke: And we're not used to it, really.

Micaela: They would need to be a little dirtier for that.

Keisuke: And we would have to cheat.

Seiichiro: And we don't have big negotiators. I mean, the professionals we have like doctors, lawyers … but few entrepreneurs; although, of course, some run their little shop.

Seiichiro reminded the others that while "Japanese values" make it difficult for Nikkei entrepreneurs to emerge in Bolivia, Peruvian descendants have more 'big' businesspersons because they have already become "peruvianised" in the course of a much longer history of migration. Consequently, he thinks that they do not fear open conflict, in contrast to the "more Japanese" Bolivian Nikkei. When justifying bribes with the need to survive, Seiichiro and his friends hold that while adhering to "Japanese values," one cannot be a "big" entrepreneur in Latin America.

Nisei Tsuyoshi Kato, too, calls himself an entrepreneur referring to a small export business he runs together with a partner. He thinks that in order to be successful with a bigger business, one would need strong networks. Instead, he found it easy to attain a position at the top of the graduate institute of one of Santa Cruz' major universities. Nevertheless, he summarises that if he has not encountered any difficulties in his career, it may be connected to the fact that academic positions are not disputed:

> Without belonging to any group, I've reached a certain level, for example, I've been president of the administrators throughout Bolivia […]. One can reach these spaces if one wants to serve people […], but there are other spaces with more economic interests or political power […]. You also have a certain influence of certain groups [in academia], but it's less […] compared to other institutions like the department's government, the town hall.

With the "groups," he alludes especially to economic entities such as CAO, CAINCO and CADEX,[5] dominated by the elites. Members of these chambers also meet in their free time, they thereby belong to overlapping circles. Famous examples of such leisure time groups are the *fraternidades* clubs or carnival *comparsas* (Waldmann 2008: 96ff.). Moreover, the mysterious *logias* are said to control the service cooperatives COTAS, CRE and SAGUAPAC (Waldmann 2008: 100ff.). Although circles of powerful *cruceños* have lost influence on a national level, contacts with such groups may be essential for entrepreneurs to survive in the regional economy.

Whether or not Nikkei are "too honest" to become large-scale entrepreneurs, a critical factor for the lack of big companies is that Tsuyoshi and other Nikkei lack strong networks. Since they were supported by Japan for a long time, investing in social capital outside the *comunidad* seemed not necessary.

The Nikkei as a bridge? – Nikkei business relations with Japan

Even though they have not founded any large companies, Bolivian Nikkei should enjoy privileged access to Japanese markets due to the cultural closeness they are often eager to emphasise. Nevertheless, few Nikkei focus on import from or export to Japan and few Japanese have established business relations with Bolivia. The Nikkei have not taken advantage of the popularity of Japanese technology

194 *Searching for an economic basis*

and not even the old Toyota Corollas and the second-hand minibuses from Japan, omnipresent in Santa Cruz, have gone through the Nikkei's hands.

One exception is a salt and treacle company owned by a Nikkei from Santa Cruz that mainly exports to Japan since the products are expensive by Bolivian standards. Also Hakuo Tamanaha, the already mentioned entrepreneur who went to Japan for *dekasegi* and networking, exports now agricultural products to Japan, the Americas and Europe. He sees his ethnic identity and his language skills as a great advantage and is proud to understand both sides, arguing that it might be more difficult for Latin Americans without his cultural knowledge to enter the Japanese market (Berríos 2001). Interestingly, Hakuo Tamanaha was the only interviewee who had consciously pursued such a strategy.

In the 1960s and 1970s, several Japanese companies came to Bolivia to invest in transport, construction, automobile imports, mineral extraction, etc., but they withdrew in the course of the Latin American economic crisis of the 1980s. They also employed some Nikkei. However, compared to Peru and Brazil, very few Japanese companies are currently doing business in Bolivia, most of them in the raw materials sector. Whereas Bolivia imports mostly automobiles and machines from Japan, it almost exclusively exports minerals such as zinc, silver and lead to Japan. Only around 5% of all Bolivian exports go to Japan, and less than 5% of the imports are Japanese (Fujimoto 2016; Furuki 2013: 79ff.). While imports from Japan stagnate, Bolivia's economic relations with China are growing steadily. To my knowledge, no detailed research exists on the topic so far, but Fernández Saavedra et al. (2014: 279) estimate that in the first half of 2012, imports grew by 36% compared to the same period the year before. In 2015, imports from China reached USD 1,747 million, compared to USD 507 million from Japan (Fujimoto 2016). According to the same author, imports from South Korea amounted to only one-third of Japanese imports in 2015, but they increased by 7.1% from 2014 to 2015.

No chamber of foreign commerce relates Bolivia and Japanese companies. An attempt to found such an institution has not been successful. Some interview partners criticised the initiator, a directory member of an important business association in Santa Cruz. They complained that he was managing the group for his own personal benefit; thus, his unpopularity reflected in the association. Other Nikkei regret that the national Nikkei association ANBJ does not promote such activities. The chamber's failure also points to the fact that Bolivian Nikkei do not perceive a need for joint action. Since they work in extremely different branches, they lack a common interest in more than sporadic and independent business associations outside agriculture.

Japanese businesspersons do not seem overly interested in building up business relations with Nikkei, either: Bolivia is a small, land-locked country without much technology and infrastructure, unstable in terms of legal security and economic policies. Nisei engineer Shusei Iha participated in a joint initiative to invite some entrepreneurs, but he experienced that the Japanese are cautious for cultural reasons:

> The Japanese entrepreneur sees the situation here, and it's very difficult to convince a Japanese from Japan so that he wants to do business [...]. It works

Searching for an economic basis 195

once they are confident, but until there it takes time. Instead, the Koreans are more practical, more agile.

Critics like Yamagata (2009) claim that while in the 1970s and 1980s, the Japanese were regarded as proactive businesspersons devoted to their companies, they now rest on their laurels and do not take any risks to explore new markets in lower income countries, unlike the Chinese or Koreans. Kazuyuki Hamaoka voices similar criticism. He has already contacted his alma mater in Japan, in case they are looking for contacts in Bolivia. However, nothing happened. Kazuyuki concludes that the Nikkei's expertise is not in demand since the Japanese are simply too chauvinist to be interested in the diaspora. He feels that they do not take him seriously since he is "not really Japanese." However, as a Nikkei, he would possess useful cultural knowledge regarding legal issues, language, etc., to help the Japanese:

> If you see a company like Samsung, it's everywhere, whereas for Japan, its main market is only Japan [...] and it was never interested in expanding. And if yes, it would send its worst employee to Bolivia as representative. Only recently have they noted that it's important; and they are looking for people who speak English, Spanish, but it's very late. The Korean market has already arrived.

Japanese authorities seem to have recognised as well that the Nikkei could become a "bridge." While it is too early for concrete results, Japanese politics has started to put more importance on their relations with Nikkei. It becomes clear that particular leaderships influence policies as well. Unlike his predecessors, Japan's premier Shinzō Abe visited Latin America several times. He spoke about a possible mutual benefit during his visits to Brazil in 2014 and Argentina in 2016 and emphasised that "Japanese descendants have won the faith of Latin America and the Caribbean on which lies the trust that they extend to Japan" (Ministério das Relações Exteriores 2014; Palácio do Planalto 2014; Straschnoy 2016; Gaimushō 2014).

Following these objectives, JICA Bolivia started some initiatives to strengthen business relations between the two countries, addressing both Nikkei and non-Nikkei. According to vice-director Ichiro Ninomiya, JICA hopes to establish public-private partnerships between small and medium companies in both countries. It invited some Japanese companies to come to Latin America, and together with the Peruvian office of the Japan External Trade Organisation JETRO, it organised a seminar with around 100 non-Nikkei participants in La Paz and Santa Cruz (Embajada del Japón en Bolivia 2016). As Ichiro explains, his local office also hopes to strengthen local agribusiness and to make Nikkei more competitive in a globalised world (JICA 2018a).

The Japanese government's goal is to strengthen the Nikkei's heritage notion, but also to take advantage of their relations and experiences. As Matsumoto (2016) argues, the Nikkei might for example help with *trámites* since Japanese

196 *Searching for an economic basis*

companies often do not understand their importance. JICA has thus expanded its short-term programmes and long-term scholarships for Nisei and Sansei. One of these initiatives is "Nikkei Next Generation," a one month-programme for 50 young Latin American Nikkei. Another is the reactivated Nikkei leader exchange (Gaimushō 2015; JICA 2018b, 2018c; Matsumoto 2015; Shushō Kantei 2015): a group of prominent Nikkei from different countries travels to Japan to meet representatives of the government and the economy like the prime minister. Nevertheless, Matsumoto (2015) thinks that all these initiatives still need to follow a more precise strategy, requiring more involvement of the different actors.

"The true Japanese flavour" – Merchandising Japanese food

Bolivia participates in international ethnic cuisine trends. Urban Bolivians consume Swiss-style cheese fondue, Indian-style curries and Brazilian-style buffets, but they may also enjoy Japanese food. Around five Japanese restaurants exist in Santa Cruz with a medium or expensive price level, plus some Asian fusion restaurants. In addition, especially women prepare and sell Japanese food on demand. In La Paz, one finds around seven Japanese restaurants with both Nikkei and non-Nikkei clients.

Nevertheless, Japanese dishes were considered unpalatable on a global level at least until the Second World War. One descendant remembers the nickname "rabbit" because of their diet rich in vegetables. According to Furuki (2013: 60), Japanese migrants in La Paz were ashamed of the strange-smelling lunch they used to take to work.

Since the 1980s, Japanese food has become globally popular (Sakamoto und Allen 2011). Moreover, it has been declared an Intangible Cultural Heritage (UNESCO 2013). This means that especially sushi stands nowadays, as Bestor (2000: 57) points out, for a cosmopolitan lifestyle that pays attention to global health trends. Hence, this popularisation of Japanese food in Bolivia has taken place because of Japan's popularity as a whole and not so much because of the Nikkei's presence. As Sugimoto (2009: 14f.) writes:

> If *sushi* were a delicacy of a country without industrial might or *sashimi* a health food of a remote village in a technologically disadvantaged region, it is doubtful that the cultural diffusion of these foodstuffs around the world would have been possible.

Although not all globally available food is healthy, many Nikkei and non-Nikkei justify the popularity of Japanese cuisine with its benefits for health,[6] contrasting it with the "unhealthy Bolivian cuisine." The argument is sometimes reinforced with Japan's high life expectancy. Kentsu Hanashiro, a Nikkei in his thirties, says proudly:

> Sushi is becoming known, sushi is Japan. So the Bolivians know what it is, there are several Japanese restaurants that are expanding. So they like the food because before they didn't know what it was […]. They look for it in

> the supermarket. I find this interesting because they already want to eat something healthy. That's important so that they can slowly get to know [Japanese culture]. It has helped us as Nikkei, for the restaurants, the shops.

As Kentsu mentions, non-Nikkei Bolivians usually equate the "true Japanese flavour" with sushi. Santa Cruz' most expensive Japanese restaurant, for example, promotes the dish with pictures on its web page as "*el verdadero sabor japonés*" [the true Japanese flavour]. Enjoying sushi is also an important reason for non-Nikkei to attend events such as Bon Odori. At the same time, nameless everyday meals that a Japanese family may prepare at home, such as combining soup vegetable leftovers with rice and ad hoc prepared fish, do not appear on restaurant menus. The process of commodification and branding of ethnic identities means essentialisation and homogenisation: restaurants celebrate and present a specific selection. As in the case of other regional dishes that have become representations of national cuisines – for example, Neapolitan pizza for Italy – through the creation of national dishes or even "gastrodiplomacy" (Pham 2013; Rockower 2014), ethnic identity may not only be reproduced but also transformed.

The definition of "typical dishes" may have different outcomes in different settings. Okinawa Soba, an Okinawan-style noodle soup with pork, has become by far the most popular Okinawan food in Bolivia; but it does not have the same meaning in Japan. Nevertheless, in Bolivia, one does not find *goya* bitter gourd and sweets from *beniimo* purple yam that are ubiquitous in Naha's tourist shops and even as comic characters. Not even the ingredients of Japanese dishes in Bolivia need to be from Japan: expensive imported soy sauce may be regarded as qualitatively better and used for special occasions. Many ingredients are produced locally like tofu or *manjū* [small cakes with sweet bean filling]. One may buy *udon* noodles produced by Brazilian and Peruvian Nikkei companies. Many Korean or Chinese items are considered acceptable, too.[7]

When visiting a festival or restaurant, customers mainly from the middle and upper class want to experience a foreign and even exotic culture. They can discover the "other" in a sensual but secure way following well-known scripts (Möhring 2012: 39ff.). Their names and decoration shape them as spaces of experience and consumption: pictures of stereotypical tourist sites, landscapes and festivals as well as background music create imagined geographies that do not show a differentiated social or political reality, but widespread stereotypes. To give the reader an idea, the Japanese restaurants in La Paz and Santa Cruz have names such as Sakura, New Tokyo and Samurai, but also less well-known names with a Japanese sound such as Ken-chan, Yorimichi and Furusato. One owner decorated the rooms with bamboo; others display lanterns, Japanese-style paintings, figurines, fans, Japanese calligraphy or *noren*, a kind of Japanese curtain that is used at the entrance to shops and restaurants. Some restaurants have a "Japanese lounge" one enters without shoes. Whereas waiters are often non-Nikkei, the dishes on the menu bear Japanese names – of course, a direct Spanish translation might not even exist – and sometimes pictures of the dishes. Free cold tea and soy sauce are common. While cutlery is available, eating with chopsticks means

Figure 8.1 Entrance to a Japanese restaurant.

an exotic touch, as I experienced several times when having lunch or dinner with non-Nikkei acquaintances (Figure 8.1).

Food could become a primary means to promote Nikkei ethnic identity and to find a stable income. But the Nikkei only partly control the reproduction of Japanese cuisine in Bolivia.[8] Several times I found advertisements of non-Nikkei chefs who give sushi-cooking courses and not even all sushi-selling restaurants are owned by Nikkei. The Nikkei are divided regarding Japanese restaurants owned by non-Nikkei and/or mixing different styles. In 2018, a Nikkei opened a restaurant serving Peruvian-style Nikkei fusion cuisine, visited regularly by descendants. After our interview, Shusei Iha bought sushi for me from a Korean restaurant, assuring that it was excellent. However, Ryoichi Sunagawa only smiled condescendingly when mentioning a restaurant owned by a non-Nikkei:

the food was not "authentic," according to him, because the chef mixed different cuisines. Like him, several Nikkei establish a hierarchy between restaurants offering also non-Japanese dishes like sweet-sour pork and accessible to customers with a smaller budget, and one restaurant that is more expensive, offers exclusively Japanese food and is said to be "just like in Japan." Several descendants also recommended an inconspicuous small restaurant offering only three dishes as especially "authentic" to me.

It is also in Japan's interest to control this reproduction of food: the Japan External Trade Organisation has certified Japanese restaurants in several Latin American countries in order to promote "authentic" Japanese food and to ensure quality, but so far not in Bolivia (JETRO 2018). Nevertheless, it is questionable that these restaurants have not adapted to their Bolivian customers.

Even if the Nikkei may not have influenced the spread of sushi, its popularity has certainly not been harmful to them. The consumption of food with an ethnic label parallels the acceptance of Japanese descendants in Bolivia. While Chinese restaurants are said to be cheap and unhygienic, many non-Nikkei acquaintances regarded Japanese food as sophisticated and belonging to an elevated standard of life. Japanese restaurants can therefore ask for higher prices.

A look across the border gives interesting insights. The popular "Nikkei cuisine," a Japanese Peruvian cooking style, combines, for instance, fish and seafood, "Japanese" soy sauce and wasabi paste with "Peruvian" *ají* chili pepper. "Nikkei cuisine" stands for descendants' incorporation into a multi-ethnic society, but also for their distinctiveness from other Peruvians and Japan. "Nikkei cuisine" has become commercialised and, with support of the Peruvian government, it has been exported to other countries, including Bolivia. This popularity also means that some Peruvian Nikkei fear a loss of control, since many chefs are non-Nikkei. As a result, they try to claim their authority over this cooking style in order to protect the brand (Comaroff and Comaroff 2009). For example, some of them plan to create a formal school to promote the "authentic" Nikkei cooking style (Takenaka 2017). However, neither has a Bolivian-Japanese fusion cuisine emerged so far, nor have Japanese descendants in Bolivia taken any measures against others appropriating 'their' food.

"Serious institutions" – Nikkei cooperatives as an expression of Japanese-ness

Many Nikkei proudly claim that the two cooperatives are model institutions in present-day Bolivia: apart from the fashion company mentioned above, they are probably the most famous Bolivian Nikkei enterprises. They represent the Nikkei's symbolic capital and prosperity and are a place where ethnic identity is negotiated; but they might also act as guarantors of social peace.

To be able to stand against large-scale farmers and companies, the Issei founded the two cooperatives CAICO in Colonia Okinawa and CAISY in San Juan shortly after their arrival. Almost all farmers in the *colonias* are affiliated: CAICO has approximately 125 members, CAISY around 100. They run major facilities in Santa Cruz and the *colonias* and, in the case of CAISY, a small office in La Paz. In recent years, the Nisei have taken over the operative management; according to a recent law, only Bolivian nationals are allowed to become part of the executive board. The two cooperatives administrate the small experimental station Cetabol near Okinawa II that carries out soil and other analyses.

Each Japanese family obtained 50 hectares upon arrival. 60 years later, CAICO members own 30,000 hectares within Colonia Okinawa; furthermore, some members have bought land outside the *colonia*. Whereas descendants have given up the cultivation of cotton and sugar cane, a representative of ABJ Okinawa estimates that Okinawan Nikkei possess 15,000 hectares of wheat and 28,000 of soybeans in- and outside the *colonia*. Most Nikkei farmers in Colonia Okinawa own around 250 or 300 hectares on average; one farmer is estimated to hold 1,500 hectares. Nikkei from San Juan have purchased less land, due to different crops and their concentration on poultry. Rice, mainly wet varieties, grows on approximately 8,500 hectares in San Juan, allowing two harvests per year. This corresponds to around 20% of the national production, according to CAISY's president. Nikkei in San Juan grow 4,000 and 1,500 hectares of soybeans in winter and summer, respectively, apart from some corn. Moreover, the *colonia* produces more than 750,000 eggs per day, being one of the largest producers in Bolivia and providing approximately 25% of the national yield, according to its president Hideo Iwamatsu and Página Siete (2014) (Figure 8.2).

Figure 8.2 Chicken house in San Juan.

Searching for an economic basis 201

Agricultural cooperatives are not only common in Japan but exist throughout the Japanese diaspora. Many Nikkei presented agriculture and the foundation of cooperatives as an almost natural combination. The most prominent was the Brazilian Cotia cooperative (1928–1994), uniting more than 15,000 members in the 1980s (Staniford 2004: 176ff.; Taniguti 2015). Nikkei cooperatives have also been the focus of JICA's assistance. For small and medium farmers, this type of organisation offers many advantages: farmers can share the storage, transport and commercialisation of crops. They jointly raise a credit or purchase seeds, tools, fuel, fertilisers and insecticides together, having more power when negotiating as a group. They can also share expertise. However, one disadvantage is that non-affiliated members may sell products at a cheaper price on the market. Furthermore, rather than as a harmonic and solidary association promoting equality, Staniford (2004: 163ff.) describes the cooperative of the Brazilian Nikkei settlement Tomé Açu as a powerful organisation able to sanction members, for instance, expelling those unable to fulfil quotas.

On closer observation, cooperatives are equally common among non-Nikkei Bolivians. They are not restricted to agriculture but are prominent in the transport sector, in mining, finance and handicrafts. Each *cruceña* and *cruceño* knows the cooperatives SAGUAPAC, CRE and COTAS as the city's water, electricity and communication suppliers. Although some scholars have argued that cooperatives were a dominant social institution in the pre-Columbian Andes, in their investigations, Heath et al. (1969: 393) did not find any evidence for such an orientation. Instead, they mostly observed failures, not least because the systematic attempt to teach the basics of cooperativism lacked and because members expected huge profits without elaborating long-term plans.

For this reason, CAICO general manager Mitsuo Ishimine thinks that Bolivian cooperatives are cooperatives in name only. Against this background, many Nikkei are proud that CAICC and CAISY are among the few functioning and economically successful agricultural cooperatives in Bolivia. Many Nikkei explain this stability and prosperity with their "Japanese values." CAISY president Hideo Iwamatsu states, for example, that cooperativism is embedded in Japanese and Central European culture, mentioning the well-functioning Mennonite cooperatives that dominate Paraguay's dairy market. Accordingly, the Nikkei feel committed to the group even though they may have advantages as individuals. They are convinced that they can trust their disciplined, honest and responsible co-ethnics. Therefore, Hideo Iwamatsu and other Nikkei regard the cooperatives' prosperity as a materialisation of "Japanese values." Descendants create ties of affection and identification with the cooperatives. At the same time, non-Nikkei social scientist Fernando Prado says: "*Cruceños* admire [...] the organisational capacity they have, the seriousness of their institutions [...]. They are real role models".

Nevertheless, Staniford (2004: 174) relativises the importance of "Japanese values": "As in Japan, where cooperation does exist, loyalty is not the outgrowth of ideological adherence to cooperative principles, but arises from calculations of self-interest." On a closer look, the picture becomes more complex also with

202 *Searching for an economic basis*

regard to corruption. Irregularities may be the exception rather than the rule, but I did hear rumours accusing a Nikkei of embezzling money from a cooperative. Hiraoka (1980: 63f.) as well as Fukaura und Nagai (2013: 257ff.) describe how the failure of San Juan's first cooperative in the 1960s brought much conflict into the settlement; thus, settlers were initially reluctant to join the newly-founded CAISY. However, such occurrences are not widely known to the outside world. Moreover, JICA's technical support has certainly played a role in establishing the cooperatives successfully, whereas non-Nikkei did not enjoy such assistance.

Cooperative officials emphasised their openness to non-Nikkei during interviews. Many non-Nikkei Bolivians work especially in CAISY's administration, although not in management. CAICO's factory employs around 100 non-Nikkei as blue-collar workers or lower administrative staff. In other words, openness to non-Nikkei is limited. An ethnic boundary also exists regarding membership. Several non-Nikkei Bolivians have been calling Colonia Okinawa's cooperative to apply for membership, as Yoshio Shimajiri from CAICO management told me smilingly – so far, none of them has been accepted. When I addressed this question at CAISY, general manager Manabu Yamashita answered vaguely that the affiliation of non-Nikkei members would have to be discussed with all members and that in every country, cooperatives work well if their members are disciplined and educated enough to comply with the basic rules.[9]

Despite these practices, the cooperatives want to be perceived as supportive. As Yoshio Shimajiri emphasises, CAICO as a reliable and exemplary employer pays its workers on time, insinuating that this is not evident in Bolivia. Colonia Okinawa's cooperative also financed a part of the town's gas pipeline with a benefit for all inhabitants, although Yoshio regrets that such facts may not be generally known. Cooperative officials emphasise their regular training sessions for non-Nikkei in their experimental station Cetabol. They underline their leading role when organising Día del Trigo [Wheat Day] or Día del Arroz [Rice Day], including conferences and the demonstration of varieties and machines. Alluding to the discourse on the introduction of crops, CAISY president Hideo Iwamatsu emphasises that envy would not be justified. He complains, contrary to all other interviewees, that the non-Nikkei do not recognise the Nikkei's pioneer role:

> We're visited by the Movimiento Sin Tierra [landless people's movement], we have farmers from all over Bolivia, rice, poultry or fruit growers, and we tell them our history since the beginning. That we started to clear the land, how they suffered, under which conditions they worked. And if you show them everything that you have now today, they say: "The Japanese government put it, the Bolivian government made the road." They practically don't recognise our parents' efforts to have a situation like today. They think that everything is easy.

His statement points to the fact that counselling sessions for non-Nikkei farmers or events like Rice Day are not held out of mere altruism. Activities can also be understood as a preventive measure against possible hostilities. As I will show

Searching for an economic basis 203

below, being excluded or aggressed by non-Nikkei is a latent concern. Hiraoka (1980: 123), for example, notes that mechanisation may have made agriculture more attractive to young Nikkei while it was harmful regarding the solidarity with non-Nikkei; the same holds true for the introduction of cotton.

Why it is difficult to sell noodles in Bolivia – The cooperatives at a time of increasing competition

The small cooperatives have to confront increasing competition and difficult market conditions as well. Some Nikkei have even come to think that "Japanese values" are not helpful to survive in the greater Bolivian economy.

On the local level, Nikkei cooperatives may exert much influence, and they still account for a significant share of the country's egg and rice production. However, competition does not rest and workforce becomes more expensive. Many Nikkei are becoming aware that their small cooperatives cannot confront the power of multinational companies. Therefore, they have to find another niche in order to survive in the Bolivian market. As CAISY general manager Manabu Yamashita explains: "We try to live up to our reputation as agricultural pioneers" and: "We try not to do the most common." JICA as well wants to transform assistance into partnership, arguing that descendants should work as Bolivians for Bolivia's progress; therefore, it aims at increasing the diversification and competitiveness of Nikkei agribusiness. At the same time, a long-term goal is the Nikkei's contribution to food security in Japan (Endōh 2009: 178ff.).

CAISY tried macadamia production for some time, but the local climate has turned out to be only partly suitable for this sensitive plant. Furthermore, especially CAICO is taking the first steps towards industrialisation. Apart from the flour mill, the cooperative started producing noodles some years ago, with an output of 500 to 600 tons per month. The noodle package features a sumo wrestler, symbolising health, strength and energy in an aestheticisation of difference – but with modest success among non-Nikkei customers (Figure 8.3).

Even though no interview partner observed any generalised discrimination for Nikkei products, the macroeconomic situation is not very favourable. Bolivia's domestic market depends heavily on the politics of its neighbours Brazil and Argentina. Farmers from Colonia Okinawa complain that the national government prefers a clandestine market with inexpensive foreign food items to sustain low-income families. Indeed, according to Tassi et al. (2013: 91), smuggling is not only faster than legal imports, but bribes equal taxes, making it a profitable business. Farthing and Kohl (2014: 88) estimate that 70% of the economy runs on contraband, without counting the extraction of minerals, oil and gas. Hence, Nikkei noodles are not competitive. The Nikkei might hold products from Nikkei producers in higher esteem because of their "Japanese-style" quality, but this is not sufficient for CAICO's noodles to be sold on the Bolivian market where a lower-class client looks first at the price. Similarly, San Juan's sushi rice as a highly specialised product is not in great demand in Bolivia. Finally, as discussed below, national agrarian policies control the export of several of the *colonias'* products.

204 *Searching for an economic basis*

Figure 8.3 CAICO's noodle factory.

While many of my non-Nikkei acquaintances had at least heard about CAICO's noodles, I could not find any products from Colonia Okinawa during a visit to the most important supermarkets in Santa Cruz. CAICO manager Yoshio Shimajiri explained this situation with the intense competition. In 2017, he hoped to be successful with the flour production initiated shortly before. He pointed to cultural reasons: Nikkei in Bolivia are too timid and consequently bad at self-marketing. Instead, Yoshio argued, they should be more "aggressive." In other words, he thought that embodying "Japanese values" is a disadvantage in an environment where small cooperatives do not wield much influence.

A comparison with Paraguay shows a similar picture. In Asunción, too, some descendants think that the Nikkei should do more self-marketing to be present on the Paraguayan market. One Nikkei entrepreneur holds the highest share of the country's egg market and has expanded into finance and other industries. However, he remains the exception, Paraguayan Nisei engineer Akiyoshi Chiba regrets: "It seems that even if they [the Nikkei] have high earnings, they are not really on the public agenda, [they maintain] a low profile." At the same time, a number of Mennonite dairy cooperatives have become well known to Paraguayan consumers; thus, Akiyoshi thinks that the Nikkei could follow that example instead of hoping that customers will seek "Japanese quality" by themselves. One step into that direction is the "Okinawa Sunday Market." I 2019, it was held once per month in front of Multimercado Okinawa and was advertised on

Searching for an economic basis 205

Facebook in Spanish. Nikkei from Colonia Okinawa sell their products to Nikkei and non-Nikkei consumers looking for organic vegetables and difference. Nikkei from San Juan have started a similar initiative.

Mai Amuro, wife of a CAICO associate, concludes that the cooperatives will only become more successful when they understand the need to create networks, for example in the powerful chambers of commerce, in order to survive in the polarised and conflictive environment. She thinks that the cooperatives should follow the example of the Brazilian farmers who successfully lobby for their interests in Bolivia, as described in Chapter 9. At the same time, she criticises that the cooperatives, like the entire community, have not been innovative and have not taken enough advantage of the "Japanese quality" discourse. For a long time, when prices were more favourable and competition weak, there was no need to improve products and seek risks: prosperity made them feel too comfortable, Mai concludes.

In contrast to flour and noodles from Colonia Okinawa, different rice varieties from San Juan dominated all visited supermarkets in Santa Cruz and La Paz. The same holds for CAISY's eggs that I found in markets and supermarkets in Santa Cruz, La Paz and Sucre. Many non-Nikkei Bolivian acquaintances had heard about CAISY, but they did not know that it had something to do with the Nikkei. When I asked Manabu Yamashita why they did not put "Colonia Japonesa de San Juan" more prominently on rice packages, his answer illustrates that despite their symbolic capital, Nikkei do not feel completely safe as an ethnic minority:

> We were cautious at the moment this government [referring to Evo Morales and the MAS] came to power because there were conflicts or misunderstandings with foreigners. And putting the name of the Japanese *colonia*, we thought that they would maybe reject us. So we maintained a low profile, but always complying with quality.

However, Yoshio objects that merely writing "Okinawa" on a package does not mean that it will be sold automatically. One reason is that some farmers from neighbouring Montero have started to put "Okinawa" on their products while selling them for a lower price without fearing any consequences.

Painful decisions – Coping with a changing environment

At a time of decreasing support from Japan, the Nikkei have to realise that they are not only dependent on economic conditions in Bolivia, but also on price fluctuations on the world market. In early 2014, farmers were confident about the future. At the beginning of the millennium, selling raw materials was lucrative and many Latin Americans were able to rise to the middle class. Manabu Yamashita's opinion at that time can be taken as representative when he speaks about contributing to Bolivia's well-being:

> We want to continue in this branch, in this challenge, to improve productivity, all the cultivations we have, rice, corn and new species, to support the

206 *Searching for an economic basis*

country's food security. I think that in all countries in the world, agriculture will continue being a really important and responsible activity to guarantee the alimentation of the whole population [...]. There's much future in South America and Bolivia in particular.

However, sinking prices resulted in a Latin America-wide economic crisis, showing that economies were far from diversified (Comisión Económica para América Latina y el Caribe 2017). Trade disputes as well as price and currency fluctuations had a huge impact on Bolivia's soybean, rice, sugarcane and corn growers. In 2019, climatic and financial reasons led to losses of about USD 300 million, while growers had become indebted with more than USD 400 million at seed and machine companies (Rojas 2019). As a result, unemployment was rising in the city, causing fear among the middle class. One friend told me, shaking her head in disbelief, that even some beauty parlours were closing. Mai Amuro, however, noticed that her once party-loving neighbours had become much quieter, concluding with a happy smile: "Thanks to God that we're in crisis!"

In their history, both *colonias* have suffered also from adverse climatic conditions with increasing extreme weather events. Natural hazards like El Niño, pests and crop failures affect them and other farmers. A combination of economic and climatic factors generated serious difficulties for CAICO around the year 2000 (Amemiya 2001). In 2015, Colonia Okinawa had problems after soybean prices decreased; moreover, it was also a difficult time for wheat cultivation. San Juan was hit by droughts in 2015 and 2016. While chicken food became expensive, the price of eggs decreased and a bacterial infection affected rice cultivations. Ichiro Ninomiya, JICA's vice-director in Bolivia, estimates their losses to be USD 2 million. When I met him in August 2017, Yoshio consoled himself that agriculture is a business with ups and downs, hoping for better harvests in the following years. Technological preparation may be one possibility to maintain socioeconomic stability. Manabu Yamashita from CAISY has observed that due to climate change, the amount of rain remains equal but becomes irregular. One measure to cope with it is the irrigation system that farmers from San Juan installed already 20 years ago, with loans from JICA and local banks.

In order to combat such challenges, both cooperatives declare that they aim at diversification. On an individual level, one farmer in Colonia Okinawa grows chia and moringa, plants commercialised as "superfood" because of their supposed health benefits. Keisuke Sakata has started cultivating coconuts; others plant guavas, whereas Ryoji Nakaima in Colonia Okinawa has gone into cattle farming. Eventually, Colonia Okinawa might need to cultivate more lucrative crops than wheat. Also, Manabu points out that San Juan's farmers cannot continue producing only raw materials. He thinks of liquid egg or prepared rice for microwaves, pointing to changing consumption patterns. He dreams of his cooperative as a forerunner of globalisation in Santa Cruz and Bolivia to fulfil once again a pioneer role.

To cope with changing market realities and to be competitive on the organisational level, CAICO has been divided into a cooperative and two companies,

Searching for an economic basis 207

similar to some Brazilian cooperatives. With this transformation, they hope to be more independent: they can for example rent their silo to third parties. However, these developments mean that the cooperative model as a symbol of ethnic solidarity and Nikkei identity is slowly abandoned. As described above, CAICO together with JICA and the department of Santa Cruz have started a programme for Nikkei start-up entrepreneurs. CAISY has not yet initiated such a process since they do not sell industrialised products, Manabu explains.

Another question is if cooperatives are organisationally able to react to change. Unlike private companies, the introduction of changes might be complex and slow due to its participatory organisation. Moreover, one key challenge in these processes is succession and the active involvement of young descendants. Apart from fearing an excessive split of land in economically favourable times, Yoshio Shimajiri sees risks in the transferring process itself: the lack of support for the young generation may impede necessary changes in the cooperative.

> We've a member who sent his son to study economics. This son did an internship in CAICO [...] and now, he works with his father. So the father said: "You will work on this land [...]." He gave him machines and everything, but the father won't interfere [...]. That's a case that seems good to me. The other case is of sons who start to work with their fathers, they work with them for years, but they don't take any decisions. The son does what the father says. Agriculture is very dynamic [...], so this son should take some decisions, but that doesn't happen [...]. And you're more audacious and tend to progress or improve more when you're young. After some time, you don't take any risks.

Similarly, Matsumoto (2017) argues that the Nisei are not strict enough in transforming the Issei's institutions. They avoid taking painful decisions, perhaps because of respect – but according to the author, such a step would be necessary in a globalised and competitive economy.

The new law on cooperatives is not helpful, either, Yoshio criticises. According to this law, only Bolivian citizens can become part of the executive board – this excludes many Issei – and cooperatives must pay a new tax, interpreted by some as an abuse since they suspect that funds will go directly to corrupt bureaucrats' pockets. Moreover, the law does not differentiate between different types of cooperatives and gives state legislation more possibilities to influence elections and other decisions (CRE 2010; Heredia García 2016). Some cooperatives all over the country, unsatisfied with such developments, have decided to form companies.

A cooperative may be more suitable for small farmers with financial difficulties than for the contemporary *colonias*. Ichiro Ninomiya from JICA has as well observed that more and more prosperous Brazilian Nikkei farmers quit their cooperatives to be more independent, whereas in Bolivia, few descendants have left so far. Many Bolivian Nikkei are still convinced of the cooperative system regarded as an inherent part of the *colonias'* organisation. However, San Juan's former mayor Katsumi Bani thinks that in order not to risk a breakup like the Brazilian Cotia Cooperative, the Nikkei might have to abandon the organisational model,

208 *Searching for an economic basis*

retaining only a few useful elements. It is unclear if such transformations will lead to other forms of cohesion with Nikkei or non-Nikkei farmers.

Changing infrastructure and growing interconnectedness will have an additional effect on the two *colonias* and their cooperatives. With support from JICA, the bumpy dirt road from Santa Cruz via the sleepy hamlet Okinawa III will be paved, offering an alternative to the slightly longer route through Warnes and Montero – it was still not finished by mid-2019. Moreover, the road to Beni via Okinawa I will be improved. Opinions on these infrastructure projects are divided. Yoshio Shimajiri sees the new bridge, inaugurated in September 2017, as a chance since farmers on the other side of the nearby Rio Grande might take their grain to be processed and stored in Colonia Okinawa; whereas inhabitants might sell seeds, food, etc., to visitors. In short, he thinks that new economic opportunities will emerge. Others, like ABJ employee Keita Itosu, fear that urbanisation will foster traffic and insecurity and that some farmers will sell their land to non-Nikkei if property prices increase. In the long term, Santa Cruz' metropolitan area might extend to Colonia Okinawa and cultivations might be transformed into urbanisations or production plants. All these developments would deeply change the *colonias'* organisation.

Whereas San Juan is located further away from the city, it might face disintegration for a different reason, San Juan's former mayor Katsumi Bani notes. The region is plagued by drug trafficking. The most affected towns and villages are at some distance, but the side effects can be felt in San Juan, like the considerable gain for ABJ's gas station. Apart from a range of obvious social problems, Katsumi fears that drug trafficking will result in money laundering and land sales.

Conclusion

Many descendants connect their prosperity to Japanese culture: they imagine a Japanese way to success as exemplified in the cooperatives, widely considered model institutions. At second glance, this economic basis is not sustainable: they struggle with increasing competition and unfavourable macroeconomic circumstances. Also, their claim that they have better chances in the labour market because of good education is doubtful, since studying was not considered a promising way to success in the socioeconomic crisis of the 1990s. Moreover, although some Nikkei claim that Japanese descendants are born entrepreneurs, one does not find many bigger Nikkei-led companies. Descendants explain this fact with a dislike for the corrupt environment, but also with a lack of networks in the Bolivian economy and politics. Instead, descendants have avoided risks in their economic activities and preferred to maintain a low profile. Finally, few Nikkei take advantage of their connections to Japan for economic enterprises, nor has Japan been overly interested in small, underdeveloped Bolivia. Despite Japan's popularity in Bolivia, the Nikkei have almost not tried to "sell" their ethnic identity; they do not control the production of the popular Japanese cuisine. Not even Japanese food or its local varieties have become as popular as in neighbouring Peru.

All this means that their ethnic identity as well as their symbolic capital have been strongly related to financial resources from Japan. Nevertheless, the Nikkei's economic situation may become more difficult with decreasing Japanese support. Even the once successful cooperatives wonder if in times of macroeconomic difficulties and climate change, they have to change to other crops or forms of organisation in order to survive. Suzuki (2010: 62f.) seems to be right when stating that the Nikkei cannot translate their symbolic capital in society into significant influence on the regional or even national economy.

Notes

1 The term refers to a person of European origin and fair complexion.
2 Some Nikkei house owners pursue a similar strategy of access control when they rent out rooms to students.
3 Cooperativa Rural de Electrificación: Santa Cruz' electricity supplier.
4 Cooperativa de Telecomunicaciones: Santa Cruz' main telecommunication supplier.
5 The regional agroneconomic chamber, the chamber of industry and commerce and the exporters' association.
6 The equation "Japanese food means health" is an oversimplification, since Japanese cuisine is manifold and has, of course, changed over time, as Ishige (2009: 314) writes. For a long time, Japanese food lacked animal protein and fats. Therefore, the Japanese government promoted meat dishes and the use of oil until in the 1960s; while today, excessive consumption of greasy fast food has become a problem for some parts of the population.
7 Although many Nikkei explained proudly that they always cook Japanese-style food at home, it is questionable what 'Japanese-style food' means. As Lie (2001: 77ff.) notes, many Japanese dishes and drinks are at least partly of foreign origin, even tea and tofu. Well-known dishes such as *omuraisu* [omelette with rice filling], *karēraisu* [curry rice], *korokke* [croquette], *tonkatsu* [pork cutlet], *yakisoba* [stir-fried noodles] and *tenpura* [fried vegetables], to name but a few, were significantly influenced by other cuisines.
8 Neither do the Nikkei control the distribution of anime and manga in Bolivia. However, this topic is beyond the scope of this book.
9 According to Staniford (2004: 179), some cooperatives in southern Brazil accepted a number of prosperous non-Nikkei Brazilians to prevent anti-Japanese sentiments in the 1970s. Yoshio Shimajiri, too, has observed that several German and Italian descendants have entered Brazilian Nikkei cooperatives.

9 How the Nikkei relate to the Bolivian state

One Wednesday morning in March 2014, the day after a visit to Colonia Okinawa, I visit San Juan for the third time. I want to learn more about daily life in the other *colonia* since, due to the Okinawan dominance in Santa Cruz and the greater distance, one hears much less about San Juan. It is the first time I go on my own, after two visits with friends. During these two trips, I had known several families and the mayor Katsumi Bani. I had also visited the Japanese restaurant and the library. Today's journey starts with fighting for a seat in the *trufi*[1] to Yapacaní. One way from Santa Cruz to San Juan's town centre, with a change in Yapacaní, takes around two and a half hours. It is a beautiful day, neither very hot nor windy but still sunny. After leaving the busy city and its surroundings, one sees the silhouette of the Andes at the horizon and passes through the beautiful village of Buena Vista. With a north–south extension of about 34 km, San Juan hosts many fields, little woods and isolated houses as well as the town centre at 12 km, "Kilómetro Doce." Some of these constructions are large, sometimes with a characteristically blue Japanese-style roof, whereas others are small houses built in the typical fashion of the lowlands, apparently belonging to non-Nikkei. Trees along the roadside are green, compared to drier Colonia Okinawa. Everything seems peaceful.

The day before, CAICO's manager had proudly shown me Colonia Okinawa's new noodle fabric, the former president of Bolivia's Ryūkyūkoku Matsuridaiko chapter had enthusiastically talked to me about the dance, and during lunch at my friend's home, her lively little kittens had been the main attraction. However, Hideo Iwamatsu, the elderly president of San Juan's cooperative CAISY who I interview in his office next to the central plaza, seems somewhat preoccupied. With a serious expression on his face, he notes that the Nikkei live in permanent insecurity: "There is practically always discrimination against foreigners. Even if you have the *libreta* [document obtained after the completion of military service]." And he adds, referring to the Nikkei's physiognomy: "All this because of the face." Since it is the first time I meet him, I am not sure if such grim statements are merely related to his character, if they have something to do with the fact that he is coming from a funeral or if there are other reasons. He cheers up only when he starts speaking about cooperativism; during lunch in the small Japanese restaurant, we thoroughly discuss the topic. Hideo also tells me that he recently sent his

DOI: 10.4324/9781003228295-9

son to a farm for Latin American Nikkei in Hawai'i that has an excellent concept, according to him: hard work and no comfort.

Hideo Iwamatsu's daughter Mayumi happens to be the current *seinenkai* president. She had previously agreed to be interviewed, but without my knowledge, she has organised five other *seinenkai* members, two females and three males, for a group interview in the *colonia's* cultural centre. The young people arrive separately in pickups. For some minutes, I try to make them talk, but then, the conversation gathers a momentum of its own. Although the young adults are generally satisfied with their lives and the *colonia's* economic progress, they are not entirely optimistic regarding their future in Bolivia. One says that contacts to non-Nikkei – mostly employees of their parents and therefore socially distant – are limited. Although nobody directly refers to it, we are all aware of the current land occupation. I remember the graffiti at the shelter marking the entrance to the *colonia*, signed by the landless people's movement Movimiento Sin Tierra – Bolivia (MST-B). The graffiti, with incorrect spelling, include "*Katsumi viola los derechos humanos* [Katsumi violates human rights]," "*50 años de Convenio Bolivia-Japon vencio se le ordena Retiro voluntario de lo contrario seran expulsados de acuerdo a nuestra Constitucion del Estado* [50 years of agreement Bolivia-Japan expired they are ordered to leave voluntarily if not they will be expelled according to our constitution]" and "*organizaciones sociales haran respetar sus Derechos como Bolivianos* [social organisations will make respect their rights as Bolivians]" (Figure 9.1).

Figure 9.1 Shelter with graffiti at the entrance to San Juan.

212 *How the Nikkei relate to the Bolivian state*

Together with Mayumi, I decide to make a spontaneous visit to mayor Katsumi Bani. The tomatoes grown on compost and the garbage bins for waste separation – two of Katsumi's projects I saw during my last visit three months ago – are still there, but the building seems deserted this afternoon. When I had seen him the last time, the mayor, a Nisei in his late 40s, had talked about the death threats he received for about one and a half years and about his fear of being imprisoned again at any moment. He had been accused of administrative irregularities by the municipal council after purchasing second-hand *micros* [minibuses] in 2008. They served as school buses for the non-Nikkei school children since many of them used to arrive at school on trucks. In 2012, he had been sent to the notorious Palmasola prison for some days, followed by a two-week stay in hospital for heart problems. Many Nikkei and non-Nikkei spoke about power games in order to intimidate the popular mayor. Now, Mayumi and I visit him in his dark office full of folders and a large map of San Juan on the wall. He seems calm, but he says that he is waiting for the end of his second term. In this context, I do not know how to understand his comment that the man whose funeral was held in the morning was lucky to pass away peacefully at 94 years.

Without giving any context, Katsumi asks me if I already took a picture of the shelter and proposes that we go together. Mayumi will drive and I will take the picture from the car: "It's better if you don't get out, and take care that nobody sees you." As he says, the situation in San Juan is tense. He feels powerless and does not see any other solution than evacuating the occupied land that once belonged to his family. At the same time, he regrets that the occupiers will use their children as human shields. Katsumi also tells us that some days ago, a municipal councillor said that the Bolivians must confiscate the land from the Japanese: "Obviously they are a little crazy, but still … ." He looks at Mayumi and says that it is important to travel and not only to Japan. Eventually, he announces that he will run a public speaking course for young adults. The course will be in Spanish, not in Japanese, he emphasises. "You can't say: 'I will just drive my tractor, I do not want to get involved because I am Japanese, I will stay in my corner.' You have to defend yourselves." And he adds, laughingly: "Or with karate and judo!"

We take the picture without any problems. While sitting at the corner of the quiet plaza in the Japanese shop and eating *anpan* [a Japanese sweet roll filled with red bean paste], Mayumi remembers the year she studied in Gunma Prefecture and used to go to Brazilian shops to buy meat and manioc "to feel at home." Around 4 o'clock, I cautiously ask her about the end of her noon break, but she answers that her boss, at the same time her uncle, is not very strict in this regard. After her father has offered me a surprising but much appreciated gift – some packages of macadamia nuts with chocolate produced in San Juan – we drive to the nearby public school to speak with the school director, an interview recommended and organised by the mayor. For once, Mayumi seems on unknown territory. Classes are finished and the courtyard is full of non-Nikkei children playing basketball and football, looking at us without saying anything. The walls are full of murals encouraging pupils to throw garbage into the garbage bin. With the mayor's help, the school has been taking part in a garbage separation programme supported by

How the Nikkei relate to the Bolivian state 213

a Swiss non-governmental organisation. School director Cecilia Arancibia arrives late and out of breath at the minuscule teachers' room, since the *trufi* was delayed. She is very friendly and she speaks full of admiration about Japanese descendants. Cecilia recognises some problems such as the Nikkei's paternalistic attitude, but she prefers to tell us about the excellent cooperation. With a strong highland accent, she speaks about the mutual help between Nikkei and non-Nikkei, mentioning the mayor and a group of about ten Nisei who have created a scholarship for non-Nikkei students from San Juan. Finally, she offers me an image of St. Bernhard. It is already getting dark outside, and I have to return to the city. Without many words, we go back to the car, and Mayumi drives me to the *trufi* stop.

The anecdote captures many of the dynamics I will describe in this chapter. The visit was insightful to understand the Nikkei's ambivalent position in the economic and political landscape of the region. As Vink und Bauböck (2013: 622) note, citizenship means the formal equality of all members in a political community, based on belonging to a state: it gives individuals certain rights and obligations towards other members of society. Hence, in this chapter, I discuss how Nikkei as citizens and members of an ethnic minority relate to other political actors in order to assert their interests and how this influences their negotiations of identity.

The Nikkei have mostly maintained a low profile in an environment marked by clientelism and corruption. Apart from a former mayor, a university professor and a former diplomat, I do not know any post-war Nikkei who work for the state or a related institution. Instead, the Nikkei's relation to the Bolivian state has been marked by distrust since they construct it as profoundly corrupt and as opposed to their own "Japanese values." However, one has to acknowledge that many non-Nikkei Bolivians try to maintain a distance to the state as well: instead of feeling part of it and channeling frustrations via democratic participation, they think that any issue related to public administration is more of a nuisance than anything else.

As a consequence of Japanese state support, Nikkei in Bolivia did not need to form alliances with powerful local actors. Thus, the Nikkei might be comparatively prosperous and well regarded in daily life, but they lack the power to assert themselves in case of conflict and may even feel threatened as "foreigners."

Maintaining a low profile – Why the Nikkei lack influence in Santa Cruz

If it is true that power in Santa Cruz is directly connected to land ownership and agroindustry, then the Nikkei are not influential in Santa Cruz Department. Hence, the case of recent Brazilian migrants in Santa Cruz is instructive to understand the Nikkei's vulnerability. The border to Brazil is less than 600 km away from Santa Cruz, and this proximity is notable not only because of Brazilian restaurants, imported products and telenovelas. Urioste (2012: 445) even speaks about a Brazilian elite in Santa Cruz, important not only in agriculture but also with subtle influence in politics, although the relation between political groups

214 *How the Nikkei relate to the Bolivian state*

favouring autonomy on the one hand and Brazilian soybean farmers on the other hand has not been researched in detail.

According to the classification of soy cultivators elaborated by Pérez Luna (2007: 100), some non-Nikkei Bolivians as well as a number of Brazilians and different business corporations are considered large-scale cultivators, each possessing more than 1,000 hectares. He classifies Nikkei as middle-scale landowners. Together with some non-Nikkei Bolivian farmers and the Mennonites, they constitute a numerically small group. With 50 hectares or less, small non-Nikkei Bolivian soy growers account for the most significant share.

Numbers collected by Mackey (2011: 11) show that while Brazilians increased land ownership for soybeans cultivation by 82% from 1993 to 2009, Nikkei enlarged the same cultivations by merely 19% in the same period. Many Brazilians have entered the market almost without competition, being able to purchase land from indebted Bolivian farmers in the 1990s, a time of adverse climatic conditions. They had connections to the world market after training by Brazilian state agencies and private companies, since Brazil is one of the continent's leader in oilseed production (Medeiros 2008; Urioste 2012). Although Bolivian agriculture lacks modernisation, mechanisation and competitiveness and despite the poor road infrastructure, it is increasingly integrated into the global market and offers Brazilian farmers favourable circumstances. The Bolivian state has assisted the agrarian sector with tax reductions and inexpensive fuel: through diesel subsidiaries, Bolivia's soy production was supported with more than USD 20 million in 2009 and USD 1,000 million in 2012 (Farthing and Kohl 2014: 149; Urioste 2011: 58). Many Brazilians in Bolivia are organised in groups for joint commercialisation. While they enjoy high yields, they control about 40% of soy production in Bolivia on more than half a million hectares of land. Gimenez (2010: 127ff.) puts forward that the Brazilian presence in Bolivia, rather than being the result of a specific geopolitical strategy, is individually motivated and driven by favourable market conditions.

Social scientist and urban planner Fernando Prado (2007: 157ff.) differentiates between several densely interwoven forms of power in the city: the civic power of Comité Cívico Pro Santa Cruz, the traditional elite's symbolic-ideological power and the agricultural power. Some of the elite families have stayed exclusively in large-scale agriculture and speculative landholding; others have expanded into finance and mass media.[2] Some Brazilian farmers have accessed these circles via business associations and marriage. According to Prado, a position in the economic and agroeconomic chambers is an important way to obtain political influence since these associations have contributed to promote a specific regional identity as supporters of autonomy opposed to the Morales administration. While several of the around 300 Brazilian farmers have entered these institutions, only two Japanese descendants as representatives of CAICO and CAISY are part of the steering committee of the wheat and oilseed growers' association ANAPO (Asociación de Productores de Oleaginosas y Trigo), together with eleven other representatives.

ANAPO is a member of the regional agroeconomic chamber Cámara Agropecuaria del Oriente (CAO), the most important economic association in

How the Nikkei relate to the Bolivian state   215

Santa Cruz. Around 70,000 farmers from 16 member associations are organised in CAO which is part of CAINCO, Santa Cruz' and Bolivia's largest chamber of commerce. CAO is politically influential up to the national level and in favour of regional autonomy. Although they include small peasants, CAO and ANAPO mainly represent the interests of large-scale farmers. Genetically modified seeds, an important issue for CAO, are for example only rentable for farmers with a certain amount of land. Nevertheless, since small soy producers do not have much power vis-à-vis international seed companies or other multinational companies, they may still benefit from ANAPO membership.

Despite the MAS government's nationalist rhetoric, agrarian laws still allow foreign residents to purchase land with certain restrictions – but one may circumvent this rule through business associations, marriage with a Bolivian national or naturalisation. Moreover, the Morales administration has not implemented any de facto prohibition of large-scale landholdings. It is not clear if the Brazilian foreign ministry has influenced the elaboration of the new Bolivian constitution, lobbying against such a prohibition – Brazil as the largest country in Latin America is an important export partner and creditor of Bolivia (Urioste 2012: 448). Even though Brazilian farmers in Bolivia do not always possess a legal land title (see below), soy production is still rentable enough to accept possible legal risks. Farmers may rely on Brazil's support if problems arise.

The example of Brazilian farmers sharply contrasts with the Nikkei and the Mennonites, although both have been living in Santa Cruz for a much longer time. In an interview, Fernando Prado expressed his surprise that the Nikkei have never reached prominent positions in CAO, ANAPO or similar entities, despite their reputation as agricultural pioneers. In contrast to some of the Brazilian farmers, they have not entered the elites through marriage, nor did they attain similar wealth, nor have they officially aligned with the dominant anti-Morales forces in Santa Cruz. Discussing with many Nikkei, we eventually agreed that descendants have consciously opted for a low profile in both the economy and in politics. Moreover, Comité Cívico, CAO and other entities representing regional power have not searched for the small Nikkei minority's support. As discussed in Chapter 4, social scientist Fernando Prado thinks that the Nikkei were too foreign to be readily accepted; as a result, they may have been unable to enter the networks of powerful *cruceños*.

> It's not that the *cruceños* are selective towards foreigners, because foreigners […] even had an advantage. Germans, French people have been in the Chamber of Commerce. Except if for *cruceños* the Japanese were not the same as Europeans […]. The Europeans are white, so they had access. They rapidly married the daughter of a millionaire and appeared on the top.

Nevertheless, Fernando Prado concludes that cultural factors on the Nikkei's side were more important than the *cruceño* elites' rejection, even though he also acknowledges that the *colonia's* settlement patterns did not encourage interaction with other parts of society. I argue that post-war Nikkei did not need to seek

216 *How the Nikkei relate to the Bolivian state*

alliances in Bolivia in order to achieve upward mobility: the Issei received land from the state and their children could enjoy all rights of Bolivian citizenship and the right to *dekasegi*. As Amemiya (2001) notes: "Until recent years, the Japanese immigrant community set itself apart as if it were an isolated oasis in the desert, with a special endowment from afar called Japanese governmental aid."

The Nikkei have strategically avoided any open conflict with non-Nikkei. No major disputes have taken place about scarce resources, unlike for example in the United States where descendants demanded reparations for being imprisoned in concentration camps in the Second World War. Their most prominent activity is agriculture, and in the 1950s and 1960s, sufficient land existed for all newcomers to the lowlands. Unlike the middlemen minorities Bonacich (1973) describes, the Nikkei do not dominate any branch; non-Nikkei Bolivians are unlikely to feel dominated or exploited by a seemingly homogeneous group of greedy foreigners. While the Nikkei have not sought contact with the Bolivian state, they have not questioned existing power relations, either.

"One is never sure to be the owner of that land" – Confronting land reforms and occupations

Land in the *colonias* is related to identity: Colonia Okinawa and San Juan are regarded as the Nikkei's imagined homeland in Bolivia. However, the Nikkei have often felt threatened by land occupations and land reforms. The way they handle these conflicts also gives an insight into the complex minority–majority relations in Bolivia.

INRA law[3] has been the most crucial law regarding land ownership since the Revolution of 1952. From 1996 onwards, it has promised legal security and transparency with the clarification of land rights (*saneamiento*). The objective was to map property boundaries in a correct cadastral survey until 2006. With the introduction of the socioeconomic function (*función económica social*, FES), the state can now confiscate land without compensation if it is not productive. Productivity can be proven, for instance, by cattle birth certificates or timely tax payment. Confiscated fallow land should be given free of charge to indigenous groups, small farmers and landless people.

In other words, MAS and its programme for the redistribution of wealth seemed a possible threat for the Nikkei since it questioned the security of their land title. As one might expect, actors such as CAO strongly opposed the process, considering INRA to be politicised and biased. CAO argued that the reform impeded flexible capitalist production, making it impossible to adapt to changing market and climate conditions (Chumacero Ruiz 2015: 162f.; Radhuber 2009: 59ff.; Valdivia 2010). In early 2014, Hideo Iwamatsu was suspicious that INRA and the landless people's movement were allies:

> One is never sure that one has the INRA title, the *función económica social*... [...], one is never sure to be the owner of that land. And they [the landless people's movement] enter with any pretext, and then, if you don't

How the Nikkei relate to the Bolivian state 217

use the land for two years, you're already against the nation [...]. I don't know if I will have the certainty one day, because these occupiers enter to occupy.

INRA's objectives have mostly not been fulfilled: titling was slow, ineffective, disorganised and full of irregularities. The process was not yet finished by mid-2019. Eventually, not much land has been confiscated: since the government increasingly relied on agribusiness, seizing properties from large-scale owners was no priority (Fabricant 2012: 173ff.). Chumacero Ruiz (2015: 173f.) argues that once the autonomy movement had lost force, the national government deemed it no longer necessary to seek support among indigenous and landless peasant groups. The Nikkei's anxieties have not been fulfilled, either, although Hideo Iwamatsu remembers that the process had been a headache for him: a company appointed by INRA registered a piece of land under his neighbour's name. Thus, he had to pay USD 2,500 for a lawyer in order to correct it.

For the most part, Nikkei preferred not to fight for their land, especially when their opponent was a member of the elites. While several Nikkei have lost such lawsuits in Bolivian courts, at least one of these land conflicts has been solved with the help of Japanese diplomacy that put Bolivian authorities under pressure (Amemiya 2001; Suzuki 2010: 61f.). When I asked her for an evaluation of the described case, Kozy Amemiya, a Japanese sociologist who has written several articles on Bolivian Nikkei, answered that the case she describes was an exception, both that the farmer stood up for his rights and that the embassy intervened. Against the local elites, the Nikkei did not have any chance to win, but having provided much development assistance while occasionally cancelling Bolivia's debts, Japan can now assist its citizens abroad. Nevertheless, relying permanently on such support might become dangerous if nationalist currents prevail, accusing Japanese descendants of harming non-Nikkei with the help of a foreign power.

Whereas the state has not confiscated much land for the benefit of landless peasants, some of them, like the above-mentioned MST-Bolivia, have started acting by themselves. Most landowners consider occupiers to be invaders of foreign property, while the landless peasants have been using anti-capitalist and nationalist narratives mixed with human rights discourses (Fabricant 2012: 40f.). The Nikkei were depicted as wealthy imperialists, while indigeneity served as an overarching political weapon: the occupiers claimed that they had more right to the land than the 'foreigners' who did not enjoy symbolic capital in their eyes.

But the Nikkei knew that despite this graffiti, right was on their side. As a reaction to such conflicts, the national government had issued a law to defend private property by the end of 2013 (Kopp 2015: 43f.). Despite a judgment of the Constitutional Court, the department's police would only act with an eviction order that the national authorities were not willing to give. Hence, most descendants did not have confidence in the Bolivian state as protector of their rights. Without evidence, some even suspected MST-B to be supported by MAS. The Nikkei justified their land claim with the argument that they had worked hard on their small pieces of land while supporting their non-Nikkei neighbours, being

218 *How the Nikkei relate to the Bolivian state*

by no means greedy agrocapitalists. Thus, some descendants concluded that they needed to better communicate their belonging to Bolivia.

After six years of occupation, the dispute was eventually decided in favour of the Nikkei. Some time after my visit, 800 police officers drove away the occupiers without casualties. Mayor Katsumi Bani thereby took advantage of dynamics at the local, international and national level – without Japanese state support. The area surrounding San Juan is marked by cocaine trafficking because it is easy to hide cultivations and installations in nearby Amboró national park. The national government, under pressure from European donors, planned to install an anti-drug police station in the region since it feared losing financial support. Conflicts emerged between those regional representatives who more or less voluntarily offered land for the police station and those who were against it, either because they feared police abuse or because they were involved in drug trafficking. When mayor Katsumi Bani offered land in San Juan, he received death threats once more, but he stayed firm (Fernández Reyes 2015). In exchange for the now operating police station, the government accepted his claim to evacuate the occupied land. One of the occupation's leaders went to prison for one year. The shelter has been painted and the atmosphere in San Juan has become more relaxed.

Interestingly, most Okinawan Nikkei were not even aware of these disputes, illustrating once again the figurative distance between the colonies. While CAICO manager Yoshio Shimajiri had heard about the conflict, he did not interpret it as an expression of anti-Nikkei sentiments, but even showed a certain understanding for the occupiers.

> San Juan is enclosed by Bolivian *colonias*, but of new colonisers. And these are the most radical. Here we have colonisers from the highlands, but these are old *colonias*, already the children of these people. You talk to them, and they are already like *cambas*, calmer, more understanding. Instead, the people [from San Juan] [...], it's said that the people from the highlands are more resentful, because of years of exploitation since colonisation, mining, slavery.

Three years later, Manabu Yamashita from San Juan explains the described land occupation by its attractive localisation close to the road to Cochabamba and thinks that such an occupation would not repeat itself. Accordingly, he does not observe any resentment against Nikkei. In sum, despite the Morales administration's nationalist rhetorics, not all descendants feel threatened as an ethnic minority.

A comparison with other groups perceived as foreigners does not show a clear pattern. According to Mackey (2011: 14f.), Brazilian farmers think that in the current political climate, landownership may be more difficult for foreigners, citing statements from the peasant syndicate and the landless movement. However, such statements do not necessarily result in land occupations. Kopp (2015: 90ff.) observes that some peasant syndicates have accused the Mennonites of accumulating land. The latter's insecurity is even more pronounced than in San Juan since the recently founded *colonias* seldom possess a legal land title. In the few cases of land

How the Nikkei relate to the Bolivian state   219

occupation, the Mennonites have tried to defend their land either by legal means or by force; sometimes, they have also ceded to the occupiers' claims. At the same time, surrounding villages and local authorities strongly support the Mennonites since they benefit financially from their neighbours. Therefore, it remains an open question if an ethnic minority in Bolivia is more at risk of losing their land. Notwithstanding, social capital appears to be essential to manage such difficulties.

Trámites and *coimas* – How Nikkei deal with bureaucracy and state policies

As citizens, Nikkei do not only enter in contact with the state in the case of land conflicts, but they also have to deal with public administration in daily life; moreover, they are affected by state policies. At the same time, daily conversations about bureaucracy signify imagining the state and giving meaning to it (Galtung 1969; Gupta 2012).

Bolivians mainly describe their encounters with the state as a nuisance: bureaucracy is described as a kind of structural violence against citizens. Furthermore, Bolivian bureaucracy is slow, disordered and scarcely digitalised. When I went to the residence registration office at the beginning of my research stay, a state employee typed my dossier on a writing machine without any haste. After different formalities in the next three days, these and other documents were eventually sent to La Paz for the last signature that took two months. In sum, *trámites* are a constant worry for all Bolivians – the sentence "I am waiting for my documents" is as typical as the sight of people carrying around beige folders with documents to obtain other documents. Working for the state is not attractive, either: many parts of Bolivia's public administration are politicised and jobs often depend on party leaders' goodwill (Gingerich 2010).

Hideo Iwamatsu from CAISY gives an example for these preoccupations: according to him, bureaucratic inflexibility makes exportation of agricultural products almost impossible.

> You need to have a permit from SENASAG [the national agency for food safety]. So, if it expires, you need a new one. But you can't renew it unless it's expired. You do the *trámite* and that takes three, four months that you lose [...]. It's a long *trámite* [...]. The products expire in the meantime.

However, few Nikkei were suspicious that such problems were rooted in anti-Nikkei sentiments. One is the hairdresser Shizuka Arai who sees a relation between the Nikkei's difficulties with bureaucracy and the Morales administration.

> They control the foreigners very much in Bolivia [...]. We recently had a problem because this Monday the government evaluated all hair salons [...]. They didn't want to give the certificate to the five Japanese, because they said: "You're foreigners and we can't give it to you." But all these people already live here for more than 40 years. They have their residence permit

220 *How the Nikkei relate to the Bolivian state*

> here in Santa Cruz. Now we don't know yet because everything has to be sent
> to La Paz [...]. [But] it's good [that they control], maybe in other countries,
> it's the same [with foreigners].

However, the problem affects those Issei without Bolivian nationality, but not the
Nisei hairdressers. As a result, these occurrences are probably not based on a dislike of "foreigners," but are the outcome of an intransparent bureaucratic process
or of civil servants trying to receive bribes. Shizuka, too, finishes her anecdote
with the sentence: "But above all, it costs money."

Popular discourse considers corruption, i.e., the divergence of institutions from
their intended functions and the misuse of public authority for individual benefit
(Gupta 2012: 79) as well as for political gain, to be the main characteristic of
Bolivian bureaucracy. In such a setting, informal rules appear to be more important than legal ones. Consequently, a lack of networks means vulnerability and the
risk of becoming a victim of arbitrary authority decisions. Not only lower bureaucracy but also state legislation as a whole is regarded as unpredictable, one reason
being that laws are passed without broad consultation. In short, Bolivians, Nikkei
included, usually characterise themselves as victims rather than as citizens, claiming to be morally superior to the state as an antagonistic "other." Nevertheless, at a
closer look, the division between a corrupt state and the non-corrupt citizens is less
clear-cut. Compare to Gupta (2007: 148): "We complain against corruption when
we are not its beneficiaries, but otherwise conveniently call it duty and obligation."

When telling stories about daily corruption, many Nikkei emphasise their supposedly natural integrity based on their ethnic identity. While civil servants in
Japan are indeed famous for not being inclined to petty corruption, its political
and economic elites are closely interwoven and mutual relations are reinforced by
gifts (Sugimoto 1997: 204f.). Therefore, it is questionable that corruption in general is only related to poverty and weakly institutionalised states. Nevertheless,
when making normative assumptions, many Nikkei interpret corruption as a sign
of dysfunctionality, underdevelopment and a failure of moral standards in Bolivia.
For example, Nataly Yonamine who took over her mother's hair salon after coming back from Japan complains that she has still not become used to Bolivian
trámites. For Nataly, Japan means the normal state where citizens are not betrayed
of their fundamental rights, while Bolivia means the deviation.

> [In Japan,] you can plan everything. In six months, I reach this target and in
> one year, two, three, four, five years, I will reach that target. I started to plan,
> I made a five years plan, [...] [but in Bolivia] I haven't achieved 20%. It
> depends on so many things. It depends on [...] third persons and public insti-
> tutions. In this country, when you want to become legal as a company, to pay
> your bills and so on, you have to pay *coimas* [bribes], so that your documents
> get ready [...]. It's impossible to imagine that in another place.

Therefore, CAISY president Hideo Iwamatsu thinks that there is no other way
than adapting to such practices: "This is a country where the only way is *coimear*

How the Nikkei relate to the Bolivian state 221

[paying bribes]." Accordingly, he describes petty corruption as a phenomenon deeply rooted in Bolivian society:

All the time and before elections, [state representatives] visit us. And these visits are not for free. ' This is not o.k., that is not o.k., you have to stop it, I will close it for 10 or 15 days." You have to get used to this country […]. It's a culture they have maybe already since they were born and it will never change here. But we have to get used to living here [laughs].

According to Hideo, the Nikkei are powerless when confronted with the amount of corruption they encounter in everyday life. This is also true for Japanese businesspersons who, as he says, prefer a Nikkei to deal with Bolivia's public administration. Hideo thinks that "Japanese values" are a disadvantage when dealing with corruption, informality, bureaucracy and the "culture of *mañana* [tomorrow]": extra-legal methods become an acceptable reaction to an externally imposed ill if objectives cannot be reached otherwise. Following Hideo's argumentation, such practices also demonstrate that the Nikkei show the necessary flexibility one needs in Bolivia, unlike the inexperienced Japanese.

Another strategy when dealing with the state is personalising relations with key actors. Citizens may seek mediating individuals with political, social or economic influence, albeit they run the risk of becoming dependent. Several Nikkei observe that personal relations become more important than impersonal bureaucratic rules: one has to find non-Nikkei friends. Since it is a moral imperative to help one's friends, such relations can be a vital resource without being morally reprehensible. This is also Nisei Kentsu Hanashiro's strategy to facilitate *trámites*. He is about to open a small business with a non-Nikkei partner. While he acknowledges that such a plan is difficult to realise for anybody in Bolivia, he thinks that if one is fluent in Spanish, there is no problem to find helpful contacts to deal with lower bureaucracy.

To make something legal, it's a *trámite* here in Bolivia […]. There is always something that's not legal. So, unfortunately, you have to pay to make things faster. This happens here, it's normal [laughs]. So it's always good to have contact with Bolivians here that can do you such favours.

Nevertheless, the line between building up a network of mutual obligations and being accused of clientelism might be thin: at some point, it might become difficult for an "honest Japanese" to convincingly present the state as the antagonistic "other."

Nevertheless, many Nikkei regret that they do not possess relations to the higher economical and political spheres to influence decisions in their favour. CAICO manager Yoshio Shimajiri criticises export controls, for example for soybeans. Farmers were especially unsatisfied in 2015 and 2016 when the price for soybeans was low. After complaints by CAO, the national government allowed more export quotas (Fernández 2017; Quispe 2014). Moreover, many Nikkei regret that it is generally impossible to export sorghum or corn, since the domestic demand has to

222 *How the Nikkei relate to the Bolivian state*

be met first, making it difficult to plan. With such measures, the government tries to maintain the price for chicken as a major staple food low. Nevertheless, Yoshio speaks of failed agricultural policies: only one-third of the demanded wheat can be produced internally since Bolivia does not offer many suitable cultivation areas. But according to him, corn and sorghum could be planted in the whole of Santa Cruz to meet both the domestic demand and to export. Furthermore, since the price for soybeans is higher than for corn, rice and sorghum, it is not attractive to plant these crops for the soil to rest. Yoshio deplores that this lack of crop rotation damages land fertility and impedes the accumulation of organic material and water, favouring pests. Shaking his head, he regrets that the government does not take any measures to prevent such outcomes. Other Nikkei cooperative members criticise that the government lumps them together with farmers from the Andes, despite different cultivation conditions, and hold that the national government should instead invest in road infrastructure to be more competitive with other Mercosur countries. As Fukui (2017: 8f.) writes, Nikkei farmers – as well as non-Nikkei employers – are also unsatisfied with specific government decisions without broad-based consensus such as the double Christmas bonus (*doble aguinaldo*) for employees, the minimum wage rise or the increased protection against dismissal. Hideo Iwamatsu from CAISY is suspicious that the government favours its electorate: "For the export of quinoa, the Indians made that product, it's said that there are no restrictions."

Apart from export limitations, CAISY manager Manabu Yamashita deplores that Bolivian laws prohibit the use of genetically modified seeds except for one variety of soybeans, although the ban is often violated (Estremadoiro Flores 2017; Heras 2016; Heredia García 2017). According to Manabu, such seeds should be called "genetically improved seeds." He sees biotechnology as a means for progress and food security, but also as a way to subsist under adverse climatic conditions and to combat pests with less pesticide. He is also convinced that such seeds enable Bolivian farmers to compete in price and productivity with neighbouring countries. Much like the exponents of CAO propagating neoliberalism and free markets, he favours free exports to choose the right moment for sales on international markets. According to him, it is essential for the Nikkei cooperatives to belong to a powerful entity like ANAPO in order to survive in the increasingly competitive agriculture. Only through these associations, farmers are able to negotiate with the national government, he emphasises. Nevertheless, whereas fighting for genetically modified seeds and free markets is a priority for CAO, it has not influenced state legislation in the case of the new law on cooperatives that directly affects the Nikkei farmers, as mentioned in Chapter 8.

Politics means dirty hands – Do "Japanese values" impede political engagement in Bolivia?

It comes as no surprise that few Nikkei are interested in running for public office. I will describe concrete cases in the next subchapter and focus here on the discussion if it is feasible for descendants to engage in Bolivian politics.

How the Nikkei relate to the Bolivian state   223

Indeed, I never witnessed ideological discussions among descendants. I was sometimes told that the Nikkei were just not interested in politics. Although public administration was regularly brought up as a daily nuisance, they almost never commented on specific political parties, personalities or ideologies. Interview partners considered Nikkei engaged in politics as candidates or party members to be the exception rather than the rule. I have not heard, either, of post-war Nikkei actively supporting the regional autonomy movement, although some expressed sympathy for a *cruceño* identity. Nisei lawyer Tomoji Yamashita thinks that this attitude has even influenced professional choices: he argues that more Nikkei have become doctors and engineers rather than lawyers because the former can avoid power struggles. Only Hirabayashi (2002) compares influencing factors and motives for the Nikkei's political commitment in the United States, Mexico and Peru and no research seems to exist on descendants in guerrilla and as opposition activists under dictatorship, although Hurtado und Solares Maemura (2006) as well as Oshiro (2016) wrote on a family member's commitment.

Identities can become political if groups make claims for rights from the state and society based on ethnic identity. The mobilisation of ethnic identity is a conscious decision: groups rely on collective identity in order to take advantage of opportunities when leaders are capable and willing to frame issues. New formulations of identity, too, can become a key for mobilisation (Glidden 2011). In recent years, indigenous people in Bolivia have been organising themselves around identity – but not the Nikkei.

Nikkei engaging in Japanese politics after the Second World War are hard to find as well. Overseas Japanese could not vote for elections in Japan before 1998 (Matsui 2007); according to Roth (2003b: 105), this change occurred as a consequence of the growing number of Japanese businesspersons abroad, not because of the Nikkei. Latin American Nikkei associations focus on cultural and social activities and generally claim to be politically neutral; there has not been any effort to build up political leaders. Mai Amuro assumes that after the end of Japanese ultranationalism, associations might also have had a "trauma," preferring to abstain from politics. This lack of engagement stands in contrast to the Brazilian Jewish organisations described by Grün (1994): their Zionist or Marxist orientation possibly serves as an inspiration for future politicians. Politically active diasporas and ethnic associations appear to be related to conflicts between different ethnic groups or to nation-building processes.

Moreover, the Latin American political arena can undoubtedly be an uncomfortable field of activity. With few exceptions, political parties, as well as parliaments and justice systems, do not enjoy symbolic capital, see, for instance, the LAPOP poll (Cohen et al. 2017). As Mansilla (2016) analyses, most Latin American politicians try to resemble TV stars or PR experts, but they do not show social responsibility, critical spirit or intellectual inclinations. Latin American elections are usually considered fair and free, but politicians do not necessarily use democratic mechanisms to stay in power and secure their income, changing from one party to another. Furthermore, party leaders have much power, making

224 *How the Nikkei relate to the Bolivian state*

it difficult for independent candidates to be elected (Gingerich 2010). Political commitment may even mean being physically aggressed.

As a result, Latin American politicians are often collectively accused of being only interested in their personal benefit instead of dedicating themselves to public service. Many Latin Americans suppose that politicians have dirty hands almost by definition. It comes to no surprise that some parts of society prefer to make demands through roadblocks or the destruction of public property. Nevertheless, it is not possible to sharply separate corrupt politicians from a clean civil society: clientelism has been a dominant feature of politics, with politicians openly proclaiming that they would reward support with jobs and funds. Although many Bolivians regard clientelism as an obstacle to progress, volunteering for a candidate can still be a means to attain upward social mobility.

Consequently, some Nikkei argue that non-Nikkei Bolivians are not able to run a country since they consider them to be too individualistic, immature and selfish. Paralleling the discussion on entrepreneurship, many believe that being a politician, at least in Latin America, is not only troublesome but also incompatible with their identity: they fear that building alliances with an established party means becoming corrupted. Nisei engineer Shusei Iha says: "To be a politician, you have to have a big throat [laughs], and moreover, you have to be a liar, so it's not easy for a Japanese to be a politician." Paulo Yokotani shares this opinion. He is the director of an economic development unit of the Brazilian federal state of São Paulo, an area with 41 million inhabitants. He admits that being too correct "like a Japanese" may be harmful for a Latin American politician, since, in his words, they have to be flexible – perhaps even too flexible, he adds. It is telling that Ryoji Nakaima, the Nisei cattle breeder from Santa Cruz, constructs a difference between Nikkei in Brazil and Bolivia: "In Brazil, for example, they live there more than 100 years, they have politicians [...]. They are more Brazilian than Japanese, they also steal [laughs]."

An important question is therefore how a Nikkei positions him- or herself in the polarised environment and if political commitment would mean entering an established but potentially corrupt party. Despite the dependencies this creates, it is easier for members of an established party to obtain the financial means for a campaign. Moreover, being a party member may be helpful to obtain voters' support outside of his or her ethnic community of only around 2,400 people – while not even all descendants may support a candidate (Hirabayashi 2002).[4] As outsiders, the Nikkei might have the advantage to be considered neutral in a polarised environment where they belong neither to the wealthy, white elite nor to the indigenous poor. Nevertheless, most interview partners doubted that Nikkei politicians had such an advantage.

All politicians are confronted with conflicting demands from different actors; and allegations of self-interest are often a political tactic. Since everybody has an issue that is not completely legal – see the subchapter on *trámites* – it is not difficult to construct an accusation. As Shakow (2014: 120) notes in her study on the town of Sacaba near Cochabamba, corruption allegations were a very current weapon in the struggle for scarce funds and jobs and may even come from one's

How the Nikkei relate to the Bolivian state   225

own group. Indeed, the fear that a politician would harm their symbolic capital was a reason for many Peruvian Nikkei voters not to support Alberto Fujimori's candidature, as described below.

Nevertheless, the Nikkei's distance to Bolivian politics may not be the result of supposedly static and superior "Japanese values," but above all of a lack of need. The Nikkei relied on Japanese state support; and, as farmer Seiichiro Takaki from San Juan resumes: "We could always escape. If I don't have success here, I go to Japan. So we weren't very determined in this respect." With the exception of land disputes, it was never necessary to claim rights from the Bolivian state, compared to fostering relations with Japan. Bolivian Nikkei do not suffer from discrimination and a deprivation of rights – in short, they might lack sufficient common goals for political action. Mai Amuro concludes that the Nikkei "have always had a low profile, they don't claim for spaces, they don't claim political power, economically either [...]. So this kind of things makes that a group has a low profile, but [lives] quiet and [...] well respected."

However, several Nikkei like Mai and Shusei did enjoy discussing political issues with me. Some Nisei and Sansei even argue that it may be necessary to be more active in Bolivian politics instead of relying on Japan. Already around the year 2000, one of Amemiya's (2001) interview partners lamented that the lack of political networks meant that the Nikkei are unable to control their life conditions, e.g., the prices of their products: "We are regarded like dolls, that is, lovable and neat and do-nothing." Even though she underlines that the governor of Santa Cruz has publicly voiced his admiration for Nikkei, Nisei Kaede Itokazu still expresses to feel threatened by *collas* – a statement that strikingly resembles the discourse of the autonomy movement. Similarly, Yoshio Shimajiri from CAICO thinks that the Nikkei may need protection against a MAS government in the future: "Maybe they would be more protected also if there were people above [...] since the current government grumbles a lot against foreigners. If they had more politicians there, they could maybe attenuate this." Descendants like Yoshio and Kaede have come to regard such a political commitment not as an engagement contradicting "Japanese values," but as a way to defend their group's position at a time when Japan reduces its assistance. Accordingly, the Nikkei know best what they need. However, no concrete political strategy has emerged from such ideas so far – and those with concrete political experiences are much less optimistic, as the next subchapter shows.

"The Nikkei has to eat more manioc" – The multiple difficulties of being a Nikkei politician

The most Nikkei politician is Peru's former president Alberto Fujimori, whose trajectory is instructive to understand the Bolivian Nikkei's attitudes towards Nikkei politicians. As regards Bolivia, Katsumi Bani, the former mayor of San Juan, is well known at least within the metropolitan region of Santa Cruz. Without aiming at a comparison, I want to show how they came to power, how they used their ethnic identity and how far Nikkei and non-Nikkei identified with them.

226   *How the Nikkei relate to the Bolivian state*

It is not surprising that the absolute number of Nikkei politicians is higher in Brazil and Peru than in other countries of Latin America. The first Brazilian Nikkei went into politics shortly after the Second World War: Yukishigue Tamura is reported to be the first *vereador* [city councillor] of São Paulo in 1947. He was later elected state deputy and federal deputy (Salvadori Filho 2014). In 1969, former cooperative manager Fábio Yassuda became federal minister for industry and commerce as the first Nikkei member of government. As regards North America, several Nikkei governors and vice-governors have been elected in Hawai'i. With the Nisei Alberto Fujimori, Peru has even had a Nikkei president: perhaps the first time that many people outside the Americas and Japan heard about Nikkei was in 1990 when *"el chino Fujimorí"* [Fujimori, the Chinese] was elected president. Apart from Fujimori, the country has seen a Nikkei premier and a president of Congress, as well as some other members of Congress like Fujimori's son Kenji and his daughter Keiko. The latter ran several times for president unsuccessfully.

In Bolivia, most public personalities of Japanese origin have been of pre-war origin, such as Pando Department's former prefect Ernesto Shimakawa as well as Jorge Yoshida, former general manager of the Central Bank of Bolivia. A post-war descendant was appointed as Bolivian ambassador in Japan under Evo Morales, another was director of a YPFB[5] subsidiary. The former was accused of irregularities and recalled, similar to the latter who was dismissed under corruption allegations. On a local level, Colonia Okinawa and San Juan have elected Nikkei mayors, in the case of San Juan until 2015. I have not heard of any post-war descendants in Comité Cívico; and as previously mentioned, they are almost not visible in CAO or similar entities. This stands in contrast to other descendants of recent migration: Arab surnames appear to be much more prominent in the Bolivian political arena.[6] I have not heard, either, of Nikkei in labour unions, organisations known as an important but also militant political force, nor of descendants in comparable grassroots organisations.

Especially well known has been Adalberto "El Chino" Kuajara, a Nikkei of pre-war origin and a former minister of health. Once a member of the Communist party, he became affiliated to the dictatorial government of Hugo Banzer and later minister of labour under Sánchez de Lozada until the latter was expulsed in 2003 – in other words, a political commitment that brought him to court and that will not have increased his popularity among Nikkei. Although he was of pre-war origin, neither engaged in *nihonjinkai* nor spoke Japanese, he has found his final resting place in the Japanese mausoleum in Santa Cruz' central cemetery.

Among post-war Nikkei, one national deputee and candidate for Bolivia's presidency became known around ten years ago. For some voters, it might have been a bonus that the *"samurai camba,"* as a newspaper wrote, was of Japanese origin. However, most Nikkei voters did not feel represented by this candidate. He had not held any responsibility in Nikkei associations and some remarked that "he's not a stable personality," "he doesn't enter the profile of the correct Japanese," "we were afraid that he would make us look bad" and "he doesn't have the necessary merits to be a dignified representative of the Japanese community." Moreover, he belonged to a practically defunct party and was related to

How the Nikkei relate to the Bolivian state   227

an ex-president wanted for trial by the MAS government. Eventually, he obtained only around 6% of all votes. He disappeared from the public and could not be located for an interview. Non-Nikkei Ruy Villanueva analyses that this candidate was not somebody Nikkei had expected, but considers him an opportunist:

> It was a surprise even for the Japanese descendants [...]. "Where is this *señor* from?" They even said: "He's an agronomist, what is he doing in politics?" [...] Those from [the party] obviously took him to benefit from the good image of the Japanese, because the party was in a bad state. In the end, the result wasn't really good because he was totally unknown.

The internationally most famous Nikkei politician is, without doubt, Alberto Fujimori. Although one might suppose that his candidacy proves a minority's increasing commitment to Peruvian society or that he stands for a politicised ethnic identity, the situation turns out to be more complex on a closer look. Fujimori's connections with the local Nikkei community were weak, and rather than being proud, most Peruvian Nikkei had mixed feelings about his first candidacy in 1990. Many disliked his populist statements; furthermore, the violent anti-Japanese incidents of the 1940s are deeply etched in the collective memory (Kushner 2001). In Peru, the Nikkei had regarded politics as a taboo for a long time. Endōh (2009: 20) states: "Fearful to the negative reaction of Peruvian society, the Japanese-Peruvian community, including Fujimori's own mother it is said, hesitated to endorse his presidential candidacy."[7] However, especially towards voters from the lower classes, Alberto Fujimori successfully cultivated his outsider role against opponent Mario Vargas Llosa, a white upper-class member of an established conservative party, an acclaimed writer and Nobel laureate (Oliart 1996).

As Murakami (2008) analyses, Peru with its weakly institutionalised democracy was looking for a saviour rather than for a supposedly honest Japanese descendant. This observation is consistent with the fact that Fujimori had no prior political experience on the national level. In the absence of a political programme, Fujimori used "*honradez, tecnología, trabajo*" [honesty, technology, work] as his slogan (Fujimori 1990), instrumentalising his Japanese origin to obtain votes. Despite this declaration, Peru suffered a systematic disrespect for democracy and human rights during his presidency, and he was eventually sentenced to 25 years in prison. By Christmas 2017, Peruvian President Pedro Pablo Kuczynski pardoned him, hoping for the support of Fujimori's children in order to survive an impeachment vote. However, Kuczynski was finally deposed and in January 2019, Fujimori returned to prison.

After Alberto Fujimori's assumption of office in 1990, Japanese development assistance for Peru almost tenfold from one year to the other (Takenaka 2003b: 478). The Japanese government thought that Fujimori's failure might bring negative consequences for both Japanese descendants and Japan's reputation. However, one should not overvalue this interest. At the time of the Latin American debt crisis, Fujimori's election initially enhanced the amount of foreign

228 *How the Nikkei relate to the Bolivian state*

aid, but Japanese foreign direct investments decreased, as Berríos (2014: 102) observes: political and economic motives were more important than any common ancestry. In the 1990s, Japan had started to support Latin America's democratising processes, but it entered a dilemma when Fujimori became increasingly authoritarian. It tried to convince him to stick to the democratic rules, but without much success (Tsunekawa 1998: 1107ff.).

Despite initial scepticism, when Fujimori was elected president, many Nikkei defended him. Nowadays, they are much more ambivalent since he turned out to be as corrupt and selfish "as any Latin American politician" (see, e.g., Morimoto 2002b: 148ff.).[8] The Japanese-Peruvian social activist, writer and researcher Doris Moromisato Miasato (2008) describes these mixed feelings in an article with the title "*Amor y Odio a Alberto Fujimori*" [Love and hate for Alberto Fujimori]. While she accuses him of human rights violations, she was shocked about the racism she experienced after Fujimori's election, feeling solidarity with him because of a shared ethnic background. Never were other Peruvian presidents punished as harshly as Fujimori has been, even though they had committed worse crimes, she argues. Other Nikkei still vigorously defend the former president like the Chilean Nikkei Ariel Takeda (2017). Peruvian society in general is also polarised regarding Fujimori's daughter Keiko. When she was not elected president in 2017, not least because she was constantly associated with her father's acts and involved in a corruption scandal, some Nikkei supported her, whereas others vehemently rejected the association between the politician and the *comunidad* (Hiyane Yzena 2017; Prado 2016).

Also Nikkei in other Latin American countries are now much more ambivalent. A Peruvian Nikkei in Santa Cruz told me that despite all controversial behaviour, Fujimori had not been that bad since he had built up schools and taught punctuality to Peruvians – ironically, she had migrated to Bolivia with her entire family in the early 1990s during his presidency. Bolivian Nikkei generally try to relativise that they do not know what has occurred exactly, arguing that Fujimori took controversial decisions because of the inaccurate advice from his counsellors. Tsuyoshi Kato expresses this ambivalence:

> Fujimori did many good things, but he also made many mistakes, so we're sorry about the situation how it is. But we don't know how it was, either. But one thing that he did was to eradicate terrorism that was widespread in Peru. But how he did it and how he administrated the country we don't know […]. We would have appreciated as Japanese that he would have passed into history as a good president.

One might suppose that it is easier to be a Nikkei politician at the local level with a more significant ethnic basis, but the following example does not confirm this assumption. The former mayor of San Juan, Katsumi Bani, is well respected among Japanese descendants while also enjoying popularity among non-Nikkei. I have not heard of anybody accusing him of embezzling money or committing another morally controversial action. Katsumi, a Nisei, started in ABJ as leader of a neighbourhood section. Around the year 2000, he helped to establish San Juan as an independent town, when the new law of popular participation enabled more decentralisation and local autonomy. As Katsumi told me, the implementation of this law was vital for him since his main motivation was to enhance social development in his immediate environment. However, he recognised that ABJ was not the right place since it was dominated by conservative Issei. Outside established networks, he ran for mayor in 2004 as a member of the political group he had founded himself in order to avoid the ideological warfare between left and the right so well known in Latin America.

In Bolivian media, he has many times been considered as "model mayor," not least because under his administration, San Juan saw an important improvement of infrastructure. Apart from the construction of public buildings and roads, he could provide running water to practically all inhabitants of San Juan. Ichilo province as well as Santa Cruz' major newspaper *EL Deber* have officially recognised the mayor's efforts. Even Evo Morales congratulated him in 2014 during his visit to San Juan, declaring that of all mayors, Katsumi had shown the most successful record.

In order to obtain popular support, Bolivian politicians frequently mention the infrastructure projects they realised successfully. But Katsumi says that he tried to implement certain practices he had known in Japan and other Latin American countries. Apart from garbage separation initiatives, he installed the compost field mentioned above in front of the town hall. Equally important to him were responsibility, education, hygiene and cleanliness of public spaces as well as sports as a way to bring people together. Furthermore, he emphasised specific values, as he told me in 2013. Through his Japanese origin, he wanted to bring to San Juan what he defined as progress:

> For around four years, in the parades [e.g., for Independence Day] but also in the school's graduation ceremony, we have been challenging each other to be on time [...]. If the students don't come, they don't take part in the parade. Last week, it was a little difficult because the students didn't come, we had to wait for 10 minutes, but 10 minutes for me [...], it's much, although not that much [...]. In my speech, I said that the danger is that we turn abnormal things into normal ones. Being on time, you see that in the United States, Japan, England ... but, well, in Mexico it's terrible, the Hispanic culture [laughs], it seems that it's a little tolerant [...]. The topic of being on time, of cleanliness in public spaces [...], it's difficult for us, but we insist.

Katsumi thereby points to a mixture of Japanese culture and good governance practices (United Nations Economic and Social Commission for Asia and the Pacific 2009). For him, the Japanese concept of *"mottainai"* or "do not waste" is a guiding principle, referring also to environment protection. Nikkei are among the most efficient rice cultivators in Bolivia; other Bolivians could thus take them as a role model for land use, he proposes. He puts forward that in Japanese culture, the community is more important than the individual, as are consensus and living in

230   *How the Nikkei relate to the Bolivian state*

harmony with an animated nature. He is the only Nikkei I know who draws parallels to the new constitution that mentions the indigenous alternative model of life *"vivir bien"* [living well] as a guiding principle: this concept emphasises sustainable growth and questions specific aspects of "Western" modernity, capitalism, neoliberalism and development.[9] Apparently, propagating "Japanese values" in Bolivia is appreciated as a way to progress.

While Katsumi may have successfully implemented some of his "Japanese-style" ideas and be widely regarded as an honest mayor, his problems started at the latest at his re-election. His political group did not win the majority in the municipal council, resulting in ongoing conflicts and eventually his imprisonment. Although Katsumi Bani was not accused of stealing public funds, staying neutral in the polarised environment turned out to be difficult without strong networks. In an interview with *El Deber* newspaper, he stated that he was temporarily suspended and arrested just because he refused to bribe and he explained that his goal was to improve the situation in San Juan without adhering to any political ideology. In other words, he underlined that he did not want to take sides for either MAS or the centre-right party of Santa Cruz' governor Rubén Costas that is in favour of regional autonomy (Dorado und Navia 2012). Despite his statement, a part of the population interpreted the situation differently: he never emphasised which political force was responsible for his imprisonment, but he was eventually considered a victim of MAS as *"alcalde opositor"* [mayor opposing MAS]. After being released from jail, Katsumi received money for public works from the department. Governor Rubén Costas' sympathy for the Japanese *colonias* is well known – the former Comité Cívico president has once received a JICA scholarship.

Around the time of Katsumi's imprisonment, the media spoke with many non-Nikkei supporters who wanted him to return to office, did not accept the interim mayor and called the previously mentioned disputes over *micros* [microbuses] extortion. One non-Nikkei blogger even stated that the people of San Juan were not heard since they were civilised and did not throw dynamite or kidnap people, indirectly contrasting them to groups supporting MAS and clearly assigning the roles of good and evil. He used Katsumi to criticise Bolivia's political system as undemocratic: according to this blogger, Katsumi's imprisonment definitively proved the judicial power's partiality. Bolivia was making a step towards totalitarianism with San Juan's mayor being in jail for buying used *micros* for school children, he wrote, whereas president Evo Morales would even purchase second-hand aeroplanes for millions of U.S. dollars (Ortiz Saucedo 2012).

The national government did not issue any statement regarding Katsumi's imprisonment; neither did the Japanese embassy. Instead, a representative from Bolivia's ombudsperson office (*Defensoría del Pueblo*) visited Katsumi in jail, probably on the initiative of the United Nation's office in La Paz that Katsumi had contacted shortly before. Santa Cruz' ex-prefect, a friend of Katsumi, told him that four of Bolivia's ex-presidents had prepared a public statement condemning the incident; furthermore, the then president of Comité Cívico visited the mayor in hospital, publicly speaking of injustice and human rights violation. Katsumi

How the Nikkei relate to the Bolivian state   231

assumes, without having any proof, that he was released because the judge and the politicians who had ordered his arrest had underestimated the media interest – his case was publicised even in Brazil. But he is not sure if somebody at a high political level influenced th s decision and why. In sum, support did not follow ethnic lines: many non-Nikkei protested against Katsumi's imprisonment, while descendants did not publicly ask for his release. Katsumi stated that the ABJ had been fearful of political trouble; thus, it had not assumed any responsibility, even though the *micros* had initia ly belonged to the town's Japanese association.

These events could be interpreted as an expression of anti-Nikkei sentiments among parts of the population. Katsumi thinks that in Bolivia, especially in the current political climate, non-Nikkei might not support somebody discredited as a potential instrument of foreign interest – an elected office might thereby be more problematic than an appointed position. Katsumi has heard that even in a country marked by immigration like Brazil, a Nikkei politician may evoke resentments:

> In Brazil, [the Nikkei] said [...] that it's better to be in secondary positions than in the foreground, although Brazil is one of the countries where the Japanese are well respected. But in other countries like Peru, Bolivia, there is much – I don't know, resistance to foreigners. [So they opted for] a lower profile [...]. I think that's part of the really very conservative culture, [...] very fearful towards foreigners or extra-terrestrials [laughs].

The Paraguayan Nikkei writer Emi Kasamatsu, one of the first women to take over responsibilities in Nikkei associations, is pessimistic as well. Emi has experienced that life can be difficult for somebody regarded as a foreigner when she was president of the well-known public Centro Paraguayo Japonés in Asunción. In the interview, she analyses that Latin American society will not allow Japanese descendants to achieve a critical position in a relevant institution. Instead, she puts forward that they prefer the Nikkei at an intermediate level where they can show their responsible, correct and efficient way of working without disturbing existing power relations (Kasamatsu 2007b). Emi emphasised her honesty and independence, but she doubts that it is possible to succeed without relations with a powerful group.

However, although the Nikkei's ethnic origin may give adversaries an additional reason to oppose them, other politicians experienced comparable difficulties. Around the same time, the mayor of the city of Potosí was temporarily suspended in the course of a similar dispute on second-hand vehicles (Mendoza 2013). In several towns in the department of Santa Cruz, mayors have been removed from office as well, justified by administrative irregularities, and often, MAS mayors followed them (Eju.TV 2012; El Día 2010; Mendez 2012; Rojas 2010). Farthing and Kohl (2014: 64), too, cite a mayor who fears to run again since he could be sent to jail, referring to the anti-corruption law that is used to attack political enemies rather than to prevent illicit practices.

Nevertheless, some Nikkei are cautiously optimistic. Akiyoshi Chiba from Asunción concludes that Nikkei are still regarded as too foreign to successfully

232 *How the Nikkei relate to the Bolivian state*

run for elections: "The Nikkei has to eat more manioc and be more Paraguayan." But this might change: he and his friend Shuji Ando, while claiming for more "Japanese values" in Paraguayan politics, await the next generation to see more candidacies. Also the Brazilian Nikkei Paulo Yokotani, the already mentioned director of the economic development unit of the federal state of São Paulo, thinks that more Nikkei politicians will emerge automatically in the future. Paulo even dreams of a Brazilian Nikkei president and believes that the Nikkei do not necessarily vote for non-Nikkei candidates because they see nowadays no need to be protected.

Can solar panels change society? – Nikkei civic engagement

While disenchantment with politics is common in Bolivia, several Nikkei, among them Katsumi Bani, argue that political commitment should be framed more broadly in order to include different forms of civic engagement. He puts forward that everything that is socially negotiated and involves questions of power is political; claiming an active role for citizens outside political parties and public offices.

Apart from running for office, according to Barrett und Zani (2015), political action may include participating in demonstrations, signing petitions, lobbying for legislative initiatives, writing articles on political developments, engaging in fundraising or distributing leaflets for political movements.[10] But Katsumi's argument mirrors the even broader definition proposed by Eriksen (2015: 175) who argues that politics can be understood as an encompassing system integrating citizens since actions that are not formally political may be equally important and consequential for society. Barrett und Zani (2015) note that such civic engagement includes, for example, voluntary work for non-governmental organisations, donations to charities, consumer activism and fundraising for a social cause.

Nikkei civic engagement in Bolivia is so far related to small, unconnected initiatives and private, spontaneous commitment. Practically unknown outside San Juan, a group of Nisei created a scholarship for non-Nikkei students to continue their education in Santa Cruz. While no Nikkei charity group exists comparable to the "Damas Argentinas" [Argentinean Ladies], Kaede Itokazu has participated in another well-known upper-class charity organisation. Sociedad Japonesa has constructed and supported the "Japanese Pavilion" in La Paz' orphanage (Embajada del Japón en Bolivia 2019b), and the Shimoji family's fashion company has donated to a big NGO that combats extreme poverty.

To promote a Japanese-style education, ideas have emerged to found a full-time Japanese Bolivian school in Santa Cruz with the repaid loans of Nikkei farmers. Such a school would be meant to transmit "Japanese values" to Nikkei students to strengthen their identity, but also to "sell" Japanese-ness to a broader public (Comaroff and Comaroff 2009). Their model is Liceo Mexicano Japonés in Mexico City: founded in 1977 with donations from Japan, the Japanese-Mexican community and the Mexican state, it is now a renowned school for both Nikkei and non-Nikkei, offering classes according to the official curricula of Mexico and

How the Nikkei relate to the Bolivian state 233

Japan (Akachi et al. 2002). As a non-Nikkei teacher remembers, some non-Nikkei parents were enthusiastic when some years ago, a Japanese congregation opened a school in Santa Cruz since parents supposed their children to become "as smart as those Japanese." However, not all Nikkei are convinced that creating a Japanese school for a broad public in Santa Cruz makes sense. Opponents do not see a need for such a school, criticising that the Nisei and Sansei are not sufficiently involved in the project. The idea to establish such a school is still at the planning stage: as of mid-2019, a plot had been purchased in the city's north.

The engagement for environment issues is a relatively recent phenomenon. Several Bolivian Nikkei named Carlos Kasuga, a Japanese-Mexican entrepreneur whom some of them know personally, as an inspiring role model. Among others, he established a project for garbage recollection. Hearing about such initiatives in Japan and Mexico and being aware of global environmental problems, some Nikkei from Colonia Okinawa started a garbage separation initiative. Some of Katsumi's projects in San Juan point to a similar direction, although he implemented them as a mayor and not in the course of a civic initiative. Katsumi engaged later in a new project: in early 2017, he and the students of the local secondary school won the Zayed Future Energy Prize in the category Global High School/The Americas in Abu Dhabi with USD 100,000 for the school's solar energy project and its rainwater tanks. During an interview in August 2017, he proudly showed me the pictures of the tanks' ongoing installation on his smartphone. While all these initiatives encompass "traditional" charity as well as causes related to the more recent global environmental protection movement, political ideology or denouncements of injustice do not play a role in these examples. I do not know of any Nikkei who has engaged in fundraising for a political party or taken part in demonstrations. Only Mai Amuro told me that she visited indigenous activists during a hunger strike together with her children.

In Bolivia, grassroots organisations have been prominent for at least the last 20 years. The aforementioned law of popular participation from the 1990s supposed the existence of a disinterested civil society. The new constitution of 2009 speaks of a sovereign people and the participation of civil society in public planning. Both assume erroneously that civil society, not least because of the supposedly communitarian orientation of indigenous groups, is morally superior to the state and a counter-hegemonic force (Shakow 2014: 123). However, it is an open question if civil society was strengthened under Evo Morales since the government preferred to pay attention only to those groups it favoured. Some grassroots organisations even foster conflict trying to impose their own, narrow interests with roadblocks or physical aggression.

Many Nikkei distance themselves from such actions, implicitly or explicitly contrasting them with their "good" commitment to society. They propagate an alternative way of life referring to "Japanese values" that nevertheless resembles discourses on good governance. They thereby put forward ideas of good citizenship with law-abidingness, solidarity and altruism, emphasising the importance of public goods and the local community. According to this narrative, descendants may contribute with Japanese-style collaboration, enhancing trust and

234 *How the Nikkei relate to the Bolivian state*

collaboration in society. As some authors point out, Latin American societies are marked by a climate of mutual suspicion and insecurity; trust seems to exist only in small groups (Armony 2004: 104ff.; Seleme Antelo et al. 2005: 134ff.). This stands in stark contrast to Japanese society, Mai says:

> When we talk about ideology, we also talk about values and principles, and there, I think that the Japanese have really developed things that are interesting or practical. I don't say that they are unique. But they could contribute to this construction of a more pluri-multi society.

Especially as members of a garbage collection initiative, the Nikkei can feel part of a worldwide community and relate to global narratives of sustainability, promoting the idea of active citizenship with universally applicable goals. Through such initiatives, participants stress their membership in Bolivian society at the local level. Paralleling the discussions on the introduction of crops, they claim to share their knowledge with non-Nikkei out of gratitude (Berenschot et al. 2017; Tilly 1995), while their connection to Japan supposedly means having a broader horizon.

Therefore, they claim to know better what non-Nikkei need. Non-Nikkei are thereby implicitly characterised to be passive, careless and in need of education. Especially ecological engagement is not common in Bolivia, nor may descendants' understanding of community be equal to non-Nikkei notions. Although it may not be an intended consequence, such behaviour can perpetuate power relations. Isaakyan und Triandafyllidou (2017) argue that for "expats," civic engagement serves firstly to reassess their privileged position and only secondly to help local communities that may reject such commitment. Similar initiatives, accompanied by discourses of modernity, are also promoted by Japanese development cooperation, although Japanese-style cleaning of classrooms seems not to be welcomed by all parents (Chuquimia 2019; Vaca Justiniano 2019). I have not personally heard of anybody opposing such actions, while some non-Nikkei acquaintances expressed a clearly positive opinion on such initiatives. Further research would be needed to find out if non-Nikkei regard such interventions as necessary and why.

While Katsumi and other Nikkei assume that such local informal actions may lead to changes on the meso- and macro-level of influence institutions and policymaking processes, this might be too optimistic (Armony 2004: 5ff.). A garbage recollection initiative may work as a goodwill measure and is less risky than an elected position, but may yield mainly symbolic results. It still has to be studied in how far the Nikkei are able to explain potential benefits and if receivers internalise these norms (Finnemore and Sikkink 1998). By 2017, San Juan has a MAS mayor, and as Katsumi told me, public spaces are as dirty as before his term of office since the new mayor does not show any interest in his programmes.

While protecting the environment and donating money to local organisations stand for the Nikkei's identification with Bolivia, the same can be said about Katsumi Bani's not yet concrete but far-reaching idea. Taking advantage of the

How the Nikkei relate to the Bolivian state   235

ongoing definition of the Bolivian state, he wants Nikkei to obtain rights in the Bolivian constitution, attempting to define the Nikkei as a specific ethnic group within Bolivian identity. To my knowledge, no Nikkei minority in Latin America has tried and achieved this so far.

Contrary to other ethnic groups, Japanese descendants do not enjoy specific rights based on their ethnic origin. This stands in contrast to the Mennonites who are exempted from military service and obligatory school for religious reasons. Moreover, the new constitution, written by a MAS-dominated constitutional assembly, recognises the institutions of 35 indigenous groups and Afro-Bolivians. They have a guaranteed representation in national and departmental parliaments and in the Supreme Court and they may establish special territories with distinct auto-governance rights. Through such measures, the plurinational state[11] wants to recognise its diverse ethnic and linguistic groups at the educational, administrative, economic, judicial and political level (García Linera 2012). Whereas the constitution speaks of preserving and protecting existing cultures, emphasising respect for all cultural groups and undefined "*comunidades interculturales*" [intercultural communities], it is not clear if the Nikkei as a non-indigenous minority can claim special rights.

The definition of plurinationalism is the main problem Katsumi finds in the new constitution, a charter that "reads like a laundry list rather than a unified document, and [...] lacks a clear path to move from rhetoric to practice" (Farthing and Kohl 2014: 42). He specifically criticises the notion of indigeneity, claiming that indigenous groups should not have more rights than non-indigenous minorities in a truly plurinational state and that other ethnic groups should be recognised as legitimate political actors as well. One particular consequence of the new constitution is that public workers must speak an indigenous language. This raises several issues: some indigenous groups have only around 30 members and not all of them speak the language of their ancestors (López 2005). Katsumi, however, argues that it is useless to learn whatever indigenous language if he wants to communicate with Issei citizens, explaining that also in towns next to the Brazilian border, more people speak Portuguese than there are speakers of some indigenous languages. Katsumi concludes that it is a "very closed pluriculturalism." In other words, the "plurinational state" applies double standards.

Moreover, Katsumi points to the fact that apart from the arbitrary naming of these 36 groups, it is not clear who does or does not belong to such a minority. The constitution defines indigenous groups as collectivities with common cultural and ethnic characteristics existing before Spanish colonisation. At the same time, it does not state that these groups need to have resided on Bolivian territory. It is not clear, either, if any other groups have ever lived where later San Juan was founded – the first inhabitants could, therefore, be the Japanese migrants. According to this argumentation, the Nikkei can be defined as indigenous, making the *colonias* their "ancestral land" much like the indigenous communities the constitution talks about. As a result, the obligation for a mayor of San Juan to learn an indigenous language instead of Japanese violates the constitution and the Human Rights Charter, Katsumi argues.

236 *How the Nikkei relate to the Bolivian state*

However, the Ministry of Autonomy informed him some years ago that the Constitutional Tribunal would not accept his claim to recognise the Japanese language on a local level. In mid-2017, Katsumi still planned to present a claim for discrimination to the Supreme Court and he stated that after the end of his term, he was free to submit such a constitutional complaint. Nevertheless, Katsumi is convinced that the possibilities to change society are manifold for citizens of any origin and that they are not limited to a public office – also without Japanese support.

Conclusion

The Nikkei lack not only relations to economic actors in Bolivia, but to politicians even at the regional level. Unlike those recent Brazilian migrants who have become large-scale farmers, the Nikkei did not increase their landholdings very much in the last decades. Ethnic associations did not support the emergence of political leaders, either; no politicised identity has been created so far. Peru's ex-president Alberto Fujimori, a Nisei, has not turned out to be an example.

While the state has mostly ignored the Nikkei as an ethnic minority, descendants emphasise to be honest model citizens, equalling Japan's administration with modernity and Bolivia's with backwardness. Many Nikkei see corruption as a proof that modernity has failed in Bolivia, considering themselves honest victims of bureaucracy and state policies. Accordingly, politics as a "minefield of conflicting claims and mutual suspicions" (Shakow 2014: 123) is not attractive for the Nikkei. Instead, some descendants now engage for civic society in small, unrelated initiatives, but with unclear consequences. Despite discourses on the seemingly united Japanese, Bolivian Nikkei have not been able to form any group in order to influence political processes. Exceptionally, they could solve land conflicts with the help of Japanese diplomacy. The idea of an individual Nikkei to obtain minority rights in the constitution has not been realised yet; the resistance from Bolivia's institutions would probably also impede such an attempt to give legitimation to a minority that is widely considered to be foreign.

The Nikkei have so far almost never been an aim of ethnic hostilities. But trying to stay neutral in a polarised environment like Bolivian politics is difficult, as the case of a Nikkei mayor has shown. Indeed, their symbolic capital appears to be useful only in the absence of conflicts over scarce resources. Japanese descendants are a small group without any possibilities to impose sanctions; their high socioeconomic status is, therefore, mainly a result of external assistance.

Notes

1 Abbreviation for *taxi de ruta fija*: shared taxi on fixed route.
2 Nevertheless, other actors may wield significant influence as well although they are not in power. The city of Santa Cruz, like the entire country, is characterised by a parallel economy of informal character, but also by grass root movements who often oppose the elites. As Gordillo et al. (2007: xxix) and Prado (2007: 177f.) observe, different kinds of labour unions have been quite successful defending their interests, e.g., with strikes and roadblocks.

How the Nikkei relate to the Bolivian state   237

3   INRA stands for Instituto Nacional de Reforma Agraria (National Agrarian Reform Institute).
4   For comparison, Santa Cruz Department counts more than three million inhabitants, its capital around 1.5 million.
5   Yacimientos Petrolíferos Fiscales Bolivianos, the state-owned company dedicated to the exploitation, industrialisation and distribution of oil and gas.
6   It is striking that Latin America has seen several presidents of Arab origin like Carlos Menem in Argentina, Julio César Turbay in Colombia, Abdala Bucaram and Jamil Mahuad in Ecuador and Michel Temer in Brazil, to name but a few. The Dominican Luis Abinader ran for president in 2016, the Honduran Salvador Nasralla in 2017 and the Brazilian Fernando Haddad in 2018, while Nayib Bukele was elected president of El Salvador in early 2019. However, I am not able to draw a comparison here and one has to bear in mind that Arab descendants are much more numerous.
7   Such a reaction was not unique. In 1947, a Nikkei running for city councillor in São Paulo caused rejection notably among the first generation, while many Nisei supported his candidature (Taniguti 2015: 213ff.). However, I have not found any research on the correlation of support for Fujimori with age.
8   The Brazilian Nikkei Luiz Gushiken, a minister under the Lula administration until 2005, had to appear in court for corruption as well, contrasting with the stereotypes of the "honest Japanese descendant."
9   But, as critical voices like Colque (2016) observe, the Morales government also used the concept to disguise the ongoing exploitation of nature.
10 It is beyond the scope of this study to discuss voting behaviour, not least because there are no data so far.
11 For discussion of the term "plurinational" and its contradictions, see Lazarte (2008).

10 Conclusion

Practically all studies on Nikkei conclude that Japanese descendants all over the Americas have achieved a high standard of living. Few studies, however, ask how this socioeconomic status influences Nikkei identity. Hence, the main argument of this book is that ethnic boundaries frequently overlap and interact with social boundaries. This works not only to the detriment of a group, as described in many studies on ethnic minorities, but sometimes also to its benefit.

Japanese descendants in Bolivia use pervasive narratives to define ethnic identity. With seemingly distinctive and primordial "Japanese values" such as honesty, respect, hard work and punctuality, they are able to convincingly present prosperity as a sign of morality. Such relatively stable narrative frames are also described for Japanese descendants in Peru and Brazil (Takenaka 2003b; Tsuda 1999). At the same time, narratives on "Japanese values" strikingly resemble common middle-class discourses in the past and present. Hence, the sentence "our values led to success" means that a group like the Nikkei needs to justify upward mobility (Takenaka 2009b). These narratives give legitimacy to a group's socioeconomic status in a capitalist society where supposedly anybody can succeed as long as he or she is willing. At the same time, they obscure the fact that start opportunities are in fact unequal. Nevertheless, the Nikkei's narrative is also persuasive since it refers to the quasi-inherited character of an ethnic group.

To take the example of Bolivia, its citizens are well aware of the country's comparatively low standard of living, while longing for modernity as represented by countries such as Japan. In a setting where cultural and phenotypical differences are often taken as markers for a person's socioeconomic background (Wade 2010), being of Japanese origin is generally a positive asset since most non-Nikkei think that the Nikkei's social and economic resources are justified. Hence, the Nikkei enjoy symbolic capital, defined as "the form that the various species of capital assume when they are perceived and recognized as legitimate" (Bourdieu 1989: 17). At the same time, non-Nikkei use the Nikkei as a positive counterexample to criticise the perceived flaws of their own society. Ethnic identifications cannot be reduced to a mere calculation of benefits, but in this case, giving up a distinctive identity might also mean losing concrete advantages in daily life. It comes as no surprise that practically all Nikkei declare to be proud of their ethnic identity. But even those who distance themselves from

DOI: 10.4324/9781003228295-10

Conclusion 239

other descendants and Japanese culture generally want to retain some cultural features.

At a closer look, "Japanese values" are not sufficient to explain the Nikkei's comfortable socioeconomic situation. Descendants all over Latin America are perhaps unique insofar as they have been consciously supported by a leading economic power. Few ethnic minorities enjoy such powerful economic and political support. Diasporic links to Japan remain important also to later generations not least because they have been essential to reproduce their prosperity and symbolic capital in Bolivia, but also in Brazil (Mori 2002; Suzuki 2010).

Descendants in Latin America benefit from Japan's global popularity, claiming authority over what they understand as "authentic" Japanese culture (Takenaka 2003b). Nevertheless, while Nikkei ethnic identity works now as a currency, the relationship between Nikkei and non-Nikkei has not been harmonious per se, but improved with Japan's and the Nikkei's risen socioeconomic status – a fact generally understated in Nikkei narratives and most studies on Latin American Nikkei. My study demonstrates that factors on the macro-level, such as the country of origin's economic and political power, also reflect on identities on the ground (Tsuda 2009). Hence, it is necessary for migration studies to focus more on international power relations and globally circulating images to understand minority–majority relations on the ground.

The relation between symbolic and socioeconomic capital is also evident in the case of pre-war migration to Bolivian Amazonia. To my knowledge, no systematic comparisons between descendants under such different conditions exist for Bolivia or other Latin American countries. As shown in this book, pre-war descendants in Bolivia often do not identify as Nikkei nor are they recognised as such. In contrast to pre-war migrants in Brazil (Ninomiya 2002), Bolivian pre-war Nikkei have not been part of an organised migration project – Bolivian Amazonia was uninteresting for Japan. Due to a lack of external support, most of them struggle socioeconomically until today.

The Nikkei example may seem unusual to many migration researchers, but it contributes to a better understanding of the universal features in migration. Unfortunately, there is no comprehensive theory of advantaged minorities and little research exists about concepts such as symbolic capital of social, ethnic or religious groups. In addition, especially English-language research has neglected migration to developing countries and post-colonial societies that are often marked by extreme social inequalities, a weak state and different definitions of ethnic and national identity – factors that are important to understand Bolivian Nikkei's advantaged yet vulnerable position. Also, Bolivian and Latin American studies have generally analysed the country's society with a focus on poor and marginalised groups, but not on migrants or more affluent parts of society (Barriga Dávalos 2016; O'Dougherty 2002).

Only Bonacich (1973) made an attempt for the theorisation of advantaged ethnic minorities but described a very specific example, not transferable to the Nikkei case. However, Nikkei in Bolivia bear some similarities with "expats," highly mobile migrants with professional qualifications above average – also

240   *Conclusion*

here, international power dynamics are quite obvious. They have only recently received some attention from migration scholars (Favell et al. 2008). Also, elite groups and their construction of class boundaries in Europe and North America (Abbink and Salverda 2013; Khan 2012) bear some parallels to the Nikkei case, but they have seldom considered the ethnic dimension.

While the Nikkei in Bolivia are in several aspects comparable to whites in Namibia or in Mauritius with similar boundary-making strategies (Salverda 2015; Schmidt-Lauber 1998), one can also observe important differences to these groups who dominate at least some areas since colonial times. Bolivian Nikkei have never belonged to the receiving country's elite, nor do they benefit from similar economic power or relations to influential groups.

But it may also be an advantage for Latin American Nikkei that they cannot be related to a colonial past, a fact that leads to resentments in the former two cases. At the same time, Japan is today considered a place of modernity in Bolivia and beyond – Nye (2011) even took it as an example to explain his concept of soft power. For non-Nikkei outside East Asia, Japan has the reputation of a sophisticated culture that implies ancient wisdom but remains unintelligible. Nevertheless, the Nikkei's discourses to justify power relations in Bolivia are strikingly similar to those justifying colonialism (Bhabha 2004; Scott 1998), comparable also to "expats" justifying their status (Fechter 2010; Isaakyan and Triandafyllidou 2017).

While power relations in multi-ethnic settings are complex and cannot be reduced to the simple dichotomy of "powerful – powerless," the situation is unstable for several reasons – a fact seldom covered by Nikkei studies. First, like the advantaged ethnic minorities all over the world, they may lose both their ethnic specificity and their elevated status. Even though many Nikkei present their identities as quasi-inherited, they also warn of "bolivianisation," cultural loss and eventually the group's disintegration, citing descendants of the pre-war migration in Bolivia and neighbouring countries as a case to avoid.

Second, there are limits to the construction and negotiation of ethnic boundaries. National imaginaries on the whole continent are based on the idea of ethnically mixed societies – practically all apply jus soli – but none of them integrates Asian migrants into its founding myths (Hatugai 2018; Li and Wang 2008; Wang 2008). Nikkei in Bolivia are well aware that as a visible minority, they are regarded as "foreigners" – no matter if they speak Spanish perfectly or otherwise present themselves as "completely Bolivian." Non-Nikkei frequently racialise descendants not even as Japanese, but as *chinos* [Chinese], meaning that all East Asians are equally foreign. The Nikkei thereby also tell us something about the definitions of "Bolivian."

Contrary to what many studies on migration in Europe and North America observe, Santa Cruz society did not require Nikkei to assimilate culturally to achieve social upward mobility. Moreover, in the case of Santa Cruz, the Nikkei arrived at a time when land was available for all, whereas conflicts between highlands and lowlands, adherents of different political camps and/or classes overshadowed all other possible divergences. Hence, until today, almost nobody perceives "foreigners" like the Nikkei to be a threat to "locals" (Urioste 2012).

Conclusion 241

Very few Nikkei feel isolated or discriminated against in daily life; instead, they live a middle-class life much like other parts of Santa Cruz' population.

It is interesting that almost no contemporary Nikkei studies have examined Japanese descendants' economic and political strategies in receiving countries. Although an individual Nikkei might obtain a high position because "all Japanese are trustworthy," it does not mean that they as "foreigners" have decisive influence outside the community – a contradiction that Bourdieu (1989) did not cover in his short discussion of symbolic capital. In case they did not draw on Japanese state support, their symbolic capital was not of much concrete use. While they are influential in the two *colonias*, they find it difficult to transfer this status to the outside where they lack networks to the elites. In the past, there was no need to join forces and negotiate with political actors or to influence legislative processes, either. As Amemiya's (2001) study on Bolivian Nikkei already shows, relations with non-Nikkei have been "harmonious" because the Nikkei avoided seeking attention, gave in in case of conflicts and preferred to "fly under the radar."

While Santa Cruz may celebrate differences highlighting its "foreign communities" and presenting itself as a "cosmopolitan global city," this does not have any political implications – the majority population nevertheless decides which forms of difference are accepted and which moral standards are valid. While "Japanese values" match the regional elites' discourse propagating neoliberalism and globalisation, the Nikkei are welcome as long as they do not challenge power relations. Those who seem to question the existing order – e.g., highlanders – are much less likely to be welcomed by those who benefit from that constellation (see also Jain's (2018: 221) remarks on representations of Indian culture in Switzerland). I do not have any reasons to assume that the situation in other Latin American countries is completely different, although I do not know any studies on that topic. Similarly, the term "model minority," used for citizens of East Asian origin especially in the U.S, implies that they enjoy symbolic capital, but do not question power relations and do not denounce discrimination (Li and Wang 2008; Wang 2008).

As also Salverda (2015) observes in his study on whites in Mauritius, even ethnically defined elites with more influence than the Nikkei occupy an ambivalent position and need to pursue strategies to maintain support from the rest of society. Fear might be even more accentuated in times of changing power relations, as Schmidt-Lauber (1998) observes for whites in Namibia. In other words: being a minority means vulnerability per se.

In order to maintain their status as a socioeconomically advantaged minority even without Japanese support, the Nikkei need a more effective lobby and network in Bolivia, for instance, in the chambers of commerce, while trying to relate to Japan as a partner and not simply as an aid receiver. In order to maintain the socioeconomic fundament of their symbolic capital, they will have to find a more solid economic basis. But reacting to change might also mean sacrificing "traditional" emblematic institutions like the cooperatives.

In the past few years, the political climate in Bolivia did not favour the engagement of Japanese descendants, either. Instead, the small ethnic minority feels increasingly vulnerable. Evo Morales' election in 2003 brought many changes to

242 *Conclusion*

the political landscape: for the first time, a non-elite indigenous leader won the presidential elections. His declared goal was to strengthen the country's indigenous ethnic minorities, democracy and inclusion. Morales was celebrated internationally for these intentions, but as Santos (2010) argues, indigenous protagonism might also mean the marginalisation and invisibilisation of other parts of society instead of a political consensus between ethnic and cultural groups. Indeed, it seems that the Constitutional Court would not accept a Nikkei's claim for minority rights. However, these aspects have so far not been discussed in research on Bolivia. As Rahier (2019: 292ff.) in his comparison of Afrodescendants in different Latin American countries concludes, non-indigenous minorities may have more chances to obtain minority rights if they use similar strategies as indigenous minorities, for example, proving their relationship to the land. It remains an open question if this would be a viable path for the Nikkei.

As Manzenreiter (2017a: 208f.) writes, Nikkei communities have been looking for a future vision for many years, but in the insecure environment, they have not found a magic formula: both seclusion and assimilation create a range of problems. Moreover, the growing urbanisation and the possible disintegration of the *colonias* will have profound consequences in the long term. This can already be witnessed in Brazil with its much bigger Nikkei population (Adachi 2006). The elderly Nikkei population is growing fast, whereas many descendants of working-age reside with their children in Japan. While more and more descendants move to urban areas, the *colonias* might one day become a kind of open-air museum with few Nikkei residents, similar to the Liberdade neighbourhood in São Paulo.

Finally, for many Nikkei, the permeability of ethnic boundaries is both a reason to celebrate and to worry: while "mestizos," people with Japanese and non-Japanese ancestry, are often considered "less Japanese," some interview partners considered them a desirable outcome of the Nikkei's adaptation to Bolivia. Although both Nikkei and non-Nikkei often presented the Nikkei community as a clearly definable entity, the *comunidad japonesa* has increasingly fuzzy boundaries (Eriksen 2010: 79f.; Moromisato Miasato 2002).

At the same time, the meaning of being Nikkei is changing. Especially, younger and urban Nikkei attach less importance to the Japanese language. Nikkei cultural activities nowadays do not require deep cultural knowledge while they undergo changes in meaning and become adapted to the Nikkei's needs and wants. Similar to Brazil, the tendency in Bolivia is that the fourth generation maintains a Japanese name – and in the Bolivian case, even a Japanese passport – but only knows some basic facts about the country and cherishes some symbolic practices.

Okinawan descendants' identifications tend to be even more complex. They constitute the majority of Bolivian Nikkei, maybe a unique situation in the diaspora. Rather than being discriminated against by Japanese and mainland Nikkei, as described in research for the middle of the 20th century in Japan and abroad, Okinawan Nikkei dominate Santa Cruz' Nikkei activities (Suzuki 2006). Many non-Nikkei have even come to consider Okinawa-related activities to be typical for Japan as a whole. While Okinawan and mainland Nikkei are becoming culturally similar, many Okinawan descendants insist on ethnic or at least cultural

Conclusion 243

differences. Okinawan Nikkei thereby try to mediate between otherwise tightly defined categories, proudly putting forward that as Okinawan Nikkei, they are culturally "more Bolivian." At the same time, Okinawan Nikkei also benefitted from their Japanese passports when receiving financial support from JICA or during *dekasegi* migration.

Also, individual Nikkei's relation to the *comunidad* is changing. Formal ethnic associations and Japanese schools lose importance. Social life especially in the city becomes increasingly fragmented between different groups. Moreover, the expansion of institutionalised social security has made associations obsolete. They are too small to offer attractive leisure time facilities for an ethnically defined segment of the urban middle class. All this might have an impact on the Nikkei's identifications or at least on their self-presentations in the future.

But another development may also strengthen their identification as Nikkei. While especially Nisei and Sansei increasingly refer to themselves as Bolivians with Japanese ancestry, some of them consciously create relations to descendants elsewhere, a topic scarcely researched so far. They try to construct a supranational Nikkei identity, while simultaneously seeking to emancipate from the older generation. This engagement also shows the ethnogenesis of something distinct from Japan (Hirabayashi et al. 2002). Participants aim at preserving "Japanese values" and uniting descendants from different countries, trying to present themselves as cosmopolitans and successful citizens of their countries. Moreover, especially Okinawa Prefecture has successfully contributed to creating networks in order to gain power vis-à-vis Tōkyō, although overseas descendants themselves may have a different understanding of these relations. Nevertheless, Pan-American Nikkei affinities have limits – events show for example the gap between Latin American and English-speaking descendants.

But while Bolivian post-war Nikkei often emphasise that they have maintained many cultural features from Japan, their relation to Japan becomes increasingly ambivalent. Even though many Nikkei and non-Nikkei presume that Japanese migrants and their offspring automatically maintain a particular relation to Japan, they increasingly identify as Bolivians with Japanese ancestry. This is also a result of the sometimes troubling *dekasegi* experience, extensively documented for the Brazilian and Peruvian case (Takenaka 2009a; Tsuda 2001a). In Japan, ethnic and national origin is often correlated with culture (Yoshino 1992; Lie 2001). But while most post-war Nikkei are Bolivian nationals by birth, not least the fact that the majority has a Japanese passport challenges the well-known concept of a clearly definable Japanese people.

In this context, the word "Nikkei" has become prominent in recent years. Interestingly, I do not know any study on this gradual change in self-designation. While many Bolivian descendants still call themselves "*japoneses*" or "*nihonjin*," a growing number of individuals present themselves as *cruceño/cruceña*, as Bolivian or as "Japanese camba." With the term "Nikkei," they emphasise their belonging to a Japanese diaspora. They thereby also insist that they are no longer Japanese migrants, while still referring to Japan as a place of origin and one source of identity.

Glossary

(Sp. = Spanish; Jp. = Japanese; Ok. = Okinawan)

ABJ   Asociación Boliviano-Japonesa: Nikkei association of San Juan and Colonia Okinawa, respectively

anime **(Jp.)**   Japanese-style animation

ANBJ   Asociación Nikkei Boliviano-Japonesa: Bolivia's national Nikkei organisation, formerly FENABOJA

APN   Asociación Panamericana Nikkei/Associação Panamericana Nikkei: Pan-American Nikkei Association

Bon Odori **(Jp.)**   Originally referring to the dance performed during the ancestor-worshipping festival Obon in July/August, it has become the name of the annual festival of Centro Social in October

camba **(Sp.)**   Inhabitant of the Bolivian lowlands

Centro Social Japonés **(Sp.)**   Nikkei association in Santa Cruz de la Sierra

chino, china **(Sp.)**   Chinese

colla **(Sp.)**   Inhabitant of the Bolivian highlands

colonia **(Sp.)**   Agricultural settlement central to Latin American Nikkei imaginary

Comité Cívico Pro Santa Cruz   Important civil society association in Santa Cruz

Confra   Pan-American sports tournament for Nikkei

COPANI   Convención Panamericana Nikkei/Convenção Panamericana Nikkei: Pan-American Nikkei conference

cruceña, cruceño **(Sp.)**   Inhabitant of Santa Cruz

Day Service (Jp.)   Monthly meeting for the elderly in Centro Social Japonés

dekasegi **(Jp.)**   Work migration, now mostly referring to the migration of Latin American Nikkei to Japan

eisā **(Ok.)**   Okinawan type of dance for young people, performed during Obon festival

FENABOJA   see ANBJ

246 *Glossary*

fujinbu, fujinkai **(Jp.)**   Women's section of an association

hiragana **(Jp.)**   Syllabary used for native Japanese words and grammatical elements

issei **(Jp.)**   First generation

JICA   Development cooperation agency of the Japanese government

kanji **(Jp.)**   Chinese characters adopted into Japanese

katakana **(Jp.)**   Japanese syllabary used for foreign words or for emphasis

kenjinkai **(Jp.)**   Associations for descendants from a specific Japanese prefecture

koseki **(Jp.)**   Japanese family register

manga **(Jp.)**   Japanese-style comics

MAS   Movimiento al Socialismo; dominant political party in Bolivia 2005–2019

Meiji era   1868–1912, marked by Japan's rapid modernisation

nihon(go)gakkō **(Jp.)**   Japanese school

nihonjinkai **(Jp.)**   Japanese association, often abbreviated as Nikkai

nihonjinron **(Jp.)**   Genre of texts focusing on Japanese cultural and national identity

Nikkei **(Jp.)**   Japanese (descendants) abroad, usually in the Americas

nisei **(Jp.)**   Second generation

Obon **(Jp.)**   Festival to honour the ancestors' spirits in July/August

paceña, paceño **(Sp.)**   Inhabitant of La Paz

Policonsultorio Nikkei   Joint medical practice, part of Centro Social

Ryūkyūkoku Matsuridaiko   Modernised form of the Okinawan *eisā* dance

sansei **(Jp.)**   Third generation

sanshin **(Jp.)**   Three-stringed instrument from Okinawa

seinenkai, seinenbu **(Jp.)**   Youth section of an association

Sociedad Japonesa de La Paz   La Paz' Nikkei association

tanomoshi **(Jp.)**   Rotating credit association

trámite **(Sp.)**   Dealings with public administration

uchināguchi **(Ok.)**   Okinawan language

uchinānchu **(Ok.)**   Okinawan

undōkai **(Jp.)**   Sports festival

Yonsei **(Jp.)**   Fourth generation

References

Abbink, Jon; Salverda, Tijo (Hg.) (2013): *The Anthropology of Elites. Power, Culture, and the Complexities of Distinction*. New York: Palgrave Macmillan.

Adachi, Nobuko (2006): Constructing Japanese Brazilian Identity. In: Nobuko Adachi (ed.): *Japanese Diasporas: Unsung Pasts, Conflicting Presents, and Uncertain Futures*. London, New York: Routledge, 102–120.

Agencia Boliviana de Información (2016): Alistan feria para incentivar e incrementar consumo de frutas y verduras, 21-04-2016. http://www1.abi.bo/abi/?i=348480, accessed 09-04-2018.

Akachi, Jesús K.; Kasuga, Carlos T.; Murakami, Manuel S.; Ota Mishima, María Elena; Shibayama, Enrique; Tanaka, René (2002): Japanese Mexican Historical Overview. In: Akemi Kikumura-Yano (ed.): *Encyclopedia of Japanese Descendants in the Americas. An Illustrated History of the Nikkei*. Walnut Creek [etc.]: AltaMira Press, 203–221.

Akamine Núñez, Miriam (2004): *Inmigración japonesa y otros países a Bolivia*. Santa Cruz de la Sierra: Gráfica Serrano.

Åkesson, Lisa (2011): Multicultural Ideology and Transnational Family Ties among Descendants of Cape Verdeans in Sweden. In: *Journal of Ethnic and Migration Studies* 37 (2), 217–235. DOI: 10.1080/1369183X.2010.521322.

Allen, Matthew (2009): Okinawa, Ambivalence, Identity, and Japan. In: Michael Weiner (ed.): *Japan's Minorities: The Illusion of Homogeneity*. London: Routledge, 188–205.

Amemiya, Kozy (1998): Being 'Japanese' in Brazil and Okinawa. In: *JPRI Occasional Paper* 13. http://www.jpri.org/publications/occasionalpapers/op13.html, accessed 22-05-2009.

Amemiya, Kozy (2001): The Importance of Being Japanese in Bolivia. In: *JPRI Working Paper* 75. http://www.jpri.org/publications/workingpapers/wp75.html, accessed 09-05-2009.

Amemiya, Kozy (2002): Reinventing Population Problems in Okinawa: Emigration as a Tool of American Occupation. In: *JPRI Working Paper* 90. http://www.jpri.org/publications/workingpapers/wp90.html, accessed 26-01-2015.

Amster, Matthew (2004): The "Many Mouths" of Community. Gossip and Social Interaction among the Kelabit of Borneo. In: *Asian Anthropology* 3 (1), 97–127. DOI: 10.1080/1683478X.2004.10552544.

Anderson, Benedict Richard O'Gorman (2006): *Imagined Communities. Reflections on the Origin and Spread of Nationalism*. London: Verso.

Ang, Ien (2004): Beyond Transnational Nationalism: Questioning the Borders of the Chinese Diaspora in the Global City. In: Brenda S.A. Yeoh und Katie Willis (eds.):

248   References

State/Nation/Transnation. Perspectives on Transnationalism in the Asia Pacific. London: Routledge, 179–196.

Aniya, Susumu (2013): La comunidad *nikkei* en la ciudad de Santa Cruz de la Sierra. In: Iyo Kunimoto (ed.): *Los japoneses en Bolivia. 110 años de historia de la inmigración japonesa a Bolivia.* La Paz: Federación Nacional de Asociaciones Boliviano-Japonesas; Asociación Nippon-Bolivia; Plural editores, 163–197.

Aoki, Hideo (2009): *Buraku* Culture. In: Yoshio Sugimoto (ed.): *The Cambridge Companion to Modern Japanese Culture.* Melbourne: Cambridge University Press, 182–198.

Appadurai, Arjun (1996): *Modernity at Large: Cultural Dimensions of Globalization.* Minneapolis: University of Minnesota Press.

Arakaki, Makoto (2002a): Hawai'i Uchinanchu and Okinawa. Uchinanchu Spirit and the Formation of a Transnational Identity. In: Ronald Y. Nakasone (ed.): *Okinawan Diaspora.* Honolulu: University of Hawai'i Press, 130–141.

Arakaki, Robert K. (2002b): Theorizing on the Okinawan Diaspora. In: Ronald Y. Nakasone (ed.): *Okinawan Diaspora.* Honolulu: University of Hawai'i Press, 26–43.

Armony, Ariel C. (2004): *The Dubious Link. Civic Engagement and Democratization.* Stanford: Stanford University Press.

Asato, Matías (2012): Qué son, hoy, nuestras instituciones: intercambio internacional Dale! In: *La Plata Hochi,* 05-08-2012. http://www.laplatahochi.com.ar/index.php ?option=com_content&view=article&id=360:que-son-hoy-nuestras-instituciones-inte rcambio-internacional-dale&catid=52:institucional&Itemid=68, accessed 18-01-2018.

Ashikaga, Ensho (1950): The Festival for the Spirits of the Dead in Japan. In: *Western Folklore* 9 (3), 217–228.

Asociación Peruano-Japonesa (2017): Departamentos. http://www.apj.org.pe/oganizacion -interna/departamentos, accessed 11-09-2017.

Association of Nikkei and Japanese Abroad (2017a): About Us. http://www.jadesas.or.jp/ en/about/index.html, accessed 27-08-2018.

Association of Nikkei and Japanese Abroad (2017b): Who are "Nikkei & Japanese Abroad"? http://www.jadesas.or.jp/en/aboutnikkei/index.html, accessed 27-08-2018.

Azuma, Eiichiro (2002a): Historical Overview of Japanese Migration, 1868–2000. In: Akemi Kikumura-Yano (ed.): *Encyclopedia of Japanese Descendants in the Americas. An Illustrated History of the Nikkei.* Walnut Creek [etc.]: AltaMira Press, 32–48.

Azuma, Eiichiro (2002b): Japanese American Historical Overview, 1868–2001. In: Akemi Kikumura-Yano (ed.): *Encyclopedia of Japanese Descendants in the Americas. An Illustrated History of the Nikkei.* Walnut Creek [etc.]: AltaMira Press, 275–292.

Bahrdt, Carl Friedrich (1790): *Handbuch der Moral für den Bürgerstand.* Frankenthal: Gegel.

Banco Interamericano de Desarrollo (2016): Bolivia. Estrategia del BID con el país (2016– 2020). http://www.iadb.org/document.cfm?id=40128335, accessed 26-09-2017.

Barrett, Martyn D.; Zani, Bruna (2015): Political and Civic Engagement. Theoretical Understandings, Evidence and Politics. In: Martyn D. Barrett und Bruna Zani (eds.): *Political and Civic Engagement. Multidisciplinary Perspectives.* London: Routledge, 3–25.

Barriga Dávalos, Pablo (2016): *Nos reservamos el derecho de admisión. Jerarquía y estatus en la clase alta de Sucre.* La Paz: Colectivo Editorial Pirata.

Barth, Fredrik (1994): Introduction. In: Fredrik Barth (ed.): *Ethnic Groups and Boundaries: The Social Organization of Culture Difference.* Oslo: Pensumtjeneste, 9–38.

References 249

Beer, Bettina (2002): *Körperkonzepte, interethnische Beziehungen und Rassismustheorien. Eine kulturvergleichende Untersuchung*. Berlin: Reimer.

Befu, Harumi (2009): Concepts of Japan, Japanese Culture and the Japanese. In: Yoshio Sugimoto (ed.): *The Cambridge Companion to Modern Japanese Culture*. Melbourne: Cambridge University Press, 21–37.

Benson, Michaela; Osbaldiston, Nick (2016): Toward a Critical Sociology of Lifestyle Migration. Reconceptualizing Migration and the Search for a Better Way of Life. In: *The Sociological Review* 64 (3), 407–423. DOI: 10.1111/1467-954X.12370.

Berenschot, Ward; Schulte Nordholt, Henk; Bakker, Laurens (2017): Introduction: Citizenship and Democratization in Postcolonial Southeast Asia. In: Ward Berenschot, Henk Schulte Nordholt und Laurens Bakker (eds.): *Citizenship and Democratization in Southeast Asia*. Leiden: Brill, 1–28.

Berríos, Rubén (2001): Japan's Economic Presence in Latin America. In: *Latin American Politics and Society* 43 (2), 147–162.

Berríos, Rubén (2014): Peru and Japan. An Uneasy Relationship. In: *Canadian Journal of Latin American and Caribbean Studies* 30 (59), 93–129. DOI: 10.1080/08263663.2005.10816868.

Bestor, Theodore C. (2000): How Sushi Went Global. In: *Foreign Policy* 121, 54–63.

Bestor, Theodore C. (2003): Inquisitive Observation: Following Networks in Urban Fieldwork. In: Theodore C. Bestor, Patricia G. Steinhoff und Victoria Lyon-Bestor (eds.): *Doing Fieldwork in Japan*. Honolulu: University of Hawai'i Press, 315–344.

Bestor, Theodore C.; Steinhoff, Patricia G.; Lyon-Bestor, Victoria (2003): Introduction: Doing Fieldwork in Japan. In: Theodore C. Bestor, Patricia G. Steinhoff und Victoria Lyon-Bestor (eds.): *Doing Fieldwork in Japan*. Honolulu: University of Hawai'i Press.

Bhabha, Homi K. (2004): *The Location of Culture*. London: Routledge.

Bieber, León Enrique (2012): *Jüdisches Leben in Bolivien. Die Einwanderungswelle 1938–1940*. Berlin: Metropol

Bonacich, Edna (1973): A Theory of Middleman Minorities. In: *American Sociological Review* 38 (5), 583–594.

Bourdieu, Pierre (1979a): *La distinction. Critique sociale du jugement*. Paris: Les éditions de minuit.

Bourdieu, Pierre (1979b): Les trois états du capital culturel. In: *Actes de la recherche en sciences sociales* 30 (1), 3–6.

Bourdieu, Pierre (1989): Social Space and Symbolic Power. In: *Sociological Theory* 7 (1), 14–25.

Bourdillon, Michael; Shambare, Michael (2002): Gossip in a Shona Community. In: *Anthropology Southern Africa* 25 (3/4), 78–85.

Bryant, Taimie L. (1991): For the Sake of the Country, for the Sake of the Family. The Oppressive Impact of Family Registration on Women and Minorities in Japan. In: *UCLA Law Review* 39 (1), 109–168.

Busdiecker, Sara (2011): Researching While Black: Interrogating and Navigating Boundaries of Belonging in the Andes. In: Benjamin Talton (ed.): *Black Subjects in Africa and Its Diasporas. Race and Gender in Research and Writing*. New York: Palgrave Macmillan, 15–30.

Butler, Kim D. (2001): Defining Diaspora, Redefining a Discourse. In: *Diaspora* 10 (2), 189–219.

Caldeira, Teresa P.R. (2000): *City of Walls. Crime, Segregation, and Citizenship in São Paulo*. Berkeley: University of California Press.

250 *References*

Carré, Guillaume (2009): L'époque prémoderne. In: Francine Hérail und Guillaume Carré (eds.): *Histoire du Japon: des origines à nos jours*. Paris: Hermann, 491–894.

Carvalho, Daniela de (2003): *Migrants and Identity in Japan and Brazil: The Nikkeijin*. London [etc.]: RoutledgeCurzon.

Castles, Stephen; Miller, Mark J. (2009): *The Age of Migration. International Population Movements in the Modern World*. Basingstoke: Palgrave Macmillan.

Chumacero Ruiz, Juan Pablo (2015): Dinámicas cíclicas de la ejecución del saneamiento de tierras en Bolivia. In: Pablo Regalsky, José Núñez del Prado, Sergio Vásquez Rojas und Juan Pablo Chumacero (eds.): *La problemática de la tierra luego de 18 años de titulación: Territoros, minifundio, individualización*. La Paz: Fundación Tierra, accessed 30-11-2017.

Chuquimia, Leny (2019): "Si los niños limpian su escuela siembran conciencia solidaria". In: *Página Siete*, 24-02-2019. https://www.paginasiete.bo/sociedad/2019/3/18/si-los -ninos-limpian-su-escuela-siembran-conciencia-solidaria-212270.html, accessed 05-04-2019.

Clarke, Peter B.; Somers, Jeffrey (Hg.) (1994): *Japanese New Religions in the West*. Sandgate: Curzon Press; Japan Library.

Cohen, Anthony P. (1992): *The Symbolic Construction of Community*. London: Routledge.

Cohen, Mollie J.; Lupu, Noam; Zechmeister, Elizabeth J. (2017): The Political Culture of Democracy in the Americas, 2016/17. A Comparative Study of Democracy and Governance. Hg. v. USAID, Vanderbilt und LAPOP. https://www.vanderbilt.edu/ lapop/ab2016/AB2016-17_Comparative_Report_English_V2_FINAL_090117_W. pdf, accessed 17-05-2018.

Colque, Gonzalo (2016): Auge y caída del "Vivir Bien". http://www.ftierra.org/index.php/ opinion-y-analisis/702-auge-y-caida-del-vivir-bien, accessed 17-01-2018.

Comaroff, John L.; Comaroff, Jean (2009): *Ethnicity, Inc*. Chicago: University of Chicago Press.

Comisión Económica para América Latina y el Caribe (2017): América Latina y el Caribe volverá a tener un crecimiento positivo en 2017, señala informe de las Naciones Unidas. https://www.cepal.org/es/comunicados/america-latina-caribe-volvera-tener-un -crecimiento-positivo-2017-senala-informe-naciones, accessed 31-10-2017.

Confra XXIII (2018): Reglamento general. https://www.clubnikkei.cl/confra/reglamento/ Confra2018-Reglamentogeneral.pdf, accessed 25-08-2018.

COPANI (2017a): Programa. https://copanilima.com/espanol#programa, accessed 25-08-2018.

COPANI (2017b): Tarifas. https://copanilima.com/espanol/#tarifas, accessed 25-08-2018.

Correo del Sur (2016): Empresa china Sinohydro incumple normas y Ministerio busca sancionarla, 04-06-2016. http://correodelsur.com/seguridad/20160406_empresa -china-sinohydro-incumple-normas-y-ministerio-busca-sancionarla.html, accessed 11-04-2018.

Covell, Stephen (2009): Religious Culture. In: Yoshio Sugimoto (ed.): *The Cambridge Companion to Modern Japanese Culture*. Melbourne: Cambridge University Press, 147–165.

CRE (2010): Advierten intromisión del Estado en elecciones de las cooperativas. Experto dice que se invade el derecho privado. http://www.cre.com.bo/webcre/VerNoticia.asp ?Id=fkcb, accessed 10-02-2018.

Creighton, Millie (2010): Metaphors of Japanese-ness and Negotiations of Nikkei Identity. The Transnational Networking of People of Japanese Descent. In: Nobuko Adachi

References 251

(ed.): *Japanese and Nikkei at Home and Abroad. Negotiating Identities in a Global World.* Amherst: Cambria Press, 134–162.

Dai-6 Sekai no Uchinānchu Taikai Jikkō Iinkai Jimukyoku (2016a): 10-gatsu 30-nichi-wo sekai no uchinānchu no hi toshite seitei shimashita. http://wuf2016.com/jp/?p=6030, accessed 02-05-2017.

Dai-6 Sekai no Uchinānchu Taikai Jikkō Iinkai Jimukyoku (2016b): Chiji-kara no messēji. http://wuf2016.com/jp/?p=135, accessed 31-08-2018.

Dai-6 Sekai no Uchinānchu Taikai Jikkō Iinkai Jimukyoku (2016c): Taikai konseputo. http://wuf2016.com/jp/?page_id=195, accessed 02-05-2017.

Dale, Peter N. (1986): *The Myth of Japanese Uniqueness.* New York: St. Martin's Press.

Daliot-Bul, Michal (2009): Japan Brand Strategy. The Taming of 'Cool Japan' and the Challenges of Cultural Planning in a Postmodern Age. In: *Social Science Japan Journal* 12 (2), 247–266. DOI: 10.1093/ssjj/jyp037.

Davis, Winston (1992): Fundamentalism in Japan: Religious and Political. In: Martin E. Marty und R. Scott Appleby (eds.): *Fundamentalisms Observed. A Study Conducted by the American Academy of Arts and Sciences.* Chicago [etc.]: The University of Chicago Press, 782–813.

Delgado, Carmen (2017): 6 de cada 10 extranjeros que llegan a Bolivia viven en Santa Cruz. In: *El Deber*, 16-07-2017. http://www.eldeber.com.bo/septimodia/6-de-cada -10-extranjeros-que-llegan-a-Bolivia-viven-en-Santa-Cruz-20170714-0083.html, accessed 07-05-2018.

Dogan, Mattei (2003): Is there a Ruling Class in France? In: *Comparative Sociology* 2 (1), 17–89.

Domenech, Eduardo; Magliano Maria José (2007): Políticas migratoria en Bolivia. El estado nacional frente a las migraciones internacionales. In: *IX Jornadas Argentinas de Estudios de Población.* Asociación de Estudios de Población de la Argentina, Huerta Grande, Córdoba. https://www.aacademica.org/000-028/142, accessed 13-11-2018.

Dorado, Cecilia; Navia, Roberto (2012): Katsumi Bani: "No recibir diezmo me generó este problema". In: *El Deber*, 30-09-2012.

D'Orbigny, Alcides (1945): *Viaje a la América Meridional. Brasil, República del Uruguay, República Argentina, La Patagonia, República de Chile, República de Bolivia, República del Perú. Realizado de 1826 a 1833.* Tercer Tomo. Buenos Aires: Editorial Futuro.

Douglass, Lisa (1992): *The Power of Sentiment. Love, Hierarchy, and the Jamaican Family Elite.* Boulder [etc.]: Westview Press.

Dresner, Jonathan (2006): Instructions to Emigrant Laborers, 1885–94: 'Return in Triumph' or 'Wander on the Verge of Starvation'. In: Nobuko Adachi (ed.): *Japanese Diasporas: Unsung Pasts, Conflicting Presents, and Uncertain Futures.* London, New York: Routledge, 52–68.

Dufoix, Stéphane (2008): *Diasporas.* Berkeley: University of California Press.

Earhart, H. Byron (1982): *Japanese Religion. Unity and Diversity.* Belmont: Wadsworth.

Eisenstadt, Shmuel Noah (1954) *The Absorption of Immigrants: A Comparative Study Based Mainly on the Jewish Community in Palestine and the State of Israel.* London: Routledge & Kegan Paul.

Eju.TV (2012): Tensión en San Ignacio por cambio de alcalde, 24-10-2012. http://eju.tv /2012/10/tensin-en-san-ignacio-por-cambio-de-alcalde, accessed 15-11-2017.

El Deber (2006): Centro Social Japonés celebra sus 50 años junto a Santa Cruz, 16-09-2006.

252 *References*

El Deber (2016): El empleo informal en Bolivia supera el 70%, 22-06-2016. http://www. eldeber.com.bo/economia/El-empleo-informal-en-Bolivia-supera-el-70-20160622 -78381.html, accessed 20-10-2017.

El Día (2010): Temen violencia en Warnes; el MAS busca sacar a Carmona de la alcaldía, 24-08-2010. http://eju.tv/2010/08/temen-violencia-en-warnes-el-mas-busca-sacar-a -carmona-de-la-alcalda, accessed 15-11-2017.

El Diario (2015): Bolivia registra bajo consumo de hortalizas, 21-12-2015. http://www. eldiario.net/noticias/2015/2015_12/nt151221/economia.php?n=40&-bolivia-registra -bajo-consumo-de-hortalizas, accessed 09-04-2018.

Embajada del Japón en Bolivia (2016): Seminario de promoción comercial entre Japón y Bolivia. http://www.bo.emb-japan.go.jp/itpr_es/seminario-comercial-japon.html, accessed 15-11-2017.

Embajada del Japón en Bolivia (2019a): Asistencia japonesa para las comunidades Nikkeis. https://www.bo.emb-japan.go.jp/files/000444241.pdf, accessed 08-09-2019.

Embajada del Japón en Bolivia (2019b): Contribución de la Sociedad Japonesa de La Paz a Bolivia. https://www.bo.emb-japan.go.jp/files/000444243.pdf, accessed 08-09-2019.

Embajada del Japón en Bolivia (2019c): Convivencia de los japoneses con Bolivia. En conmemoración del 120 aniversario de la inmigración japonesa a Bolivia. https://www. youtube.com/watch?v=LAGcxS7lRI0&feature=youtu.be, accessed 09-08-2019.

Embajada del Japón en Bolivia (2019d): Exhibición Histórica del 120 Aniversario de la Inmigración Japonesa a Bolivia. https://www.bo.emb-japan.go.jp/itpr_ja/120exhibicion .html, accessed 09-08-2019.

Endōh, Toake (2009): *Exporting Japan. Politics of Emigration towards Latin America.* Urbana: University of Illinois Press.

Eriksen, Thomas Hylland (2010): *Ethnicity and Nationalism. Anthropological Perspectives.* London: Pluto Press.

Eriksen, Thomas Hylland (2013): Ethnicity: From Boundaries to Frontiers. In: James G. Carrier und Deborah B. Gewertz (eds.): *The Handbook of Sociocultural Anthropology.* London: Bloomsbury, 280–300.

Eriksen, Thomas Hylland (2015): *Small Places, Large Issues. An Introduction to Social and Cultural Anthropology.* London [etc.]: Pluto Press.

Esmein, Jean (2009): De 1868 à nos jours. In: Francine Hérail und Guillaume Carré (eds.): *Histoire du Japon: des origines à nos jours.* Paris: Hermann, 985–1408.

Estremadoiro Flores, Ernesto (2017): Productores revelan uso de semilla de maíz transgénico de contrabando. In: *El Deber*, 29-09-2017. https://www.eldeber.com. bo/economia/Revelan-uso-de-semilla-de-maiz-transgenico-20170928-0073.html, accessed 15-11-2017.

Fabricant, Nicole (2012): *Mobilizing Bolivia's Displaced. Indigenous Politics & the Struggle over Land.* Chapel Hill: University of North Carolina Press.

Faist, Thomas (2010): Diaspora and Transnationalism: What Kind of Dance Partners? In: Rainer Bauböck und Thomas Faist (eds.): *Diaspora and Transnationalism. Concepts, Theories and Methods.* Amsterdam: Amsterdam University Press, 9–34.

Farthing, Linda C.; Kohl, Benjamin H. (2014): *Evo's Bolivia. Continuity and Change.* Austin: University of Texas Press.

Favell, Adrian; Feldblum, Miriam; Smith, Michael Peter (2008): The Human Face of Global Mobility: A Research Agenda. In: Michael Peter Smith und Adrian Favell (eds.): *The Human Face of Global Mobility. International Highly Skilled Migration in Europe, North America and the Asia-Pacific.* New Brunswick: Transaction Publishers, 1–25.

References 253

Fechter, Anne-Meike (2010): Gender, Empire, Global Capitalism. Colonial and Corporate Expatriate Wives. In: *Journal of Ethnic and Migration Studies* 36 (8), 1279–1297. DOI: 10.1080/13691831003687717.

Fernández, Juan Carlos (2017): Gobierno da luz verde para exportar 300.000t de soya. In: *El Deber*, 30-03-2017. http://www.eldeber.com.bo/economia/Gobierno-da-luz-verde -para-exportar-300.000-t-de-soya-20170329-0124.html, accessed 20-10-2017.

Fernández Reyes, Nelfi (2015) Los diferentes rostros de una realidad. Ichilo, Víctima y cómplice del narcotráfico. In: Boris Miranda und Daniel Agramont (eds.): *El rostro de la (in)seguridad en Bolivia. Siete crónicas sobre circuitos delictivos*. La Paz: Friedrich Ebert Stiftung, Fundación para el Periodismo.

Fernández Saavedra, Gustavo; Chávez Álvarez, Gonzalo; Zegada, María Teresa (2014): *La Bolivia del siglo XXI, nación y globalización. Enfoque internacional y estudios de caso*. La Paz: PIEB.

Finnemore, Martha; Sikkink, Kathryn (1998): International Norm Dynamics and Political Change. In: *International Organization* 52 (4), 887–917.

Fish, Robert A. (2009): 'Mixed-Blood' Japanese: A Reconsideration of Race and Purity in Japan. In: Michael Weiner (ed.): *Japan's Minorities: The Illusion of Homogeneity*. London: Routledge, 40–58.

Foucault, Michel (1975): *Surveiller et punir. Naissance de la prison*. Paris: Gallimard.

Freddi, Valentino (2003): *Presencia italiana en Santa Cruz. Actores y pioneros en el desarrollo cruceño desde 1900 al 2000*. Santa Cruz de la Sierra: Sirena.

Frühstück, Sabine; Manzenreiter, Wolfram (2002): Neverland Lost. Judo Cultures in Austria, Japan and Everywhere. In: Harumi Befu und Sylvie Guichard-Anguis (eds.): *Globalizing Japan. Ethnography of the Japanese Presence in Asia, Europe, and America*. London, New York: RoutledgeCurzon, 69–93.

Fuess, Harald (2004): *Divorce in Japan. Family, Gender, and the State, 1600–2000*. Stanford: Stanford University Press.

Fujimori, Alberto (1990): Mensaje del presidente constitucional del Perú, ingeniero Alberto Fujimori Fujimori, ante el congreso nacional, el 28 de Julio de 1990. http:// www4.congreso.gob.pe/museo/mensajes/Mensaje-1990-2.pdf, accessed 07-10-2017.

Fujimoto, Masayuki (2016): Panorama general del comercio entre Japón y Bolivia y los instrumentos disponibles para la promoción del comercio por JETRO. http://www.bo .emb-japan.go.jp/files/000208068.pdf, accessed 15-02-2017.

Fukaura, Haruko; Nagai, Kazuo (2013): Fundación y desarrollo de la Colonia San Juan. In: Iyo Kunimoto (ed.): *Los japoneses en Bolivia. 110 años de historia de la inmigración japonesa a Bolivia*. La Paz: Federación Nacional de Asociaciones Boliviano-Japonesas; Asociación Nippon-Bolivia; Plural editores, 239–287.

Fukui, Chizu (2017): Boribia ni okeru nikkeijin ijūchi no rekishiteki keisei to kadai. In: *Kokusai kankei gakubu kenkyū nenbō* 38 (2), accessed 10-10-2018.

Furuki, Toshihiro (2013): 100 años de la comunidad *nikkei* de La Paz. In: Iyo Kunimoto (ed.): *Los japoneses en Bolivia. 110 años de historia de la inmigración japonesa a Bolivia*. La Paz: Federación Nacional de Asociaciones Boliviano-Japonesas; Asociación Nippon-Bolivia; Plural editores, 47–85.

Gaceta Oficial de Bolivia (1976): Decreto Ley n° 13344. http://www.gacetaoficialdebolivia. gob.bo/index.php/normas/descargar/20790, accessed 13-11-2018.

Gaimushō (2014): Speech by Prime Minister Abe. Juntos!! Bringing infinite depth to Japan - Latin America and the Caribbean Cooperation. https://www.mofa.go.jp/la_c/sa/br/ page3e_000208.html, accessed 21-06-2018.

254 References

Gaimushō (2015): Jisedai nikkeijin shidōsha kaigi no kaisai. http://www.mofa.go.jp/mofaj/press/release/press4_001894.html, accessed 11-04-2018.

Gaimushō (2016): Boribia Taminzoku Kuni. http://www.mofa.go.jp/mofaj/area/bolivia/data.html, accessed 30-10-2017.

Gaimushō (2017a): Countries and Regions. Japan-Latin America and the Caribbean Relations. http://www.mofa.go.jp/mofaj/area/latinamerica.html, accessed 12-02-2017.

Gaimushō (2017b): Japan's Diplomacy Open to the Public. Cooperation with Emigrants and Japanese Descendants, Nikkei. https://www.mofa.go.jp/policy/other/bluebook/2017/html/chapter4/c040203.html, accessed 27-08-2018.

Galtung, Johan (1969): Violence, Peace, and Peace Research. In: *Journal of Peace Research* 6 (3), 167–191.

Gamlen, Alan (2008): The Emigration State and the Modern Geopolitical Imagination. In: *Political Geography* 27, 840–856.

Gans, Herbert J. (1979): Symbolic Ethnicity. The Future of Ethnic Groups and Cultures in America. In: *Ethnic and Racial Studies* 2 (1), 1–20.

Gapp, Rod; Fisher, Ron; Kobayashi, Kaoru (2008): Implementing 5S within a Japanese Context. An Integrated Management System. In: *Management Decision* 46 (4), 565–579. DOI: 10.1108/00251740810865067.

García Linera, Álvaro (2012): Del Estado aparente al Estado integral. http://blogs.ffyh.unc.edu.ar/garcialinera/files/2015/10/Conferencia-UNC.pdf, accessed 12-08-2017.

Gaudioso, Tomoko Kimura; Soares, André Luis Ramos (2010): Entre o Butsudan e a missa: Práticas religiosas de imigrantes japoneses no Rio Grande do Sul, Brasil. In: *Amérique Latine: Histoire et Mémoire* 20, accessed 30-11-2017.

Gimenez, Heloisa Marques (2010): O desenvolvimento da cadeia da soja na Bolívia e a presença brasileira: uma história comum. M.A. thesis. Universidade de São Paulo, São Paulo. Programa de Pós-Graduação em Integração da América Latina. www.teses.usp.br/teses/disponiveis/84/84131/tde-18122012-114938/publico/2010_HeloisaMarquesGimenezv1.pdf, accessed 30-11-2017.

Gingerich, Daniel W. (2010): Bolivia: Traditional Parties, the State, and the Toll of Corruption. In: Stephen D. Morris und Charles H. Blake (eds.): *Corruption & Politics in Latin America. National and Regional Dynamics.* Boulder: L. Rienner Publishers, 55–87.

Glidden, Lisa M. (2011): *Mobilizing Ethnic Identity in the Andes. A Study of Ecuador and Peru.* Lanham: Lexington Books.

Gluckman, Max (1963): Gossip and Scandal. In: *Current Anthropology* 4 (3), 307–316.

Gobernación Autónoma de Santa Cruz (2009): 110 años de la colonia japonesa en Bolivia. https://www.youtube.com/watch?v=oBF4MObL6vU, accessed 11-09-2017.

Goldstein, Daniel M. (2004): *The Spectacular City. Violence and Performance in Urban Bolivia.* Durham: Duke University Press.

Gómez Vaca, Rómulo (1928): Desde mi umbral. http://www.soysantacruz.com.bo/Contenidos/1/ArteYCultura/Textos/B03-GomezVR.asp, accessed 09-07-2021.

Gordillo, José Miguel; Alberto Rivera Pizarro; Sulcata, Ana Evi (2007): *¿Pitaq kaypi kamachiq? Las estructuras de poder en Cochabamba, 1940 - 2006.* La Paz: Fundación PIEB.

Gordon, Andrew (2014): *A Modern History of Japan. From Tokugawa Times to the Present.* New York: Oxford University Press.

Gordon, Milton M. (1964): *Assimilation in American Life: The Role of Race, Religion, and National Origins.* New York: Oxford University Press.

Graham, Richard (1990): Introduction. In: Richard Graham (ed.): *The Idea of Race in Latin America, 1879–1940.* Austin: University of Texas Press, 1–5.

References 255

Grün, Roberto (1994): Identidade e representação: Os judeus na esfera política e a imagem na comunidade. In: *Revista Brasileira de Ciências Sociais* 9, 123–148, accessed 30-11-2017.

Gupta, Akhil (2012): *Red Tape. Bureaucracy, Structural Violence, and Poverty in India.* Durham: Duke University Press.

Gupta, Dipankar (2007): *Mistaken Modernity. India between Worlds.* New Delhi: HarperCollins Publishers.

Gustafson, Bret (2006): Spectacles of Autonomy and Crisis: Or, What Bulls and Beauty Queens have to do with Regionalism in Eastern Bolivia. In: *Journal of Latin American Anthropology* 11 (2), 351–379.

Guttmann, Allen; Thompson, Lee (2001): *Japanese Sports. A History.* Honolulu: University of Hawai'i Press.

Hardacre, Helen (2003): Fieldwork with Japanese Religious Groups. In: Theodore C. Bestor, Patricia G. Steinhoff und Victoria Lyon-Bestor (eds.): *Doing Fieldwork in Japan.* Honolulu: University of Hawai'i Press, 71–88.

Hatugai, Érica Rosa (2018): Um corpo como fronteira. Parentesco e identificações entre descendentes nipônicos "mestiços". PhD thesis. Universidade Federal de São Carlos. Centro de Educação e Ciências Humanas, Departamento de Antropologia Social.

Hauser-Schäublin, Brigitta (2008): Teilnehmende Beobachtung. In: Bettina Beer (ed.): *Methoden und Techniken der Feldforschung.* Berlin: Reimer, 33–54.

Heath, Dwight B.; Erasmus, Charles J.; Buechler, Hans C. (1969): *Land Reform and Social Revolution in Bolivia.* New York [etc.]: Frederick A. Praeger.

Heckmann, Friedrich (1992): *Ethnische Minderheiten, Volk und Nation: Soziologie inter-ethnischer Beziehungen.* Stuttgart: Ferdinand Enke Verlag.

Hedberg, Anna Sofia (2007): *Outside the World. Cohesion and Deviation among Old Colony Mennonites in Bolivia.* Uppsala: University Library.

Heiman, Rachel; Liechty, Marc; Freeman, Carla (2012): Introduction: Charting an Anthropology of the Middle Class. In: Rachel Heiman, Carla Freeman und Marc Liechty (eds.): *The Global Middle Classes. Theorizing through Ethnography.* Santa Fe: SAR Press, 3–29.

Hein, Laura; Selden, Mark (2003): Culture, Power, and Identity in Contemporary Okinawa. In: Laura Hein und Mark Selden (eds.): *Islands of Discontent. Okinawan Responses to Japanese and American Power.* Lanham: Rowman & Littlefield, 1–35.

Heinrich, Patrick (2004): Language Planning and Language Ideology in the Ryūkyū Islands. In: *Language Policy* 3, 153–179.

Heras, Carlos (2016): Tira y afloja en Bolivia sobre el uso de semillas transgénicas. In: *Página Siete*, 01-12-2016. http://www.paginasiete.bo/miradas/2016/1/12/tira-afloja-bolivia-sobre-semillas-transgenicas-83066.html, accessed 15-11-2017.

Heredia García, Hilton (2016): Rige otra tasa de regulación y genera rechazo de sectores. In: *El Deber*, 15-08-2016. https://www.eldeber.com.bo/economia/Rige-otra-tasa-de-regulacion-y-genera-rechazo-de-sectores-20160815-84959.html, accessed 10-02-2018.

Heredia García, Hilton (2017): Crece importación de maíz transgénico de Argentina. In: *El Deber*, 17-02-2017. http://www.eldeber.com.bo/economia/Crece-importacion-de-maiz-transgenico-de-Argentina-20170216-0135.html, accessed 20-10-2017.

Hertog, Ekaterina (2009): *Tough Choices. Bearing an Illegitimate Child in Contemporary Japan.* Stanford: Stanford University Press.

Higa, Hiroshi (2013): Establecimiento y desarrollo de la Colonia Okinawa. In: Iyo Kunimoto (ed.): *Los japoneses en Bolivia. 110 años de historia de la inmigración*

256 References

japonesa a Bolivia. La Paz: Federación Nacional de Asociaciones Boliviano-Japonesas; Asociación Nippon-Bolivia; Plural editores, 199–238.

High Level Committee on the Indian Diaspora (2001): Report of High Level Committee on the Indian Diaspora. Estimated Size of Overseas Indian Community: Country-wise. http://www.indiandiaspora.nic.in/diasporapdf/part1-est.pdf, accessed 01-10-2017.

Hirabayashi, James A.; Kikumura-Yano, Akemi (2002): The Pan-American Nikkei Association: A Report on the Tenth and Eleventh Meetings. In: *Amerasia Journal (Special Issue)* 28 (2), 147–157.

Hirabayashi, Lane Ryo (2002): Pathways to Power. Comparative Perspectives on the Emergence of Nikkei Ethnic Political Traditions. In: Lane Ryo Hirabayashi, Akemi Kikumura-Yano und James A. Hirabayashi (eds.): *New Worlds, New Lives: Globalization and People of Japanese Descent in the Americas and from Latin America in Japan.* Stanford: Stanford University Press, 159–178.

Hirabayashi, Lane Ryo; Kikumura-Yano, Akemi; Hirabayashi, James A. (Hg.) (2002): *New Worlds, New Lives: Globalization and People of Japanese Descent in the Americas and from Latin America in Japan.* Stanford: Stanford University Press.

Hiraoka, Mário (1980): *Japanese Agricultural Settlement in the Bolivian Upper Amazon: A Study in Regional Ecology.* Tsukuba: University of Tsukuba Press.

Hiyane Yzena, Christian (2017): La hoguera de los sueños. In: *Perú Shimpo*, 06-08-2017. http://www.perushimpo.com/noticias.php?idp=8033, accessed 11-10-2017.

Hobsbawm, Eric J. (2008): *The Invention of Tradition.* Cambridge: Cambridge University Press.

Höhe, Sybille (2011): *Religion, Staat und Politik in Japan. Geschichte und zeitgeschichtliche Bedeutung von Sōka Gakkai, Kōmeitō und Neuer Kōmeitō.* München: Iudicium.

Hollweg, Mario Gabriel (1995): *Alemanes en el oriente boliviano. Su aporte al desarrollo de Bolivia.* Santa Cruz de la Sierra: Sirena.

Horst, Oscar H.; Asagiri, Katsuhiro (2000): The Odyssey of Japanese Colonists in the Dominican Republic. In: *Geographical Review* 90 (3), 335–358.

Hu-DeHart, Evelyn (2002): *Huagong* and *Huashang*: The Chinese as Laborers and Merchants in Latin America and the Caribbean. In: *Amerasia Journal (Special Issue)* 28 (2), 64–90.

Hurtado, Mary; Solares Maemura, Hector (2006): *El samurai de la revolución: Los sueños y la lucha de Freddy Maemura junto al Che.* [La Paz]: Editorial Maemura.

Ibuki, Norm Masaji (2013): Francisco Miyasaka On Being a Cuban Nisei. http://www.discovernikkei.org/en/journal/2013/10/01/francisco-miyasaka-being-cuban-1, accessed 12-02-2017.

Imamura, Anne E. (2009): Family Culture. In: Yoshio Sugimoto (ed.): *The Cambridge Companion to Modern Japanese Culture.* Melbourne: Cambridge University Press, 76–91.

Inoue, Masamichi S. (2017): *Okinawa and the U.S. Military. Identity Making in the Age of Globalization.* New York: Columbia University Press.

Instituto Boliviano de Comercio Exterior (2016): Santa Cruz: Economía y comercio exterior (Boletín Electrónico Bisemanal, 544). http://www.ibce.org.bo//images/ibcecifras_documentos/CIFRAS-544-Santa-Cruz-Economia-Comercio-Exterior.pdf, accessed 11-10-2017.

Instituto Boliviano de Comercio Exterior (2017): Bolivia: Exportaciones de soya y sus derivados (Boletín Electrónico Bisemanal, 594). http://ibce.org.bo/images/ibcecifras_documentos/Cifras-594-Bolivia-Exportaciones-de-Soya-y-sus-derivados.pdf, accessed 16-11-2017.

References 257

Instituto Nacional de Estadística (2012): Resultos Censo nacional de población y vivienda. http://fm.ine.gob.bo/censofichacomunidad, accessed 09-01-2017.

Instituto Nacional de Estadística (2017a): Aspectos Geográficos. http://www.ine.gob.bo/index.php/bolivia/aspectos-geograficos, accessed 09-01-2017.

Instituto Nacional de Estadística (2017b): Gas Natural, Zinc y Soya, representan el 54,8% de las exportaciones bolivianas. http://www.ine.gob.bo/index.php/component/k2/item/1141-gas-natural-zinc-y-soya-representan-el-54-8-de-las-exportaciones-bolivianas?highlight=WyJleHBvcnRhY2lvbmVzIl0=, accessed 15-11-2017.

Instituto Nacional de Estadística (2017c): Población. http://www.ine.gob.bo, accessed 09-01-2017.

Instituto Nacional de Estadística (2019): Bolivia - salario mínimo nacional. https://www.ine.gob.bo/index.php/descarga/487/salario-minimo-nacional/46077/bolivia-salario-minimo-nacional-1991-2019.xlsx, accessed 09-07-2021.

International Organization for Migration (2018): Bolivia - IOM Migration Activities. https://www.iom.int/es/countries/bolivia, accessed 07-05-2018.

Ionescu, Sanda (2002): Soka Gakkai in Germany: The Story of a Qualified Success. In: Harumi Befu und Sylvie Guichard-Anguis (eds.): *Globalizing Japan. Ethnography of the Japanese Presence in Asia, Europe, and America*. London, New York: RoutledgeCurzon, 94–108.

Iraola Mendizábal, Guillermo (2014): La nueva cocina del oriente boliviano y su toque japonés. In: *Página Siete*, 30-09-2014. http://www.paginasiete.bo/revmiradas/2014/10/5/nueva-cocina-oriente-boliviano-toque-japones-33761.html, accessed 09-04-2018.

Isaakyan, Irina; Triandafyllidou, Anna (2017): Reflections on Diaspora and Soft Power. Community Building among Female US Expats in Southern Europe. In: *Identities* 24, 1–18. DOI: 10.1080/1070289X.2017.1291000.

Ischida, Camila Aya (2010): A experiência nikkei no Brasil: uma etnografia sobre imaginários e identidades. M.A. thesis. Universidade de São Paulo, São Paulo. Departamento de Antropologia da Faculdade de Filosofia, Letras e Ciências Humanas. www.teses.usp.br/ teses/ disponiveis/ 8/ 8134/ tde-08022011-094359/ publico/ 2010_CamilaAyaIschida.pdf, accessed 09-11-2014.

Ishige, Naomichi (2009): Food Culture. In: Yoshio Sugimoto (ed.): *The Cambridge Companion to Modern Japanese Culture*. Melbourne: Cambridge University Press, 300–316.

Iwabuchi, Koichi (2002): "Soft" Nationalism and Narcissism: Japanese Popular Culture Goes Global. In: *Asian Studies Review* 26 (4), 447–469.

Jain, Rohit (2018): *Kosmopolitische Pioniere. »Inder_innen der zweiten Generation« aus der Schweiz zwischen Assimilation, Exotik und globaler Moderne*. Bielefeld: transcript-Verlag.

Jansen, Marius B. (2000): *The Making of Modern Japan*. Cambridge: The Belknap Press of Harvard University Press.

Japan-Tag Düsseldorf/NRW e.V. (2018): Japan in Düsseldorf und NRW. http://www.japantag-duesseldorf-nrw.de/japan-in-duesseldorf, accessed 28-04-2018.

Jenkins, Richard (1994): Rethinking Ethnicity: Identity, Categorization and Power. In: *Ethnic and Racial Studies* 17 (2), 197–223.

Jenkins, Richard (1997): *Rethinking Ethnicity: Arguments and Explorations*. London [etc.]: Sage Publications.

JETRO (2018): The Certification Program of Japanese Food and Ingredient Supporter Stores Overseas. https://www.jetro.go.jp/en/trends/foods/supporter.html, accessed 25-08-2018.

258 *References*

JICA (2018a): Activity Report 2017: Latin America and the Caribbean. https://www.jica. go.jp/english/publications/reports/annual/2017/c8h0vm0000bws721-att/2017_08.pdf, accessed 22-08-2018.

JICA (2018b): FY2018: Education Program for Nikkei Next Generation (High-school Students). Application Guide. https://www.jica.go.jp/peru/espanol/activities/ c8h0vm0000baizrl-att/activity03_06_01_en.pdf, accessed 24-08-2018.

JICA (2018c): FY2018: Education Program for Nikkei Next Generation (University Students). Application Guide. https://www.jica.go.jp/mexico/office/activities/nikkei/ ku57pq000029iokr-att/college_application_guide_e.pdf, accessed 24-08-2018.

Jones, Randall S.; Fukawa, Kohei (2015): Achieving Fiscal Consolidation while Promoting Social Cohesion in Japan. In: OECD Economics Department Working Papers 1262. DOI: 10.1787/5jrtpbs9fg0v-en.

Jones-Correa, Michael (2001): Under Two Flags: Dual Nationality in Latin America and Its Consequences for Naturalization in the United States. In: *International Migration Review* 35 (4), 997–1029.

Kasamatsu, Emi (2002): Japanese Paraguayan Historical Overview. In: Akemi Kikumura-Yano (ed.): *Encyclopedia of Japanese Descendants in the Americas. An Illustrated History of the Nikkei.* Walnut Creek [etc.]: AltaMira Press, 229–238.

Kasamatsu, Emi (2005): *Historia de la Asociación Panamericana Nikkei. Presencia e inmigración japonesas en las Américas.* Asunción: Servilibro.

Kasamatsu, Emi (2007a): ¿Es o no una ventaja ser Nikkei? Características peculiares de los Nikkei del Paraguay. Estudio comparativo con los Nikkei de las Américas. http://www. discovernikkei.org/es/journal/2007/6/6/ventaja-ser-nikkei/, accessed 21-10-2017.

Kasamatsu, Emi (2007b): ¿Es o no una ventaja ser Nikkei? Discriminación y exclusión social y acceso a la política de los Nikkei en las Américas. http://www.discovernikkei. org/es/journal/2007/6/19/ventaja-ser-nikkei, accessed 10-07-2017.

Katz, Jonathan M. (2006): Japan Families Come to Dominican Republic. In: *Washington Post,* 25-07-2006. http://www.washingtonpost.com/wp-dyn/content/article/2006/07/25 /AR2006072500193.html, accessed 27-01-2015.

Kerr, George H. (1964): *Okinawa: The History of an Island People.* Rutland [etc.]: Charles E. Tuttle.

Khan, Shamus Rahman (2012): The Sociology of Elites. In: *Annual Review of Sociology* 38, 361–377.

Khosravi, Shahram (2010): *"Illegal" Traveller. An Auto-Ethnography of Borders.* Basingstoke: Palgrave Macmillan.

Kikumura-Yano, Akemi (Hg.) (2002a): *Encyclopedia of Japanese Descendants in the Americas. An Illustrated History of the Nikkei.* Walnut Creek [etc.]: AltaMira Press.

Kikumura-Yano, Akemi (2002b): Introduction. In: Akemi Kikumura-Yano (ed.): *Encyclopedia of Japanese Descendants in the Americas. An Illustrated History of the Nikkei.* Walnut Creek [etc.]: AltaMira Press, 1–5.

Kim, Youna (Hg.) (2013): *The Korean Wave. Korean Media Go Global.* London: Routledge.

Kirshner, Joshua (2011): Migrants and Citizens. Hygiene Panic and Urban Space in Santa Cruz. In: Nicole Fabricant und Bret Gustafson (eds.): *Remapping Bolivia. Resources, Territory, and Indigeneity in a Plurinational State.* Santa Fe: School for Advanced Research Press, 96–115.

Klein, Herbert S. (2003): *A Concise History of Bolivia.* Cambridge: Cambridge University Press.

Klein, Misha (2012): *Kosher Feijoada and Other Paradoxes of Jewish Life in São Paulo.* Gainesville: University Press of Florida.

References 259

Kobayashi, Audrey; Ayukawa, Midge (2002): A Brief History of Japanese Canadians. In: Akemi Kikumura-Yano (ed.): *Encyclopedia of Japanese Descendants in the Americas. An Illustrated History of the Nikkei.* Walnut Creek [etc.]: AltaMira Press, 149–161.

Kopp, Adalberto J. (2015): *Las colonias menonitas en Bolivia. Antecedentes, asentamientos y propuestas para un diálogo.* La Paz, Bolivia: Fundación Tierra.

Koronia Okinawa Nyūshoku 50 Shūnen Kinenshi Hensan Iinkai (Hg.) (2005): *Boribia no taichi ni ikiru Okinawa imin.* Santa Kurusu: Okinawa Nihon Boribia Kyōkai.

Koser, Khalid; Salt, John (1997): The Geography of Highly Skilled International Migration. In: *International Journal of Population Geography* 3, 285–303.

Kunimoto, Iyo (1990): *Un pueblo japonés en la Bolivia tropical. Colonia San Juan de Yapacaní en el Departamento de Santa Cruz.* Santa Cruz de la Sierra: Ed. Casa de la Cultura "Raúl Otero Reiche".

Kunimoto, Iyo (2013a): De los Andes a la cuenca amazónica. In: Iyo Kunimoto (ed.): *Los japoneses en Bolivia. 110 años de historia de la inmigración japonesa a Bolivia.* La Paz: Federación Nacional de Asociaciones Boliviano-Japonesas; Asociación Nippon-Bolivia; Plural editores, 21–46.

Kunimoto, Iyo (Hg.) (2013b): *Los japoneses en Bolivia. 110 años de historia de la inmigración japonesa a Bolivia.* La Paz: Federación Nacional de Asociaciones Boliviano-Japonesas; Asociación Nippon-Bolivia; Plural editores.

Kushner, Eve (2001): Japanese Peruvians: Reviled and Respected. http://www.evekushner. com/writing/index.php?p=28, accessed 22-05-2009.

La Gaceta del Norte (1923): *Factores de progreso en el Noroeste desde el año 1912, 14-04-1923.*

La Razón (2013): Censo 2012: El 69% de los bolivianos dice no pertenecer a ninguno de los 36 pueblos indígenas reconocidos por la Constitución, 31-07-2013. http://www.la -razon.com/index.php?_url=/sociedad/Censo-bolivianos-pertenecer-pueblo-indigena _0_1879612128.html, accessed 27-11-2017.

La Razón (2018): Bolivia registró en 2017 su mayor déficit comercial, 31-01-2018. http:// www.la-razon.com/economia/Comercio-deficit-Bolivia-registro_0_2866513374.html, accessed 11-04-2018.

Lamont, Michèle (1992): *Money, Morals, and Manners. The Culture of the French and American Upper-Middle Class.* Chicago [etc.]: University of Chicago Press.

Lan, Pei-Chia (2003): "They Have More Money but I Speak Better English!": Transnational Encounters between Filipina Domestics and Taiwanese Employers. In: *Identities: Global Studies in Culture and Power* 10 (2), 132–161, accessed 13-11-2014.

Laumonier, Isabel (2002): Japanese Argentine Historical Overview. In: Akemi Kikumura-Yano (ed.): *Encyclopedia of Japanese Descendants in the Americas. An Illustrated History of the Nikkei.* Walnut Creek [etc.]: AltaMira Press, 71–82.

Lazarte, Jorge (2008): ¿Multiculturalismo o multinacionalismo? El incordio de la asamblea constituyente de Bolivia. In: *Seminario internacional justicia intercultural: Conflictos normativos e integración de minorías en las sociedades plurales. Fundación Manuel Giménez Abad,* 1–14.

Lebra, William P. (1966): *Okinawan Religion. Belief, Ritual, and Social Structure.* Honolulu: University of Hawai'i Press.

Lesser, Jeffrey (2002): In Search of the Hyphen. Nikkei and the Struggle over Brazilian National Identity. In: Lane Eyo Hirabayashi, Akemi Kikumura-Yano und James A. Hirabayashi (eds.): *New Worlds, New Lives: Globalization and People of Japanese Descent in the Americas and from Latin America in Japan.* Stanford: Stanford University Press, 37–58.

260 References

Lesser, Jeffrey (2008): How the Jews Became Japanese and Other Stories of Nation and Ethnicity. In: Jeffrey Lesser und Raanan Rein (eds.): *Rethinking Jewish-Latin Americans*. Albuquerque: University of New Mexico Press, 41–54.

Levitt, Peggy; Jaworsky, B. Nadya (2007): Transnational Migration Studies: Past Developments and Future Trends. In: *Annual Review of Sociology* 33, 129–156.

Ley, David (2010): *Millionaire Migrants. Trans-Pacific Life Lines*. Malden: Wiley-Blackwell.

Li, Guofang; Wang, Lihshing (Hg.) (2008): *Model Minority Myth Revisited. An Interdisciplinary Approach to Demystifying Asian American Educational Experiences*. Charlotte: Information Age Publishing.

Lie, John (2001): *Multiethnic Japan*. Cambridge: Harvard University Press.

Liechty, Mark (2003): *Suitably Modern. Making Middle-Class Culture in a New Consumer Society*. Princeton: Princeton University Press.

Lien, Pei-te; Affigne, Tony (2002): Peoples of Asian Descent in the Americas: Theoretical Implications of Race and Politics. In: *Amerasia Journal (Special Issue)* 28 (2), 1–26.

López, Luis Enrique (2005): *De resquicios y boquerones. La educación intercultural bilingüe en Bolivia*. La Paz: Plural editores.

Los Tiempos (2016): Trabajadores de Sinopec mantienen su huelga, 28-01-2016. http://www.lostiempos.com/actualidad/economia/20170130/trabajadores-sinopec-mantienen-su-huelga, accessed 11-04-2018.

Mackey, Lee (2011): Legitimating Foreignization in Bolivia: Brazilian agriculture and the relations of conflict and consent in Santa Cruz, Bolivia. Paper presented at the International Conference on Global Land Grabbing, 6–8 April 2011. https://www.iss.nl/fileadmin/ASSETS/iss/Documents/Conference_papers/LDPI/23_Lee_Mackey.pdf, accessed 22-10-2017.

Maeyama, Takashi (1972): Ancestor, Emperor, and Immigrant: Religion and Group Identification of the Japanese in Rural Brazil (1908–1950). In: *Journal of Interamerican Studies and World Affairs* 14 (2), 151–182.

Maeyama, Takashi (1979): Ethnicity, Secret Societies, and Associations: The Japanese in Brazil. In: *Comparative Studies in Society and History* 21 (4), 589–610.

Majewicz, Alfred F. (2006): Is Ryūkyūan Endangered? Worried Impressions from the Outside. In: Josef Kreiner (ed.): *Japaneseness versus Ryūkyūanism*. Bonn: Bier'sche Verlagsanstalt, 31–47.

Mansilla, H.C.F. (2016): Las transformaciones de las élites políticas en América Latina. Una visión inusual de la temática. In: *Revista de Ciencias Sociales* 12 (1), accessed 30-11-2017.

Manzenreiter, Wolfram (2013): Diaspora ohne Heimat: Einfluss der Rückkehrmigration auf japanische Auswanderergemeinschaften in Südamerika. In: *Asiatische Studien/ Etudes Asiatiques* 67 (2), 651–680.

Manzenreiter, Wolfram (2014): Diasporapolitiken: Der japanische Emigrationsstaat in historischer Perspektive. In: Ilker Ataç, Michael Fanizadeh, Albert Kraler und Wolfram Manzenreiter (eds.): *Migration und Entwicklung: Neue Perspektiven*. Wien: Promedia-Verlag, 223–242.

Manzenreiter, Wolfram (2017a): Living Under More than One Sun: The Nikkei Diaspora in the Americas. In: *Contemporary Japan* 29 (2), 193–213.

Manzenreiter, Wolfram (2017b): Squared Diasporas: Representations of the Japanese Diaspora Across Time and Space. In: *Contemporary Japan* 29 (2), 106–116.

Masterson, Daniel M. (2006): The Japanese of Peru. The First-Century Experience and Beyond. In: Nobuko Adachi (ed.): *Japanese Diasporas: Unsung Pasts, Conflicting Presents, and Uncertain Futures*. London, New York: Routledge, 142–158.

References   261

Matsue, Regina Yoshie (2002): A Expansão Internacional das Novas Religiões Japonesas: Um Estudo sobre a Igreja Messiânica Mundial no Brasil e na Austrália. In: *Revista de Estudos da Religião* 4, 1–19, accessed 30-11-2017.

Matsui, Shigenori (2007): The Voting Rights of Japanese Citizens Living Abroad. In: *International Journal of Constitutional Law* 5 (2), 332–342. DOI: 10.1093/icon/mom012.

Matsumori, Akiko (1995): Ryūkyuan: Past, Present and Future. In: John Christopher Maher (ed.): *Multilingual Japan*. Clevedon [etc.]: Multilingual Matters, 19–44.

Matsumoto, Alberto (2015): Líderes Nikkei de América Latina invitados por el gobierno de Japón – su rol y expectativas. http://www.discovernikkei.org/es/journal/2015/6/19/lideres-nikkei, accessed 09-04-2018.

Matsumoto, Alberto (2016): Los nikkei de la siguiente generación y su relación con el Japón. Cambios que se están produciendo en las comunidades japonesas de Sudamérica. http://www.discovernikkei.org/es/journal/2016/9/30/siguiente-generacion, accessed 09-04-2018.

Matsumoto, Alberto (2017): Desafíos y oportunidades para las colonias japonesas de Santa Cruz, Bolivia. http://www.discovernikkei.org/es/journal/2017/9/29/nikkei-latino, accessed 09-04-2018.

McClain, James L. (2002): *Japan: A Modern History*. New York: W.W. Norton.

Medeiros, Gustavo (2008): Evolución y características del sector soyero en Bolivia. In: Ximena Soruco (ed.): *Los barones del Oriente. El poder en Santa Cruz ayer y hoy*. Santa Cruz de la Sierra, 173–229.

Melgar Tísoc, Dahil M. (2012): La migración japonesa en México y su relación con los imaginarios urbanos. In: Nora Kuperszmit, Teresa Lagos Mármol, Leonardo Mucciolo und Mariana Sacchi (eds.): *Entre pasados y presentes III. Estudios contemporáneos en ciencias antropológicas*. Buenos Aires: Mnemosyne, 188–204.

Mendez, Roberto (2012): Suspenden a su alcalde y La Guardia se moviliza. In: *El Día*, 27-04-2012. https://www.eldia.com.bo/index.php?cat=150&pla=3&id_articulo=90117, accessed 15-11-2017.

Mendoza, Luz (2013): Termina calvario de alcalde Joaquino; es absuelto del caso "compra de autos usados". In: *Eju.TV 2013*, 12-04-2013. http://eju.tv/2013/12/termina-calvario-de-alcalde-joaquino-es-absuelto-del-caso-compra-de-autos-usados/, accessed 01-11-2018.

Ministério das Relações Exteriores (2014): Visita ao Brasil do Primeiro-Ministro do Japão, Shinzo Abe - Comunicado Conjunto da Visita Oficial de Trabalho. http://www.itamaraty.gov.br/pt-BR/notas-a-imprensa/5777-visita-ao-brasil-do-primeiro-ministro-do-japao-shinzo-abe-comunicado-conjunto-da-visita-oficial-de-trabalho-declaracao-conjunta-sobre-cooperacao-na-area-de-construcao-naval-para-facilitacao-do-desenvolvimento-de-recursos-offshore, accessed 07-10-2017.

Mitchell, Jon (2016): Welcome home, Okinawa. In: *Japan Times*, 22-10-2016. http://www.japantimes.co.jp/news/2016/10/22/national/history/welcome-home-okinawa, accessed 02-05-2017.

Mitre, Antonio (2006): *Náufragos en tierra firme. Bloqueo comercial, despojo y confinamiento de japoneses de Bolivia durante la Segunda Guerra Mundial*. Santa Cruz de la Sierra: Editorial El País.

Miyahira, Katsuyuki; Petrucci, Peter R. (2011): Reaching Out with *Chimugukuru*: Positioning Okinawan Identity at the Fourth Worldwide Uchinānchu Festival and Beyond. In: Jacob Edmond, Henry Johnson und Jacqueline Leckie (eds.): *Recentring Asia. Histories, Encounters, Identities*. Leiden, Boston: Global Oriental, 285–309.

262 References

Möhring, Maren (2012): *Fremdes Essen. Die Geschichte der ausländischen Gastronomie in der Bundesrepublik Deutschland*. München: Oldenbourg.

Molasky, Michael S. (2001): *The American Occupation of Japan and Okinawa: Literature and Memory*. London: Routledge.

Monheim, Felix; Köster, Gerrit (1982): *Die wirtschaftliche Erschliessung des Departements Santa Cruz (Bolivien) seit der Mitte des 20. Jahrhunderts*. Wiesbaden: Franz Steiner.

Montero, Baldwin (2018): Sinohydro denuncia bloqueo de su campamento en Padilla y agresión a su personal. In: *La Razón*, 31-01-2018. http://www.la-razon.com/sociedad /Bolivia-Sinohydro-empresa-Padilla-pelea-protesta-conflicto_0_2866513370.html, accessed 11-04-2018.

Mooney, Nicola (2011): *Rural Nostalgias and Transnational Dreams. Identity and Modernity among Jat Sikhs*. Toronto, Buffalo, London: University of Toronto Press.

Mori, Edson (2002): The Japanese-Brazilian Dekasegi Phenomenon: An Economic Perspective. In: Lane Ryo Hirabayashi, Akemi Kikumura-Yano und James A. Hirabayashi (eds.): *New Worlds, New Lives: Globalization and People of Japanese Descent in the Americas and from Latin America in Japan*. Stanford: Stanford University Press, 237–248.

Mori, Koichi (2003): Identity Transformations among Okinawans and Their Descendants in Brazil. In: Jeffrey Lesser (ed.): *Searching for Home Abroad. Japanese Brazilians and Transnationalism*. Durham: Duke University Press, 47–65.

Mori, Koichi (2011): Transformations of the *Nissei* Educational Model in a Japanese-Brazilian Ethnic Community. From *wakon-hakusai-ron* (Japanese-Spirits/Brazilian-Skills model) to *hakkon-wasai-ron* (Brazilian-spirits/Japanese-skills model). In: Junji Koizumi und Mayumi Kudo (eds.): *Conflict Studies in the Humanities*. Osaka: Global COE Program, 151–183.

Morimoto, Amelia (2002a): Japanese Immigrants and Their Descendants in Peru: 1899–1998. In: Akemi Kikumura-Yano (ed.): *Encyclopedia of Japanese Descendants in the Americas. An Illustrated History of the Nikkei*. Walnut Creek [etc.]: AltaMira Press, 247–257.

Morimoto, Amelia (2002b): Peruvian Nikkei. A Sociopolitical Portrait. In: Lane Ryo Hirabayashi, Akemi Kikumura-Yano und James A. Hirabayashi (eds.): *New Worlds, New Lives: Globalization and People of Japanese Descent in the Americas and from Latin America in Japan*. Stanford: Stanford University Press, 141–158.

Morimoto, Amelia (2007): La religión entre los Nikkei del Perú. http://www.discovernikkei. org/es/journal/2007/5/1/religon, accessed 26-01-2015.

Moromisato Miasato, Doris (2002): I Woman, I Man, I Nikkei. Symbolic Constructions of Femininity and Masculinity in the Japanese Community of Peru. In: Lane Ryo Hirabayashi, Akemi Kikumura-Yano und James A. Hirabayashi (eds.): *New Worlds, New Lives: Globalization and People of Japanese Descent in the Americas and from Latin America in Japan*. Stanford: Stanford University Press, 187–204.

Moromisato Miasato, Doris (2008): Amor y odio a Alberto Fujimori: testimonio de una nikkei peruana. http://www.discovernikkei.org/es/journal/2008/4/15/ser-nikkei-peru, accessed 30-11-2017.

Mouer, Ross; Norris, Craig (2009): Exporting Japan's Culture: From Management Style to Manga. In: Yoshio Sugimoto (ed.): *The Cambridge Companion to Modern Japanese Culture*. Melbourne: Cambridge University Press, 352–368.

Moya, Jose C. (2005): Immigrants and Associations. A Global and Historical Perspective. In: *Journal of Ethnic and Migration Studies* 31 (5), 833–864. DOI: 10.1080/13691830500178147.

References   263

Müller, Bernadette (2011): *Empirische Identitätsforschung. Personale, soziale und kulturelle Dimensionen der Selbstverortung.* Wiesbaden: VS Verlag für Sozialwissenschaften.

Murakami, Yusuke (2008): Interpretando los años de vigencia del fujimorismo. In: *Argumentos* 4, accessed 27-10-2017.

Murphy-Shigematsu, Stephen (1993): Multiethnic Japan and the Monoethnic Myth. In: *MELUS* 18 (4), 63–80.

Nader, Laura (1972): Up the Anthropologist - Perspectives Gained from Studying Up. In: Dell Hymes (ed.): *Reinventing Anthropology.* New York: Pantheon Books, 285–311.

Nagase, Atsuka Anne (2017): Personal Reflection on My First COPANI Experience, at COPANI Lima 2017. http://www.discovernikkei.org/en/journal/2017/12/27/copani-2017/, accessed 28-08-2013.

Naikaku-fu (2016): Kuuru Japan senryaku. https://www.cao.go.jp/cool_japan/index.html, accessed 10-04-2018.

Nakamaki, Hirochika (2003): *Japanese Religions at Home and Abroad. Anthropological Perspectives.* London: RoutledgeCurzon.

Nakane, Chie (1973): *Japanese Society.* Harmondsworth, Ringwood: Pelican Books.

Nakasone, Ronald Y. (2002): An Impossible Possibility. In: Ronald Y. Nakasone (ed.): *Okinawan Diaspora.* Honolulu: University of Hawai'i Press, 3–25.

Nakato, Yasue (2012): Japanese Immigrants in Brazil and 'Colonia-go': Japanese as an Immigrant Language. In: Naoki Yoshihara (ed.): *Global Migration and Ethnic Communities. Studies of Asia and South America.* Balwyn North: Trans Pacific Press, 211–231.

Neary, Ian J. (2009): Burakumin in Contemporary Japan. In: Michael Weiner (ed.): *Japan's Minorities: The Illusion of Homogeneity.* London: Routledge, 59–83.

Ninomiya, Masato (2002): Japanese Brazilian Historical Overview. In: Akemi Kikumura-Yano (ed.): *Encyclopedia of Japanese Descendants in the Americas. An Illustrated History of the Nikkei.* Walnut Creek [etc.]: AltaMira Press, 115–126.

Nishida, Mieko (2009): 'Why Does a Nikkei Want to Talk to Other Nikkeis?': Japanese Brazilians and Their Identities in São Paulo. In: *Critique of Anthropology* 29, 423–445.

NotiBoliviaRural (2012): El INIAF impulsa la horticultura de hortalizas en los hogares de Cochabamba, 02-04-2012. http://www.notiboliviarural.com/index.php?option=com_content&view=article&id=1641:el-iniaf-impulsa-la-horticultura-de-hortalizas-en-los-hogares-de-cochabamba&catid=293:agricola&Itemid=543, accessed 09-04-2018.

Nye, Joseph; Kim, Youna (2013): Soft Power and the Korean Wave. In: Youna Kim (ed.): *The Korean Wave. Korean Media Go Global.* London: Routledge, 31–42.

Nye, Joseph S. (2011): *The Future of Power.* New York: PublicAffairs.

O'Dougherty, Maureen (2002): *Consumption Intensified. The Politics of Middle-Class Daily Life in Brazil.* Durham: Duke University Press.

Ohnuki-Tierney, Emiko (1993): *Rice as Self. Japanese Identities Through Time.* Princeton: Princeton University Press.

Okihiro, Gary Y. (2002): Turning Japanese American. In: Akemi Kikumura-Yano (ed.): *Encyclopedia of Japanese Descendants in the Americas. An Illustrated History of the Nikkei.* Walnut Creek [etc.]: AltaMira Press, 9–27.

Oliart, Patricia (1996): "A President Like You": Fujimori's Popular Appeal. In: *NACLA Report on the Americas* 30 (1), 19.

Ölschleger, Hans Dieter (2004): Minorities in the Americas. In: Josef Kreiner, Ulrich Möhwald und Hans Dieter Ölschleger (eds.): *Modern Japanese Society.* Leiden, Boston: Brill, 525–548.

264   References

Omori, Hisako (2017): Eating Japanese Food in Diaspora as Identity Building: The Case of a Japanese Canadian Church. In: *Contemporary Japan* 29 (2), 148–161.

Ong, Aihwa (2005): *Flexible Staatsbürgerschaften. Die kulturelle Logik von Transnationalität*. Frankfurt am Main: Suhrkamp.

Ortiz, Ana Isabel; Soliz, Lorenzo (2007): *El arroz en Bolivia*. La Paz: CIPCA.

Ortiz Saucedo, Jimmy (2012): Cárcel para Katsumi, impunidad para Evo. http://www.icees.org.bo/2012/09/carcel-para-katsumi-impunidad-para-evo, accessed 11-09-2017.

Oshikawa, Susumu (2013): La comunidad *nikkei* en el departamento de Pando. In: Iyo Kunimoto (ed.): *Los japoneses en Bolivia. 110 años de historia de la inmigración japonesa a Bolivia*. La Paz: Federación Nacional de Asociaciones Boliviano-Japonesas; Asociación Nippon-Bolivia; Plural editores, 143–161.

Oshiro, Gaby (2016): *Desaparecidos* Nikkei: Reappeared in the Argentinian Conscience. http://www.discovernikkei.org/en/journal/2016/3/23/desaparecidos-nikkei-1, accessed 07-10-2017.

Osterweil, Marc J. (1998): The Economic and Social Condition of Jewish and Arab Immigrants in Bolivia, 1890–1980. In: Ignacio Klich und Jeffrey Lesser (eds.): *Arab and Jewish Immigrants in Latin America. Images and Realities*. London: Frank Cass, 146–166.

Osumi, Midori (2006): Language Endangerment: An Okinawan Case. In: Josef Kreiner (ed.): *Japaneseness versus Ryūkyūanism*. Bonn: Bier'sche Verlagsanstalt, 49–57.

Ota Mishima, María Elena (1993): El Japón en México. In: Guillermo Bonfil Batalla (ed.): *Simbiosis de culturas. Los inmigrantes y su cultura en México*. México: Consejo Nacional para la Cultura y las Artes [etc.], 181–215.

Página Siete (2014): Avicultoras produjeron 1.500 millones de huevos en 2013, 25-07-2014. http://www.paginasiete.bo/economia/2014/7/26/avicultoras-produjeron-1500-millones-huevos-2013-27719.html, accessed 11-04-2018.

Página Siete (2016): Centenares de vecinos de la zona Sur de La Paz protestan por falta de agua ante embajada china, 20-11-2016. http://www.paginasiete.bo/sociedad/2016/11/20/centenares-vecinos-zona-protestan-falta-agua-ante-embajada-china-117702.html, accessed 11-04-2018.

Página Siete (2017): El déficit fiscal de 8,3% en 2018 se aproxima al de 2002, 12-03-2017. http://www.paginasiete.bo/economia/2017/12/3/deficit-fiscal-83-2018-aproxima-2002-161705.html, accessed 04-11-2018.

Paine, Robert (1967): What is Gossip About? An Alternative Hypothesis. In: *Man* 2 (2), 278–285.

Palácio do Planalto (2014): Palavras da Presidenta da República, Dilma Rousseff, durante almoço em homenagem ao Primeiro-Ministro do Japão, Shinzo Abe - Palácio Itamaraty. http://www2.planalto.gov.br/acompanhe-o-planalto/discursos/discursos-da-presidenta/palavras-da-presidenta-da-republica-dilma-rousseff-durante-almoco-em-homenagem-ao-primeiro-ministro-do-japao-shinzo-abe-palacio-itamaraty, accessed 07-10-2017.

Pardo, Italo; Prato, Giuliana B. (2012): Introduction. The Contemporary Significance of Anthropology in the City. In: Italo Pardo und Giuliana B. Prato (eds.): *Anthropology in the City. Methodology and Theory*. Farnham: Ashgate, 1–28.

Parejas Moreno, Alcides (1981): *Colonias Japonesas en Bolivia*. La Paz: Talleres-Escuela de Artes Gráficas del Colegio "Don Bosco".

Park, Kyeyoung (2002): "10,000 Señora Lees": The Changing Gender Ideology of Korean-Latina-American Women in the Diaspora. In: *Amerasia Journal (Special Issue)* 28 (2), 160–180.

References 265

Peguero, Valentina (2015): Japanese Immigration in the Dominican Republic. http://www.discovernikkei.org/en/journal/2015/11/13/dominican-republic, accessed 12-02-2017.

Pellegrini Calderón, Alessandra (2016): *Beyond Indigeneity. Coca Growing and the Emergence of a New Middle Class in Bolivia*. Tucson: The University of Arizona Press.

Peña Claros, Claudia (2009): Santa Cruz: el poder y sus resistencias. Claves para entender la reivindicación autonomista cruceña. In: Fernanda Wanderley (ed.): *Estudios urbanos en la encrucijada de la interdisciplinaridad*. La Paz: CIDES-UMSA, 151–177.

Pérez Luna, Mamerto (2007): *No todo grano que brilla es oro. Un análisis de la soya en Bolivia*. La Paz: CEDLA. http://cedla.org/sites/default/files/no_todo_grano_que_brilla_es_oro_un_analisis_de_la_soya_en_bolivia.pdf, accessed 30-11-2017.

Pham, Mary Jo A. (2013): Food + Diplomacy = Gastrodiplomacy. *The Diplomatist*. https://thediplomatistdotcom.wordpress.com/2013/04/05/eat-drink-gastrodiplomacy, accessed 30-10-2017.

Pina-Cabral, João de (2000): How Do the Macanese Achieve Collective Action? In: João de Pina-Cabral und Antónia Pedroso de Lima (eds.): *Elites. Choice, Leadership and Succession*. Oxford: Berg, 201–225.

Plata Quispe, Wilfredo (2008): El discurso autonomista de las élites de Santa Cruz. In: Ximena Soruco (ed.): *Los barones del Oriente. El poder en Santa Cruz ayer y hoy*. Santa Cruz de la Serra, 101–172.

Prado, César (2016): El Oriente Disidente, 25-06-2016. http://caretas.pe/Main.asp?T=3082&id=12&idE=1260&idA=75540, accessed 25-06-2016.

Prado, Fernando (2007): Poder y elites hoy: quienes son y como ejercen su poder. In: Fernando Prado (ed.): *Poder y elites en Santa Cruz. Tres visiones sobre un mismo tema*. Santa Cruz de la Sierra: Editorial El País, 147–210.

Quispe, Aline (2014): El agro prevé exportar 25.000 TM de maíz y 110.000 de sorgo. In: *La Razón*, 18-10-2014. http://www.la-razon.com/economia/Productores-agro-preve-exportar-maiz-sorgo_0_2145985427.html, accessed 20-10-2017.

Radhuber, Isabella Margerita (2009): *Die Macht des Landes. Der Agrardiskurs in Bolivien - eine Analyse der sozialen, politischen und wirtschaftlichen Vorstellungen und der Machtbeziehungen*. Wien: LIT.

Radhuber, Isabella Margerita (2013): *Der plurinationale Staat in Bolivien. Die Rolle der Ressourcen- und Budgetpolitik*. Münster: Westfälisches Dampfboot.

Rahier, Jean Muteba (2019): The Multicultural Turn, the New Latin American Constitutionalism, and Black Social Movements in the Andean Sub-Region. In: Linda J. Seligmann und Kathleen Sue Fine-Dare (eds.): *The Andean World*. London: Routledge, 389–402.

Ramírez, Ana María (2013): El boom coreano. Triunfan su música, idioma y novelas. In: *La Razón*, 28-07-2013 http://www.la-razon.com/ index.php?_url=/ suplementos/ escape/ coreano-Triunfan-musica-idioma-novelas_0_1876612404.html, accessed 01-01-2015.

Reichl, Christopher A. (1995): Stages in the Historical Process of Ethnicity: The Japanese in Brazil, 1908–1988. In: *Ethnohistory* 42 (1), 31–62.

Riley, John (1999): Japanese Farms Feed Dominican Republic. In: *The Seattle Times*, 12-05-1999. http://community.seattletimes.nwsource.com/archive/?date=19991205&slug=2999516, accessed 27-01-2015.

Rocha, Cristina Moreira da (1999): Identity and Tea Ceremony in Brazil. In: *Japanese Studies* 19 (3), 287–295.

Rockower, Paul (2014): The State of Gstrodiplomacy. In: *Public Diplomacy Magazine*, accessed 30-10-2017.

266   References

Rojas, Aidée (2010): El MAS se hace de otra alcaldía; destituyen al alcalde de Buenavista. In: *El Deber*, 12-05-2010. http://eju.tv/2010/12/el-mas-se-hace-de-otra-alcalda -destituyen-al-alcalde-de-buenavista, accessed 15-11-2017.

Rojas, Fernando (2019): Crisis de precios debilita economía de productores de soya, caña, arroz y maíz. In: *El Deber*, 09-06-2019. https://www.eldeber.com.bo/economia/Crisis -de-precios-debilita-economia-de-productores-de-soya-cana-arroz-y-maiz-20190608 -8552.html, accessed 22-09-2019.

Rojas Jordán, Gary (2013): En Mitsuba, al igual que en Japón, si no es de calidad no se vende. In: *El Deber*, 07-09-2013.

Roos, Vera; Lombard, Antoinette (2003): Interdisciplinary Collaboration. An Ongoing Community Narrative. In: *Journal of Community Psychology* 31 (5), 543–552. DOI: 10.1002/jcop.10061.

Ropp, Steven Masami (2002): The Nikkei Negotiation of Minority/Majority Dynamics in Peru and the United States. In: Lane Ryo Hirabayashi, Akemi Kikumura-Yano und James A. Hirabayashi (eds.): *New Worlds, New Lives: Globalization and People of Japanese Descent in the Americas and from Latin America in Japan*. Stanford: Stanford University Press, 279–295.

Ropp, Steven Masami; Chávez de Ropp, Romy (2002): An Interview with Francisco Miyasaka, President of the Japanese Cuban Association. In: *Amerasia Journal (Special Issue)* 28 (2), 128–146.

Roth, Joshua Hotaka (2003a): Responsibility and the Limits of Identification: Fieldwork among Japanese and Japanese Brazilian Workers in Japan. In: Theodore C. Bestor, Patricia G. Steinhoff und Victoria Lyon-Bestor (eds.): *Doing Fieldwork in Japan*. Honolulu: University of Hawai'i Press, 335–351.

Roth, Joshua Hotaka (2003b): Urashima Taro's Ambiguating Practices: The Significance of Overseas Voting Rights for Elderly Japanese Migrants to Brazil. In: Jeffrey Lesser (ed.): *Searching for Home Abroad. Japanese Brazilians and Transnationalism*. Durham: Duke University Press, 103–119.

Ryūkyū shinpō (2016): Okinawa damashii netsuku keishō, uchinānchu taikai, 1-man 5395 nin tsudoi heimaku, 31-10-2016. http://ryukyushimpo.jp/movie/entry-385868.html, accessed 02-05-2017.

Sahoo, Ajaya Kumar (2006): Issues of Identity in the Indian Diaspora: A Transnational Perspective. In: *Perspectives on Global Development and Technology* 5 (1–2), 81–98.

Sakamoto, Rumi; Allen, Matthew (2011): There's Something Fishy About That Sushi. How Japan Interprets the Global Sushi Boom. In: *Japan Forum* 23 (1), 99–121. DOI: 10.1080/09555803.2011.580538.

Sakurai, Célia (1993): *Romanceiro da imigração japonesa*. São Paulo: Editora Sumaré.

Salvadori Filho, Fausto (2014): A felicidade do pioneiro. Quando o Brasil tratava japoneses com desconfiança, ele se tornou o primeiro político nipônico eleito fora do Japão. In: *Apartes Janeiro/Fevereiro*, 16–24, accessed 30-11-2017.

Salverda, Tijo (2015): *The Franco-Mauritian Elite. Power and Anxiety in the Face of Change*. New York: Berghahn Books.

Salverda, Tijo; Abbink, Jon (2013): Introduction: An Anthropological Perspective on Elite Power and the Cultural Politics of Elite. In: Jon Abbink und Tijo Salverda (eds.): *The Anthropology of Elites. Power, Culture, and the Complexities of Distinction*. New York: Palgrave Macmillan, 1–28.

Sandoval, Carmen Dunia (2003): *Santa Cruz: Economía y poder 1952–1993*. La Paz: Fundación PIEB.

References 267

Sansone, Livio (1997): The New Politics of Black Culture in Bahia, Brazil. In: Cora Govers und Hans Vermeulen (eds.): *The Politics of Ethnic Consciousness*. New York, London: St. Martin's Press; Macmillan Press, 277–309.

Santa Kurusu Chūō Nihonjinkai Sōritsu 50 Shūnen Kinenshi (Hg.) (2006): *Tomoni gojūnen, soshite mirai-he*. Santa Kurusu: Santa Kurusu Nihonjinkai.

Santos, Boaventura de Sousa (2010): *Refundación del Estado en América Latina. Perspectivas desde una epistemología del Sur*. Mexico: Siglo XXI.

Schmidt-Lauber, Brigitta (1998): *"Die verkehrte Hautfarbe": Ethnizität deutscher Namibier als Alltagspraxis*. Berlin: Reimer.

Schoop, Wolfgang (2008): Inseguridad ciudadana y segregación residencial en Santa Cruz, Bolivia. In: Barbara Potthast (ed.): *Ciudadanía vivida, (in)seguridades e interculturalidad*. Buenos Aires: Fundación Foro Nueva Sociedad, 169–182.

Schubert, Jon (2017) *Working the System. A Political Ethnography of the New Angola*. Ithaca: Cornell University Press.

Scott, James C. (1985): *Weapons of the Weak. Everyday Forms of Peasant Resistance*. New Haven, London: Yale University Press.

Scott, James C. (1998): *Seeing Like a State. How Certain Schemes to Improve the Human Condition Have Failed*. New Haven: Yale University Press.

Scott, John (2003): Transformations in the British Economic Elite. In: *Comparative Sociology* 2 (1), 155–173.

Seleme Antelo, Susana (2007): Marco teórico y conceptual sobre poder, clases sociales, elites, Estado y región. In: Fernando Prado (ed.): *Poder y elites en Santa Cruz. Tres visiones sobre un mismo tema*. Santa Cruz de la Sierra: Editorial El País.

Seleme Antelo, Susana; Prado Salmón, Fernando; Prado Zanini, Isabella; Ledo García, Carmen (2005): *Santa Cruz y su gente. Una visión crítica de su evolución y de sus principales tendencias*. Santa Cruz de la Sierra: CEDURE, accessed 09-11-2014.

Shakow, Miriam (2014): *Along the Bolivian Highway. Social Mobility and Political Culture in a New Middle Class*. Philadelphia: University of Pennsylvania Press.

Shimose, Pedro (2012): Los otros japoneses. In: *El Deber*, 26-12-2012.

Shioiri, Yumi (2013): La comunidad *nikkei* en el departamento de Beni. In: Iyo Kunimoto (ed.): *Los japoneses en Bolivia. 110 años de historia de la inmigración japonesa a Bolivia*. La Paz: Federación Nacional de Asociaciones Boliviano-Japonesas; Asociación Nippon-Bolivia; Plural editores, 87–142.

Shōno, Eriko; Sugiura, Atsushi (2013): Las comunidades bolivianas *nikkei* en Japón. In: Iyo Kunimoto (ed.): *Los japoneses en Bolivia. 110 años de historia de la inmigración japonesa a Bolivia*. La Paz: Federación Nacional de Asociaciones Boliviano-Japonesas; Asociación Nippon-Bolivia; Plural editores, 289–324.

Shushō Kantei (2015): Chūnanbei jisedai nikkeijin shidōsha ni yoru hyōkei. http://www.kantei.go.jp/jp/97_abe/actions/201503/19chunanbei_jisedai_hyoukei.html, accessed 11-04-2018.

Siemann, Yvonne (2017): "Transmitting the Message of Okinawa by Drums". Representations of Japaneseness and Okinawanness in Okinawan Dance in Santa Cruz, Bolivia. In: *Contemporary Japan* 29 (2), 177–192. DOI: 10.1080/18692729.2017.1351026.

Siemann, Yvonne (2013): Se perdió un eslabón en la cadena. El impacto de la migración de descendientes de japoneses de Bolivia a Japón. In: *Revista Boliviana de Investigación* 13 (2), 57–74.

Siu, Lok (2002): Cultural Citizenship of Diasporic Chinese in Panama. In: *Amerasia Journal (Special Issue)* 28 (2), 181–202.

268 References

Siu, Lok (2007): The Queen of the Chinese Colony: Contesting Nationalism, Engendering Diaspora. In: Rhacel Salazar Parreñas und Lok Siu (eds.): *Asian Diasporas. New Formations, New Conceptions*. Stanford: Stanford University Press, 105–139.

Smith, Barbara B. (1962): The Bon-Odori in Hawaii and in Japan. In: *Journal of the International Folk Music Council* 14, 36–39.

Sociedad Japonesa de La Paz (2012): *90 Años de Historia - Sociedad Japonesa de La Paz. 1922–2012*. La Paz: Sociedad Japonesa de La Paz; Imprenta Quatro Hermanos.

Soka Gakkai International (2015): SGI: A Snapshot. http://www.sgi.org/snapshot, accessed 30-11-2017.

Sōmushō (2015): 3–14: Kenmin Keizai Keisan. A: Keizai Seichōritsu Oyobi Hitoriatari Kenmin Shotoku (Heisei 17–24 nenbo). http://www.stat.go.jp/data/nenkan/back64/zuhyou/y0314a00.xls, accessed 30-10-2016.

Sōmushō (2016a): F. Rōdō. https://www.e-stat.go.jp/SG1/estat/GL32020101.do?method=xlsDownload&fileId=000007581645&releaseCount=1, accessed 31-10-2018.

Sōmushō (2016b): J. Fukushi. Shakai Hoshō. https://www.e-stat.go.jp/SG1/estat/GL32020101.do?method=xlsDownload&fileId=000007581653&releaseCount=1, accessed 31-10-2018.

Sōmushō (2017): Nihon tōkei nenkan. http://www.stat.go.jp/data/nenkan/66nenkan/zenbun/jp66/top.html, accessed 30-11-2017.

Soruco, Ximena (2006): La ininteligibilidad de lo cholo en Bolivia. In: *Tinkazos* 9 (21), accessed 13-08-2018.

Soruco, Ximena (2008): De la goma a la soya: el proyecto histórico de la élite cruceña. In: Ximena Soruco (ed.): *Los barones del Oriente. El poder en Santa Cruz ayer y hoy*. Santa Cruz de la Sierra, 1–172.

Staniford, Philip (2004): *Pioneers in the Tropics. The Political Organization of Japanese in an Immigrant Community in Brazil*. Oxford: Berg.

State of Hawai'i (2013): American Community Survey 2013 Hawaii Selected Population Profiles (3-Year Estimates). Race Alone or in Combination With One or More Races. http://files.hawaii.gov/dbedt/census/acs/ACS2013/ACS2013_3_Year/ACS_HI_Select_Pop_Profiles_13_3yr_files/ACS_13_3YR_S0201_alone_combo.pdf, accessed 12-02-2017.

Statistics Canada (2016): Data Tables: Ethnic Origin. http://www12.statcan.gc.ca/census-recensement/2016/dp-pd/dt-td/Rp-eng.cfm?LANG=E&APATH=3&DETAIL=0&DIM=0&FL=A&FREE=0&GC= 0&GID=0&GK=0&GRP=1&PID=110528&PRID=10&PTYPE=109445&S=0&SHOWALL=0&SUB=0&Temporal=2017&THEME=120&VID=0&VNAMEE=&VNAMEF=, accessed 12-02-2017.

Stearman, Allyn MacLean (1985): *Camba and Kolla. Migration and Development in Santa Cruz, Bolivia*. Orlando: University Press of Florida.

Stefanoni, Pablo (2010): *"Qué hacer con los indios..." y otros traumas irresueltos de la colonialidad*. La Paz: Plural editores.

Straschnoy, Camil (2016): Abe: "Estamos del lado opuesto del mundo, pero nos une un vínculo eterno". El primer ministro japonés mantuvo un encuentro con la comunidad nipona en Buenos Aires como antesala a su encuentro con el presidente Macri. In: *Télam*, 21-11-2016. http://www.telam.com.ar/notas/201611/171065-primer-ministro-japon-shinzo-abe-visita-argentina-comunidad-nikkei.html, accessed 25-11-2017.

Sugimoto, Yoshio (1997): *An Introduction to Japanese Society*. Cambridge [etc.]: Cambridge University Press.

References 269

Sugimoto, Yoshio (2009): 'Japanese Culture': An Overview. In: Yoshio Sugimoto (ed.): *The Cambridge Companion to Modern Japanese Culture*. Melbourne: Cambridge University Press, 1–20.

Suzuki, Taku (2005): Viewing Nations, Narrating Hybridity: Okinawan Diasporic Subjectivity and Japanese Satellite Telecasts in Colonia Okinawa, Bolivia. In: *Diaspora* 14 (1), 75–107.

Suzuki, Taku (2006): Becoming 'Japanese' in Bolivia: Okinawan-Bolivian Trans(national) Formations in Co onia Okinawa. In: *Identities: Global Studies in Culture and Power* 13, 455–481.

Suzuki, Taku (2010): Embodying Belonging: Racializing Okinawan Diaspora in Okinawa and Japan. Honolulu: University of Hawai'i Press.

Taira, Teruyuki (2005): Santa Kurusu shi ni okeru okinawakenijn no seikatsu. In: Koronia Okinawa Nyūshoku 50 Shūnen Kinenshi Hensan Iinkai (ed.): *Boribia no taichi ni ikiru Okinawa imin*. Santa Kurusu: Okinawa Nihon Boribia Kyōkai, 354–355.

Takeda, Ariel (2002) Japanese Immigrants and Nikkei Chileans. In: Akemi Kikumura-Yano (ed.): *Encyclopedia of Japanese Descendants in the Americas. An Illustrated History of the Nikkei*. Walnut Creek [etc.]: AltaMira Press, 177–191.

Takeda, Ariel (2017): Por n Vez: Fujimori. http://www.discovernikkei.org/es/journal/2017 /2/20/fujimori, accessed 30-10-2017.

Takenaka, Ayumi (1999): Japanese Peruvians and Their Ethnic Encounters. In: Roshni Rustomji-Kerns (ed.): *Encounters. People of Asian Descent in the Americas*. Lanham [etc.]: Rowman & Littlefield, 113–118.

Takenaka, Ayumi (2003a): Paradoxes of Ethnicity-Based Immigration: Peruvian and Japanese-Peruvian Migrants in Japan. In: Roger Goodman, Ceri Peach, Ayumi Takenaka und Paul White (eds.): *Global Japan. The Experience of Japan's New Immigrant and Overseas Communities*. London: RoutledgeCurzon, 222–235.

Takenaka, Ayumi (2003b): The Mechanisms of Ethnic Retention: Later-Generation Japanese Immigrarts in Lima, Peru. In: *Journal of Ethnic and Migration Studies* 29 (3), 467–483.

Takenaka, Ayumi (2005): Nikkeis y peruanos en Japón. In: Ulla D. Berg und Karsten Paerregaard (eds.): *El 5to suyo*. Lima: Instituto de Estudios Peruanos, 205–227.

Takenaka, Ayumi (2009a): Ethnic Hierarchy and Its Impact on Ethnic Identities: A Comparative Analysis of Peruvian and Brazilian Return Migrants in Japan. In: Takeyuki Tsuda (ed.): *Diasporic Homecomings. Ethnic Return Migration in Comparative Perspective*. Stanford: Stanford University Press, 260–280.

Takenaka, Ayumi (2009b): How Diasporic Ties Emerge: Pan-American Nikkei Communities and the Japanese State. In: *Ethnic and Racial Studies* 32 (8), 1325–1345.

Takenaka, Ayumi (2017): Immigrant Integration through Food: Nikkei Cuisine in Peru. In: *Contemporary Japan* 29 (2), 117–131.

Tamayo, Franz (1986) *Creación de la pedagogía nacional*. La Paz: Librería Editorial "Juventud".

Tambiah, Stanley Jeyaraja (1994): The Politics of Ethnicity. In: Robert Borofsky und American Anthropological Association (eds.): *Assessing Cultural Anthropology*. New York [etc.]: McGraw-Hill, 430–442.

Taniguti, Gustavo Takeshy (2015): Cotia: imigração, política e cultura. PhD thesis. Universidade de São Paulo. Faculdade de Filosofia, Letras e Ciências Humanas, Departamento de Sociologia. www.teses.usp.br/teses/disponiveis/8/8132/tde-16072015 -122819/publico/2015_GustavoTakeshyTaniguti_VCorr.pdf, accessed 30-11-2017.

270　References

Tassi, Nico; Medeiros, Carmen; Rodriguez-Carmona, Antonio; Ferrufino, Giovana (2013): *Hacer plata sin plata. El desborde de los comerciantes populares en Bolivia.* La Paz: PIEB.

Taylor, Charles (2002): Modern Social Imaginaries. In: *Public Culture* 14 (1), 91–124.

Thompson, Stephen Ide (1968): Religious Conversion and Religious Zeal in an Overseas Enclave: The Case of the Japanese in Bolivia. In: *Anthropological Quarterly* 41 (4), 201–208.

Thompson, Stephen Ide (1977): Separate but Superior: Japanese in Bolivia. In: George L. Hicks und Philip E. Leis (eds.): *Ethnic Encounters: Identities and Contexts.* Belmont: Wadsworth Publishing Company, 89–101.

Tilly, Charles (1995): Citizenship, Identity and Social History. In: *International Review of Social History* 40 (S3), 1–17. DOI: 10.1017/S0020859000113586.

Tomita, Andréa Gomes Santiago (2004): As Novas Religiões Japonesas como instrumento de transmissão de cultura japonesa no Brasil. In: *Revista de Estudos da Religião* 3, 88–102, accessed 30-11-2017.

Tsuda, Takeyuki (1999): Ethnic Preferences: Positive Minority Status of Japanese Brazilians and Their Ethnic Encounters with Other Minority Groups in Brazil. In: Roshni Rustomji-Kerns (ed.): *Encounters. People of Asian Descent in the Americas.* Lanham [etc.]: Rowman & Littlefield, 209–222.

Tsuda, Takeyuki (2001a): From Ethnic Affinity to Alienation in the Global Ecumene: The Encounter between the Japanese and Japanese-Brazilian Return Migrants. In: *Diaspora* 10 (1), 53–91.

Tsuda, Takeyuki (2001b): When Identities Become Modern: Japanese Emigration to Brazil and the Global Contextualization of Identity. In: *Ethnic and Racial Studies* 24 (3), 412–432.

Tsuda, Takeyuki (2007): When Minorities Migrate: The Racialization of the Japanese Brazilians in Brazil and Japan. In: Rhacel Salazar Parreñas und Lok Siu (eds.): *Asian Diasporas. New Formations, New Conceptions.* Stanford: Stanford University Press, 225–251.

Tsuda, Takeyuki (2009): Global Inequities and Diasporic Return: Japanese American and Brazilian Encounters with the Ethnic Homeland. In: Takeyuki Tsuda (ed.): *Diasporic Homecomings. Ethnic Return Migration in Comparative Perspective.* Stanford: Stanford University Press, 227–259.

Tsujimoto, Masahiro (2012): Migration, Economic Adaption and Mutual Cooperation: Japanese Rotating Savings and Credit Associations in Argentina. In: Naoki Yoshihara (ed.): *Global Migration and Ethnic Communities. Studies of Asia and South America.* Balwyn North: Trans Pacific Press, 163–175.

Tsunekawa, Keiichi (1998): Die politische Seite der japanisch-lateinamerikanischen Beziehungen. In: Japanisch-Deutsches Zentrum Berlin (ed.): *Symposium: Die Beziehungen zwischen Deutschland, Japan und Lateinamerika. 20.-22.03.1997.* Berlin: JDZB, 103–114.

UNESCO (2013): Washoku, traditional dietary cultures of the Japanese, notably for the celebration of New Year. Inscribed in 2013 (8.COM) on the Representative List of the Intangible Cultural Heritage of Humanity. https://ich.unesco.org/en/RL/washoku-traditional-dietary-cultures-of-the-japanese-notably-for-the-celebration-of-new-year-00869, accessed 25-11-2017.

Unión de Jóvenes Nikkei del Paraguay (2012): Avance - Fénix Intercambio Internacional 2012. https://www.youtube.com/watch?v=KE_pDMUimh8, accessed 20-01-2018.

Unión de Jóvenes Nikkei del Paraguay (2014): Porque están para cumplirse - Fénix Intercambio Internacional 2013. https://www.youtube.com/watch?v=Spwi1OeGiE4, accessed 19-01-2018.

References 271

United Nations Economic and Social Commission for Asia and the Pacific (2009): What is Good Governance? https://www.unescap.org/resources/what-good-governance, accessed 11-04-2018.

United States Census Bureau (2016): Asian Alone or in Any Combination with Selected Groups 2016. https://factfinder.census.gov/faces/tableservices/jsf/pages/productview.xhtml?pid=ACS_15_1YR_B02018&prodType=table, accessed 12-02-2017.

Urioste, Miguel (2011): *Concentración y extranjerización de la tierra en Bolivia*. La Paz: Fundación Tierra. http://www.ftierra.org/index.php/publicacion/libro/48-concentracion-y-extranjerizacion-de-la-tierra-en-bolivia, accessed 30-11-2017.

Urioste, Miguel (2012): Concentration and "Foreignisation" of Land in Bolivia. In: *Canadian Journal of Development Studies/Revue canadienne d'études du développement* 33 (4), 439–457.

Vaca Justiniano, Berthy (2019): Nueva política municipal: Los alumnos deben limpiar sus aulas, como disciplina. In: *El Deber*, 13-03-2019. https://www.eldeber.com.bo/santacruz/Alumnos-deben-limpiar-sus-aulas-y-cuidar-sus-pupitres-como-disciplina-20190312-8620.html, accessed 04/052019.

Valaskivi, Katja (2013): A Brand New Future? Cool Japan and the Social Imaginary of the Branded Nation. In: *Japan Forum* 25 (4), 485–504. DOI: 10.1080/09555803.2012.756538.

Valdivia, Gabriela (2010): Agrarian Capitalism and Struggles over Hegemony in the Bolivian Lowlands. In: *Latin American Perspectives* 37 (4), 67–87.

Valdivia, Gabriela (2012): Coca's Haunting Presence in the Agrarian Politics of the Bolivian Lowlands. In: *GeoJournal* 77 (5), 615–631. DOI: 10.1007/s10708-011-9407-9.

Vegas, Leopoldo; Cuéllar, Róger (2017): Zvonko Matkovic: el liderazgo cruceño tiene que despertar. In: *El Deber*, 07-09-2017, www.eldeber.com.bo/septimodia/El-liderazgo-cruceno-tiene-que-despertar-esta-con-miedo-20170707-0104.html, accessed 27-11-2017.

Vink, Maarten Peter; Bauböck, Rainer (2013): Citizenship Configurations. Analysing the Multiple Purposes of Citizenship Regimes in Europe. In: *Comparative European Politics* 11 (5), 621–648. DOI: 10.1057/cep.2013.14.

Wade, Peter (2010): *Race and Ethnicity in Latin America*. London: Pluto.

Wakatsuki, Yasuo; Kunimoto, Iyo (Hg.) (1985): *La inmigración japonesa en Bolivia. Estudios históricos y socio-económicos*. Tokio: Universidad de Chuo.

Waldmann, Adrián (2008): *El hábitus camba. Estudio etnográfico sobre Santa Cruz de la Sierra*. Santa Cruz de la Sierra: Editorial El País.

Wang, L. Ling-Chi (2008): Myths and Realities of Asian American Success: Reassessing and Redefining the 'Model Minority' Stereotype. In: Guofang Li und Lihshing Wang (eds.): *Model Minority Myth Revisited. An Interdisciplinary Approach to Demystifying Asian American Educational Experiences*. Charlotte: Information Age Publishing, 1–20.

Watanabe, José (2010): Glosario de palabras japonesas de uso en el Perú. http://www.discovernikkei.org/en/journal/2010/2/16/glosario-de-palabras-japonesas, accessed 07-05-2017.

White, Paul (2003): The Japanese in Latin America: On the Uses of Diaspora. In: *International Journal of Population Geography* 9 (4), 309–322.

Wimmer, Andreas (2013): *Ethnic Boundary Making. Institutions, Power, Networks*. New York: Oxford University Press.

Wolff, Reinhard; Fröschle, Hartmut (1979): Die Deutschen in Bolivien. In: Hartmut Fröschle (ed.): *Die Deutschen in Lateinamerika. Schicksal und Leistung*. Tübingen, Basel: Horst Erdmann, 146–168.

272   References

Yamagata, Tatsufumi (2009): Tamed Economic Animal: Conservative Japanese Businessmen in the Global Competition. http://www.ide.go.jp/English/Research/ Region/Asia/20091006.html, accessed 14-12-2017.

Yamanaka, Keiko (2000): "I Will Go Home, but When?": Labor Migration and Circular Diaspora Formation by Japanese Brazilians in Japan. In: Mike Douglass und Glenda S. Roberts (eds.): *Japan and Global Migration: Foreign Workers and the Advent of a Multicultural Society*. London: Routledge, 123–152.

Yanagida, Toshio (1998a): Einige Bemerkungen zum Austausch von Wissen zwischen Asien und Lateinamerika im 16. und 17. Jahrhundert. In: Japanisch-Deutsches Zentrum Berlin (ed.): *Symposium: Die Beziehungen zwischen Deutschland, Japan und Lateinamerika. 20.-22.03.1997*. Berlin: JDZB, 57–61.

Yanagida, Toshio (1998b): Japanische Einwanderung in Lateinamerika. In: Japanisch-Deutsches Zentrum Berlin (ed.): *Symposium: Die Beziehungen zwischen Deutschland, Japan und Lateinamerika. 20.-22.03.1997*. Berlin: JDZB, 65–77.

Yano, Christine R. (2003): Unraveling the Web of Song. In: Theodore C. Bestor, Patricia G. Steinhoff und Victoria Lyon-Bestor (eds.): *Doing Fieldwork in Japan*. Honolulu: University of Hawai'i Press, 277–293.

Yoshino, Kosaku (1992): *Cultural Nationalism in Contemporary Japan. A Sociological Enquiry*. London: Routledge.

Yoshino, Kosaku (2001): Japan's Nationalism in a Marketplace Perspective. In: Montserrat Guibernau und John Hutchinson (eds.): *Understanding Nationalism*. Cambridge, Malden: Polity Press, 142–163.

Zapana, Verónica (2014): Siete de cada 10 matrimonios terminan en divorcio en el país. Por primera vez, Bolivia celebra hoy el dia de la familia. In: *Página Siete*, 14-05-2014. https://www.paginasiete.bo/sociedad/2014/5/15/siete-cada-matrimonios-terminan -divorcio-pais-21534.html, accessed 29-01-2020.

Zhou, Min (2004): Revisiting Ethnic Entrepreneurship: Convergencies, Controversies, and Conceptual Advancements. In: *International Migration Review* 38 (3), 1040–1074.

Zöllner, Reinhard (2006): *Geschichte Japans. Von 1800 bis zur Gegenwart*. Paderborn: Ferdinand Schöningh.

Index

5S method 86, 103–4, 109n1

Abe, Shinzō 195
ABJ 140–1, 147, 153–4, 161-2, 177; and finance 67, 164; and politics 228–9, 231
acceptance of foreign migrants by non-Nikkei 32, 42–43, 53–7, 70–72
African descendants in Bolivia 71, 235
agriculture 27, 45–6; agricultural companies 68, 191–2, 195; agricultural events 202–3; agricultural policies 203, 207, 222; cattle breeding 38, 187, 191, 206; cultivation of fruits, vegetables and nuts 62–66, 203; future of 205–8; and marketing 204–5; *see also* business relations, cooperatives, land ownership
ANAPO 214–5, 222
ANBJ/FENABOJA 141–2, 159, 178, 180, 192, 194; *see also* associations
ancestor worshipping *see* religion
anime *see* Japanese pop culture
anniversary of immigration 59–61, 76, 143, 180; and exclusion of certain groups 133, 157, 163; and official visitors 105, 153; and pre-war descendants 111, 128–30
anniversary publication 57, 74, 116, 128
APJ 155, 161
APN 171, 184n4, *see also* Pan-American Nikkei networks
Arab migration to Santa Cruz and Bolivia 42, 75, 78, 143, 191, 226
Argentina, Nikkei in 1, 23, 29–30, 32, 155, 171–2
assimilation *see* loss of "Japanese values"
associations 139–43; activities 147–53, 197; in Bolivian Amazonia 111, 128, 142; crisis of 153–61; and finances 164–5; and leadership 155–162; *see also*

ABJ, ANBJ/FENABOJA, Centro Social Japonés, Fraternidad Fujii, Okinawa Kenjinkai, Sociedad Japonesa de La Paz Asunción, Nikkei in 142, 157, 163, 165, 231
autonomy movement in Santa Cruz 19, 39–41, 78, 214–5, 217, 230–1

Bani, Katsumi 211–2, 218, 228–36
baseball 1, 134, 142, 170
Beni *see* Bolivian Amazonia
Bolivia: economy of 33, 68, 186, 194, 206, 214; history of 34–8; immigration policies of 32, 74; politics of 36–8, 229–31; *see also* non-Nikkei Bolivians
Bolivian Amazonia: history of 34–6; socioeconomic situation of 110–11, 126; *see also* pre-war Nikkei
Bolivian Constitution of 2009 37, 71, 143, 215, 230, 233; and Nikkei 235–6; and Santa Cruz 39, 41
Bolivian nationality *see* nationality
Brazil, Nikkei in 77, 85n11, 106, 114, 187; and associations 139, 161; and economy 197, 201, 207, 209n9; history of 23, 27, 29–33, 46, 59, 85n9; and language 46; and marriage 93, 95; of Okinawan origin 124; and Pan-American Nikkei networks 169, 171, 175; and religion 144–5; and politics 224, 226, 231–2; in Santa Cruz 130–2
Brazilians in Bolivia and Santa Cruz 41–2, 63, 214–6
Buddhism *see* religion
bureaucracy, dealings with 77, 85n2, 115, 190, 195–6, 219–22
business relations of Bolivia to China 194–5; to Japan 193–6; to South Korea, 194–5

274   *Index*

CAICO 45, 47, 126, 199–207; donations from 177; and Bolivian bureaucracy and legislation 214, 222; *see also* cooperatives

CAISY 46–7, 199–203, 205–7; donations from 124, 153; and Bolivian bureaucracy and legislation 214, 219, 222; *see also* cooperatives

CAO 193, 214–6, 221–2

Catholicism *see* religion

Centro Paraguayo Japonés 165, 231

Centro Social Japonés 46–7, 92, 114, 140–1, 144–5; activities at 82, 119, 121, 138–9, 149–52, 160–1; conflicts over location 159–60; finances 161, 164–5; gender 161–4; leadership at 155–6, 158, 160; membership at 115, 122, 124–5, 131–3, 154–5, 158; pre-war descendants and 126, 129–30; support by JICA 153

Cetabol 87, 200, 202

charity *see* civic engagement

Chile, Nikkei in 29–30, 32, 167n8, 176, 179

Chinese migration to Santa Cruz and Bolivia 42, 70–5, 199

civic engagement of Nikkei 153, 232–236

citizenship 213, 233–4; *see also* nationality

cleanliness as "Japanese value" 51, 87, 97, 101–5, 151–3, 229

clientelism 37–8, 213, 221, 224; *see also* corruption

climate change 206

Cobija *see* Bolivian Amazonia

Cochabamba, Nikkei association of 159, 162

Colonia Okinawa 44–46, 48, 69, 77, 92; agriculture at 49n8, 200; civic engagement at 233; and Confra 177, 179; future of 208; infrastructure at 147; "Japanese values" at 107, 112, 175; language at 116–7; politics at 226; and San Juan 122–5; sports at 151; school at 87, 100, 164; *see also* CAICO

colonias in Bolivia 17n4, 20, 75, 164, 207, 235; and JICA 66–8; and language 116; and social cohesion 90, 112, 147, 154–5; *see also* Colonia Okinawa, San Juan

Comité Cívico Pro Santa Cruz 39, 78, 214

community *see* comunidad japonesa

comunidad japonesa 88–94, 112–5, 130–6; and pre-war Nikkei 110–11, 126–30

Confra 1–2, 130, 158, 170, 173, 176–80; *see also* Pan-American Nikkei events

consumption 11, 51, 95–9

contraband in Bolivia 37–8

cooperatives 116, 221; in Brazil 207, 209n9; and legislation 207–8; of non-Nikkei Bolivians 193, 201; in Paraguay 204; *see also* CAICO, CAISY

COPANI 2, 167n8, 170–80, 184n4, 190; *see also* Pan-American Nikkei events

corruption 36–7, 95, 99, 192–3, 202–3, 220–1; in politics 213, 224, 226, 228–31, 237n8

cosplay *see* Japanese pop culture

Costas, Rubén 39, 230

crime 98–9, 109, 208

cuisine *see* food

cultural loss *see* loss of "Japanese values"

Day Service 119, 138–9, 140, 146, 151, 160–1

dekasegi 8, 18n10, 33, 45, 68–9; acceptance by Japanese 34, 176; and economy 116, 185, 190; and identity 106; and language 117; and pre-war descendants 43, 111, 126–7, 129

development assistance 45, 58, 66, 189, 217, 225, 227; *see also* JICA

diaspora, theory of 7–8

discrimination of Nikkei *see* exclusion of Nikkei

domestic worker 73, 78, 85n3, 97, 102, 117

Dominican Republic, Nikkei in the 23, 29–30, 32

drug trafficking 19, 37–8, 187, 207, 218

Düsseldorf 168–9

economic engagement of Nikkei 185–6; and companies 187–8, 190–6, and entrepreneurship 190–3; and Japan 193–6; and macroeconomic influences 203, 205–8; *see also* cooperatives, labour market

education 27–8, 34, 52, 95, 187, 189; of non-Nikkei Bolivians at school and work 103–5, 212–3, 228–9, 233; inside the family; of pre-war Nikkei 127–8; at school 51, 75–6, 96–7, 109n5, 189; at university 36, 44, 52, 80, 68, 187–190; *see also* Japanese school

eisā 26, 112, 135, 151, 180, 182; *see also* Ryūkyūkoku Matsuridaiko

elite of Santa Cruz 39–42, 49n6, 78, 193, 214–5, 217

elite studies 10–11, 18n13, 214–6
empleada see domestic worker
entrepreneurs 68, 185–6, 190–3, 195–6, 204, 207
environmental protection initiatives 212–3, 229, 233–4
European migration to Santa Cruz and Bolivia 41–2, 78
ethnic identity, theory of 3–7; and diaspora 7–8; and symbolic capital 8–12
exclusion of Nikkei 45, 61, 70–9, 132–3, 196; in economy and politics 204, 219–21, 231; in Peru 31, 227; theory of 9–12
export *see* business relations

farming *see* agriculture
FEGASACRUZ 187
FENABOJA see ANBJ
Fénix 172, 174, 179; *see also* Pan-American Nikkei events, youth exchange
Festival de la Buena Cosecha *see hōnensai*
fieldwork 12–15
filial piety 52, 94, 112, 119–121, 144, 207; and associations 151, 157; and Pan-American Nikkei events 173, 178; *see also* respect
financial difficulties: of individuals 45, 69, 114–15, 120; of associations 162–5
food: from Bolivia 65; donations of 74, 178; and gender 161–3; and identity 55, 85n5, 93–4, 132, 149, 209n6; and merchandising 196–9, 203–5; and Okinawan identity 26, 125, 169, 197; in restaurants 149, 196–9; and soft power 82–3, 196–9; *see also* agriculture, Nikkei fusion cuisine, sushi
food security and Nikkei 27, 203, 205–6, 222
football 1, 3, 17n1, 170, 173
Fraternidad Fujii 47, 89, 142, 160–1
friendship between Nikkei and non-Nikkei 53–4, 72, 75–7, 88, 96–7, 221
Fujimori, Alberto 31, 71, 177, 184n4, 225–8
Fujimori, Keiko 184n4, 226, 228
fujinbu 134, 138, 140, 162–4; *see also* gender
futsal *see* football

gated community 19, 49, 51, 78, 98–9, 114
generational differences 119–121, 138–9, 156–8, 165, 189, 207, 229

gender 49n7, 133, 157–8, 161–4
genetically modified seeds 215, 222
golf 1, 142, 17, 172, 188
gossip 91, 112, 115, 192; *see also* social pressure
Guayaramerín *see* Bolivian Amazonia

hairdressers 50, 52, 90 219–20
hard work as "Japanese value" 52–3, 55, 61, 101, 104, 173
hōnensai 149–51
honesty as "Japanese value" 51, 53, 104, 173; in politics 220, 224, 227, 231; in work life 186–7
hospital 45–6, 66–8, 164

identity, theory of 4; ethnic identity 4–7; and marketing 5, 80, 199, 232; in the nation state 6; and politics 223; and race 5–6
Imperial family of Japan 128, 133, 153, 159, 175
import *see* business relations
indigenous groups 6, 13, 32, 49n5, 72; in politics 37, 223, 235; stereotypes about 56, 113
INRA *see* land reform
integration, discourses on: 75–9; *see also* loss of values

Japan: economy of 23–4; emigration policies of 23, 26–8, 74, 145; government of 100, 105, 127, 153, 176, 227; history of 21–4; identity in 24–6; immigration policies of 33–4, 111; perceptions of 105–8; *see also dekasegi,* JICA, nationality, soft power
Japanese Bolivian school, plans of 232–3
Japanese classes for adults 82, 109n6, 126, 136
Japanese companies in Bolivia 190–6, 221
Japanese consulate in Santa Cruz 46, 69, 82, 150, 153, 160
Japanese embassy in Bolivia 44, 82, 126, 217, 230
Japanese language: 100–103, 115–119, 171, 174–5, 187; *see also kanji*
Japanese migration to Bolivia: history of 43–8, 61; in recent times 120, 131–2, 165
Japanese nationality *see* nationality
Japanese pop culture 79, 81–2

276 Index

Japanese school 44, 46–7, 140; history of 27, 32, 44, 47, 117; and "Japanese values" 87, 100–3, 112; support by JICA 66–7, 164; and language 116–7, 119; prerequisites to attend 103, 147; and social meaning 89, 131; and teachers 132, 136–7; *see also* Japanese classes for adults
"Japanese values" 51–6, 73, 81, 84, 97: and the *comunidad japonesa* 89, 94, 151–2; at school 101–3; and economy 186–7, 190–3, 201, 203–4, 221; at Pan-American Nikkei events 169, 171–4, 176–9; and politics 229–30, 233–4; *see also* loss of "Japanese values"
Jewish migration from Germany to Bolivia 41–2
JICA 23, 26–7, 44–5, 52, 66–68, 84; and exchanges 120, 196; and relation to pre-war descendants 125–6, 130; and support for cooperatives 201–3, 206–8; and support for cultural activities and associations 82, 153, 164; and support for schools 103; and support for start-ups 192, 195–6; *see also* volunteers from Japan, scholarship, development assistance

Kaigai Nikkeijin Kyōkai 171
kanji characters 18n16, 101, 116
karaoke events 133, 147, 150, 154, 172, 182
Karate 79, 135, 140, 149
Kasamatsu, Emi 231
Kasuga, Carlos 104, 180, 192, 233
kenjinkai 140–1; *see also* Okinawa Kenjinkai
Korean migration to Ssanta Cruz and Bolivia 42, 72–75, 133
Korean pop culture 74–5
koseki 33, 49n4, 126–7, 157
Kuajara, Adalberto 226

labour market in Bolivia 187–190; *see also* professions
landless people's movement *see* Movimiento sin Tierra – Bolivia
land occupation 211–2, 217–19
land ownership 213–219
land reform under Morales 216–7, 237n3
La Paz 34; *see also* Sociedad Japonesa de La Paz
Latin America: economy in 68, 194–5, 206; identity in 32–3, 70, 134;

immigration policies in 31–3, 42–3, 70; Japan's interest in 27–8, 194–5; politics in 223–4, 231, 234 237n6
law of popular participation 229, 233
Liceo Mexicano Japonés 87, 232–3
Lima 142, 149, 164, 174, 179, 184n4
loss of "Japanese values" 87, 91, 94, 97, 151, 154; and generational differences 119–20; and language 117, 119; and Okinawan descendants 123; and Pan-American Nikkei events 171–2, 182–3; and pre-war Nikkei 111, 126, 131; and school 100–2

manga *see* Japanese pop culture
marginalisation in the Nikkei community 113–5, 118–1, 120–1, 123–5, 130–6; of pre-war descendants 126–30, 131–4
marriage of Nikkei and non-Nikkei 92–95, 117–8, 134, 163
MAS 40, 205, 216–7, 225, 230–1, 234–5; *see also* Morales, Evo
media consumption by Nikkei 105, 125, 128
media images of Japan 61, 83–4
media images of Nikkei 61, 78, 80, 129; of individual Nikkei 55, 143, 186, 229–31
Mennonites 42, 78, 235; and agriculture 63, 65, 201, 204, 214–15, 218–19
mestizaje see "mixed" origin
Mexico, Nikkei in 27, 29–32, 99, 223, 232–3; and Pan-American Nikkei events 1, 171, 175, 223
middle class: theory of 10–11, 189
middlemen minorities 11, 18n11, 216
"mixed" origin, Nikkei of 2–3, 132–4, 129–30, 137n4, 179
model minority 11
modernity, discourses on 9, 39, 65, 79–81, 103–7, 234
Morales, Evo 37, 229
Morales administration 37–8, 41, 214–5, 218–9, 230, 233; and foreigners 42, 56, 205; and indigenism 49n5, 237n9
Movimiento sin Tierra-Bolivia 202, 211, 216–8
Multimercado Okinawa 89–90, 141, 204
museums of migration 59–61

nationality: Bolivian nationality 33, 41, 69–70, 216, 200, 220; double nationality 25, 33, 69, 125; Japanese nationality 8, 45–6, 120; of pre-war descendants 61, 69, 85n9, 126–7, 132
natural disasters 45, 67, 130, 206

networks *see* social capital
nihongogakkō see Japanese school
nihonjinkai see associations, Centro Social Japonés, Sociedad Japonesa de La Paz
nihonjinron 24, 55
nikkai see associations, Centro Social Japonés, Sociedad Japonesa de La Paz
Nikkei fusion cuisine 199
Nikkei: definition of 2–3, 171, 174–5, 242; numbers 28–32
Nikkei from other countries living in Bolivia: 118–9, 131–2
non-Nikkei Bolivians: conflicts between Nikkei and 45, 211–3, 217; participation in Nikkei networks 135–6, perceptions of Nikkei and Japan 53–8, 82–3, 149, 197–8, 225; *see also* marriage, friendship, stereotypes
North America, Nikkei in 25, 29–32, 74, 175–6, 184n3, 226

Obon 149, 151 *see also* Bon Odori
Okinawa prefecture: emigration from 29; history of 21–4, 127; identity of 2, 25–6, 168–9, 180, 197; political agenda of 8, 125, 169, 182–3; *see also* Pan-Okinawan identity
Okinawan Nikkei's identity in Bolivia 121–126, 178, 182–3, 197; *see also* Pan-Okinawan identity
Okinawa Kenjinkai 46, 89, 122, 141, 163; membership 154–5, 158. 160–1; leadership 158, 186
Okinawa Kenjinkai in Germany 168
Okinawan language 25, 49n2, 112, 117, 124–5, 169

PAN *see* APN
PANA convention *see* COPANI
Pan-American Nikkei networks 170–1; costs of 178–9; and identity 171, 174–8; and language 118, 175; perception in Bolivia 178–80; and "Japanese values" 171–4; *see also* COPANI, Confra, Pan-Okinawan identity
Pan-Okinawan identity 133, 148. 168–9, 171, 180–3; *see also* Uchinanchu Taikai, Wakamono Taikai
Pando *see* Bolivian Amazonia
Paraguay, Nikkei in: associations of 142, 157, 159, 163, 165; in economy 192, 204; history of 23, 29–32; and Pan-American Nikkei events 1, 171–5, 178; and politics 231–2

Peru, Nikkei in: associations 147, 155, 159, 161, 164; and *dekasegi* 33; in economy 192–3; history of 27, 29–32; and language 46; and nationality 106; and Pan-American Nikkei events 1, 173, 175, 177; and politics 227–8; and religion 144
physiognomy 25, 70, 122, 126, 133, 210
plurinationalism 6, 37, 235–6, 237n11
Policonsultorio Nikkei 80, 140, 156–7, 164
political engagement of Nikkei 177, 225–232, lack of interest in 222–5; *see also* civic engagement
positive minority 11
pre-war Nikkei 43, 89, 92, 110–11, 116, 126–32, 226: and associations 128, 139–40, 142, 146, 158; history of 46, 61, 74; and JICA 130; and Pan-American Nikkei events 179; and nationality 69; *see also* Bolivian Amazonia
professions 52–3, 68–9; *see also* labour market
prosperity of Nikkei 47–8, 78–9, 115, 177, 187, 192; and dangers 96–9; and *dekasegi* 68–9; and "Japanese values" 50–5, 58–62; and JICA 66–8; and pre-war Nikkei 43, 111, 127–8, 177
punctuality 71, 101, 105, 123, 152, 228–9; as key factor for success 51, 54–5, 186; at work 103, 128–129

religion 48–9n1, 134, 143–5, 148–9, 166–7n4
remigration *see* dekasegi
respect as "Japanese value" 51–2, 55, 89–94, 101, 175, 186; as example for non-Nikkei 151–2, 178; in Japan 106; lack of 57, 121, 155, 158; *see also* filial piety
restaurants *see* food
Revolution of 1952 6, 21, 36–7, 44, 62, 67, 71, 191
Riberalta *see* Bolivian Amazonia
rotating credit associations *see* tanomoshi
Rurrenabaque *see* Bolivian Amazonia
Ryūkyūkoku Matsuridaiko dance 101, 124–5, 134–135, 147–9, 180; *see also* eisā

San Juan 27, 45–6, 53, 58–60, 192, 210–13; agriculture at 49n8, 63, 200; associations at 83, 147, 154, 158, 161; and civic engagement 233; and Colonia Okinawa 122–5; future of 208;

278 *Index*

and "Japanese values" 112; and land
occupations 211–12, 218; and language
116–7; and non-Nikkei 77, 92, 213; and
politics 226, 228–32, 234; and religion
144–5; school at 100, 164; sports at
150–1; *see also* CAISY
sanshin 26, 112, 149, 168, 180, 182
Santa Cruz, city of 19–21; history of 34–6;
identity of 19, 38–41, 49n6, 78; *see also*
autonomy movement in Santa Cruz,
Comité Cívico Pro Santa Cruz, elite of
Santa Cruz
São Paulo 31, 59, 129, 224, 237n7, 242
school *see* education, Japanese school
seinenkai 83, 117, 124, 133, 158, 211
self-employment 52, 191
Shimose, Pedro 129–30
social capital 9, 187–90, 193, 205,
213–6, 220–2
social engagement *see* civic engagement
social pressure 90–92, 112, 147
Sociedad Japonesa de La Paz 140;
activities at 150; donations of 232;
history of 44, 57, 74; and finance 162–5;
membership and participation at 92,
131, 135–6, 146–8, 158
soft power 51, 79–84, 196–9
Sōka Gakkai 144, 166n3; *see also* religion
Soranbushi dance 83, 124
Spanish language 69–70, 102, 106, 116–9,
137, 221; at Pan-American Nikkei
events 174; at school 46, 100
sports festival *see undōkai*
status symbols 96–7
stereotypes: about Japan and the Japanese
61, 95, 106–8, 221; about other Latin

Americans 175; about lower classes
77–8; about non-Nikkei Bolivians 56–8,
93–8, 103–5, 134–136, 186, 188
sushi 79, 196–9; *see also* food
symbolic capital, theory of 8–12

Taiwanese migration to Santa Cruz 65,
72, 74
Tamayo, Franz 6
tanomoshi 86–9, 142
tea ceremony 83, 147–8
trámite see bureaucracy
Trinidad *see* Bolivian Amazonia

uchināguchi see Okinawan language
Uchinanchu Taikai 26, 168, 180–3
undōkai 60, 87, 124, 150–2,
157, 160
upward social mobility of Nikkei *see*
prosperity
urban-rural differences among Nikkei 77,
87, 111–113, 117, 147, 155

values *see* Japanese values
vivir bien, concept of 230
volleyball 1, 89, 101, 141, 170
volunteers from Japan 59, 66, 101, 108,
130, 165

Wakamono Taikai 168–9, 180, 182
see also Pan-Okinawan identity
wealth *see* prosperity
work life 77, 103–5, 187–90

youth exchanges 26, 133, 168–9, 171–3,
180, 183

Printed in the United States
by Baker & Taylor Publisher Services